Visual Basic .NET Introductory Concepts and Techniques

Gary B. Shelly

Thomas J. Cashman

Jeffrey J. Quasney

THOMSON

COURSE TECHNOLOGY

COURSE TECHNOLOGY
25 THOMSON PLACE
BOSTON MA 02210

SHELLY
CASHMAN
SERIES®

Australia • Canada • Denmark • Japan • Mexico • New Zealand • Philippines • Puerto Rico • Singapore
South Africa • Spain • United Kingdom • United States

THOMSON ™

COURSE TECHNOLOGY

COPYRIGHT © 2003 Course Technology, a division of Thomson Learning.
Printed in the United States of America

Asia (excluding Japan)
Thomson Learning
5 Shenton Way #01-01
UIC Building
Singapore 068808

Latin America
Thomson Learning
Seneca, 53
Colonia Polanco
11560 Mexico D.F. Mexico

Canada
Nelson/Thomson Learning
1120 Birchmount Road
Scarborough, Ontario
Canada M1K 5G4

Japan
Thomson Learning
Nihonjisyo Brooks Bldg 3-F
1-4-1 Kudankita, Chiyoda-Ku
Tokyo 102-0073 Japan

South Africa
Thomson Learning
15 Brookwood Street
P.O. Box 1722
Soverset West 7120
South Africa

UK/Europe/Middle East
Thomson Learning
Berkshire House
168-173 High Holborn
London, WC1V 7AA United Kingdom

Australia/New Zealand
Nelson/Thomson Learning
102 Dodds Street
South Melbourne, Victoria 3205
Australia

Spain
Thomson Learning
Calle Magallanes, 25
28015-MADRID
ESPANA

ISBN 0-7895-6547-1

1 2 3 4 5 6 7 8 9 10   BC   06 05 04 03 02

Visual Basic .NET
Introductory Concepts
and Techniques

Contents

CHAPTER 1

An Introduction to Visual Basic .NET and Program Design

CHAPTER 2

The Visual Basic .NET Integrated Development Environment

CHAPTER 3

Building an Application in the Visual Basic .NET Environment

CHAPTER 4

Working with Variables, Constants, Data Types, and Expressions

APPENDIX A

Flowcharting, Pseudocode, and the Unified Modeling Language (UML)

APPENDIX B

Changing Screen Resolution and the IDE Layout

APPENDIX C

Visual Basic .NET Common Control Summary

APPENDIX D

General Forms of Common Visual Basic .NET Statements

APPENDIX E

The .NET Framework Class Library Overview

APPENDIX F

ASCII Character Codes

Shelly Cashman Series — Traditionally Bound Textbooks

The Shelly Cashman Series presents the following computer subjects in a variety of traditionally bound textbooks. For more information, see your Course Technology representative or call 1-800-648-7450. For Shelly Cashman Series information, visit Shelly Cashman Series at course.com/shellycashman.

COMPUTERS	
Computers	Discovering Computers 2003: Concepts for a Digital World, Web Enhanced, Complete Edition
	Discovering Computers 2003: Concepts for a Digital World, Web Enhanced, Introductory Edition
	Discovering Computers 2003: Concepts for a Digital World, Web Enhanced, Brief Edition
	Teachers Discovering Computers: Integrating Technology in the Classroom 2e
	Exploring Computers: A Record of Discovery 4e
	Study Guide for Discovering Computers 2003: Concepts for a Digital World, Web Enhanced
	Essential Introduction to Computers 4e (32-page)

WINDOWS APPLICATIONS	
Microsoft Office	Microsoft Office XP: Essential Concepts and Techniques (5 projects)
	Microsoft Office XP: Brief Concepts and Techniques (9 projects)
	Microsoft Office XP: Introductory Concepts and Techniques, Course One (15 projects)
	Microsoft Office XP: Advanced Concepts and Techniques, Course Two (11 projects)
	Microsoft Office XP: Post Advanced Concepts and Techniques, Course Three (11 projects)
	Microsoft Office 2000: Essential Concepts and Techniques (5 projects)
	Microsoft Office 2000: Brief Concepts and Techniques (9 projects)
	Microsoft Office 2000: Introductory Concepts and Techniques, Enhanced Edition (15 projects)
	Microsoft Office 2000: Advanced Concepts and Techniques (11 projects)
	Microsoft Office 2000: Post Advanced Concepts and Techniques (11 projects)
Integration	Integrating Microsoft Office XP Applications and the World Wide Web: Essential Concepts and Techniques
PIM	Microsoft Outlook 2002: Essential Concepts and Techniques
Microsoft Works	Microsoft Works 6: Complete Concepts and Techniques[1] • Microsoft Works 2000: Complete Concepts and Techniques[1] • Microsoft Works 4.5[1]
Microsoft Windows	Microsoft Windows XP: Complete Concepts and Techniques[1]
	Microsoft Windows XP: Brief Concepts and Techniques
	Microsoft Windows 2000: Complete Concepts and Techniques (6 projects)[1]
	Microsoft Windows 2000: Brief Concepts and Techniques (2 projects)
	Microsoft Windows 98: Complete Concepts and Techniques (6 projects)[2]
	Microsoft Windows 98: Essential Concepts and Techniques (2 projects)
	Introduction to Microsoft Windows NT Workstation 4
Word Processing	Microsoft Word 2002[2] • Microsoft Word 2000[2] • Microsoft Word 97[1]
Spreadsheets	Microsoft Excel 2002[2] • Microsoft Excel 2000[2] • Microsoft Excel 97[1]
Database	Microsoft Access 2002[2] • Microsoft Access 2000[2] • Microsoft Access 97[1]
Presentation Graphics	Microsoft PowerPoint 2002[2] • Microsoft PowerPoint 2000[2] • Microsoft PowerPoint 97[1]
Desktop Publishing	Microsoft Publisher 2002[1] • Microsoft Publisher 2000[1]

PROGRAMMING	
Programming	Microsoft Visual Basic.NET: Complete Concepts and Techniques[2] • Microsoft Visual Basic 6: Complete Concepts and Techniques[1] • Programming in QBasic • Java Programming: Complete Concepts and Techniques[1] • Structured COBOL Programming 2e

INTERNET	
Browser	Microsoft Internet Explorer 6: Introductory Concepts and Techniques • Microsoft Internet Explorer 5: An Introduction • Microsoft Internet Explorer 4: An Introduction • Netscape Navigator 6: An Introduction • Netscape Navigator 4: An Introduction
Web Page Creation and Design	Web Design: Introductory Concepts and Techniques • HTML: Complete Concepts and Techniques 2e[2] • Microsoft FrontPage 2002: Essential Concepts and Techniques • Microsoft FrontPage 2002[2] • Microsoft FrontPage 2000[1] • JavaScript: Complete Concepts and Techniques 2e[1]

SYSTEMS ANALYSIS	
Systems Analysis	Systems Analysis and Design 4e

DATA COMMUNICATIONS	
Data Communications	Business Data Communications: Introductory Concepts and Techniques 3e

[1]Also available as an Introductory Edition, which is a shortened version of the complete book
[2]Also available as an Introductory Edition, which is a shortened version of the complete book and also as a Comprehensive Edition, which is an extended version of the complete book

Preface

The Shelly Cashman Series® offers the finest textbooks in computer education. We are proud of the fact that our previous *Microsoft Visual Basic* books have been so well received by instructors and students. The *Microsoft Visual Basic .NET* books continue with the innovation, quality, and reliability found in the previous editions. In particular, a new step-by-step pedagogy has been integrated with an in-depth discussion of programming concepts and techniques. In addition, the end-of-chapter exercises are enhanced with critical-thinking problems.

Visual Basic .NET is the most significant upgrade since the introduction of Visual Basic. Some of the major enhancements to Visual Basic .NET include: (1) an easier-to-use integrated development environment (IDE); (2) support for Web Forms and XML Web services; (3) Windows Forms that provide a clear, object-oriented, extensible set of classes that enable you to develop rich Windows applications; (4) Project templates that allow you easily to create various types of Windows and Web applications and controls; (5) new features that incorporate resources such as message queues, event logs, and performance counters into applications; and (6) new debugging features.

In our *Visual Basic. NET* books, you will find an educationally sound and easy-to-follow pedagogy that combines a step-by-step approach with corresponding screens. The Other Ways and Tip features offer in-depth suggestions about alternative ways to complete a task and programming techniques. Every programming chapter builds an application from start to finish following a disciplined development cycle defined in Chapter 1. The Shelly Cashman Series *Microsoft Visual Basic .NET* books will make your programming class exciting and dynamic and one that your students will remember as one of their better educational experiences.

Objectives of This Textbook

Microsoft Visual Basic .NET: Introductory Concepts and Techniques is intended for a one-credit course or a full-semester course that includes a survey of programming using Visual Basic .NET. No experience with a computer is assumed, and no mathematics beyond the high school freshman level is required. The objectives of this book are:

- To teach the fundamentals of the Microsoft Visual Basic .NET programming language
- To emphasize the development cycle as a means of creating applications
- To illustrate well-written and readable programs using a disciplined coding style, including documentation and indentation standards
- To teach the basic concepts and methods of object-oriented programming and object-oriented design
- To use practical problems to illustrate application-building techniques
- To encourage independent study and help those who are working alone in a distance education environment

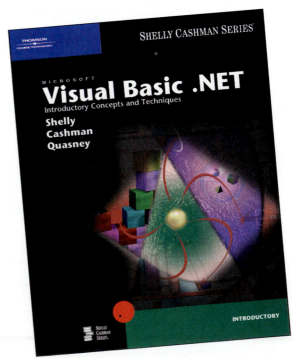

The Shelly Cashman Approach

Features of the Shelly Cashman Series *Microsoft Visual Basic .NET* books include:

- **Building Applications** Each programming chapter builds a complete application using the six phases of the development cycle: (1) analyze requirements; (2) design solution; (3) validate design; (4) implement design; (5) test solution; and (6) document solution.

- **Step-by-Step, Screen-by-Screen Methodology** Each of the tasks required to build an application within a chapter is identified using a step-by-step, screen-by-screen methodology. Students have the option of learning Visual Basic .NET by reading the book without the use of a computer or by following the steps on a computer and building a chapter application from start to finish.

- **More Than Just Step-By-Step** This book offers extended but clear discussions of programming concepts. Important Visual Basic. NET design and programming tips are interspersed throughout the chapters. When a Visual Basic .NET statement is introduced, one or more tables follow showing the general form of the statement and the various options available. With in-depth appendices on the Visual Basic .NET common controls, general forms of statements, and .NET Framework class library, the book can be used as a Visual Basic .NET reference manual.

- **Other Ways Boxes for Reference** Visual Basic .NET provides a variety of ways to carry out a given task. The Other Ways boxes displayed at the end of many of the step-by-step sequences specify the other ways to do the task completed in the steps. Thus, the steps and the Other Ways box make a comprehensive reference unit.

Organization of This Textbook

Microsoft Visual Basic .NET: Introductory Concepts and Techniques provides detailed instruction on how to use Visual Basic .NET. The material is divided into four chapters and six appendices as follows:

Chapter 1 – An Introduction to Visual Basic .NET and Program Design Chapter 1 provides an overview of the capabilities of Visual Basic .NET, application development, program development methodology, program design tools, object-oriented design and object-oriented programming, and the .NET architecture.

Chapter 2 – The Visual Basic .NET Integrated Development Environment Chapter 2 introduces students to the major elements of the Visual Basic .NET integrated development environment. Students modify the Take-Home Pay Calculator. The modifications consist of changing a property of a control and changing code. Topics include starting Visual Basic .NET; customizing the development environment; opening a project; running a project; setting a property on a control; modifying code; saving a project; printing a form and code; and accessing and using the Visual Basic .NET Help system.

Chapter 3 – Building an Application in the Visual Basic .NET Environment Chapter 3 introduces students to the process of building a complete application in the Visual Basic .NET environment. The chapter begins with a requirements document for the State Tax Computation application and shows the process of proper design and analysis of the program. Topics include designing a Visual Basic .NET application; changing form properties; adding controls to a form; moving and resizing controls; changing properties of controls; writing code for an event procedure; commenting code; and using the assignment statement.

Chapter 4 – Working with Variables, Constants, Data Types, and Expressions Chapter 4 presents students with the fundamental concepts of programming, including variables, constants, data types, and expressions. The chapter introduces two new controls in the development of the Automobile Loan Calculator. Topics include proper alignment and sizing of controls; setting a default button on a form; locking controls on a form; coding a form Load event; declaring variables and constants; using data types properly; using arithmetic expressions; understanding operator precedence; converting data types; and using intrinsic functions.

Appendices This book concludes with six appendices. Appendix A covers program design tools, including flowcharting and the Unified Modeling Language (UML). Appendix B demonstrates how to take full advantage of the .NET IDE by setting the proper screen resolution and arranging windows to maximize productivity. Appendix C summarizes the common controls used in the book along with common properties, methods, and events for those controls. Appendix D summarizes the Visual Basic .NET statements introduced in the book. Appendix E provides an overview of several common classes in the .NET Framework class library that a beginning programmer will find useful. Appendix F provides students with an ASCII chart.

End-of-Chapter Activities

A notable strength of the Shelly Cashman Series *Microsoft Visual Basic .NET* books is the extensive student activities at the end of each chapter. Well-structured student activities can make the difference between students merely participating in a class and students retaining the information they learn. The end-of-chapter activities in the Shelly Cashman Series *Visual Basic .NET* books are detailed below.

- **What You Should Know** A listing of the tasks completed in the chapter in order of presentation together with the pages on which the step-by-step, screen-by-screen explanations appear. This section provides a perfect study review for students.

- **Key Terms** This list of the key terms found in the chapter together with the pages on which the terms are defined aid students in mastering the chapter material.

- **Homework Assignments** The homework assignments are divided into three sections: Label the Figure, Short Answer, and Learn It Online. The Label the Figure section in the chapters where it applies, involves a figure and call outs that students fill in. The Short Answer section includes fill in the blank and short essay questions. The Learn It Online section is comprised of Web-based exercises that include chapter reinforcement (true/false, multiple choice, and short answer), practice tests, learning games, and Web exercises that require students to extend their learning beyond the material covered in the book.

- **Debugging Assignment** This exercise requires students to open an application with errors from the Visual Basic .NET Data Disk that accompanies the book and debug it. Students may obtain a copy of the Visual Basic .NET Data Disk by following the instructions on page xvi in the preface of this book.

- **Programming Assignments** An average of ten programming assignments per chapter require students to apply the knowledge gained in the chapter to build applications on a computer. The initial programming assignments step students through building the application and are accompanied by screens showing the desired interface. Later assignments state only the problem, allowing students to create on their own.

Shelly Cashman Series Teaching Tools

The two categories of ancillary material that accompany this textbook are Teaching Tools (ISBN 0-7895-6550-1) and Online Content. These ancillaries are available to adopters through your Course Technology representative or by calling one of the following telephone numbers: Colleges and Universities, 1-800-648-7450; High Schools, 1-800-824-5179; Private Career Colleges, 1-800-347-7707; Canada, 1-800-268-2222; Corporations with IT Training Centers, 1-800-648-7450; and Government Agencies, Health-Care Organizations, and Correctional Facilities, 1-800-477-3692.

Teaching Tools

The Teaching Tools for this textbook include both teaching and testing aids. The contents of the Teaching Tools CD-ROM are listed below.

- **Instructor's Manual**   The Instructor's Manual consists of Microsoft Word files that include lecture notes, solutions to laboratory assignments, and a large test bank. The files allow you to modify the lecture notes or generate quizzes and exams from the test bank using your own word processing software. Where appropriate, solutions to laboratory assignments are embedded as icons.

- **Figures in the Book**   Illustrations for every screen in the textbook are available. Use this ancillary to create a slide show from the illustrations for lecture or to print transparencies for use in lecture with an overhead projector.

- **ExamView**   ExamView is a state-of-the-art test builder that is easy to use. ExamView enables you quickly to create printed tests, Internet tests, and computer (LAN-based) tests. You can enter your own test questions or use the test bank that accompanies ExamView. The test bank is the same as the one described in the Instructor's Manual section.

- **Lecture Success System**   This ancillary, which consists of intermediate files that correspond to certain figures in the book, allows you to step through the creation of an application in a chapter during lecture without entering large amounts of data.

- **Instructor's Lab Solutions**   Solutions and required files for all the Chapter projects, Debugging Assignments, and Programming Assignments at the end of each chapter are available.

- **Student Files**   Most of the projects created in this book do not use files supplied by the authors. In the few instances, however, where students are instructed to open a project to complete a task, the files are supplied.

- **Course Syllabus**   Any instructor who has been assigned a course at the last minute knows how difficult it is to come up with a course syllabus. For this reason, sample syllabi are included that can be customized easily to a course.

- **Chapter Reinforcement**   True/false, multiple choice, and short answer questions help students gain confidence.

- **Interactive Labs**   Eighteen completely updated, hands-on Interactive Labs that take students from ten to fifteen minutes each to step through help solidify and reinforce mouse and keyboard usage and computer concepts. Student assessment is available.

- **PowerPoint Presentation**   PowerPoint Presentation is a multimedia lecture presentation system that provides PowerPoint slides for each chapter. Presentations are based on the chapters' objectives. Use this presentation system to present well-organized lectures that are both interesting and knowledge based. PowerPoint Presentation provides consistent coverage at schools that use multiple lecturers in their programming courses.

Online Content

If you use Blackboard or WebCT, the test bank for this book is free in a simple, ready-to-use format. Visit the Instructor Resource Center for this textbook at course.com to download the test bank, or contact your local sales representative for details.

Acknowledgments

The Shelly Cashman Series would not be the leading computer education series without the contributions of outstanding publishing professionals. First, and foremost, among them is Becky Herrington, director of production and designer. She is the heart and soul of the Shelly Cashman Series, and it is only through her leadership, dedication, and tireless efforts that superior products are made possible.

Under Becky's direction, the following individuals made significant contributions to these books: Doug Cowley, production manager; Ginny Harvey, series specialist and developmental editor; Ken Russo, senior Web and graphic designer; Mike Bodnar, associate production manager; Mark Norton, technical analyst; Siva Gogulapati, interactive media manager; Doug Cowley, Betty Hopkins, and Christy Pardini, interior designers; Michelle French, cover designer; Kellee LaVars, interior illustrator; Betty Hopkins, Jeanne Black, and Christy Pardini, QuarkXPress compositors; Richard Hansberger, developmental/copy editor; Ginny Harvey, proofreader; Cristina Haley, indexer.

Finally, we would like to thank Richard Keaveny, associate publisher; Cheryl Ouellette, managing editor; Jim Quasney, series consulting editor; Alexandra Arnold and Erin Runyon, product managers; Katie McAllister, marketing manager; Reed Cotter, associate product manager; and Emilie Perreault, editorial assistant.

Gary B. Shelly
Thomas J. Cashman
Jeffrey J. Quasney

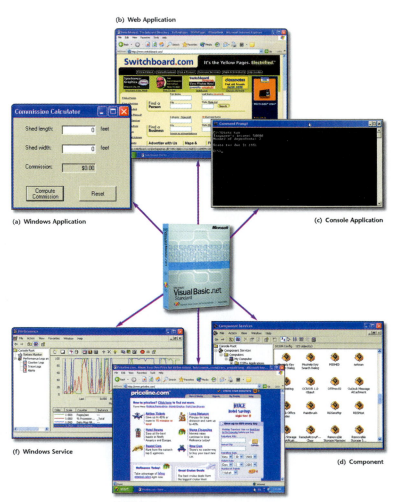

(a) Windows Application
(b) Web Application
(c) Console Application
(d) Component
(e) Web Service
(f) Windows Service

Visual Studio .NET Professional 60-Day Trial Edition

A copy of the complete version of the Microsoft Visual Studio .NET Professional 60-Day trial edition on DVD, which includes Microsoft Visual Basic .NET, can be found on the inside back cover of this book. When you activate the software, you will receive a license that allows you to use the software for 60 days. Course Technology and Microsoft provide no product support for this trial edition. When the trial period ends, you can purchase a copy of Microsoft Visual Studio .NET or Microsoft Visual Basic .NET, or uninstall the trial edition and reinstall your previous version.

> **Tip**
>
> **Installation Recommendations**
> To complete the programming assignments in this book, visit scsite.com/vsinstall for recommendations on to how to install the 60-Day trial edition or any edition of Visual Studio .NET or Visual Basic .NET.

Minimum System Requirements

The minimum system requirements are a Pentium II-class processor, 450 MHz; Windows XP Professional (160 MB RAM) or Windows 2000 Professional (96 MB RAM) or Windows 2000 Server (192 MB RAM) or Windows NT 4.0 Workstation with SP6 (64 MB RAM) or Windows NT 4.0 Server with SP6 (160 MB RAM); 3.5 GB on installation drive and 500 MB on system drive; DVD-ROM drive; Super VGA 800 x 600 or higher resolution monitor; mouse or compatible pointing device; and an Internet connection for activation.

To the Student Getting the Most Out of Your Book

Welcome to *Microsoft Visual Basic. NET: Introductory Concepts and Techniques*. You can save yourself a lot of time and gain a better understanding of Visual Basic .NET if you spend a few minutes reviewing the figures and call outs in this section.

1 Each Chapter Builds an Application

Each programming chapter builds a complete application, which is carefully described and shown in the first figure of the chapter.

2 Consistent Presentation

The authors use a disciplined approach to building all chapter applications using the six phases of the development cycle. By the end of the course, you will be building applications using this methodology by habit.

3 Pedagogy

Chapter applications are built using a step-by-step, screen-by-screen approach. This pedagogy allows you to build the application on a computer as you read the chapter. Generally, each step is followed by an italic explanation that indicates the result of the step.

4 More Than Just Step-By-Step

This book offers extended but clear discussions of programming concepts. Important Visual Basic. NET design and programming concepts are interspersed throughout the chapters.

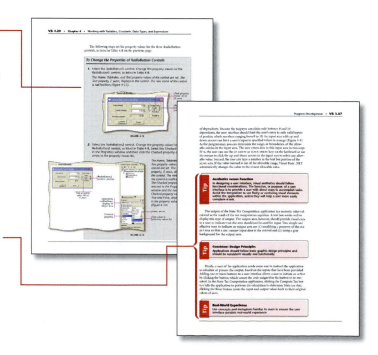

5 Review

After successfully stepping through the chapter, a section titled What You Should Know lists the Visual Basic .NET tasks with which you should be familiar in the order they are presented in the chapter.

6 Test Preparation

The Key Terms section lists the bold terms in the chapter you should know for test purposes.

7 Reinforcement and Extension

The Short Answer exercises are the traditional pencil-paper exercises. The Learn It Online exercises are Web based. Some of these Web-based exercises, such as the Practice Test and Crossword Puzzle, are for reinforcement. Others take you beyond the Visual Basic .NET topics covered in the chapter.

8 In the Lab

If you really want to learn how to program in Visual Basic .NET, then you must design, program, and debug applications using Visual Basic .NET. Every programming chapter includes a Debugging Assignment and several carefully developed Programming Assignments.

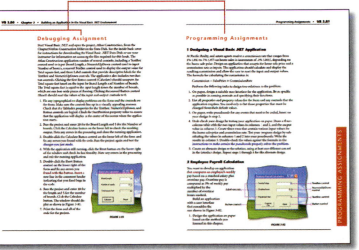

Data Disk Download Instructions

A few of the exercises in this book require that you begin by opening a data file from a Data Disk. Choose one of the following to obtain a copy of the Data Disk.

Instructors

- A copy of the Data Disk is on the Teaching Tools CD-ROM below the category Student Data Files, which you can copy to your school's network for student use.
- Download the Data Disk via the World Wide Web by following the instructions below.
- Contact us via e-mail at reply@course.com.
- Call Course Technology's Customer Service department for fast and efficient delivery of the Data Disk.

Students

- Check with your instructor to determine the best way to obtain a copy of the Data Disk.
- Download the Data Disk via the World Wide Web by following the instructions below.

Instructions for Downloading the Data Disk from the World Wide Web

1 Insert a formatted floppy disk in drive A. Start your browser and then enter the URL scsite.com.

2 When the SCSITE.COM page displays, perform **one** of the following procedures: (a) *Browse by Subject area:* Click the subject category to which your book belongs. When the category list expands, click the title of your textbook. When the Textbook page displays, scroll down to the Data Files area and then click From FTP Site. Follow the instructions beginning with step 3 below. (b) *Support area:* Click Download Instructions. Follow the instructions on the screen.

3 If the Save As dialog box displays, click the Save button.

4 When the Save As dialog box displays, select a folder on your hard disk to download the file to. Write down the folder name listed in the Save in box and the file name listed in the File name box for use in step 6, and then click the Save button.

5 When a dialog box displays indicating the download is complete, click the OK button. Close your browser.

6 Open Windows Explorer and display the contents of the folder to which you downloaded the file. Double-click the downloaded file name on the right side of the Windows Explorer window.

7 When the WinZip Self-Extractor dialog box displays, type a: in the Unzip To Folder text box, and then click the Unzip button.

8 When the WinZip Self-Extractor displays the number of files unzipped, click the OK button. Click the Close button in the WinZip Self-Extractor dialog box. Close Windows Explorer.

9 Remove the floppy disk from drive A and label it Shelly Cashman Data Disk. You now are ready to insert the Data Disk and open the required files.

1

An Introduction to Visual Basic .NET and Program Design

Objectives

You will have
mastered the material in
this chapter when you can:

- Describe Visual Basic .NET
- Describe the Visual Basic programming language
- Describe programs, programming, applications, and program development
- Identify each of the phases in the development cycle
- Define an algorithm
- Define objects, attributes, and methods
- Explain object-oriented programming (OOP) and object-oriented design (OOD)
- Describe rapid application development (RAD)
- Identify the key components of .NET

Introduction

Before a computer can produce a desired result, it must have a step-by-step series of instructions that tells it exactly what to do. The step-by-step series of instructions is called a **program**. The process of writing the sets of instructions for the computer to follow is called **programming**. **Programmers**, also called **software developers**, design and write programs. An **application** is a collection of one or more programs that is designed to complete a specific task, such as word processing or accounting. The process of using a programming language or programming environment to build software applications is called **program development**.

Microsoft Visual Basic .NET encompasses a set of tools and technologies that helps developers build programs quickly. Visual Basic .NET's user-friendly programming environment, along with the relative simplicity of its programming language, allows individuals with little programming experience to create a wide range of programs.

This chapter concentrates on the many uses of Visual Basic .NET and how Visual Basic .NET can help you develop programs. The chapter first covers the types of programs that you create using Visual Basic .NET and then covers the fundamental program design concepts and tools used to design a program logically to solve a problem. You also will learn about .NET and the technologies involved in Visual Basic .NET programs.

What Is Microsoft Visual Basic .NET?

Microsoft Visual Basic .NET is a programming environment that allows you to build programs for the Windows operating system or any operating system that supports Microsoft's .NET architecture. **.NET** (pronounced *dot net*) encompasses a series of technologies that allows almost any type of program to run in a common environment, which is discussed in more detail later in the chapter. Visual Basic .NET is the seventh version of Microsoft's Visual Basic programming environment. By adding .NET to the name, Visual Basic, Microsoft indicates Visual Basic's tight integration with Microsoft's .NET initiative. You often will see Visual Basic .NET referred to with the abbreviation, VB .NET. Visual Basic .NET is based on the **Visual Basic programming language**, which evolved from BASIC (Beginner's All-purpose Symbolic Instruction Code).

The Visual Basic .NET programming environment allows you to create programs for the Windows operating system and the Web. Figure 1-1 illustrates the types of programs you can create with Visual Basic .NET. A **Windows application** (Figure 1-1a) is a program with a graphical user interface that runs in the Windows environment. A **Web application** (Figure 1-1b) is a program that a user accesses through a Web browser. **Console applications** (Figure 1-1c) run in a text environment such as the Windows MS-DOS prompt or Command Prompt interface. **Components** (Figure 1-1d) are programs that serve as helpers or prebuilt pieces of other programs. A **Web service** (Figure 1-1e) is a program that receives a request for information from another program over the Web and returns data to the requesting program. A **Windows service** (Figure 1-1f) performs maintenance or data-gathering tasks without requiring user intervention.

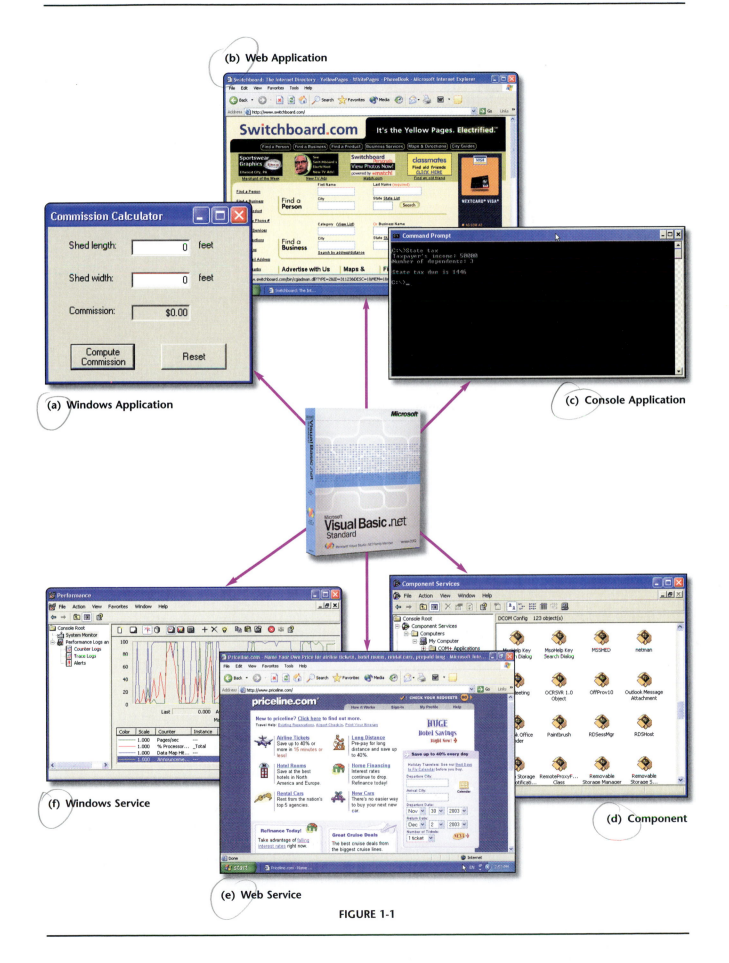

(b) Web Application

(a) Windows Application

(c) Console Application

(f) Windows Service

(e) Web Service

(d) Component

FIGURE 1-1

As shown in Table 1-1, Visual Basic .NET is available in a stand-alone edition, Visual Basic .NET Standard. It also is packaged in several editions of **Microsoft Visual Studio .NET**, which is a comprehensive set of programming languages and tools for building Windows applications, Web applications, and other programs and services. The edition of Visual Studio .NET or Visual Basic .NET most appropriate for you depends on the programming tasks you want to accomplish.

Table 1-1   Editions of Visual Basic .NET

EDITION	TYPICAL USE
Visual Basic .NET Standard	Hobbyist or small corporation with a small software development team
Visual Studio .NET Professional	Software developer, small or mid-sized corporation
Visual Studio .NET Academic	Student learning or instructor teaching Visual Basic .NET in an academic environment; includes everything in Visual Studio .NET Professional, plus additional samples and tools for creating classroom and lab materials
Visual Studio .NET Enterprise Developer (VSED)	Large corporation developing complex applications that interact with other systems and many data sources; includes everything in Visual Studio .NET Professional, plus additional tools to support larger development teams
Visual Studio .NET Enterprise Architect (VSEA)	Large corporation designing large applications; includes everything in Visual Studio .NET Enterprise Developer, plus additional tools for designing large applications

Programming and Application Development

When a program starts to run, its instructions are placed into the computer's memory, and the program is called a **stored program**. Memory also stores any data that the instructions process or manipulate.

Once the program is stored, the first instruction is located and sent to the control unit (**fetched**) where it is translated into a form the computer can understand (**decoded**), and then carried out (**executed**) (Figure 1-2). The result of the instruction is placed in memory (**stored**). Then, the next instruction is fetched, decoded, and executed, and the results are stored again in memory. This process, called a **machine cycle**, continues under the direction of the operating system, instruction by instruction, until the program is completed or until the computer is instructed to halt.

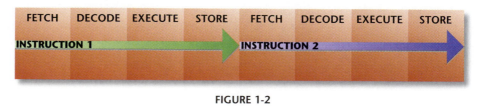

FIGURE 1-2

Programming also is referred to as **coding**, because the instructions written by a computer programmer are called computer code, or **code** (Figure 1-3).

```
[Design] Form1.vb
Form1                                          ▼   (Declarations)                                        ▼
   1 ⊟ Public Class Form1
   2       Inherits System.Windows.Forms.Form
   3
   4 ⊞   Windows Form Designer generated code
 136 ⊟     ' Chapter 3:     State Tax Computation
 137       ' Programmer:    J. Quasney
 138       ' Date:          September 2, 2003
 139       ' Purpose:       This project calculates state income tax due based
 140       '                on income level and number of dependents.
 141 ⊟     Private Sub btnCompute_Click(ByVal sender As System.Object, ByVal e As System.EventArgs) Handles btnCompute.Clic
 142           ' Calculate tax and display the result in the txtTaxDue text box
 143           txtTaxDue.Text = 0.03 * (txtIncome.Text - 600 * nudDependents.Value)
 144       End Sub
 145
 146 ⊟     Private Sub btnReset_Click(ByVal sender As System.Object, ByVal e As System.EventArgs) Handles btnReset.Click
 147           ' Set all input and output display values to 0
 148           txtIncome.Text = "0"
 149           nudDependents.Value = 0
 150           txtTaxDue.Text = "0"
 151       End Sub
 152 └ End Class
 153
```

FIGURE 1-3

The process of using a programming language or programming environment to build an application made up of one or more programs is called **application development**. An application tells a computer how to accept instructions and data from the user and how to produce information in response to those instructions. Most computer users do not code the programs that make up the applications they use for common business and personal purposes, such as word processing and spreadsheet applications, or Web browsers. Instead, they purchase the applications from software vendors or stores that sell computer products. These purchased programs often are referred to as **application software packages**.

Application Types

As shown in Figure 1-1 (on page VB 1.03), Visual Basic .NET allows you to develop different types of applications. Some programs you write will require an application that has a user interface, including Web and Windows applications, while other programs such as services and components will not. This section describes the types of applications you can develop in more detail.

Windows Applications

Visual Basic .NET allows developers to create Windows applications with a graphical user interface as shown in Figure 1-4 on the next page. The Windows graphical user interface (GUI) provides visual cues such as menus, buttons, and icons that allow a user to enter data and instructions into the computer.

Both Windows applications and Console applications, which are discussed on the next page, are called stand-alone applications. A **stand-alone application** is an application that does not require other applications or data sources to run in the operating system.

FIGURE 1-4

Web Applications

Web browsers provide another environment for Visual Basic .NET programs. Visual Basic .NET can be used to create complete Web sites and pages that run in almost any Web browser on any operating system. When you create and run a Web page using Visual Basic .NET, the program code is converted into standard Hypertext Markup Language (HTML). **Hypertext Markup Language** (**HTML**) is the Web authoring language that uses a set of special instructions called tags or markups to define the structure and layout of a Web document and specify how the page is displayed in a browser. The resulting application is called a Web application (Figure 1-5). The principles of Web page design are similar to those of Windows applications with a graphical user interface. Typically, developers work with a more limited set of buttons, menus, and other graphical interface objects when building Web pages than they would when building a Windows application.

FIGURE 1-5

Console Applications

Visual Basic .NET can be used to create Console applications that run within the Windows command prompt environment. While working with a **command prompt interface**, a user enters data and instructions into a computer by typing keywords or pressing keys on the keyboard. Figure 1-6 shows an example of a program running in a command prompt environment. The text, C:\>, is a prompt that tells the user that the application is awaiting a command from the user.

command entered by user

data entry

result of calculation

command prompt

FIGURE 1-6

Windows Services

Unlike Console, Windows, and Web applications, some programs — such as services — do not require any user interaction at all. A **service** is a program that runs in an operating system and performs such tasks as maintenance, information gathering, security, and notification but requires no user interaction. Figure 1-7 shows a view of data gathered by a Windows service that monitors the computer system's performance. A Windows service often begins when Windows is started, and performs maintenance or data gathering tasks in the background while Windows is running.

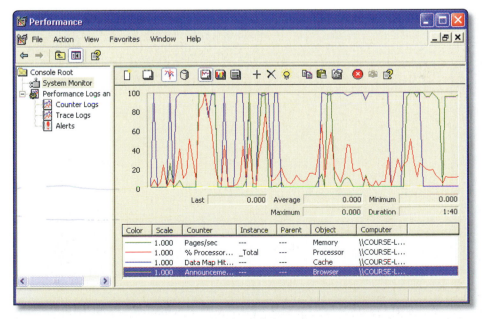

FIGURE 1-7

Visual Basic .NET allows you to create Windows services. For example, you can create a Windows service that sends an administrator an e-mail each time a user prints a document consisting of more than one hundred pages. The user will not see the Windows service running in the Windows GUI. As long as the Windows service is running on the user's computer, the service will monitor any request to print and check the page count, regardless of which application sends the request to print.

Web Services

Web services are a relatively new type of program that can be created using Visual Basic .NET. A Web service is a program that provides information to another program over the Web, but does not have a user interface. The information provided usually is specific and well defined. For example, an airline may create a Web service for programmers not associated with the airline who are developing travel-related Web applications. The airline's Web service may accept departure and arrival dates, departure and arrival cities, and the number of tickets being purchased as inputs (Figure 1-8). Based on this information, the Web service then sends a flight schedule back as output to the Web application. Once the Web application receives data from the airline's Web service, that data can be formatted for display on a Web page or used in any other way required by the programmers. A user does not provide data directly to a Web service; rather, data is sent in an electronic format from the Web application to the Web service and back again over the Internet. Web services developed in Visual Basic .NET rely on specific guidelines that determine how the input and output data should be formatted so that it can be sent electronically.

FIGURE 1-8

Components

Visual Basic .NET can create components for other programs to use (Figure 1-9). A component functions as a prebuilt program that can be used by other programs or applications to complete a task or process. Components usually have a programmatic interface, rather than a user interface. A **programmatic interface** defines the method in which other programs or applications should send and receive data from a component. A component works behind the scenes. Figure 1-9 shows the Windows Component Services Manager, which allows Windows users to view and control the components that the Windows operating system uses as part of its normal operations.

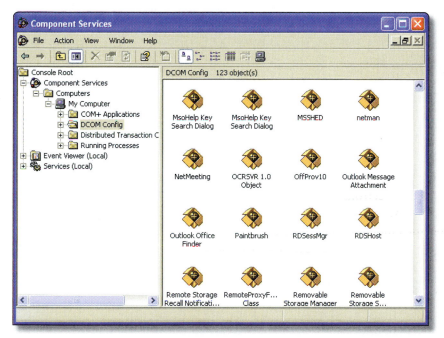

FIGURE 1-9

Components provide the benefit of **reusability**, which means they can be reused over and over by many programs developed by different programmers. Having reusable components means that companies can spend less time and money developing new programs, thus making components valuable to businesses. For example, a programmer first can develop an inventory component that knows how to get information about each product the company has in inventory. The development team then can use this inventory component in several applications to get information about a product in inventory. An accounting application, for example, can use the component to complete an end-of-month report. Another application used to create a catalog for the company's products can use the component to gather information about the product.

Windows services, Web services, and components are programs that do not have a user interface. Data is sent to the program and then data is returned or an action is performed by the program. Alternatively, the program can monitor the computer or operating system for a particular event to occur before performing an action. Often, common business functionality is programmed into a component, Web service, or Windows service, so that it can be made available to any other programmers in the organization who need that functionality for programs they are developing. For example, if a business has a component that knows how to look up an employee's telephone number when it is given an employee name, then a Windows application, Web application, or Console application all can use this same component.

The Development Cycle

Programmers do not sit down and start writing code as soon as they have a programming assignment. Instead, they follow an organized plan, or **methodology**, that breaks the development cycle into a series of tasks. Many formal program development methodologies are available to programmers.

The methodology used in this book breaks the **development cycle** into six phases: (1) analyze requirements; (2) design solution; (3) validate design; (4) implement design; (5) test solution; and (6) document solution. Figure 1-10 portrays the development cycle as a continuing, iterative process or loop. When the testing phase identifies errors or new requirements are demanded of the program, a new iteration of the cycle begins by analyzing the requirements.

Table 1-2 describes each step that a programmer takes to create a computer program that solves a problem. In the discussion that follows, the term program is used to describe the result of the development cycle. An application, which is made up of one or more programs, also can be the result of the development cycle.

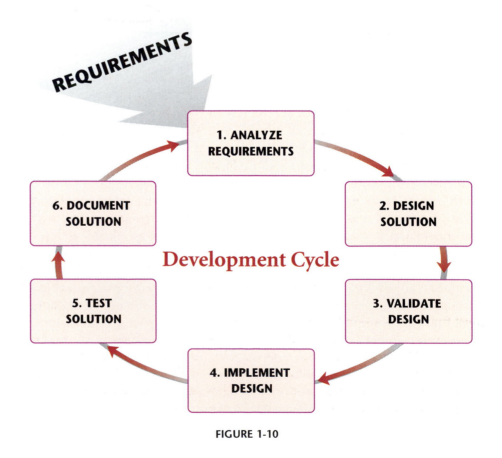

FIGURE 1-10

Table 1-2   The Development Cycle

	PHASE	DESCRIPTION
1	Analyze requirements	Verify that the requirements are complete, and translate user requirements into technical requirements, including descriptions of the program's inputs, processing, outputs, and interface.
2	Design solution	Develop a detailed, logical plan using a tool such as pseudocode, flowcharts, or class diagrams to group the program's activities into modules; devise a method of solution or algorithm for each module; and test the solution algorithms. Design the user interface for the application, including input areas, output areas, and other necessary elements.
3	Validate design	Step through the solution design with test data. Receive confirmation from the user that the design solves the problem in a satisfactory manner.
4	Implement design	Translate the design into a program using a programming language or programming environment by creating the user interface and writing code; include internal documentation, or comments, which are notes within the code that explain the purpose of code statements.
5	Test solution	Test the program, finding and correcting errors (debugging) until it is error free and contains enough safeguards to ensure the desired results.
6	Document solution	Review and, if necessary, revise internal documentation; and formalize and complete end-user (external) documentation.

Program requirements drive the development cycle. **Requirements** are supplied by the program's users or a representative of the users, and are presented in a **requirements document**. **Users** present a requirements document to programmers when they believe a particular problem can be solved by a program. A requirements document lists the functions and features that the program must provide for its users. Requirements include a statement of purpose for the requested program (also called a problem definition), the equations the program must use, and an explanation of how the program should respond to user interaction. Requirements may specify that a new program be developed or they may specify updates to an existing program. In addition, requirements indicate how the program will be made available to users or other programmers; for example, the requirements might specify that a stand-alone Windows application must be developed for the program, or they might specify that the program must function as a Windows or Web service.

An example of a requirements document is shown in Figure 1-11 on the next page. The document specifies the requirements for a new program that must be made available to users as both a Web application and a Windows application. The program's main purpose is to allow sales people inside and outside a company to calculate a commission on the sale of storage sheds.

REQUEST FOR NEW APPLICATION

Date submitted:	August 1, 2004
Submitted by:	Margaret Stevens
Purpose:	Inside and outside sales representatives request a quick method of verifying the correct commission they should receive on storage sheds that the company builds and they sell.
Application title:	Commission Calculator

Algorithms:	Commission is based on the square footage of the storage shed sold. The sales person knows the length and width of the shed. If the number of square feet is less than 200, then the commission is 7% of the total sales price. Otherwise, the commission is 11%. This year, prices are $5.00 per square foot.
	
	Calculations can be summarized as follows:
	
	SquareFeet = Length × Width
	TotalPrice = SquareFeet × $5.00
	
	If SquareFeet is less than 200:
	    Commission = TotalPrice × 7%
	Otherwise:
	    Commission = TotalPrice × 11%

Notes:	1) The outside sales force requires a Web interface for the program. Inside sales people do not have Web access and a Windows application is required for inside sales people. 2) Sales associates are accustomed to the following terminology: *Shed length, Shed width, and Commission.* 3) The application should allow the user to enter values for the length and width of the shed. 4) Due to state regulations, we do not make sheds whose length or width is greater than 30 feet. 5) The application should also allow the user to reset all values on the screen to zero (0) so that another calculation can be performed. 6) The calculation of commission should be designated by the term, Compute Commission. The resetting of the values should be designated by the term, Reset.

Approvals

Approval Status:	X	Approved
		Rejected
Approved by:	Randall Washington	
Date:	August 4, 2004	
Assigned to:	J. Quasney, Programmer	

FIGURE 1-11

Analyze Requirements — Phase 1

The first step in analyzing requirements is to verify that the requirements are complete and provide all the necessary information to solve the problem. If the statement of purpose is vague or unclear, or an equation is incorrect or incomplete, the programmer must request that the requirements document be revised to address these issues. Second, the programmer should make an initial determination that it is possible to solve the problem using a program.

In order to make sure that the problem can be solved, the programmer lists the input and output data required for the program. After doing so, the programmer determines whether the input data is available to the programmer for testing purposes. Next, the programmer ensures that the information provided explains how to convert the input data into output data so that a solution, or **algorithm**, can be developed. In other words, the requirements must clearly state the rules that govern how to convert the input into output.

The requirements must state how the user will interact with the program, which includes requirements that specify whether the program must be made available in an application with a user interface such as a Windows or Web application, or whether the program will be part of a service or component. The requirements may include terminology that the user is familiar with and, therefore, must be included in the user interface. The requirements help the programmer determine which technologies to use when designing a solution to the problem. For larger problems, the analysis also should include an initial breakdown of the problem into smaller problems so that programmers can develop solutions gradually and in smaller, more manageable pieces.

The requirements for the Commission Calculator shown in Figure 1-11 specify the input data that should be entered by the user and the equation that must be used to calculate the output data. The requirements also explain how users will interact with the program, including the rules that govern valid and invalid input data entered by the user. The end result of the analyze requirements phase is that both the user and the programmer must agree in writing that the requirements for the program are clear and complete. At this point, the programmer can begin to design a solution and the user can begin designing tests to verify that the solution satisfies the program's requirements.

Design Solution — Phase 2

When you **design** the solution, you develop a logical model that illustrates the sequence of steps you will take to solve the problem. Programmers use object diagrams, flowcharts, pseudocode, and storyboards to outline the logic of the program.

Often programs can be broken in to smaller pieces, called **objects**, which represent a real person, place, event, or transaction. Object-oriented design is an approach to program design that identifies how objects must interact with each other in order to solve a problem. The end product of object-oriented design is an object model. An **object model** illustrates the attributes and methods of an object. The **attributes** of an object are values that determine, for example, the appearance of an object. The **methods** of an object are instructions that the object uses to manipulate values, generate outputs, or perform actions. Attributes and methods together comprise an object. Objects often are individual programs themselves that can be reused by other programs.

The Commission Calculator requires that users access the program using one of two methods: a Web application and a Windows application. Rather than creating two completely separate applications for these two types of users, the algorithm used to solve the problem should be programmed only once. By centralizing the program logic for the two application types, maintenance of the program is easier and the logic only needs to be programmed once, rather than twice. The algorithm can be placed in an object. The Commission object has two attributes that correspond to the inputs, length and width. The object requires one method, getCommission(), that tells the object how to manipulate the input values and generate the required output. The getCommission() method performs the calculation after the attributes, length and width, are sent to the object by the program. Figure 1-12 shows a diagram of the Commission object using a standard diagramming technique that illustrates the methods and attributes of an object.

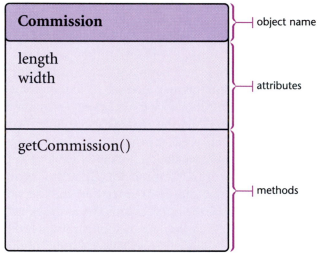

FIGURE 1-12

Programmers often create a diagram or picture called a **flowchart** that graphically represents the logic used to develop an algorithm. Table 1-3 shows a standard set of flowchart symbols used to represent various steps or operations in a program's logic. When you draw a complete flowchart, you must begin with a terminal symbol that is then connected by a flowline to the first logical step in the solution to the problem. Most of the time, each step required to solve a problem is represented by a separate symbol. Appendix A includes a more detailed discussion of how to develop flowcharts and diagram objects.

Table 1-3   Flowcharting Symbols and Their Meanings

SYMBOL	NAME	MEANING
	Process Symbol	Represents the process of executing a defined operation or group of operations that results in a change in value, form, or location of information; also functions as the default symbol when no other symbol is available
	Input/Output (I/O) Symbol	Represents an I/O function, which makes data available for processing (input) or for displaying (output) processed information
left to right, right to left, top to bottom, bottom to top	**Flowline Symbol**	Represents the sequence of available information and executable operations; lines connect other symbols, and arrowheads are mandatory only for right-to-left and bottom-to-top flow
	Annotation Symbol	Represents the addition of descriptive information, comments, or explanatory notes as clarification; vertical lines and broken lines may be placed on the left, as shown, or on the right
	Decision Symbol	Represents a decision that determines which of a number of alternative paths is to be followed
	Terminal Symbol	Represents the beginning, the end, or a point of interruption or delay in a program
	Connector Symbol	Represents any entry from, or exit to, another part of the flowchart; also serves as an off-page connector
	Predefined Process Symbol	Represents a named process consisting of one or more operations or program steps that are specified elsewhere

The next step in designing a solution is to develop the algorithm that represents the getCommission() method (Figure 1-12) of the Commission object. Figure 1-13 on the next page shows a flowchart that represents the algorithm used by the getCommission() method of the Commission object to calculate the correct commission. The flowchart includes a **control structure**, which is a portion of a program that allows the programmer to specify that code will be executed only if a condition is met. The control structure in the flowchart, for instance, illustrates how the program decides which commission rate to use based on the total number of square feet.

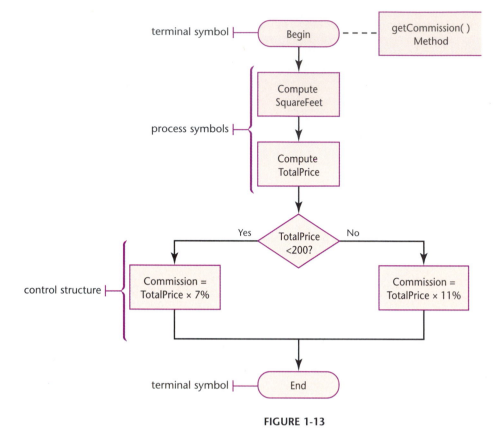

FIGURE 1-13

Programmers also use pseudocode to develop the logic of an algorithm for a program. **Pseudocode** expresses the step-by-step instructions using keywords, and depicts logical groupings or structures using indentation. Figure 1-14 shows the pseudocode for the getCommission() method of the Commission object. The pseudocode is not program code, but an English representation of how the code should be written. The pseudocode serves as an intermediary step between the requirements and the final program code. It allows the programmer to check the logic before proceeding to write code.

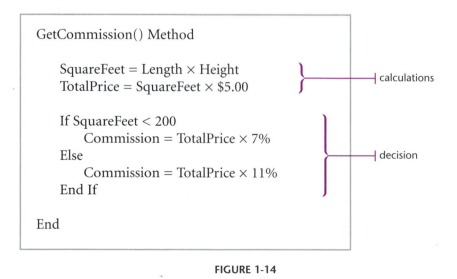

FIGURE 1-14

Because Visual Basic .NET often is used to create Web pages and Windows applications with graphical user interfaces, programmers may create a **storyboard**, or hand-drawn sketch, of how the application window or Web page will look and where the objects will be placed in the window or on the form. A storyboard also can serve as a reference for the logical names of these objects as you code your program.

The Commission Calculator application may use a similar user interface for both a Windows application and a Web application, as shown in the storyboard in Figure 1-15. Although these interfaces must be programmed separately, the user interface is similar and the same storyboard is useful for both.

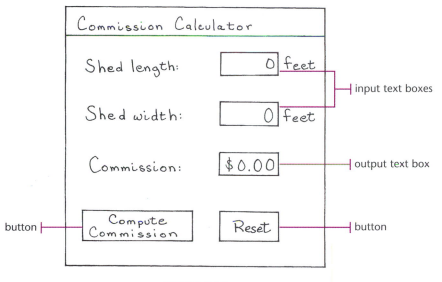

FIGURE 1-15

The end result of designing a solution includes technical documentation that explains how the program will meet the requirements. Any documents that relate to the design of the user interface should be made available to the user, who must validate that the design is correct and that the program's **usability**, which is a measure of a user's ability to interact with a program in a reasonable and intuitive manner, is acceptable.

Many programmers use combinations and variations of these program design tools. Your instructor or supervisor may prefer one type of design tool to another, and you will probably find one or two more useful than others as you develop your own programming style. In addition, companies often have written standards that specify the tools that must be used to design programs.

Validate Design — Phase 3

Both the programmer and the user must **validate**, or check, the program design. The programmer steps through the solution with test data to verify that the solution meets the requirements. The user also must agree that the design solves the problem put forth in the requirements. The validation of the design is the user's last chance to make certain that all of the requirements necessary were included in the initial requirements document. By comparing the program design with the original requirements, both the programmer and the user can validate that the solution is correct and satisfactory.

In the Commission Calculator application, the design can be validated by using a test case for input data and then stepping the test data through both the equation written in the requirements document and the algorithm presented in the program design. The results can be compared to be sure that they match.

Implement Design — Phase 4

The **implementation** of the design includes writing the code that translates the design into a program and, if necessary, creating the user interface. Coding also includes internal documentation, or **comments**, which are notes within the code that explain the purpose of the code. When programmers write the code and create the interface, their job includes testing the code as they write it. Related code that performs a specific task or function should be tested for correctness during the programming process. This type of testing is known as **unit testing**.

Based on the flowchart in Figure 1-13 on page VB 1.16 and the pseudocode in Figure 1-14 on page VB 1.16, Figure 1-16 shows some of the code necessary to implement the getCommission() method for the Commission Calculator application. Figure 1-17 shows the user interface developed for the Windows application from the original design illustrated in Figure 1-15 on the previous page.

```
5      Public Function getCommission() As Double
6          Dim dblSquareFeet, dblTotalPrice As Double
7          Dim Commission As Double
8
9          ' calculate the total number of square feet and the total price
10         ' based on the total number of square feet (square feet x $5.00)
11         dblSquareFeet = length * width
12         dblTotalPrice = dblSquareFeet * 5.0
13
14         ' if the number of square feet is less than 200, use the lower
15         ' commission rate
16         If dblSquareFeet < 200.0 Then
17             Commission = dblTotalPrice * 0.07
18         Else
19             Commission = dblTotalPrice * 0.11
20         End If
21
22         Return Commission
23     End Function
```

FIGURE 1-16

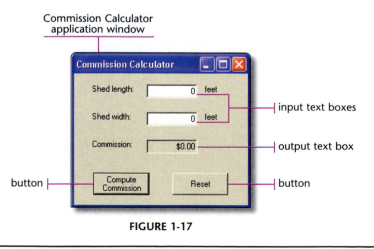

Commission Calculator application window

FIGURE 1-17

Test Solution — Phase 5

The purpose of **testing** is to verify that the program meets the requirements from the user's point of view. The program should perform its assigned function correctly under all normal circumstances. If the program includes a user interface, testing should ensure that the user interface also meets requirements. For larger projects, a test plan typically is developed at the same time that the requirements are agreed upon at the end of the analyze requirements phase. A **test plan** consists of a collection of test cases. **Test cases** are individual scenarios that include input data and expected output data and that are designed to ensure that the program solves a particular problem indicated in the program requirements.

If several programs or components comprise a finished application, then testing must ensure that all programs and components interact correctly. This is called **integration testing**.

The end result of testing the solution includes documentation of any problems with the application. If the user accepts the program as complete and correct, then the user documents this fact and the program may be put to use. If the testing results are unsatisfactory, then the results are documented and returned to the programmer. The resolution of the problems revealed during testing begins a new iteration of the development cycle, with the outstanding issues serving as requirements.

The Commission Calculator application requires testing to ensure that all possible cases of valid input data cause the program to calculate the correct result every time. The application must not allow the user to enter values disallowed by the requirements, such as a length or width greater than 30 feet. Test cases also should include input data that would result in the number of square feet being greater than 200 and less than 200. Based upon the requirements, the value of 200 for square feet is called a boundary value. **Boundary values** are values that cause a certain rule to become effective. Test cases include the testing of exact boundary values because common logic and programming mistakes occur when boundary values are reached in a problem.

Figure 1-18 shows the Commission Calculator application in the Windows environment being tested with input values of 10 feet and 20 feet for the length and width, respectively, of a shed. These input values result in an area of 200 square feet for the shed. Per the requirements, the correct commission should be calculated by multiplying the total sales price by 11%, which results in a commission of $110.00.

$$(200 \times \$5.00) \times 11\% = \$110.00$$

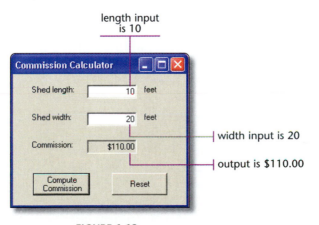

FIGURE 1-18

Document Solution — Phase 6

The final phase in the development cycle is to document the completed solution. The **documentation** for a completed programming project includes the requirements documents, program design documents, user interface documents, and documentation of the code. The code should be archived electronically so that it can be accessed in the event that a programmer must fix an error in the code or use the code for other purposes.

In the Commission Calculator project, final documentation consists of all documents generated during the development cycle. This also includes electronic archiving and printing the program code and design. The complete set of documents for the project includes the requirements document, approval of requirements by the user and programmer, program design documents, test cases, program code, and hard-copy proof that the test cases were completed successfully.

Object-Oriented Programming and Object-Oriented Design

Object-oriented programming and object-oriented design represent a recent methodology of program development. **Object-oriented programming** (**OOP**) is an approach to programming and application development in which the data and the code that operates on the data are packaged into a single unit called an object. **Object-oriented design** (**OOD**) represents the logical plan of a program as a set of interactions among objects and operations. The benefit is that programs developed using an object-oriented approach are easier to develop and maintain.

Objects

As you have learned, an object is anything real or abstract, about which you store both data and operations that manipulate the data. Each object has its own set of characteristics and behaviors, known as attributes and methods. Examples of objects are an invoice, an organization, a computer screen used to interact with a computer program, an airplane, or an employee. Parts of the Windows graphical user interface, such as windows, buttons, and text boxes, are also objects. An object may be composed of other objects, which in turn may contain other objects. For example, a window object may contain text box, check box, and button objects. **Aggregation** is the term used to describe the concept of an object being composed of other objects.

A **class** is the programmatic implementation, or description, of an object. A class is what you use to describe an object in programming terms. Once an object and its behaviors are described in a class, you can create an instance of that class in your program. Whereas a class defines a set of objects, an **instance** is a programmatic representation of a particular object.

Just as flowcharts describe the logic of algorithms, the **Unified Modeling Language** (**UML**), examples of which are shown earlier in Figure 1-12 on page VB 1.14 and later in Figure 1-20 on page 1.22, provides a standardized model for object-oriented design to depict or diagram concepts graphically for design purposes. The UML is a system of symbols used to describe object behaviors and interaction, and to represent how a system behaves or should behave. The UML is a relatively new language, having been developed in the 1990s from a number of object-oriented design tools. You will learn more about representing a program design using the UML later in this book. Appendix A includes an introduction to the use of the UML. Figure 1-12 on page VB 1.14 is an example of a type of UML diagram that shows the attributes and methods for an object.

Rapid Application Development

Rapid application development (**RAD**) refers to the use of prebuilt objects to make program and application development much faster. Using prebuilt objects is faster because you use existing objects rather than creating new ones yourself. The result is shorter development cycles, easier maintenance, and the ability to reuse objects for other projects. One of the major premises on which industry implementation of OOP is built is greater reusability of code.

As shown in Table 1-4, the adoption of an object-oriented approach to programming and program design has two primary benefits. First, using OOP means that not all members of a development team need to be proficient in an object-oriented programming language such as Visual Basic .NET, Visual C# .NET, Delphi, Java, or C++. Second, OOP provides a more practical and economical approach to programming because the task of creating objects can be separated from the task of assembling objects into applications. Some programmers can focus on creating objects while other developers leverage their knowledge of business processes to assemble applications using OOD and OOP methods and tools.

Table 1-4 Benefits of Object-Oriented Design and Programming

BENEFIT	EXPLANATION
Reusability	Classes are designed so they can be reused in many systems or so they can be used in the creation of other classes.
Stability	Classes are designed for frequent reuse and become stable over time.
Easier design	The programmer looks at objects as a black box and is not concerned with the details inside the object.
Faster design	Applications can be created from existing objects.

As you have learned, Visual Basic .NET allows you to build applications that use the Windows graphical user interface. The elements that comprise the graphical user interface are all objects. For example, a button you click in an application is an instance of a button class. An attribute of the button might be the text or icon that appears on the button face. A method of the button might be the action that is initiated when you click the button.

In Visual Basic .NET, a graphical object such as a button that is used to build the user interface is called a **control**. Controls have properties such as color or width. As well, controls have **events**, which are actions or occurrences, such as clicking a button or opening a new application window that a program can respond or react to. Events cause methods to execute in controls. When an event occurs, a message is sent to a method in the control that can be programmed to perform some task or function. A control also can have methods that are not events and are used to set or get properties. For example, a button may have a setColor() method that sets the color of the button that the user sees. The background on which the controls are drawn is called a **form**. When the application executes in the Windows environment, forms become windows. Forms are just another type of control, and they have properties, events, and methods as do other controls, such as buttons. Figure 1-19 shows a Visual Basic .NET application running in the Windows environment and the various controls used to build the graphical user interface. A partial UML diagram for a button control is shown in Figure 1-20.

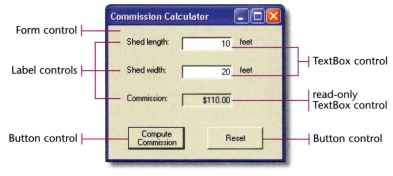

FIGURE 1-19

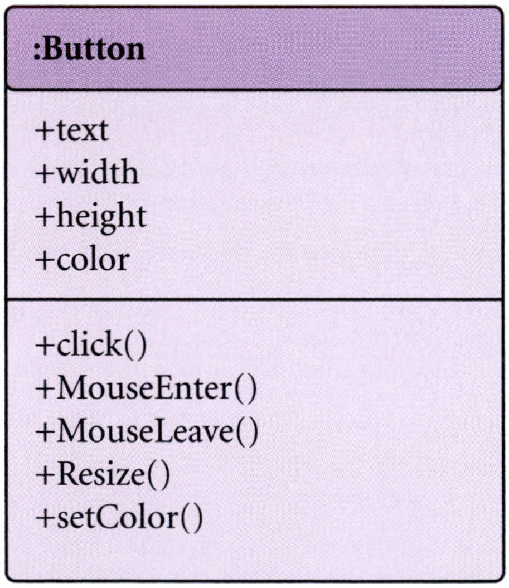

```
:Button

+text
+width
+height
+color

+click()
+MouseEnter()
+MouseLeave()
+Resize()
+setColor()
```

FIGURE 1-20

What Is .NET?

Microsoft announced its .NET initiative in 2000. As previously mentioned, .NET encompasses a series of technologies that allows almost any type of application to run in a common environment. Visual Studio .NET, which includes Visual Basic .NET, is the first major set of tools available that allow for applications to be created for .NET. The common environment in which applications created for .NET run is known as the **.NET Framework** (Figure 1-21).

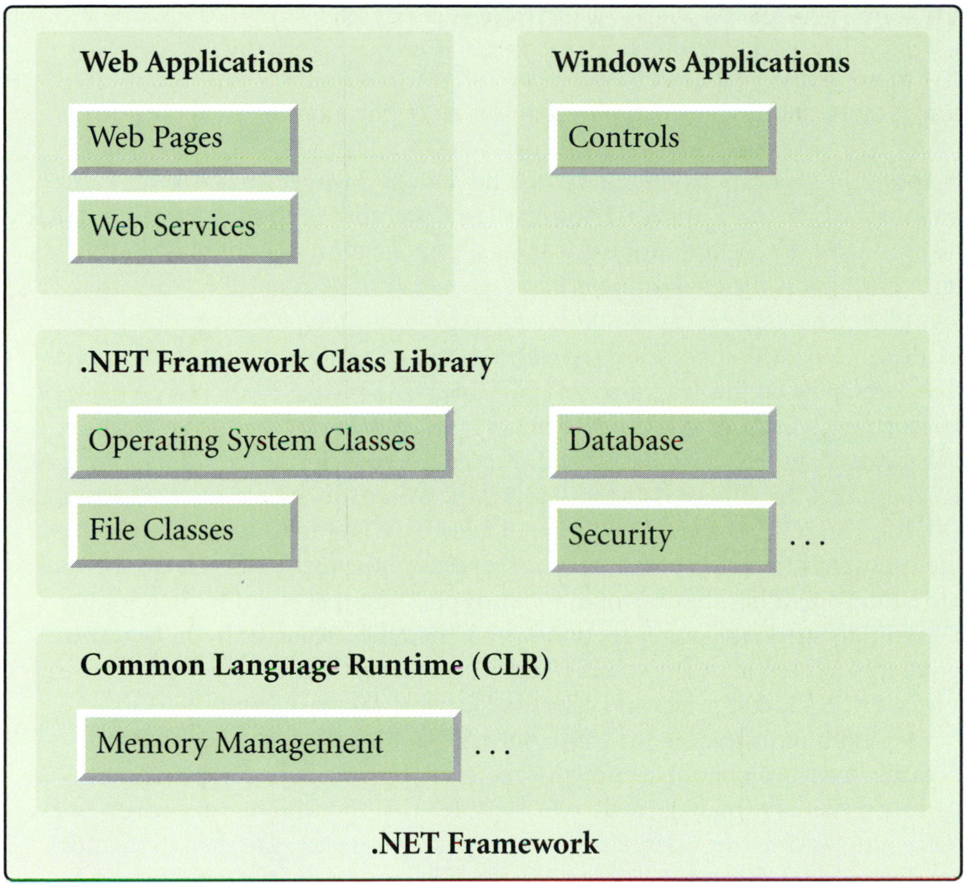

Web Applications

Web Pages

Web Services

Windows Applications

Controls

.NET Framework Class Library

Operating System Classes

File Classes

Database

Security

. . .

Common Language Runtime (CLR)

Memory Management

. . .

.NET Framework

FIGURE 1-21

The .NET Framework provides a programmer with a rich set of classes, known as the **.NET Framework class library**, which can be used to build applications. The class library offers two significant benefits to programmers. First, the class library provides commonly used classes that you do not have to spend time creating yourself. You can use these classes in your own programs. Second, it ensures that all programmers have access to the same common classes, thereby making code more understandable and reusable.

For these reasons and others, the .NET Framework is very powerful. First, it allows programmers using almost any .NET-enabled programming language to write applications and components (classes) that can be made available to others. In the past, programs written for the same operating system using different languages or technologies could not interact easily with each other. Second, the .NET Framework class library is full featured and extensible. The libraries provide almost any class that a programmer needs to interact with the operating system and other systems, such as databases and networks. In the past, programmers wrote complex code when working with other systems. Finally, the libraries provide an object view of the operating system and other systems. For example, a file in the operating system can be accessed through the library and the file will look like an object to the programmer. The file may have methods, such as readFile(), and attributes, such as fileSize.

The Common Language Runtime (CLR)

In previous versions of Visual Basic and other Windows development tools, the result of developing an application was an application that was executed in memory by the operating system, as described on page VB 1.04. In the .NET framework, applications do not execute directly in the operating system. Rather, an intermediate .NET system, known as the **Common Language Runtime** (**CLR**), takes control of the application and runs the application under the operating system. The CLR is the environment that executes Visual Basic .NET programs.

When you create an application using a programming language that is not made for .NET, the application typically contains operating system instructions that execute when the program runs. The operating system reads and executes the instructions when the operating system is instructed to execute the application. When you create .NET applications, however, the resulting applications consist of language that the CLR understands, called the **Microsoft Intermediate Language** (**MSIL**). The MSIL is sometimes referred to as IL. When the application executes, the CLR reads the MSIL and performs the steps of the machine cycle on the code, just as the operating system would for an application that is not written for the .NET Framework. All languages that work with .NET create MSIL. In fact, two programs written in different .NET languages, such as Visual Basic .NET and Visual C# .NET, that perform the same task, likely will have identical MSIL.

In addition to reading the MSIL, the CLR appropriates many tasks that typically have been performed by the operating system. For example, the CLR performs memory management, which means that the CLR decides where to execute commands in the computer's memory and where to store data in memory.

Figure 1-22 shows how a Visual Basic .NET program relates to the .NET Framework. The diagram illustrates the association between a Visual Basic .NET program, the MSIL that is created from the program, the CLR, and the Windows operating system.

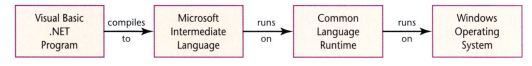

FIGURE 1-22

Visual Basic .NET Windows applications still are considered stand-alone applications, even though they require the CLR to operate. One benefit of the CLR is that a version of the CLR can be created for different operating systems. Therefore, you only need to create a .NET application once and it could run on several operating systems. In the past, creating one application to run on multiple operating systems was a very difficult undertaking. Visual Basic .NET allows you to create with relative ease programs that can run on many different types of systems.

Chapter Summary

This chapter provided an overview of application development, object-oriented design and object-oriented programming, and the Visual Basic .NET software development system. This overview has provided a context within which you can better understand the concepts and technologies involved in the chapters that follow. You also learned the fundamentals of program development, including the process and some of the tools used to assist in the process. Finally, you learned that Visual Basic .NET is a powerful programming environment that allows you to build complex object-based programs, including Console applications, Windows applications, Web applications, components, Windows services, and Web services.

Key Terms

aggregation *(VB 1.20)*
algorithm *(VB 1.13)*
application *(VB 1.02)*
application development *(VB 1.05)*
application software packages *(VB 1.05)*
attributes *(VB 1.13)*
boundary values *(VB 1.19)*
class *(VB 1.20)*
code *(VB 1.05)*
coding *(VB 1.05)*
command prompt interface *(VB 1.07)*
comments *(VB 1.18)*
Common Language Runtime (CLR) *(VB 1.24)*
components *(VB 1.02)*
Console applications *(VB 1.02)*
control *(VB 1.21)*
control structure *(VB 1.15)*
decoded *(VB 1.04)*
design *(VB 1.13)*
development cycle *(VB 1.10)*
documentation *(VB 1.20)*
events *(VB 1.21)*
executed *(VB 1.04)*
fetched *(VB 1.04)*
flowchart *(VB 1.14)*
form *(VB 1.22)*
Hypertext Markup Language (HTML) *(VB 1.06)*
implementation *(VB 1.18)*
instance *(VB 1.20)*
integration testing *(VB 1.19)*
machine cycle *(VB 1.04)*
methodology *(VB 1.10)*
methods *(VB 1.13)*
Microsoft Intermediate Language (MSIL) *(VB 1.24)*
Microsoft Visual Basic .NET *(VB 1.02)*
Microsoft Visual Studio .NET *(VB 1.04)*
.NET *(VB 1.02)*

.NET Framework *(VB 1.22)*
.NET Framework class library *(VB 1.23)*
object model *(VB 1.13)*
objects *(VB 1.13)*
object-oriented design (OOD) *(VB 1.20)*
object-oriented programming (OOP) *(VB 1.20)*
program *(VB 1.02)*
program development *(VB 1.02)*
programmatic interface *(VB 1.09)*
programmers *(VB 1.02)*
programming *(VB 1.02)*
pseudocode *(VB 1.16)*
rapid application development (RAD) *(VB 1.21)*
requirements *(VB 1.11)*
requirements document *(VB 1.11)*
reusability *(VB 1.09)*
service *(VB 1.07)*
software developers *(VB 1.02)*
stand-alone application *(VB 1.05)*
stored *(VB 1.04)*
stored program *(VB 1.04)*
storyboard *(VB 1.17)*
test cases *(VB 1.19)*
test plan *(VB 1.19)*
testing *(VB 1.19)*
Unified Modeling Language (UML) *(VB 1.20)*
unit testing *(VB 1.18)*
usability *(VB 1.17)*
users *(VB 1.11)*
validate *(VB 1.17)*
Visual Basic programming language *(VB 1.02)*
Windows application *(VB 1.02)*
Web application *(VB 1.02)*
Web service *(VB 1.02)*
Windows service *(VB 1.02)*

HOMEWORK ASSIGNMENTS

Short Answer

1. In a machine cycle, after an instruction is _____, it is then _____ and then the instruction is _____. Finally, the result of the instruction is _____.

2. A _____ is a program that does not have an interface and is accessible over the Web. A program that runs in the Windows GUI and has an interface is called a _____. A Windows program that performs maintenance tasks and does not typically have a GUI is a _____.

3. A _____ typically does not have a user interface, but serves as a helper to other programs.

4. A _____ interface allows a user to interact with the computer using buttons and other visual cues. A _____ interface requires a user to type instructions to interact with a computer.

5. The result of creating a Visual Basic .NET program is _____, which is read and executed by the _____.

6. A _____ describes something about an object. A _____ is an action that an object can perform.

7. _____ testing is performed by the programmer while the programmer writes code. _____ testing ensures that all programs that comprise an application interact correctly.

8. List the six phases of the development cycle in order and briefly describe the purpose of each phase.

9. List and describe four benefits of rapid application development and object-oriented design and object-oriented programming.

10. List three sets of test data for a program that determines the quotient A/B, where A must be an integer between -10 and -1, and B must be non-zero.

11. Which variables would you test in Figure 1-14 on page VB 1.16 to ensure the Commission result is positive? Describe the valid range of the variables you select.

12. An employee's weekly Gross Pay is determined by multiplying the hours worked by the rate of pay. Overtime (hours worked more than 40) is paid 1.5 times the hourly rate. Answer the following questions:

    a. Identify the interface input text box(es).

    b. Identify the interface output text box(es).

    c. Identify the interface button(s).

    d. Draw a flowchart to compute the gross pay.

    e. Write the pseudocode that corresponds to the flowchart in d.

13. List and describe each of the types of programs you can write using Visual Basic .NET.

14. Define the following terms: object-oriented programming; object-oriented design; aggregation; class; UML; RAD; .NET Framework; .NET Framework Class Library; CLR; and MSIL.

15. Draw a flowchart that determines the number of negative values (Negative), number of zero values (Zero), and number of positive values (Positive) in the following data set; 4, 2, 3, -9, -4, -6, -8, 3, 2, 0, 0, 8, -3, 4. When the user enters the number -999, terminate the process.

16. Draw a flowchart that accepts three values for U, V, and W, which are positive and not equal to one another. The flowchart should then determine which has the smallest value and assign this value to Smallest, before displaying it.

17. Given two positive-values (assume they are assigned to A and B), draw a partial flowchart that assigns the larger value to Big and the smaller value to Small. If A and B are equal, assign either to Same.

Learn It Online

Start your browser and visit scsite.com/vbnet/exs. Follow the instructions in the exercises below.

1. **Chapter Reinforcement TF, MC, and SA**   Click the True/False, Multiple Choice, and Short Answer link below Chapter 1. Print and then answer the questions.

2. **Practice Test**   Click the Practice Test link below Chapter 1. Answer each question, enter your first and last name at the bottom of the page, and then click the Grade Test button. When the graded practice test displays on your screen, click Print on the File menu to print a hard copy. Continue to take practice tests until you score 80% or better. Hand in a printout of the final practice test.

3. **Crossword Puzzle Challenge**   Click the Crossword Puzzle Challenge link below Chapter 1. Read the instructions, and then enter your first and last name. Click the Play button. Complete the crossword puzzle. When you are finished, click the Submit button. When the crossword puzzle redisplays, click the Print button.

4. **Tips and Tricks**   Click the Tips and Tricks link below Chapter 1. Right-click the information and then click Print on the shortcut menu. Construct a brief example of what the information relates to in Visual Basic .NET to confirm you understand how to use the tip or trick. Hand in the example and printed information.

5. **Newsgroups**   Click the Newsgroups link below Chapter 1. Click a topic that pertains to Chapter 1. Print three comments.

6. **Expanding Your Horizons**   Click the Articles for Visual Basic .NET below Chapter 1. Click a topic that pertains to Chapter 1. Print the information. Construct a brief example of what the information relates to in Visual Basic .NET to confirm you understand the contents of the article. Hand in the example and printed information.

7. **Search Sleuth**   Select three key terms from the Key Terms section of this chapter and then use the Google search engine at google.com (or any major search engine) to display and print two Web pages for each key term.

PROGRAMMING ASSIGNMENTS

1 Analyzing Requirements

Review the requirements document in Figure 1-23 and then answer the questions.

REQUEST FOR NEW APPLICATION

Date submitted:	September 13, 2004
Submitted by:	Anthony Normington
Purpose:	Phone representatives often receive phone calls from field engineers who are ordering refills for customer's cylindrical distilled water tanks that we refill. The phone representatives need to be able to convert the measurements into a reorder size in gallons.
Application title:	Water Volume Calculator
Algorithms:	The tanks may have a radius from 10 to 20 feet. The field engineer measures how far down the water level is from the top of the tank and also notes the tank's radius. Support engineers must calculate how many gallons of distilled water to send to the customer to fill the tank. If a shipment is over a certain number of gallons, the phone representative must be told by the application to notify a manager about a large shipment. Calculations can be summarized as follows: CubicFeet = 3.1416 x Radius^2 x Depth Gallons = CubicFeet x 7.47 If Gallons over certain amount then 　　Notify user to inform manager of large shipment
Notes:	1) The application should allow the user to enter values for the radius and height down to the water level (depth). 2) The end user should not be able to enter a depth greater than the maximum depth of tank that we support. 3) The application should also allow the user to reset all values on the screen to zero (0) so that another calculation can be performed. 4) In the near future, we want to allow customers to access this calculation remotely. Customers would build their own applications and remotely access the calculation on our Web server.

Approvals

Approval Status:	X	Approved
		Rejected
Approved by:	Andrew Philips	
Date:	September 15, 2004	
Assigned to:	J. Quasney, Programmer	

FIGURE 1-23

1. List at least three relevant requirements missing from the requirements document that are necessary to design a complete application. Use these new requirements when completing the remaining tasks.

2. What are the types of programs that must be created in order to meet the requirements?

3. List the inputs and outputs necessary to solve the problem.

4. Design three sets of test data and step the test data through the algorithm listed in the requirements in order to obtain the expected output of the problem.

Assignments 2 through 7 involve solving problems using pseudocode, flowcharts, and object diagrams. For additional information about these topics, see Appendix A.

2 Writing Pseudocode

Write pseudocode to describe the logic illustrated by the flowchart shown in Figure 1-24.

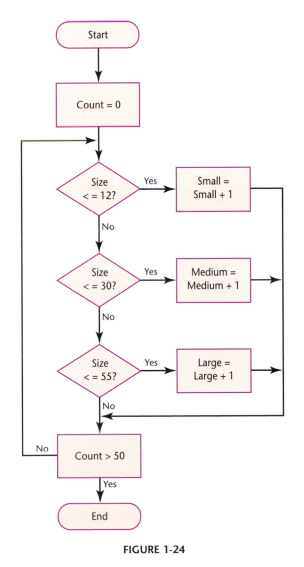

FIGURE 1-24

3 Understanding Flowcharts

A flowchart representation of part of a cardiovascular disease risk assessment is shown in Figure 1-25. The higher the point total, the greater the risk. In the spaces provided, write the point total for the following six people.

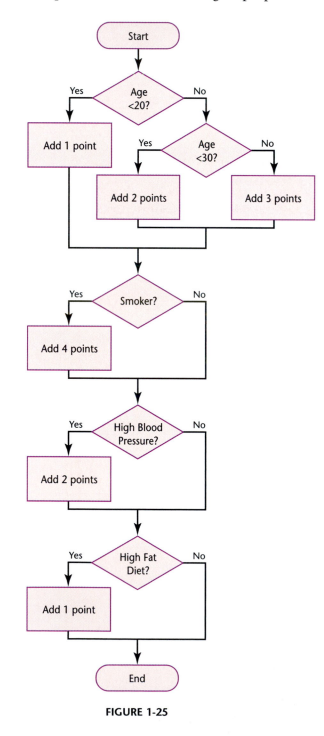

FIGURE 1-25

1. A 25-year-old smoker with high blood pressure who eats a low-fat diet.

   _____

2. A 35-year-old nonsmoker with normal blood pressure who eats a low-fat diet. _____

3. A 20-year-old nonsmoker with high blood pressure who eats a high-fat diet. _____

4. A 45-year-old smoker with high blood pressure who eats a high-fat diet. _____

5. A 61-year-old nonsmoker with high blood pressure who eats a high-fat diet. _____

6. A 16-year-old nonsmoker with normal blood pressure who eats a high-fat diet. _____

4 Drawing a Partial Flowchart

Draw a partial flowchart to calculate the commission paid to a salesperson. The salesperson receives a 14% commission if his or her sales exceed $40,000. The commission is 9% if sales are less than or equal to $40,000, but greater than $25,000. Sales less than or equal to $25,000 earn a commission of 7%.

5 Creating a Flowchart

Draw one flowchart that enables the mechanical man to complete the Phase 1 and Phase 2 movements efficiently, as illustrated in Figure 1-26.

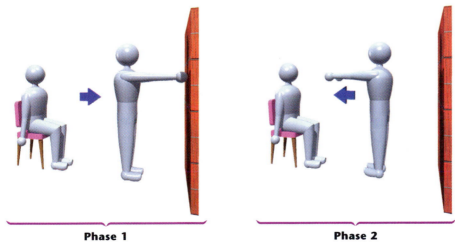

Phase 1   **Phase 2**

FIGURE 1-26

The mechanical man possesses the following properties:

1. He is restricted to a limited set of operations.
2. He is event-driven (doing nothing unless given a specific instruction).
3. He must carry out instructions one at a time.
4. He understands the following instructions:
   a. Physical movement:
      (1) Stand
      (2) Sit

(continued)

5 Creating a Flowchart *(continued)*

    (3) Take one step forward

    (4) Raise arms straight ahead

    (5) Lower arms to sides

    (6) Turn right (90 degrees without taking a step)

b. Arithmetic:

    (1) Add one to a running total

    (2) Subtract one from a running total

    (3) Store a total (any number of totals can be stored)

c. Logic:

The mechanical man can decide what instruction he will carry out next on the basis of answers to the following questions:

    (1) Arithmetic results

        (a) Is the result positive?

        (b) Is the result negative?

        (c) Is the result zero?

        (d) Is the result equal to a predetermined amount?

    (2) Physical status

        (a) Are the raised arms touching anything?

6 Creating Object Diagrams

Identify the relevant objects in the mechanical man problem. Draw an object diagram for each one. List all the possible values of each of the attributes you identify.

7 Creating a High-Level Class Diagram

Pick any class of objects that interests you (for example, clothes, musical instruments, physical fitness equipment, etc.). Create a class diagram showing at least four levels of subclasses and superclasses. For each subclass, identify several attributes inherited from each of its superclasses.

8 Designing a User Interface

Based on your previous experience with Windows applications, draw a picture of a user interface for an application that will convert any amount of U.S. dollars into the equivalent amount in an international currency. The currencies should include Euro, Yen, Pounds, and Canadian dollars. Describe the events and methods (the exact exchange rates and calculations are not necessary). Referring to the user interface you designed, what mistakes could a user make? What will your application do in response to those mistakes?

9 Identifying Events and Methods

Start any software application available to you. On your own paper, briefly describe what the application generally allows the user to do. Identify five specific events in the application and their corresponding methods (operations). Write your name on the paper and hand it in to your instructor.

2

The Visual Basic .NET Integrated Development Environment

Objectives

You will have
mastered the material in
this chapter when you can:

- Start Visual Basic .NET
- Customize the Visual Basic .NET integrated development environment
- Open a Visual Basic .NET project
- Describe the basic components of the Visual Basic .NET integrated development environment
- Run a Visual Basic .NET project
- Set a property on a control
- Navigate the code window
- Modify code in an existing project
- Save a Visual Basic .NET project
- Print a Visual Basic .NET project's forms and code
- Use Visual Basic .NET Help
- Quit Visual Basic .NET

Introduction

This chapter concentrates on the Visual Basic .NET environment in which you work when you develop a Visual Basic .NET project. A **project** is a collection of code and other files that usually encompasses one program. This chapter explains how to modify an existing Visual Basic .NET program and then test the changes made to the program. After completing this chapter, you should be able to start Visual Basic .NET, describe the components of the Visual Basic .NET environment, and run a project from within the Visual Basic .NET environment. You will learn how to modify properties and existing code in a Visual Basic .NET program, and then save the changes you have made. Finally, you will understand how to document a Visual Basic .NET project and use the Visual Basic .NET Help tools.

Chapter Two — Calculating Take-Home Pay

In this chapter, you will open and modify the program in the Take-home pay calculator project, which is a Windows application. The application is a tool used by a company's human resources department when interviewing job candidates. When job candidates are told a yearly salary amount, they often ask what their weekly take-home pay will be based on that yearly salary. The Take-Home Pay Calculator application allows the human resources employee to make that calculation quickly.

To use the Take-Home Pay Calculator application, the user enters in a yearly salary, the percentage that the employee wants to contribute to his or her retirement plan, and selects which insurance plan the employee will use. As the information is entered, the application automatically updates the weekly pay amount displayed on the screen. The application makes the calculation by dividing the yearly salary amount by 52 to find the gross weekly pay amount. The application then deducts taxes, retirement account contributions, and insurance payments from the gross weekly pay amount to determine the net weekly take-home pay. The application deducts 6.2% for Social Security tax, 1.45% for Medicare tax, 2.5% for state tax, 18% for federal tax, $20 per pay period for individual insurance, and $30 per pay period for family insurance.

Recently, the company has moved to a biweekly pay schedule, which means the company distributes paychecks every other week rather than every week. This chapter shows the changes required to modify the Take-Home Pay Calculator application to calculate the net biweekly take-home pay based on a yearly salary amount.

Figure 2-1a shows the application before modifications. Figure 2-1b shows the application after modifications. As you can see from the two figures, the label, Weekly take-home pay, is changed to Biweekly take-home pay. Also, the resulting take-home pay that the application calculates is different for the two versions of the application. The biweekly take-home pay amount is twice the weekly take-home pay amount given the same salary, retirement plan contribution rate, and insurance plan contributions.

original label reads
Weekly take-home pay

original result of
calculation

(a) Original Application

modified label reads
Biweekly take-home pay

result of calculation
after modifications

(b) Application after Modifications
FIGURE 2-1

Starting and Customizing Visual Basic .NET

You typically develop and modify Visual Basic .NET applications in the integrated development environment. The **integrated development environment (IDE)** is part of the Visual Basic .NET application and contains the windows and toolbars that allow you to develop Visual Basic .NET applications and components. Many programmers find it convenient to display as many of the windows and toolbars as possible while working in the Visual Basic .NET IDE. Professional software programmers typically work in as high a resolution as their computer will allow in order to display many of these tools at all times. Some work with multiple monitors attached to the same computer in order to see as much information as possible.

When working on a project in Visual Basic .NET, you should set your computer monitor to as high a resolution as you can tolerate, so that you can display multiple windows and toolbars. The screens shown in this book use a 1024 × 768 resolution. For instructions on how to change the resolution on your computer, see Appendix B on page VB B.01.

Resolution

When working with Visual Basic .NET, set your computer monitor to at least 1024 × 768 resolution or as high a resolution as you can tolerate.

As described, the Visual Basic .NET IDE contains the windows and toolbars that allow you to develop Visual Basic .NET applications and components. Visual Basic .NET records the size and location of these windows and toolbars when you close a project, so that the IDE displays the same configuration each time you start Visual Basic .NET.

If you are a student working in a computer lab, the IDE may look completely different every time you start Visual Basic .NET in the lab, which can be disorienting if you are new to Visual Basic .NET. To help solve that problem, Visual Basic .NET includes several profiles that customize the environment in which you work. In Visual Basic .NET, a **profile** is used to store personalized settings that define the layout of windows in the Visual Basic .NET IDE, keyboard shortcuts that apply, the default filter to use when searching for help, and other options. Once you choose a profile, Visual Basic .NET remembers it for the next time you use Visual Basic .NET on that computer.

As your proficiency in Visual Basic .NET improves, you can choose a different profile or modify the profile you are using already to change the settings for any existing projects and apply these settings when starting a new project. Each time you sit down at a computer in the lab, you should make sure to check the profile and modify it as described on the next several pages.

The following steps start Visual Basic .NET and customize the Visual Basic .NET environment.

To Start and Customize Visual Basic .NET

1. Click the Start button on the taskbar and then point to All Programs on the Start menu.

2. Point to Microsoft Visual Studio .NET on the All Programs submenu.

3. Point to Microsoft Visual Studio .NET on the Microsoft Visual Studio .NET submenu.

The Microsoft Visual Studio .NET submenu displays (Figure 2-2). Microsoft Visual Studio .NET is highlighted.

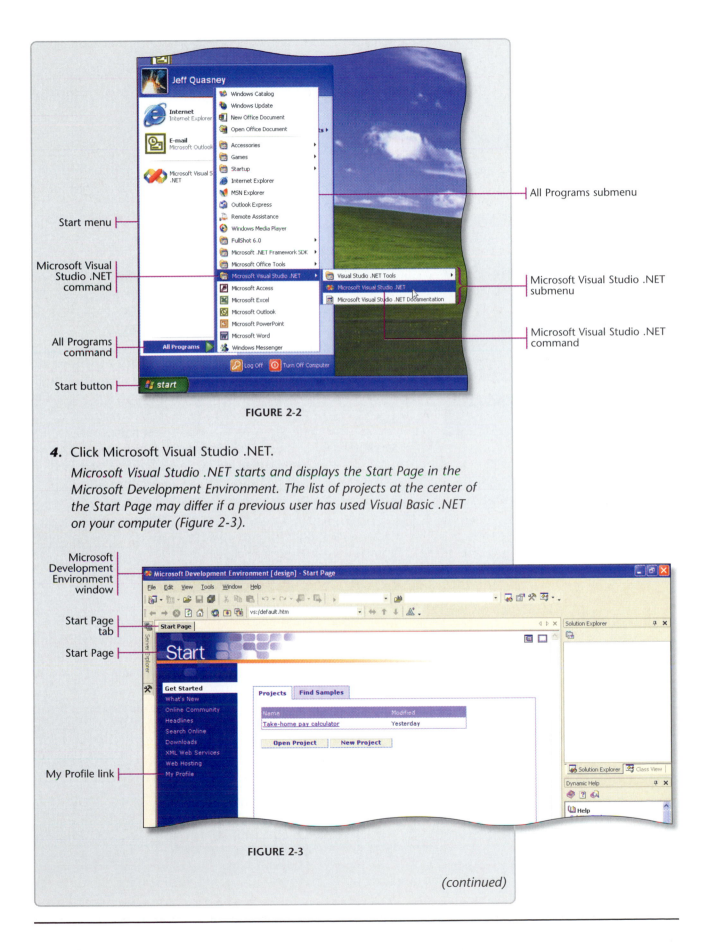

FIGURE 2-2

4. **Click Microsoft Visual Studio .NET.**

   Microsoft Visual Studio .NET starts and displays the Start Page in the Microsoft Development Environment. The list of projects at the center of the Start Page may differ if a previous user has used Visual Basic .NET on your computer (Figure 2-3).

FIGURE 2-3

(continued)

5. Click the My Profile link on the left side of the Start Page.

The Start Page displays My Profile information (Figure 2-4). The selections made for the personalized settings may differ if a previous user has modified the selections.

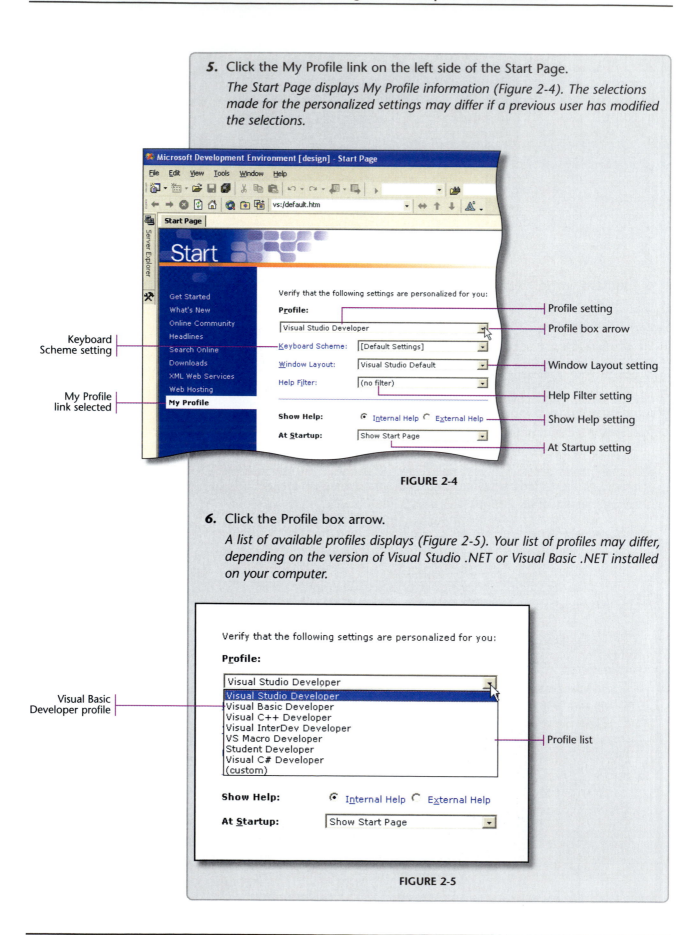

FIGURE 2-4

6. Click the Profile box arrow.

A list of available profiles displays (Figure 2-5). Your list of profiles may differ, depending on the version of Visual Studio .NET or Visual Basic .NET installed on your computer.

FIGURE 2-5

7. Click Visual Basic Developer in the Profile list.

The Profile changes to Visual Basic Developer. The Keyboard Scheme and Window Layout change to Visual Basic 6 and the Help Filter changes to Visual Basic (Figure 2-6). The Toolbox window displays with a push pin icon pointed down to indicate that the Toolbox window is pinned to the left side of the screen and will display until closed.

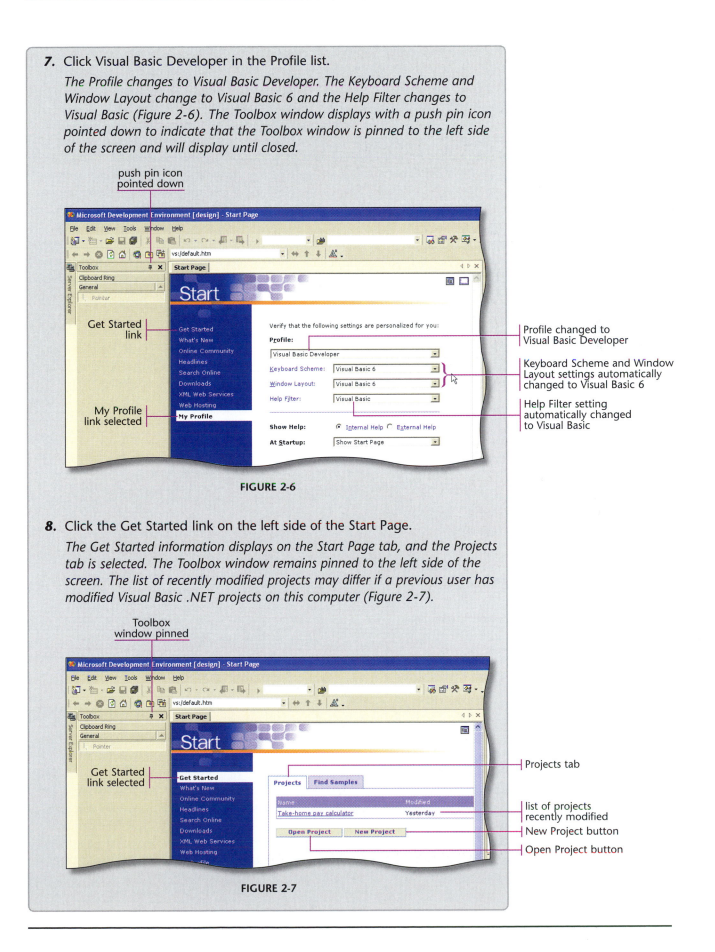

FIGURE 2-6

8. Click the Get Started link on the left side of the Start Page.

The Get Started information displays on the Start Page tab, and the Projects tab is selected. The Toolbox window remains pinned to the left side of the screen. The list of recently modified projects may differ if a previous user has modified Visual Basic .NET projects on this computer (Figure 2-7).

FIGURE 2-7

As discussed in Chapter 1, Visual Basic .NET is part of several editions of Visual Studio .NET. When you use Visual Basic .NET, you access Visual Basic .NET through Visual Studio .NET. Therefore, when you start Visual Basic .NET, the commands on the Windows Start menu are labeled as Visual Studio .NET.

You can experiment with other profiles and settings in the My Profile view of the Start Page (Figure 2-6 on the previous page) to see the changes to the development environment. Be sure to write down or remember the original settings before making any changes so that you can change them back if you do not like them. The Window Layout and Help Filter settings change the development environment most significantly. Setting the Window Layout to Visual Basic 6, for example, customizes the screen to display the Toolbox window automatically because Visual Basic developers typically use the Toolbox often. Setting the Help Filter to Visual Basic filters the large quantity of information in the Help system to focus on information most useful to a Visual Basic developer. Changing this setting reduces the time needed to navigate the Help system, which is discussed later in this chapter.

The Show Help setting determines whether Visual Basic .NET looks for Help files on your computer's hard drive, DVD-ROM drive, and CD-ROM drive, or on the Web. The At Startup setting (Figure 2-6) tells Visual Basic .NET what tab or page to display in the main work area when you start Visual Basic .NET.

> **Tip**
>
> **Profile**
> In the My Profile view on the Start Page, select the Visual Basic Developer profile if you want to display the Toolbox window and limit the contents of Help to those topics relating to Visual Basic .NET, rather than all of the products associated with Visual Studio .NET.

Opening an Existing Project

When Visual Basic .NET starts (Figure 2-7 on the previous page), you can choose to open an existing project or file or start a new project. When you choose to start a new project, you choose which type of application or Windows component you want to create. For example, you can choose to create a Web application or a Windows application. When you choose to open an existing project or file, you select the location on your hard drive or floppy disk drive where the project or file is stored.

You also can open an existing project you have recently modified in the Get Started view of the Start Page. As shown in Figure 2-7, the Projects tab of the Get Started view lists the name and last modified date for any projects on which you recently have worked. The next time you start Visual Basic .NET after opening the Take-home pay calculator project, you will see the Take-home pay calculator project listed. Instead of clicking the Open Project button to open the project, you can click the project name to open the project.

The following steps open the Take-home pay calculator project from the Data Disk.

To Open an Existing Project

1. Insert the Data Disk in drive A. See page xvi in the preface of this book for instructions for downloading the Data Disk or see your instructor for information about accessing the files required in this book.

2. Click the Open Project button.

3. If necessary, click the Look in box arrow and then click 3½ Floppy (A:).

Visual Basic .NET displays the Open Project dialog box. The names of folders on the Data Disk in drive A display in the Open Project dialog box (Figure 2-8).

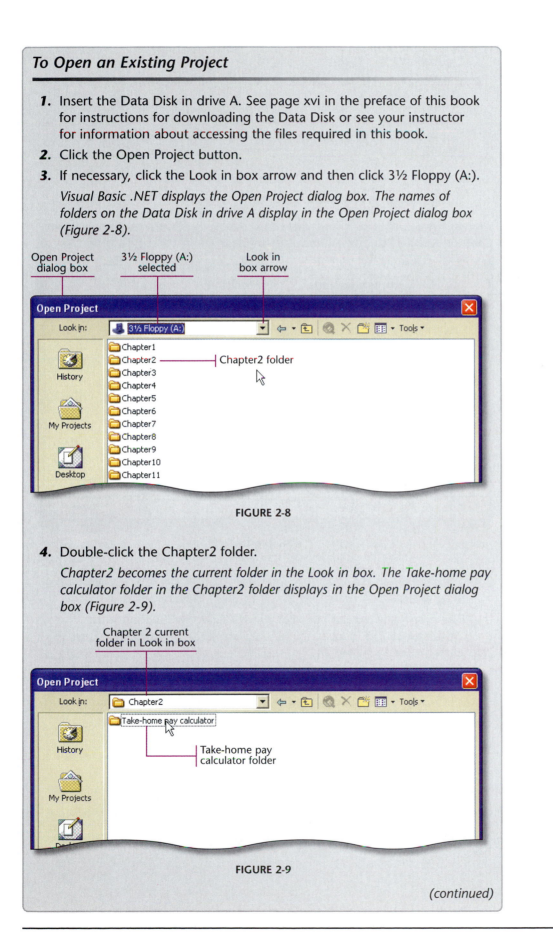

FIGURE 2-8

4. Double-click the Chapter2 folder.

Chapter2 becomes the current folder in the Look in box. The Take-home pay calculator folder in the Chapter2 folder displays in the Open Project dialog box (Figure 2-9).

FIGURE 2-9

(continued)

5. Double-click the Take-home pay calculator folder.

6. If necessary, click the Take-home pay calculator solution file (Take-home pay calculator.sln).

Take-home pay calculator becomes the current folder in the Look in box. The Take-home pay calculator solution file and folder display in the dialog box (Figure 2-10).

Take-home pay calculator is current folder in Look in box

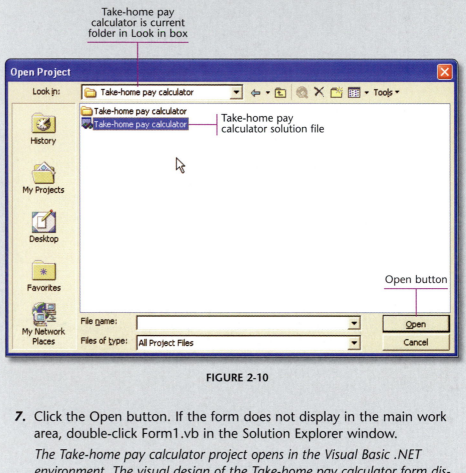

FIGURE 2-10

7. Click the Open button. If the form does not display in the main work area, double-click Form1.vb in the Solution Explorer window.

The Take-home pay calculator project opens in the Visual Basic .NET environment. The visual design of the Take-home pay calculator form displays on the Form1.vb [Design] tab in the main work area. The Solution Explorer window at the top right of the screen displays information about the project (Figure 2-11).

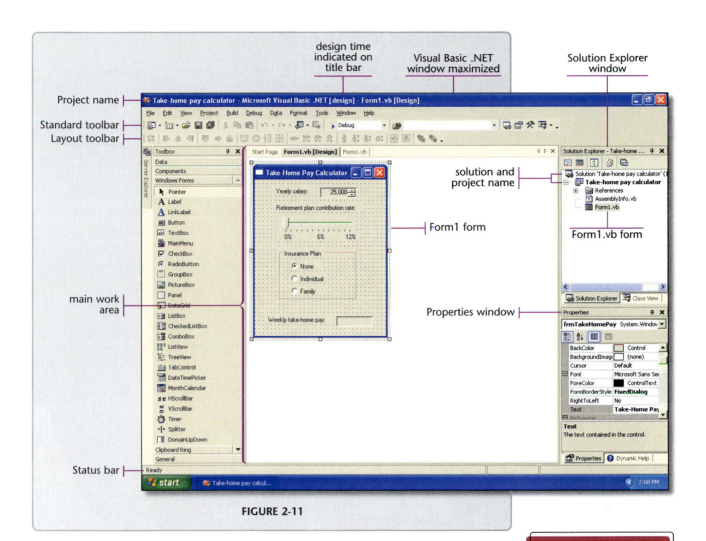

FIGURE 2-11

OTHER WAYS

1. Click Open File button on Standard toolbar
2. Press ALT+F, O, P

Visual Basic .NET opens the project as shown in Figure 2-11. When you first open a project, Visual Basic .NET enters a mode in the IDE called design time. When the IDE is in **design time**, you can make modifications to the forms and code of any program. When the IDE is in design time, the word, [design], displays on the title bar of the Visual Basic .NET window.

Exploring the Visual Basic .NET Integrated Development Environment

The Visual Basic .NET integrated development environment consists of several toolbar and window areas. Depending on the task you are performing and the options you choose, other toolbars and windows will display or replace the components shown in Figure 2-11.

Menu Bar and Toolbars

The **menu bar** displays the Visual Basic .NET menu names, each of which represents a list of commands that allow you to create, edit, save, print, test, and run a Visual Basic .NET application or component, as well as access many other essential commands. The **Standard toolbar** contains buttons that execute commonly used commands such as Open Project, Save, Cut, Copy, Paste, and others (Figure 2-12). The **Layout toolbar** contains buttons that execute commonly used formatting commands such as Align to Grid, Size to Grid, Center Horizontally, Center Vertically, and others (Figure 2-13).

The Standard and Layout toolbars allow you to perform common tasks more quickly than when using menus. For example, to save your work, you can click the Save button on the Standard toolbar instead of clicking File on the menu bar and then clicking Save on the File menu. Each button has a picture on the button face to help identify the button's function. Also, when you move the mouse pointer over a button or box, the name of the button or box displays below it in a **ScreenTip**. Each of the buttons is explained in detail when used in the steps.

FIGURE 2-12

FIGURE 2-13

Visual Basic .NET contains several other toolbars to help you perform your work. If you right-click any toolbar in the Visual Basic .NET IDE, a shortcut menu displays that lists all the available toolbars in Visual Basic .NET. Figure 2-14 shows the toolbar shortcut menu. A check mark next to a toolbar name indicates that the toolbar currently is displaying in the IDE. The last menu command, Customize, allows you to change the toolbars to fit your own needs by adding, deleting, and modifying toolbar buttons. It also allows you to create new custom toolbars.

Tip

Toolbars
Right-click any toolbar in the Visual Basic .NET IDE to display a shortcut menu that lists all the available toolbars.

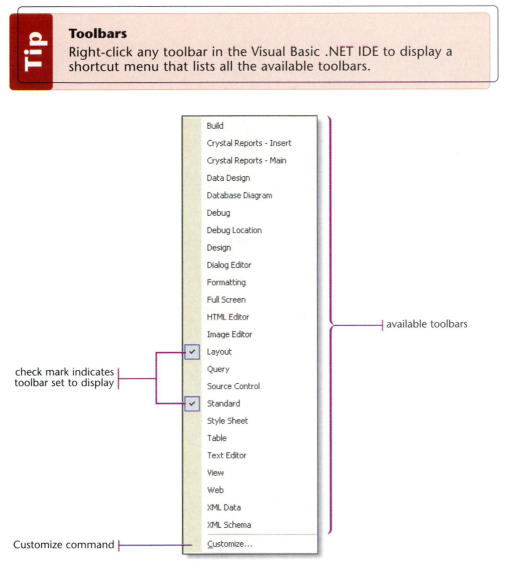

check mark indicates toolbar set to display

available toolbars

Customize command

FIGURE 2-14

Status Bar

The **status bar**, which is located above the Windows taskbar at the bottom of the Visual Basic .NET window, displays information about the current state of the Visual Basic .NET IDE (Figure 2-11 on page VB 2.11). Mode indicators, such as Ready and Building, display on the status bar and specify the current mode of Visual Basic .NET. When the mode is **Ready**, Visual Basic .NET is waiting for you to perform a task. The status bar also presents information about the location of the insertion point and the progress of current tasks.

Status indicators on the status bar, such as INS or OVR, can be double-clicked to turn certain keys or modes on or off. Double-clicking the OVR status indicator, for example, changes Visual Basic .NET from **Insert** mode, which inserts characters as you type, to **Overtype** mode, which replaces existing characters as you type. You also can press the INSERT key on the keyboard to change the status between Overtype and Insert mode.

Windows

As you perform tasks in the IDE, Visual Basic .NET automatically opens different windows to help you complete the task. You also can open a window manually by clicking commands on the Other Windows submenu of the View menu. Table 2-1 shows a summary of the windows available in the Visual Basic .NET IDE.

Table 2-1 **Visual Basic .NET IDE Windows**

WINDOW NAME	DEFAULT SCREEN LOCATION	FUNCTION
Toolbox	Left	Includes assortment of tools available for designing forms and a user interface; organized into tabs containing related components, controls, or code
Server Explorer	Left	Allows you to view and manage servers, such as database servers, available during development
Solution Explorer	Upper right	Lists all objects in a solution, including files with program code, references, and so on
Properties	Lower right	List of attributes of object currently selected in the main work area, such as a control on a form
Class View	Upper right	Lists items that make up a class
Resource View	Upper right	Allows you to view resources, or external information, that are included in the project
Output	Main work area	Displays program output during execution
Help Content	Upper right	Displays table of contents for the Help system
Help Index	Upper right	Displays index of the Help system
Dynamic Help	Lower right	Displays Help topics for item selected in the environment
Autos	Lower left	Used during debugging; displays information about variables for the line of code executing
Locals	Lower left	Used during debugging; displays information about variables in the current procedure
Watch	Lower left	Used during debugging; displays information about variables that you have asked to be watched during run time
This	Lower left	Used during debugging; displays information about the current method

Table 2-1   Visual Basic .NET IDE Windows (continued)

WINDOW NAME	DEFAULT SCREEN LOCATION	FUNCTION
Call Stack	Lower right	Used during debugging; displays information about the history of what has been executed
Breakpoints	Lower right	Lists all breakpoints that you have set for the current project
Threads	Lower right	Displays information about all threads created by the currently running program
Command Window	Bottom	Allows a Visual Basic .NET statement to be run in real time
Immediate	Lower right	Allows code to be analyzed as it runs
Find Results	Main work area	Displays results of searches run
Document Outline	Left	Used to show the elements of the Web page when designing Web pages in Visual Basic .NET
Object Browser	Main work area	Allows you to examine and learn about the structure of objects, including properties and methods of objects
Running Documents	Upper left	Used for debugging applications that use Web pages
Task List	Bottom	Displays a list of tasks maintained for a project
Macro Explorer	Upper right	Allows you to select and run macros that you have available to use in the Visual Basic .NET environment

Each of the windows will be discussed in detail when they are introduced in this book.

The Components of a Visual Basic .NET Solution

When a project is opened, Visual Basic .NET opens the project within a solution, as shown in Figure 2-11 on page VB 2.11. A **solution** is a grouping of projects and related files. Solutions can contain one project, such as the Take-home pay calculator project, or many related projects, data files, graphic files, and any other files that relate to the programming task at hand.

You work on one solution at a time in Visual Basic .NET. You can, however, run multiple instances of Visual Basic .NET at the same time on the same computer in order to work on multiple solutions. This approach can be useful when working on related solutions or project, or copying elements of one project to another.

Copying across Projects

To copy elements in one project to another project, open each project in a separate instance of Visual Basic .NET and then use the Copy and Paste commands.

Projects, such as the Take-home pay calculator project, are individual programs and are always created within solutions. Projects within solutions may be programmed in different languages within the .NET architecture. Each individual project is written in one programming language, such as Visual Basic .NET or Visual C++ .NET.

A project can include several components, including files and other objects. When you start a new project to build a Windows application, Visual Basic .NET creates at least three files with the project: References, AssemblyInfo.vb, and a default form. As shown in Figure 2-15, each of these three files displays in a tree view below the project name in the Solution Explorer window. A **tree view** is a hierarchical list of items. Groups of items in the list can be collapsed or expanded by clicking plus (+) or minus (−) signs next to the group.

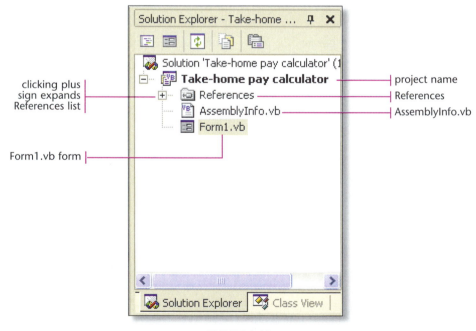

FIGURE 2-15

The first file, **References**, provides a tree view of .NET classes that are needed in the application. By default, five .NET classes are included in a new Windows application. The second file, **AssemblyInfo.vb**, is a file of code that includes information for the Visual Basic .NET compiler. This information uniquely identifies the project to the CLR. Visual Basic .NET provides the References and AssemblyInfo.vb file for a Windows application project, but you probably will never need to modify or view these files.

The third file is a default Windows form, Form1.vb. The Form1.vb file contains the information about the Take-home pay calculator form that displays in the main work area shown in Figure 2-11 on page VB 2.11. Form1.vb is highlighted in the Solution Explorer window to indicate that the form currently is active in the main work area. The Properties window is populated with information about the form that displays in the main work area. Most of this chapter concentrates on the modification of this third item, Form1.vb.

When you open a project file as shown in Figure 2-10 on page VB 2.10, you only need to open the project file. The project file knows where to locate the References, AssemblyInfo.vb file, the default form, Form1.vb, and any additional files needed for the program.

Running a Project

You can run projects within the Visual Basic .NET IDE in order to test the functionality of programs that you develop. When you **run** a project, the project is loaded into memory and the program code is executed by the .NET architecture. By running your projects often during the development phase, you can check for any problems, or **bugs**, that you may have introduced into your code inadvertently. You also can verify that the user interface displays as anticipated, to ensure that the user interface is understandable and easy to use.

Running a Project
Run your projects often during the development phase to check for any bugs that may have been introduced inadvertently.

When you run a project, the IDE enters a mode called **run time**. When run time begins, the IDE changes significantly, closing some windows and opening others. The functionality of these new windows will be discussed in later chapters.

An application is the version of your Windows application project that you distribute to end users. When users run your application, they will not need to use the Visual Basic .NET IDE. The distribution of applications to users will be discussed in a later chapter.

The steps on the following pages run the Take-Home Pay Calculator application from within the Visual Basic .NET IDE. Sample data values test the functionality and validity of the application.

To Run a Project

1. Click the Start button on the Standard toolbar.

As the application starts, Visual Basic .NET opens the Output window and displays informational messages that scroll by in the Output window. The Autos and Call Stack windows then display at the bottom of the IDE, on top of the Output window. The Toolbox and Properties windows are closed. The word, [design], on the Visual Basic .NET title bar changes to [run]. The application window displays, and the Yearly salary box is selected and ready for input. The application button displays on the Windows taskbar (Figure 2-16). The design view of the form continues to display in the background. The Weekly take-home pay result is $345.43 based on the default values for Yearly salary, the Retirement plan contribution rate, and the Insurance Plan.

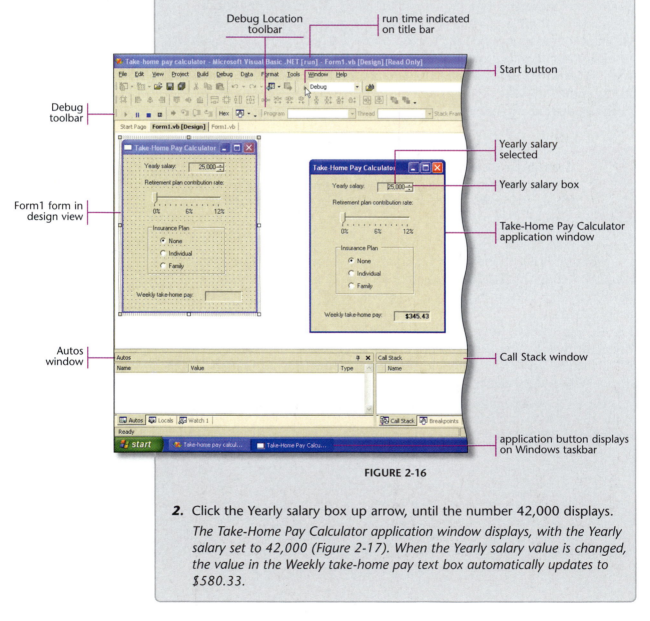

FIGURE 2-16

2. Click the Yearly salary box up arrow, until the number 42,000 displays.

The Take-Home Pay Calculator application window displays, with the Yearly salary set to 42,000 (Figure 2-17). When the Yearly salary value is changed, the value in the Weekly take-home pay text box automatically updates to $580.33.

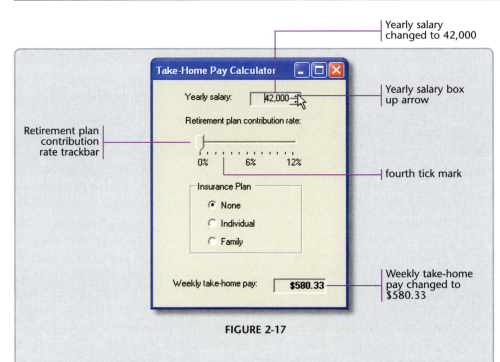

FIGURE 2-17

3. Drag the Retirement plan contribution rate trackbar to the fourth tick mark, which represents 3%.

The Retirement plan contribution rate trackbar moves to the fourth tick mark to indicate a retirement plan contribution rate of 3%. The value in the Weekly take-home pay text box automatically updates to $556.10 as the contribution rate changes (Figure 2-18).

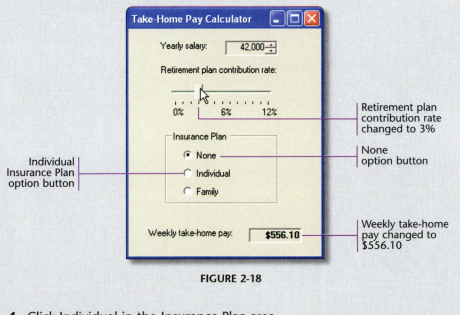

FIGURE 2-18

4. Click Individual in the Insurance Plan area.

The Individual option button is selected, and the None option button is no longer selected. The value in the Weekly take-home pay text box updates to $536.10 to reflect the deduction taken based on the change in the Insurance Plan option (Figure 2-19 on the next page).

(continued)

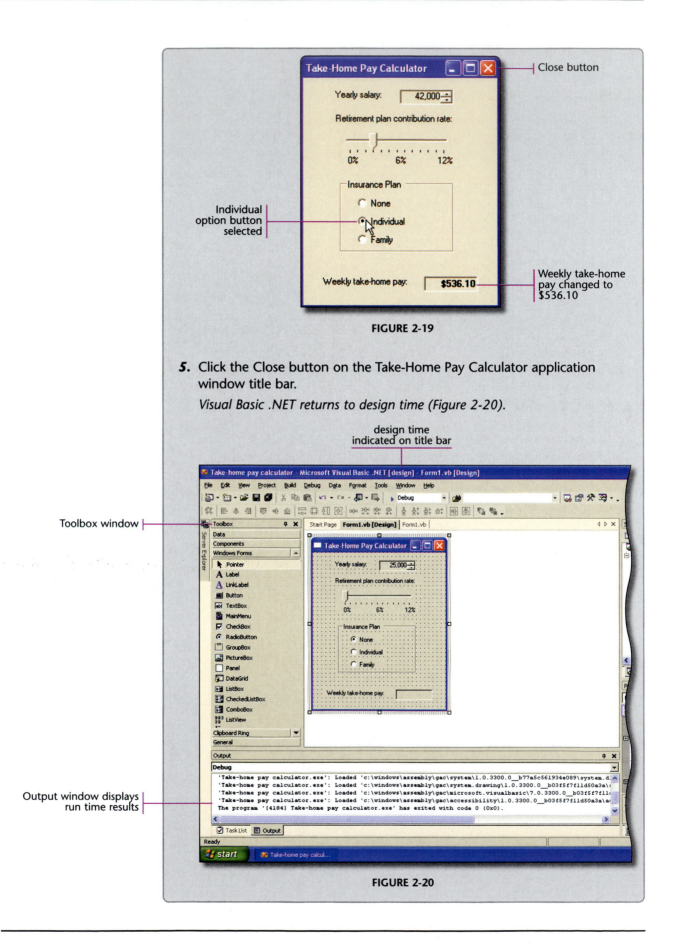

FIGURE 2-19

5. Click the Close button on the Take-Home Pay Calculator application window title bar.

Visual Basic .NET returns to design time (Figure 2-20).

FIGURE 2-20

You can click the Start button to run the application again and then use different data values for the yearly salary and retirement plan contribution rate, and select a different insurance plan option. You do not need to close and then restart the application each time you want to perform another calculation.

As just mentioned, running your projects allows you to check for bugs introduced into your code and verify that the project displays and behaves correctly. Running a project also enables you to learn about the program before you make modifications to it.

Modifying an Existing Project

One of the main tasks a programmer faces involves modifying a project rather than creating a new project. A programmer has three main tasks to consider in the implement design phase when modifying an existing project. First, the programmer gathers information about the existing program and the desired modification requirements. Second, the programmer modifies the user interface and the code in the project. Finally, the programmer unit tests the changes to ensure that they address the requirements and do not create additional problems, or bugs, in the program.

The modification requirements for the Take-Home Pay Calculator application call for a change from a weekly pay frequency to a biweekly pay frequency. This change means that the application must calculate biweekly take-home pay based on 26 pay periods in a year rather than 52. Making this modification requires two changes to the project. First, the text, Weekly take-home pay:, must be changed to the text, Biweekly take-home pay:. The text is displayed on the form using a **Label control**, which is a Visual Basic .NET control used to display text information on a Windows form. Figure 2-21 shows three Label controls in the application.

The second change involves modifying the project code that calculates the take-home pay based on 26 biweekly payments rather than 52 weekly payments.

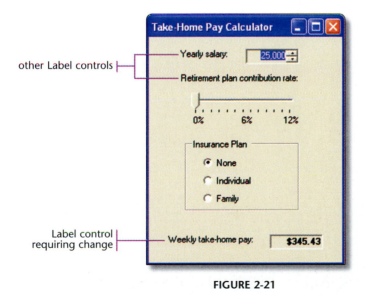

FIGURE 2-21

Modifying a Property of a Control

To make changes to an object on a user interface, such as a control, you click the item and then change the values of its properties in the Properties window. Changing a property's value is known as setting a property. A **property** is a characteristic or attribute of an object, such as its background color or the text that it displays. As described in Table 2-1 on pages VB 2.14 and VB 2.15, the **Properties window** lists the attributes for the object currently selected in the main work area.

The Properties window includes an Object box and a Properties list. The **Object box** in the Properties window displays the name of the currently selected object or control. The **Properties list** displays the set of properties and current value of the properties for the object or control named in the Object box.

The following steps use the Properties window to modify the Text property of the Label control.

To Modify the Text Property of a Label Control

1. Click the Weekly take-home pay: Label control on the Form1 form in the main work area.

The mouse pointer changes to a double two-headed arrow. A shaded outline and handles display around the selected Label control. The control's name (Label6) displays in the Object box of the Properties window. The Properties list displays the set of properties and values for the Label control (Figure 2-22).

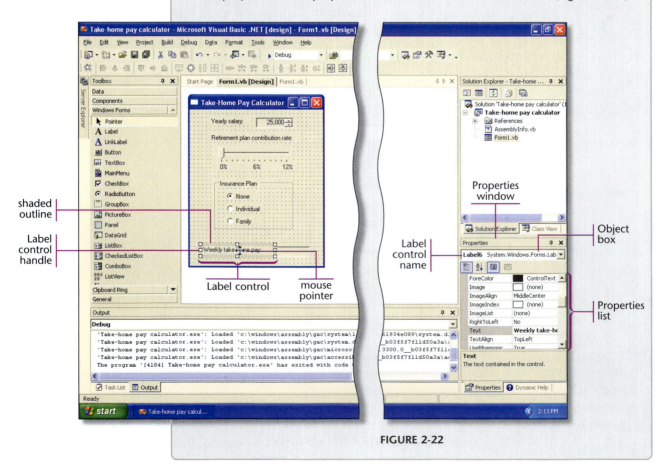

FIGURE 2-22

2. Scroll the Properties list until the Text property is visible.

3. Double-click the Text property. The Text property is the word Text in the left column of the Property list.

The Text property is highlighted in the Properties list (Figure 2-23). The Text property value is selected. A description of the Text property displays at the bottom of the Properties window.

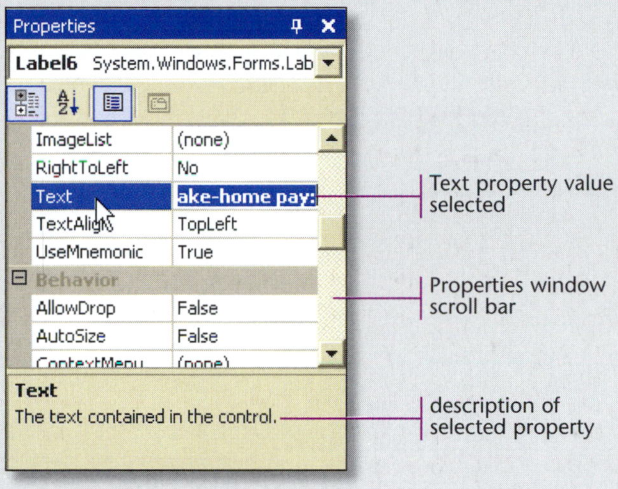

FIGURE 2-23

4. Type Biweekly take-home pay: and do not press the ENTER key.

The value of the Text property changes to Biweekly take-home pay: (Figure 2-24). You can correct mistakes made while typing by using the BACKSPACE key or the DELETE key. The Label control on the form still displays the original Text property value.

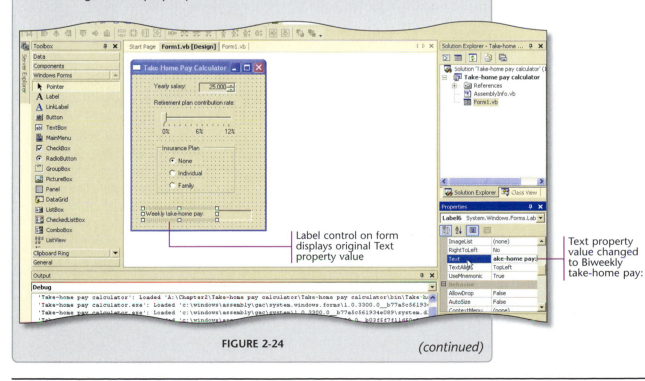

FIGURE 2-24

(continued)

5. Press the ENTER key.

The new Text property value displays on the Label control on the form (Figure 2-25).

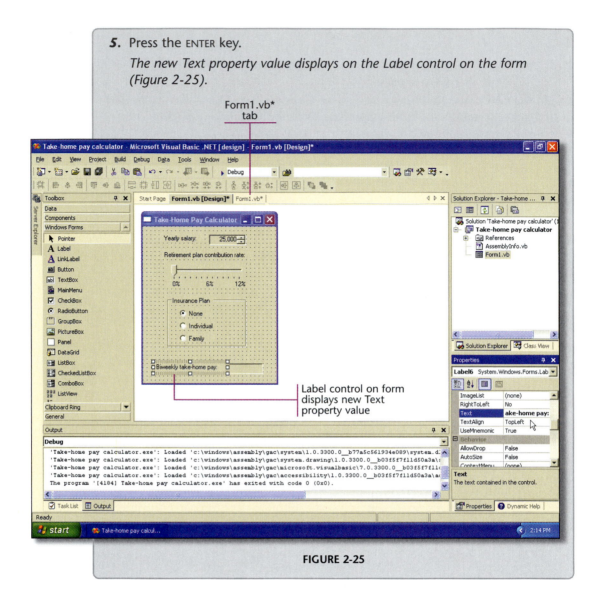

FIGURE 2-25

As shown in the Properties window in Figure 2-23 on the previous page, the Text property is just one of many properties for the Label control. The Properties window allows you to modify the value for any of these properties to change the appearance and functions of a control on a form. This same basic procedure is used for setting most of the properties of any type of control or object on a form during design time. Chapter 3 will discuss properties in more detail.

The Label control on the form now displays the text, Biweekly take-home pay, meaning the first change to update the application is complete. Next, you must modify the code that calculates the take-home pay in order to calculate take-home pay based on 26 biweekly payments rather than 52 weekly payments.

Navigating the Code Window

When you are designing the user interface of a Windows application, such as a form with controls, the main work area of the Visual Basic .NET environment contains a visual representation of the form that the user interacts with at run time. As shown in Figure 2-25, the word, [Design], on the Form1.vb [Design]* tab indicates that this view of the form is a visual representation of the user interface design.

Navigating to the Code Window

To display the design view of a form, click the tab in the main work area with the name of the form and the word, [Design], next to it. To display the code associated with a form, click the tab in the main work area with the name of the form on it.

Designing the user interface, however, is just one aspect of Visual Basic .NET programming. You also must program the actions that execute during run time. When you are programming, or coding, the main work area of the Visual Basic .NET environment displays the **code window**, which provides an area where you can view and edit code.

The code window includes an Object box and a Procedure box at the top of the window. The **Object box** of the code window (Figure 2-26 on the next page) includes a list of all of the individual forms, controls, and classes included in a project. The individual forms, controls, and classes included in a project are all objects. When you want to write or view code for a particular object in a project, you can navigate to the code by selecting it in the Object box. The **Procedure box** allows you to select individual procedures, or pieces of code, that are associated with the object currently selected in the Object box.

Writing or Viewing Code

To write or view the code associated with an object, select the object in the Object box in the code window and then select a procedure in the Procedure box.

The steps on the next page demonstrate how to navigate the code window.

To Navigate the Code Window

1. Click the Form1.vb* tab at the top of the main work area. If the Form1.vb tab does not display above the main work area, click View on the menu bar and then click Code.

The code window opens in the main work area. The name of the current form displays in the Object box in the code window. Lines of code previously entered display in the code window. The insertion point displays before the first character of the first line of code (Figure 2-26).

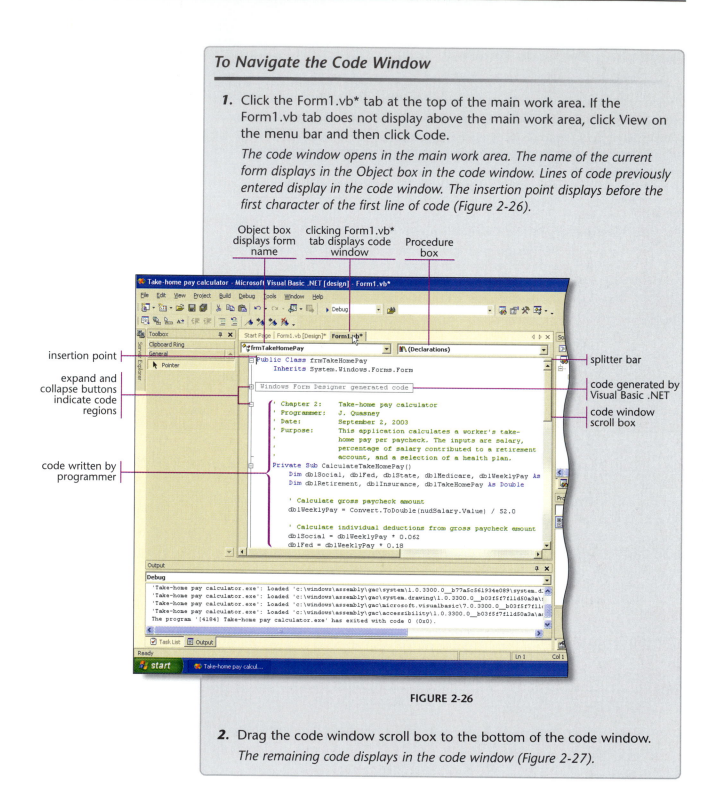

FIGURE 2-26

2. Drag the code window scroll box to the bottom of the code window.

The remaining code displays in the code window (Figure 2-27).

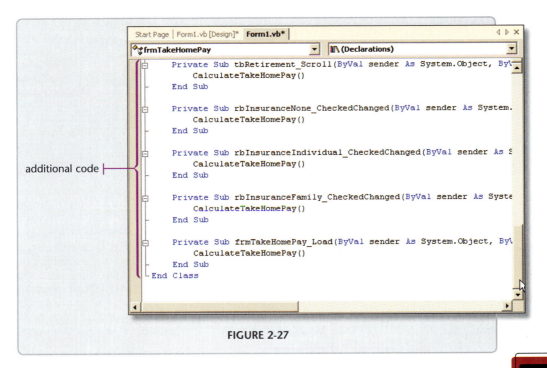

FIGURE 2-27

As shown in Figure 2-26, Visual Basic .NET displays some words in the code in color. Most of the colored words are keywords. **Keywords** are words that have special meaning within Visual Basic .NET and provide a vocabulary for the Visual Basic .NET language. Some of the keywords shown in color in the code window include Public, Class, Private, Sub, and Dim.

Collapse and expand buttons on the left side of the code window indicate code regions. A **code region** is a group of related lines of code. Visual Basic .NET automatically knows how and when to create these regions as you create your code. Visual Basic .NET also allows you to define your own code regions. Code regions are collapsible and expandable, so that you can collapse or hide large sections of code so they do not clutter the work area.

The code window shown in Figure 2-26 displays four code regions. The plus sign (+) next to the second region indicates that this code is collapsed. The boxed-in text next to the plus sign indicates that this code was written automatically by Visual Basic .NET. The minus sign (–) next to the third region indicates that this code is expanded. The code that begins the third code region was written by a programmer and includes useful notations about the authorship and purpose of the code.

If you need to work with multiple sections of code at the same time, the **splitter bar** allows you to create two or more windows within the code window. You can drag the splitter bar vertically to create or remove additional code windows.

Modifying Code in the Code Window

The code window functions as a text editor for writing code statements. You can use the keyboard and/or a mouse to navigate, select, and modify code within the code window just as you would modify text with a text editor such as WordPad.

The following steps modify the code so that the application calculates take-home pay based on 26 biweekly payments rather than 52 weekly payments.

To Modify Code in the Code Window

1. Drag the code window scroll box up until the code displays in the code window as shown in Figure 2-28.

The fourth code region, which includes the code for the CalculateTakeHomePay procedure, displays in the code window (Figure 2-28). The code requiring the change is the sixth code line of the fourth code region. This line of code currently is set to calculate gross weekly pay by dividing the yearly salary by 52.0.

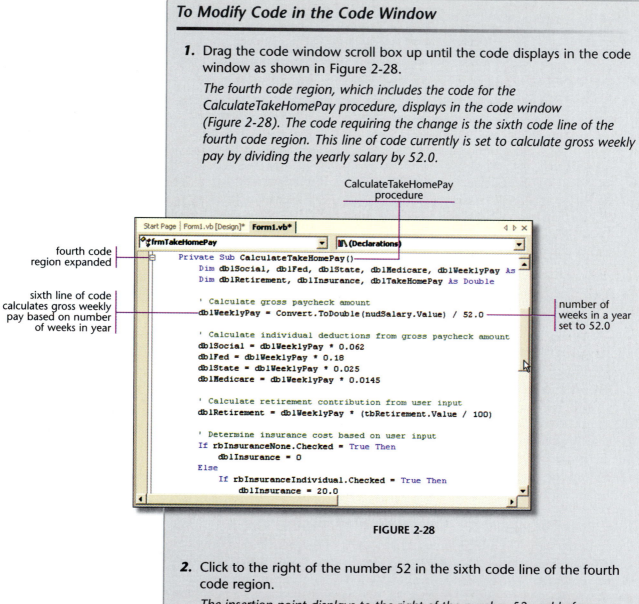

FIGURE 2-28

2. Click to the right of the number 52 in the sixth code line of the fourth code region.

The insertion point displays to the right of the number 52 and before the decimal point (Figure 2-29). CalculateTakeHomePay displays in the Procedure box.

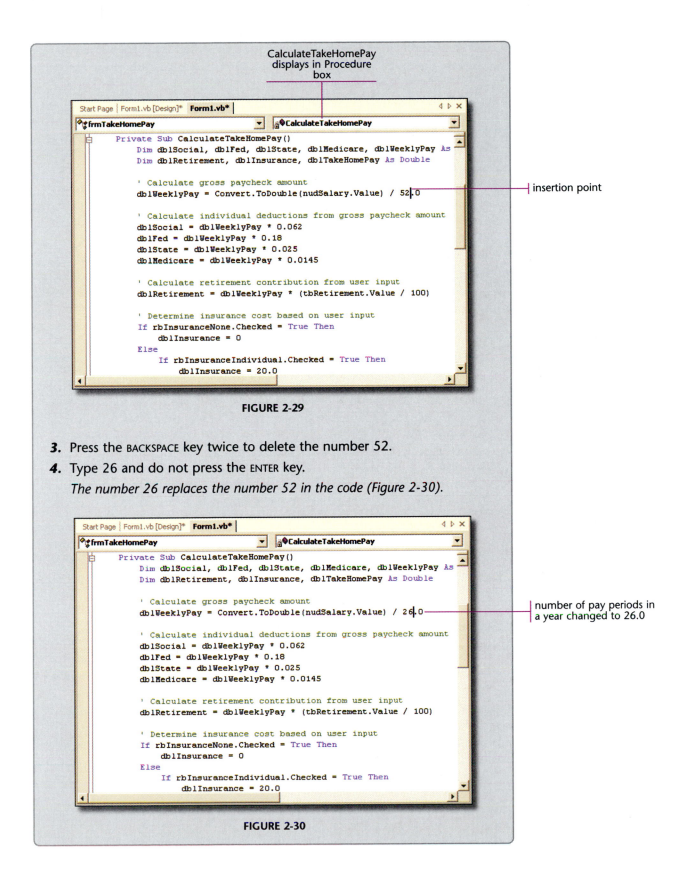

CalculateTakeHomePay
displays in Procedure
box

insertion point

```
Start Page | Form1.vb [Design]* | Form1.vb* |
frmTakeHomePay                          CalculateTakeHomePay

    Private Sub CalculateTakeHomePay()
        Dim dblSocial, dblFed, dblState, dblMedicare, dblWeeklyPay As
        Dim dblRetirement, dblInsurance, dblTakeHomePay As Double

        ' Calculate gross paycheck amount
        dblWeeklyPay = Convert.ToDouble(nudSalary.Value) / 52.0

        ' Calculate individual deductions from gross paycheck amount
        dblSocial = dblWeeklyPay * 0.062
        dblFed = dblWeeklyPay * 0.18
        dblState = dblWeeklyPay * 0.025
        dblMedicare = dblWeeklyPay * 0.0145

        ' Calculate retirement contribution from user input
        dblRetirement = dblWeeklyPay * (tbRetirement.Value / 100)

        ' Determine insurance cost based on user input
        If rbInsuranceNone.Checked = True Then
            dblInsurance = 0
        Else
            If rbInsuranceIndividual.Checked = True Then
                dblInsurance = 20.0
```

FIGURE 2-29

3. Press the BACKSPACE key twice to delete the number 52.
4. Type 26 and do not press the ENTER key.

   The number 26 replaces the number 52 in the code (Figure 2-30).

number of pay periods in
a year changed to 26.0

```
Start Page | Form1.vb [Design]* | Form1.vb* |
frmTakeHomePay                          CalculateTakeHomePay

    Private Sub CalculateTakeHomePay()
        Dim dblSocial, dblFed, dblState, dblMedicare, dblWeeklyPay As
        Dim dblRetirement, dblInsurance, dblTakeHomePay As Double

        ' Calculate gross paycheck amount
        dblWeeklyPay = Convert.ToDouble(nudSalary.Value) / 26.0

        ' Calculate individual deductions from gross paycheck amount
        dblSocial = dblWeeklyPay * 0.062
        dblFed = dblWeeklyPay * 0.18
        dblState = dblWeeklyPay * 0.025
        dblMedicare = dblWeeklyPay * 0.0145

        ' Calculate retirement contribution from user input
        dblRetirement = dblWeeklyPay * (tbRetirement.Value / 100)

        ' Determine insurance cost based on user input
        If rbInsuranceNone.Checked = True Then
            dblInsurance = 0
        Else
            If rbInsuranceIndividual.Checked = True Then
                dblInsurance = 20.0
```

FIGURE 2-30

As shown in Figure 2-30 on the previous page, when you click a line of code in a code region, the Procedure box displays the current location of the insertion point. By watching the Object box and the Procedure box, you always know where you are writing or viewing code.

The preceding steps modified the number of weeks the Take-Home Pay Calculator uses to calculate take-home pay. The code change tells Visual Basic .NET to divide the yearly salary by 26.0, instead of 52.0, to calculate a gross pay amount for a biweekly pay period.

When you change the value from 52.0 to 26.0, be sure to use the decimal representation of these numbers to ensure the application correctly calculates the values. Chapter 4 will discuss the use of decimal representation in more detail.

The modifications to the existing project are now complete. The Text property value for the Label control is modified to display the text, Biweekly take-home pay:, and the code that calculates take-home pay is modified to base take-home pay on 26 biweekly payments. With the changes complete, the project should be saved and then run, so you can test the changes.

Saving and Running a Project

Before starting a new Visual Basic .NET project or quitting Visual Basic .NET, you should save your work. You also should save your project periodically while you are working on it and before you run it for the first time. Visual Basic .NET will save your project automatically when you run it. During the process of developing a project, however, you should err on the side of caution and save your work often.

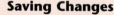

> **Tip**
>
> **Saving Changes**
> You should save your work periodically while you are working on a project and again before you run the project for the first time.

Saving a Project

Visual Basic .NET projects are saved as a set of files. For example, one of the files used extensively in the Take-home pay calculator project is the Form1.vb file, which is indicated on the tab in the main work area (Figure 2-31). The Form1.vb file contains the information that displays in both the Form1.vb [Design] window and the Form1.vb code window. Other files saved with a project contain information about the type of project and other options that are saved with the project.

The following steps save the Take-home pay calculator project on the Data Disk in drive A.

To Save a Project

1. Click the Form1.vb [Design]* tab.
2. Click the Save All button on the Standard toolbar.

   The asterisks next to Form1.vb [Design] on the window title bar and the main work area tab no longer display, indicating that the project has been saved (Figure 2-31). Because the project was opened from the Data Disk in drive A, Visual Basic .NET automatically saves the project on the Data Disk in drive A.

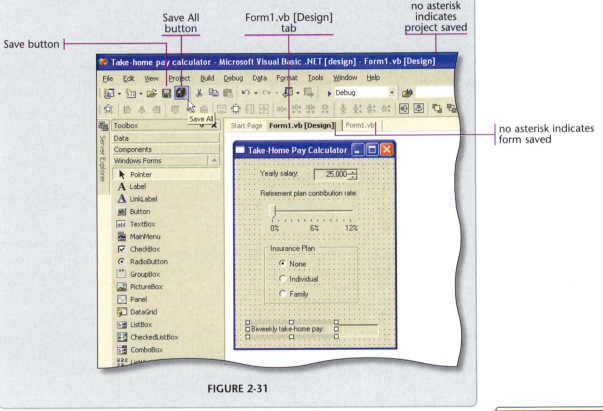

FIGURE 2-31

OTHER WAYS

1. Press ALT+F, L

Clicking the **Save All button** saves all files associated with a project. You can click the **Save button** to save only the current file you are working on in the main work area. Using the Save button is practical if you are modifying an individual file that is part of a much larger project. If you want to save your work with a different file name or in a different folder or on a different drive, click the **Save Selected Items As command** on the File menu.

Saving Projects and Files

If you are changing one file in a large project, then use the Save button to save the individual file rather than the Save All button, which saves all project files whether or not they were changed.

Running a Project to Test Changes

Once the project is saved, you should run the project to test that your changes have not introduced new bugs or caused problems with the functionality of the program or introduced invalid code. You also should test changes frequently as you are working on a project. If you have several changes to make to a program, for instance, it is important to test each change individually, so you easily can identify which change introduced a new problem into the project.

To test the changes in a project, run the project using the same steps used to run the project earlier in the chapter. The following steps run the project and test the changes made to the project.

To Run a Project to Test Changes

1. Click the Start button on the Standard toolbar.

The word, [design], on the Visual Basic .NET title bar changes to [run] as Visual Basic .NET enters run time. The Take-Home Pay Calculator application window displays in the center of the screen and the insertion point displays in the Yearly salary box (Figure 2-32). The design view of the form continues to display in the background.

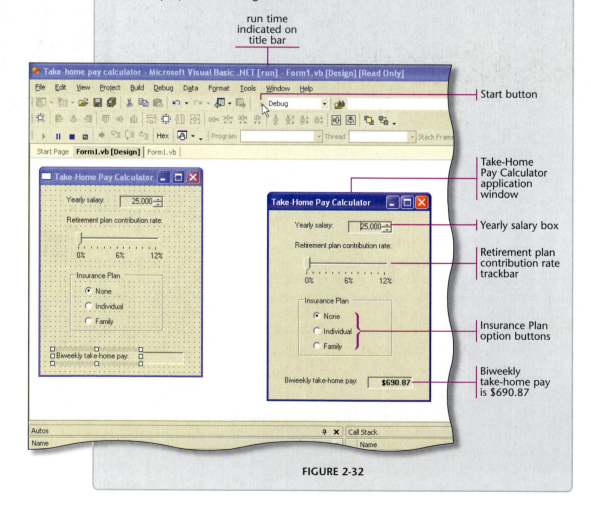

FIGURE 2-32

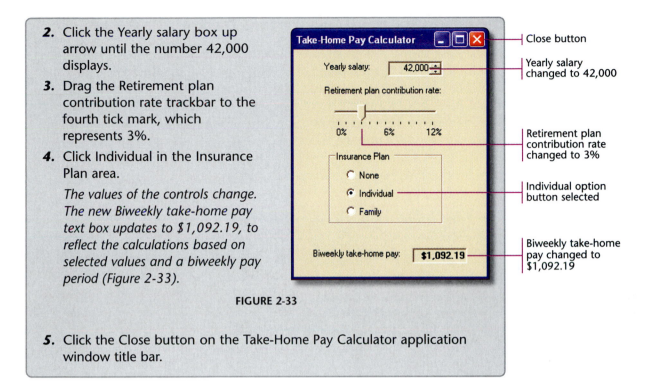

2. Click the Yearly salary box up arrow until the number 42,000 displays.

3. Drag the Retirement plan contribution rate trackbar to the fourth tick mark, which represents 3%.

4. Click Individual in the Insurance Plan area.

   The values of the controls change. The new Biweekly take-home pay text box updates to $1,092.19, to reflect the calculations based on selected values and a biweekly pay period (Figure 2-33).

FIGURE 2-33

5. Click the Close button on the Take-Home Pay Calculator application window title bar.

The same values entered earlier in this chapter (Figure 2-19 on page VB 2.20) now produce a different result. Try entering various values for the three inputs to further test the project. See the deductions listed on page VB 2.02 if you want to check a calculation by hand.

If your program does not run as expected, check the changed code and the changed property to make sure they match the specifications in this chapter. For example, you may have misspelled a change in a property or put the wrong number in the code window. The process of making your code work as expected is known as **debugging**. Continue debugging the application by changing the Text property of the label or the code and then running the project to test that it operates as expected.

Tip

Testing Changes
Run a project often as you are modifying it to test changes, and verify that they have been applied correctly.

Documenting an Application

Documenting an application refers to producing a record of the design and code used to create an application. Documentation can be electronic or printed. A printed record, also called a **hard-copy output**, can make it easier to check your program or refine it. Often, project requirements dictate that you archive a hard-copy output of an application's code and user interface to share with a client or other developers.

Documenting the User Interface Design of a Form

Because Visual Basic .NET does not include functionality that allows you to print the visual representation of a form, you must use other Windows capabilities to print a record of the user interface. One easy way to print a copy of a Visual Basic .NET form in design mode is to use Windows' built-in ability to take a picture of the screen display. After the screen display picture is taken, the image can be pasted into the Windows Paint application and then printed.

The following steps print a record of the user interface design of the Form1 form for the Take-home pay calculator project.

To Print a Record of the User Interface Design of a Form

1. With the Take-home pay calculator project open in design time, press the PRINT SCREEN key.

Windows copies an image of the screen, as shown in Figure 2-34. The image is copied on the Windows Clipboard.

design time
indicated on
title bar

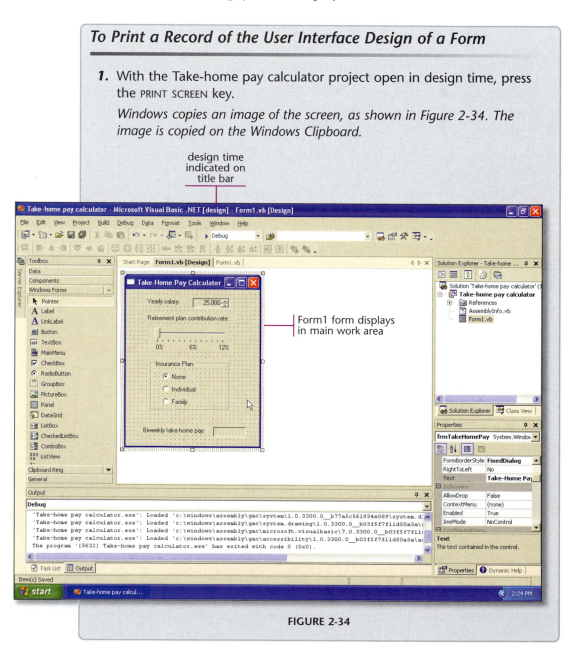

Form1 form displays
in main work area

FIGURE 2-34

2. Click the Start button on the Windows taskbar and then point to All Programs on the Start menu.

3. Point to Accessories on the All Programs submenu, and then point to Paint on the Accessories submenu.

The Accessories submenu displays, and the Paint command is highlighted (Figure 2-35).

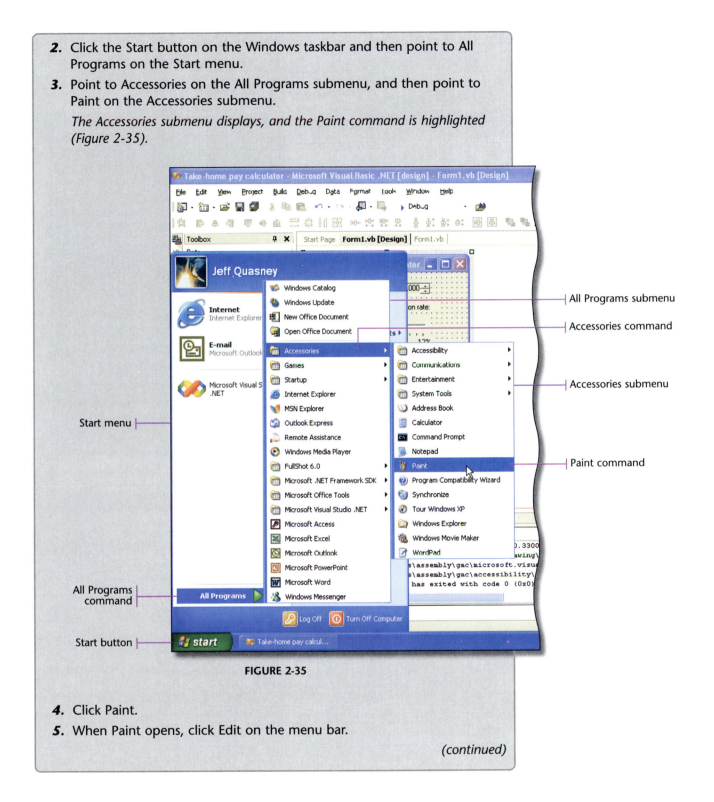

FIGURE 2-35

4. Click Paint.

5. When Paint opens, click Edit on the menu bar.

(continued)

6. Point to Paste on the Edit menu.

Paint starts and displays a blank picture area in the Paint window. The Paste command is highlighted on the Edit menu (Figure 2-36).

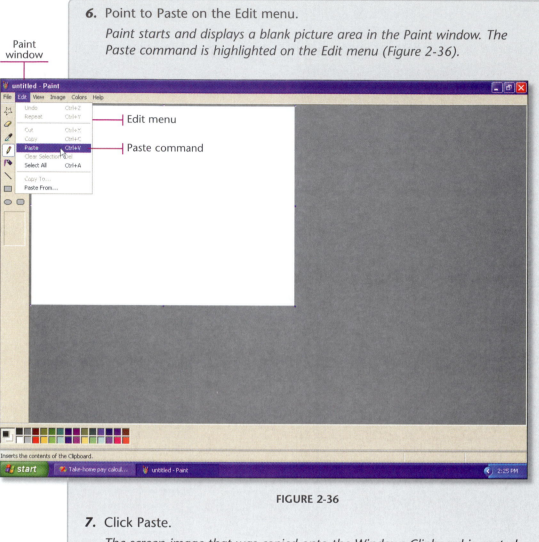

FIGURE 2-36

7. Click Paste.

The screen image that was copied onto the Windows Clipboard is pasted into the picture area in the Paint window (Figure 2-37).

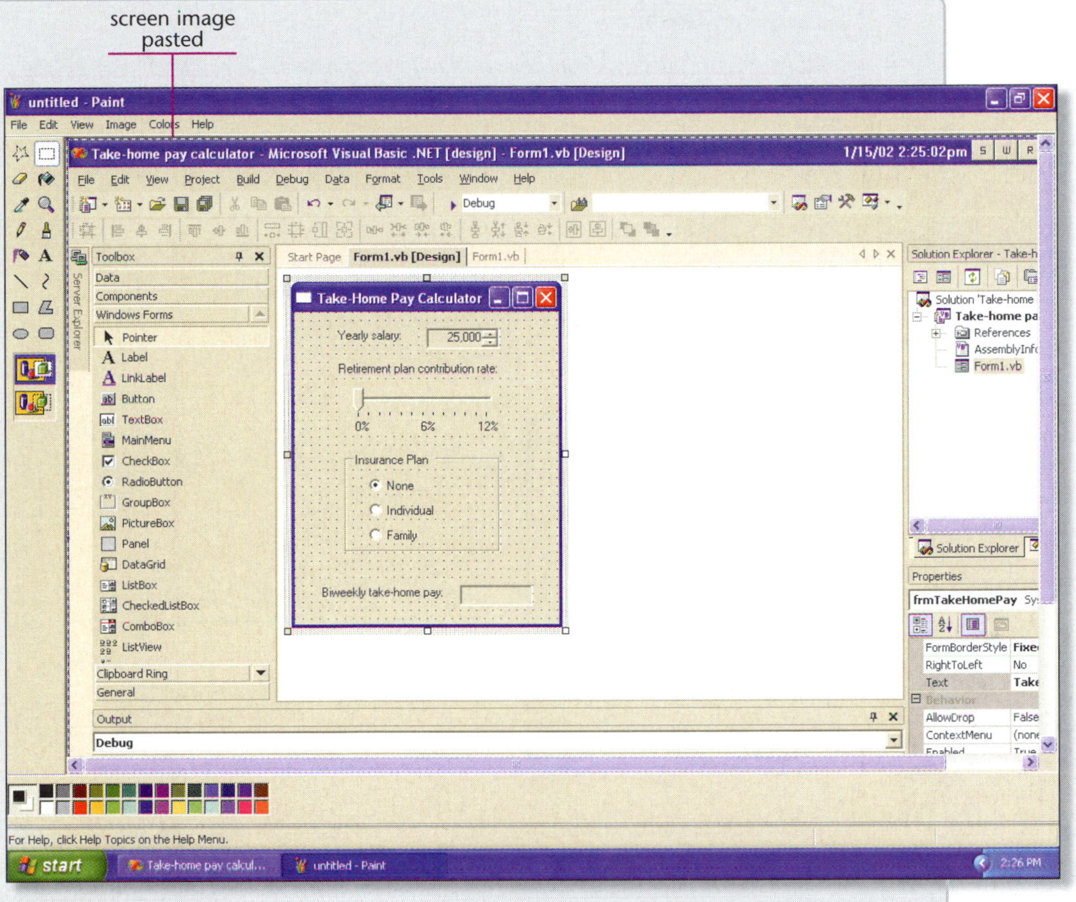

screen image
pasted

FIGURE 2-37

8. Click File on the menu bar.

The File menu displays (Figure 2-38).

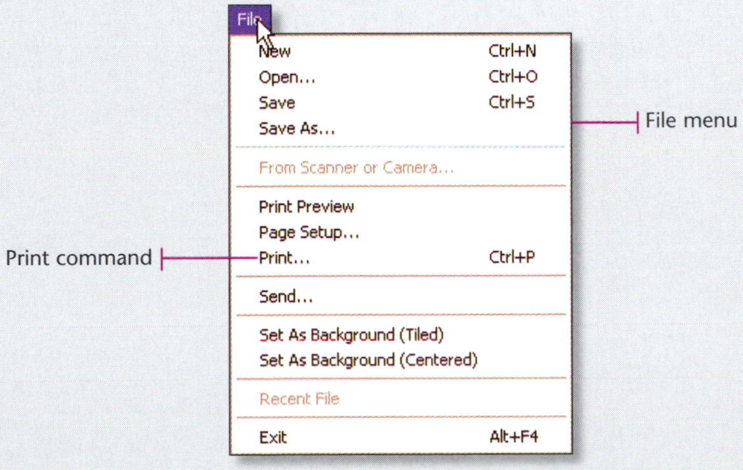

File menu

Print command

FIGURE 2-38

(continued)

9. Click Print on the File menu.

The Print dialog box displays (Figure 2-39). The available printers in the Select Printer area will differ, depending on the printers installed on your computer.

Print dialog box

Close button

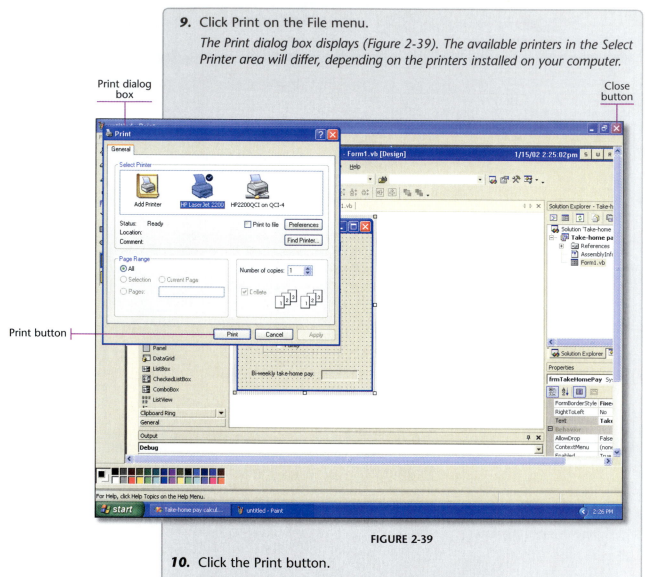

Print button

FIGURE 2-39

10. Click the Print button.

Paint prints a copy of the screen image of the user interface design from the default printer (Figure 2-40). The printout may print over several pages depending on your printer.

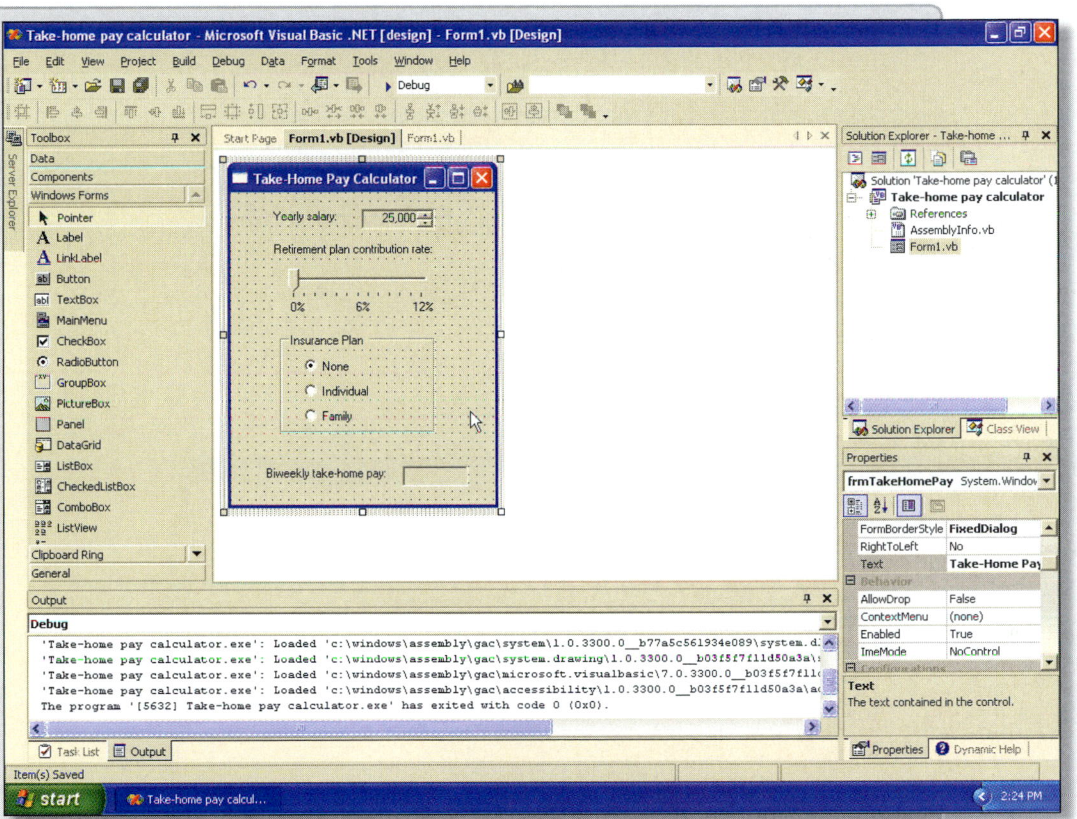

FIGURE 2-40

11. Click the Close button on the Paint window title bar. When the Paint dialog box displays to confirm whether or not you want to save the pasted image, click the No button.

The Paint window closes and the Visual Basic .NET window displays.

In addition to pasting the copied screen image from the Windows Clipboard into Paint, you also can paste the screen images into programs such as Microsoft Word or Microsoft PowerPoint. Additionally, you can save an electronic version of the screen in Paint by using the Save As command on the File menu in the Paint program.

Screen capture programs also allow you to capture a screen image and then create a printed record of a form's user interface design. Some of these programs allow you to capture only a specific rectangular area of the screen. You may need to experiment with your printer and the printer settings in order to obtain optimal results for printing a form's user interface design.

Documenting Code for a Form

Visual Basic .NET does include functionality that allows you to print a hard copy of the code used in a project. The **Print command** is available on the File menu when the active window contains printable items, such as code, help topics, Web pages, or other printable output. To print the form code, you first must display the code in the code window in the main work area.

The following steps print a record of the code in the Form1 form of the Take-home pay calculator project.

To Print a Record of the Code for a Form

1. Click the Form1.vb tab to display the form code in the code window.

2. Click File on the menu bar.

The form code displays in the code window, which is the active window. The File menu displays (Figure 2-41).

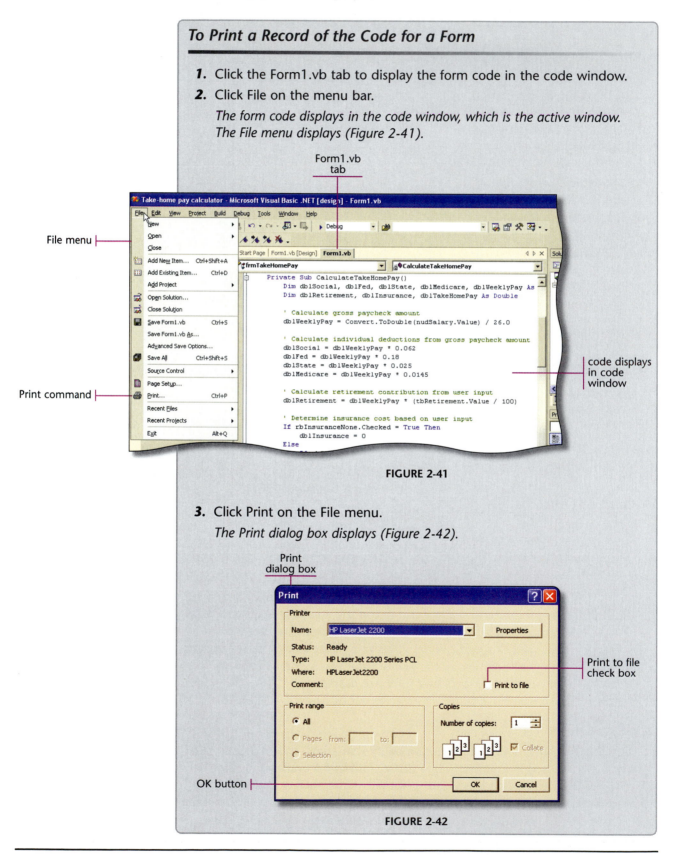

FIGURE 2-41

3. Click Print on the File menu.

The Print dialog box displays (Figure 2-42).

FIGURE 2-42

4. Click the OK button.

Visual Basic .NET prints a copy of the form code from the default printer. Continuation markers print to indicate that a line of code was too long to fit the width of the printed page (Figure 2-43).

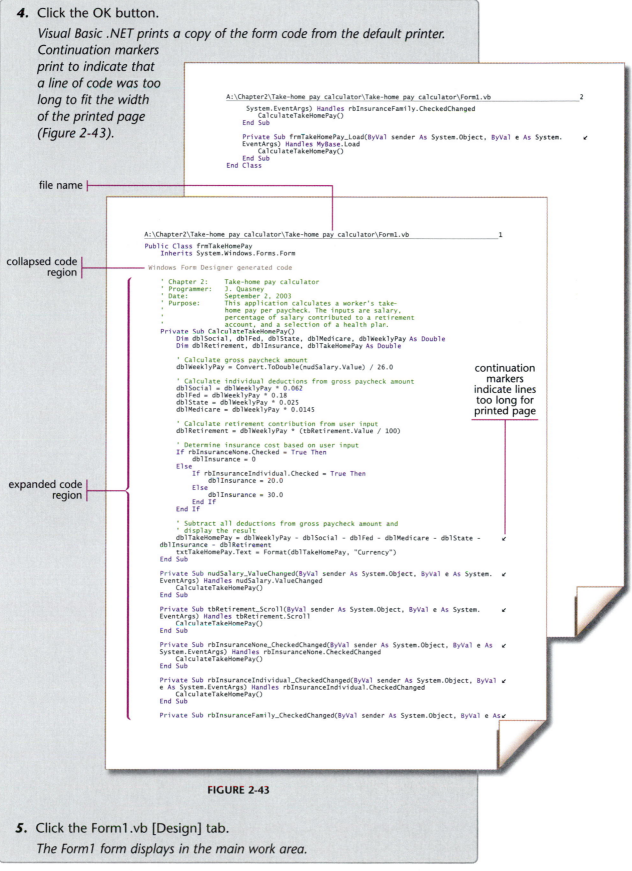

FIGURE 2-43

5. Click the Form1.vb [Design] tab.

The Form1 form displays in the main work area.

The Print dialog box also allows you to print a selection from the active window or specific pages from the active window. If the Print to file check box is selected in the Print dialog box, the print output is sent to the file specified in the Print To File dialog box that displays after you click the OK button in the Print dialog box.

The printed page shown in Figure 2-43 on the previous page contains continuation markers on the right side of the page. **Continuation markers** indicate that a line of code was too long to print on one line and is continued on the next line. The printout does not distinguish code regions or print code in any collapsed code regions; it does, however, print descriptions of any collapsed code regions.

The changes to the Take-Home Pay Calculator application now are complete.

Visual Basic .NET Help

The Visual Basic .NET IDE includes an extensive Help system. Visual Basic .NET **Help** contains documents, examples, articles, and other information about the Visual Basic .NET language and environment to assist you in using Visual Basic .NET. While working in the Visual Basic .NET IDE, you can access Help in a number of ways.

Navigating the Visual Basic .NET Help System

As shown in Figure 2-44, the Help menu in the Visual Basic .NET IDE includes a number of commands you can use to access Help.

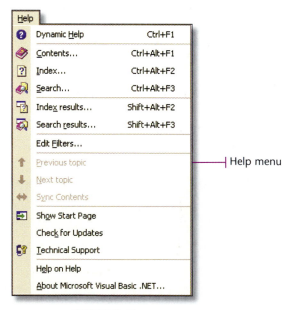

FIGURE 2-44

Table 2-2 summarizes the Help menu commands and where each command displays the Help information by default. Many of these Help menu commands also can be accessed using tabs on windows in the IDE.

Table 2-2   Help Menu Commands

MENU COMMANDS	DEFAULT DISPLAY AREA	ACTION
Dynamic Help	Lower right	Displays the Dynamic Help window
Contents	Upper right	Displays a tree view of all Help topics
Index	Upper right	Displays an alphabetical list of all Help items
Search	Upper right	Displays a search form that allows you to find topics by entering keywords
Index results	Bottom	Displays a list of Help articles related to an item that is clicked in the Index window
Search results	Bottom	Displays a list of Help articles generated from completing a search using the Search window
Edit Filters	Main work area	Allows a user to customize Help results by specifying filter criteria for all Help searches and results
Previous topic	Main work area	Allows a user to navigate to a Help article that previously displayed in the main work area
Next topic	Main work area	Allows a user to navigate to the next topic in the Search results or Index results
Sync Contents	Main work area	Causes the Contents window to navigate to the item currently being accessed in the Help system
Show Start Page	Main work area	Displays the initial Visual Basic .NET Start Page
Check for Updates	New window	Attempts to connect to Microsoft's Web site to check for new updates to the Visual Basic .NET application
Technical Support	Main work area	Displays links with contact information for Microsoft technical support
Help on Help	Main work area	Displays information on how to get the most out of using the Help system
About Microsoft Visual Basic .NET	New window	Displays copyright information, Visual Basic .NET licensing information, and system information

Depending on how Visual Basic .NET was installed on your computer, you may be required to insert one of the Visual Basic .NET CD-ROMs or DVD-ROMs when you need to access Help. If this is the case, you will need to locate the specific CD-ROM or DVD-ROM and insert it. It always is a good habit to keep the Visual Basic .NET CD-ROM or DVD-ROM in your CD-ROM or DVD-ROM drive while you are using Visual Basic .NET.

Contents, Index, and Search Windows

The Contents, Index, and Search Help menu commands display content from the Visual Basic .NET Help system. The **Contents window** shown in Figure 2-45 displays a listing of Help topics arranged much like a table of contents in a book. Expand and collapse buttons allow topics and subtopics to be displayed or hidden from view. Double-clicking any topic without a collapse or expand button displays the Help topic on a tab in the main work area.

Tip

When to Use the Contents Window
Use the Contents window for help as you would the table of contents at the front of a book or when you know the general category of the topic in question.

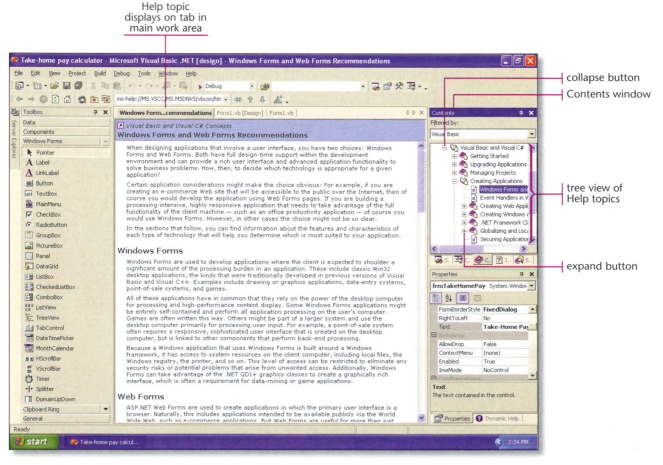

FIGURE 2-45

The **Index window** provides a navigational aid similar to a book index. Topics are listed alphabetically, and subtopics display below main topics. You also can type a topic in the Look for box to display a list of items related to that topic in the Index window. Figure 2-46 shows the Visual Basic .NET IDE. After clicking Index on the Help menu, typing Textbox in the Look for box, and then double-clicking TextBox control (Windows Forms), the topic is selected in the list in the Index window and the information displays on the tab in the main work area.

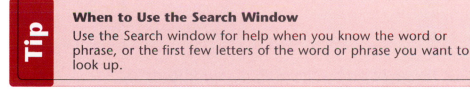

Tip

When to Use the Index Window
Use the Index window for help as you would the index in a book.

TextBox Control
topic displays on tab
in main work area

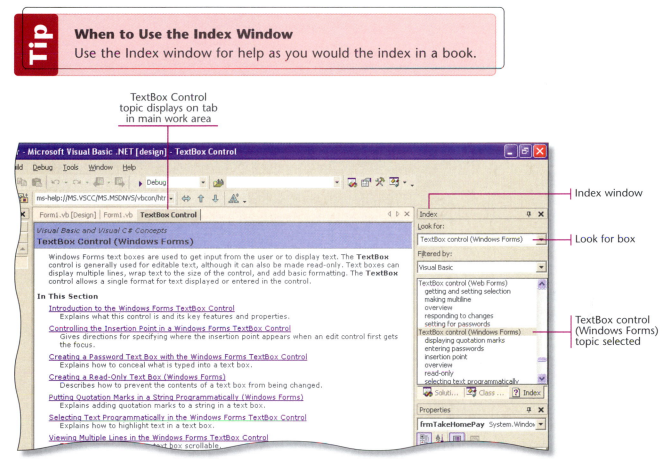

FIGURE 2-46

The **Search window** allows you to search the Visual Basic .NET Help system for a specific term or phrase. Figure 2-47 on the next page shows the IDE after clicking the Search command on the Help menu and then entering the search term, label control, in the Look for box.

Tip

When to Use the Search Window
Use the Search window for help when you know the word or phrase, or the first few letters of the word or phrase you want to look up.

Search window

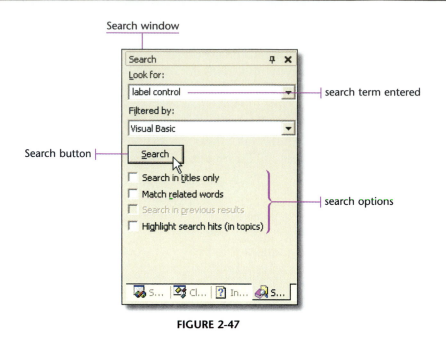

search term entered

Search button

search options

FIGURE 2-47

When a user clicks the Search button in the Search window, the Help system searches for Help topics related to the search term. Once it locates topics related to the search term entered in the Search window, it then displays the results in the **Search Results window**. Double-clicking the first topic in the Search Results window displays the Help topic in the main work area, as shown in Figure 2-48.

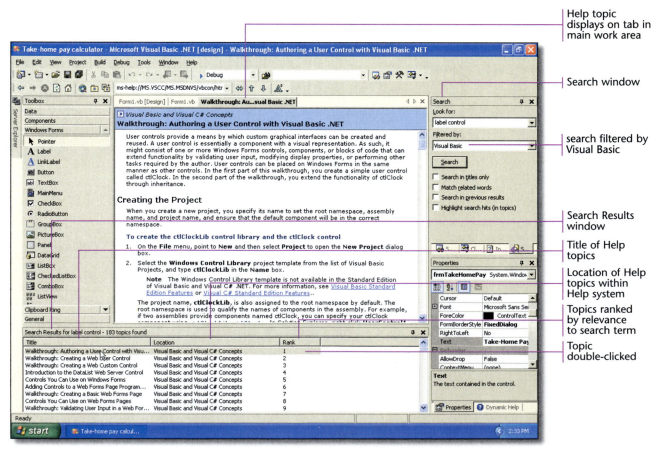

Help topic displays on tab in main work area

Search window

search filtered by Visual Basic

Search Results window

Title of Help topics

Location of Help topics within Help system

Topics ranked by relevance to search term

Topic double-clicked

FIGURE 2-48

Dynamic Help Window

In Visual Basic .NET, **Dynamic Help** displays help for whatever task or window you are working with in the IDE. As you navigate in the IDE, open new windows, or select items on a form, Dynamic Help automatically updates itself with relevant information. By default, the Dynamic Help window displays in the same window area as the Properties window. You can access Dynamic Help either by clicking the Dynamic Help tab next to the Properties tab in the Properties window or by selecting Dynamic Help on the Help menu.

Figure 2-49 shows the Dynamic Help topics that display when the Retirement plan contribution rate TrackBar control is selected on the Form1 form in the main work area. To view a Help topic displaying in the Dynamic Help window, double-click the topic in the Dynamic Help window. The Help topic will display on a new tab in the main work area.

> **Tip**
>
> **When to Use the Dynamic Help Window**
> Use the Dynamic Help window to learn more about the item selected in the main work area.

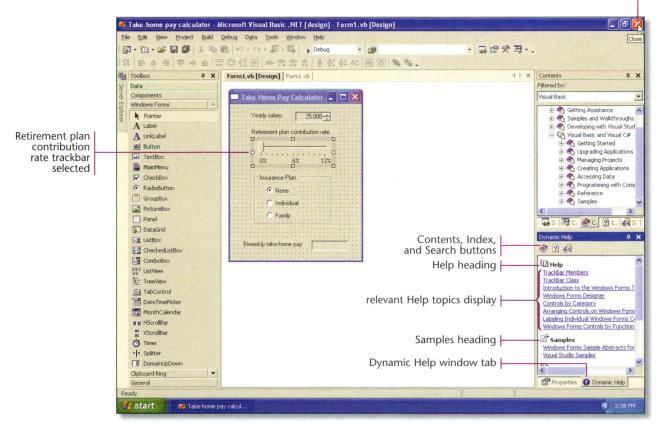

FIGURE 2-49

By clicking the headings within the Dynamic Help window, such as Help or Samples, you can collapse or expand the topic list. The Dynamic Help window also contains Contents, Index, and Search buttons on its toolbar. Clicking the

Contents, Index, or Search button will open the corresponding Help window in the upper right of the IDE.

Context-Sensitive Help

In addition to the types of Help accessed via the Help menu, you also can access Help in many areas of the Visual Basic .NET IDE by pressing the F1 key. This feature, called **context-sensitive help**, is available for most areas of the Visual Basic .NET IDE. For example, to get help about the Solution Explorer window, you would click the Solution Explorer window title bar and then press the F1 key. The Help topic about the Solution Explorer window then displays on a tab in the main work area. To close the Help tab, right-click the tab and then click Hide on the shortcut menu.

Tip

Hiding Help Windows
To hide a Help window, right-click the tab of the window and then click Hide on the shortcut menu.

Quitting Visual Basic .NET

When you have completed working with Visual Basic .NET, you should quit the Visual Basic .NET system to conserve memory for other Windows applications. Perform the following step to quit Visual Basic .NET.

To Quit Visual Basic .NET

---

1. Click the Visual Basic .NET Close button on the right side of the title bar (Figure 2-49 on the previous page).

If you made changes to the project since the last time it was saved, Visual Basic .NET displays the Microsoft Visual Basic .NET dialog box. If you click the Yes button, you can resave your project and quit. If you click the No button, you will quit without saving changes. Clicking the Cancel button will close the dialog box.

OTHER WAYS

1. Press ALT+F, X

Chapter Summary

In this chapter, you learned the fundamentals of using the Visual Basic .NET integrated development environment (IDE). You learned how to start Visual Basic .NET and then open and run a Visual Basic .NET project. You learned how to modify the properties of a control and modify code in a project. After you modified the project, you learned how to save and then test your changes. You also learned how to document an application by printing a record of the user interface design and code for a form. Finally, you learned how to access Help information about Visual Basic .NET using the Help system.

What You Should Know

Having completed this chapter, you now should be able to perform the tasks shown in Table 2-3.

Table 2-3   Chapter 2 What You Should Know

TASK NUMBER	TASK	PAGE
1	Start and Customize Visual Basic .NET	VB 2.04
2	Open an Existing Project	VB 2.09
3	Run a Project	VB 2.18
4	Modify the Text Property of a Label Control	VB 2.22
5	Navigate the Code Window	VB 2.26
6	Modify Code in the Code Window	VB 2.28
7	Save a Project	VB 2.31
8	Run a Project to Test Changes	VB 2.32
9	Print a Record of the User Interface Design of a Form	VB 2.34
10	Print a Record of the Code for a Form	VB 2.40
11	Quit Visual Basic .NET	VB 2.48

Key Terms

AssemblyInfo.vb *(VB 2.16)*
bugs *(VB 2.17)*
code region *(VB 2.27)*
code window *(VB 2.25)*
Contents window *(VB 2.44)*
context-sensitive help *(VB 2.48)*
continuation markers *(VB 2.42)*
debugging *(VB 2.33)*
design time *(VB 2.11)*
documenting an application *(VB 2.33)*
Dynamic Help *(VB 2.47)*
hard-copy output *(VB 2.33)*
Help *(VB 2.42)*
Index window *(VB 2.45)*
Insert *(VB 2.13)*
integrated development environment (IDE) *(VB 2.03)*
keywords *(VB 2.27)*
Label control *(VB 2.21)*
Layout toolbar *(VB 2.12)*
menu bar *(VB 2.11)*
Object box (Properties window) *(VB 2.22)*
Object box (code window) *(VB 2.25)*
Overtype *(VB 2.13)*

Print command *(VB 2.39)*
Procedure box *(VB 2.25)*
profile *(VB 2.04)*
project *(VB 2.02)*
property *(VB 2.22)*
Properties list *(VB 2.22)*
Properties window *(VB 2.22)*
Ready *(VB 2.13)*
References *(VB 2.16)*
run *(VB 2.17)*
run time *(VB 2.17)*
Save button *(VB 2.31)*
Save All button *(VB 2.31)*
Save Selected Items As command
  (VB 2.31)
Search window *(VB 2.45)*
Search Results window *(VB 2.46)*
ScreenTip *(VB 2.12)*
solution *(VB 2.15)*
splitter bar *(VB 2.27)*
Standard toolbar *(VB 2.12)*
status bar *(VB 2.13)*
tree view *(VB 2.16)*

Homework Assignments

Label the Figure

Identify the 18 Visual Basic .NET components shown in Figure 2-50.

1. _____
2. _____
3. _____
4. _____
5. _____
6. _____
7. _____
8. _____
9. _____

10. _____
11. _____
12. _____
13. _____
14. _____
15. _____
16. _____
17. _____
18. _____

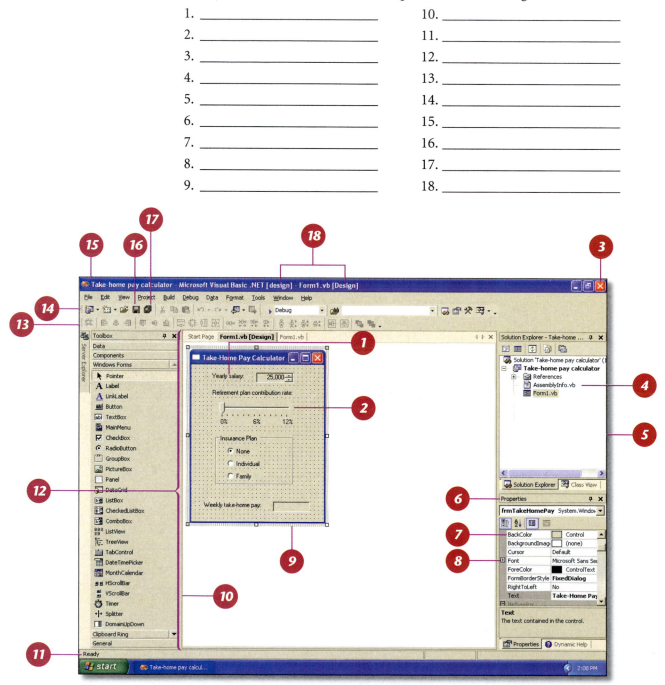

FIGURE 2-50

Short Answer

1. Which of the following Visual Basic .NET settings can you change through the My Profile link?

   a. At Startup   d. mouse scheme   g. default drive
   b. monitor   e. Window Layout   h. default browser
   c. Keyboard Scheme   f. Help Filter

2. The Solution Explorer window displays a _____ of the files that make up an application. The Properties window displays a list of the _____ of the _____ on the form.

3. When you first open a project, the IDE enters a mode called _____ time. When you run a project, the IDE enters a mode called _____ time.

4. List five items that may display on the status bar.

5. Fill in the default location and function for each of the IDE windows in Table 2-4

Table 2-4 Visual Basic .NET IDE Windows

WINDOW NAME	DEFAULT SCREEN LOCATION	FUNCTION
Class View		
Help Content		
Properties		
Solution Explorer		
Toolbox		

6. Define the following terms: Solution, References, bugs, design time, run time.

7. List the labels on the Take-Home Pay Calculator application window in Figure 2-33 on page VB 2.33.

8. Briefly explain how you print a form and the code in Visual Basic .NET.

9. List the corresponding Help function keys for context-sensitive help, dynamic help, contents, index, search, index results, and search results.

10. Explain the purpose of the collapse and expand buttons in the code window.

11. Use Help to define the function of the following buttons on the Standard toolbar shown in Figure 2-12 on page VB 2.12: New Project, Add New Item, Navigate Backward, Navigate Forward, Start, Solution Explorer, Properties Window, Toolbox, and Class View.

12. What other ways can you use to display the code window?

13. Explain the difference between clicking the Save button and clicking the Save All button on the Standard toolbar.

14. What is the purpose of the tabs at the top of the main work area?

15. If a project is made up of three forms, then how many items will display below the name of the project in the Solution Explorer window?

16. Explain what the asterisk means that follows the tab name Form1.vb [Design]*.

17. Define the term property and list five examples of the properties of a Label control.

18. What is the function of the Save Selected Items As command on the File menu?

19. Briefly summarize when you would use the following Help menu commands: Contents, Index, and Search.

20. What is Dynamic Help?

Learn It Online

Start your browser and visit scsite.com/vbnet/exs. Follow the instructions in the exercises below.

1. **Chapter Reinforcement TF, MC, and SA**   Click the True/False, Multiple Choice, and Short Answer link below Chapter 2. Print and then answer the questions.

2. **Practice Test**   Click the Practice Test link below Chapter 2. Answer each question, enter your first and last name at the bottom of the page, and then click the Grade Test button. When the graded practice test displays on your screen, click Print on the File menu to print a hard copy. Continue to take practice tests until you score 80% or better. Hand in a printout of the final practice test.

3. **Crossword Puzzle Challenge**   Click the Crossword Puzzle Challenge link below Chapter 2. Read the instructions, and then enter your first and last name. Click the Play button. Work the crossword puzzle. When you are finished, click the Submit button. When the crossword puzzle redisplays, click the Print button.

4. **Tips and Tricks**   Click the Tips and Tricks link below Chapter 2. Click a topic that pertains to Chapter 2. Right-click the information and then click Print on the shortcut menu. Construct a brief example of what the information relates to in Visual Basic .NET to confirm you understand how to use the tip or trick. Hand in the example and printed information.

5. **Newsgroups**   Click the Newsgroups link below Chapter 2. Click a topic that pertains to Chapter 2. Print three comments.

6. **Expanding Your Horizons**   Click the Articles for Visual Basic .NET below Chapter 2. Click a topic that pertains to Chapter 2. Print the information. Construct a brief example of what the information relates to in Visual Basic .NET to confirm you understand the contents of the article. Hand in the example and printed information.

7. **Search Sleuth**   Select three key terms from the Key Terms section of this chapter and then use the Google search engine at google.com (or any major search engine) to display and print two Web pages for each key term.

Debugging Assignment

Start Visual Basic .NET and open the project, Greenling Realty, from the Chapter2\ Greenling Realty folder on the Data Disk. See page xvi in the preface of this book for instructions for downloading the Data Disk or see your instructor for information about accessing the files required in this book. The project consists of one form that calculates commission on home sales for real estate agents. When a home is sold, Greenling Realty and the agent receive a total commission percentage from 1% to 6%, depending on the sale. The total commission percentage is input using the trackbar on the form. Greenling Realty receives 1.5% of the total commission percentage; the agent receives the rest. If the home sale price is at or above $300,000, then the agent receives an additional 20% commission.

The Greenling Realty project contains bugs in the user interface design and in the program code. Follow the steps below to debug the project.

1. Fix the spelling error in the Home Price Label control. The Label control currently reads Hose Price. Select the Label control and then modify the Text property value in the Properties window to make this change.

2. The Commission Rate TrackBar control currently is labeled with a rate of 0%. This label should read 1%. Select the Trackbar control and then modify the Text property value in the Properties window to make this change.

3. The Agent's Commission label contains a typographical error and currently reads Agen Commission. Select the Label control and then modify the Text property value in the Properties window to make this change.

4. Click Code on the View menu. Find the line of code that determines whether to give the 20% bonus. This line of code currently is checking for a limit of 30000, not 300000. Correct this error and return to the form design window.

5. Save the project and then run the project to test for any bugs. Use 350000 for a home sale price and 5% for the commission. The application should display as shown in Figure 2-51, with an Agent's Commission of $14,700.00.

FIGURE 2-51

6. Document the user interface design of the form using the PRINT SCREEN key on the keyboard and print it using the Windows Paint application. Document the form code by printing the code for the Form1.vb form. Circle the lines of code you modified on the code printout.

Programming Assignments

1 Opening and Modifying a Visual Basic .NET Project

Start Visual Basic .NET and open the project, Take-home pay calculator, from the Chapter2 folder on the Data Disk. See page xvi in the preface of this book for instructions for downloading the Data Disk or see your instructor for information about accessing the files required in this book. The Take-home pay calculator project must be modified because the company is moving to a monthly pay period and increasing the percentage of gross pay that employees can contribute to the retirement plan to 14%. Figure 2-52 shows the Take-Home Pay Calculator application after the changes have been made to the user interface and code.

1. Click the 6% Label control. Change the Text property value from 6% to 7% in the Properties window.

2. Click the 12% Label control. Change the Text property value from 12% to 14% in the Properties window.

3. Click the Biweekly take-home pay Label control. Change the Text property value to Monthly take-home pay: in the Properties window.

4. Click the Retirement plan contribution rate TrackBar control. Change the Maximum property value from 12 to 14.

5. Click the Form1.vb tab to display the code window. Find the line of code that divides the yearly salary by 26.0. Change 26.0 to 12.0 to indicate a monthly pay period.

6. Use the Save All button on the Standard toolbar to save your changes.

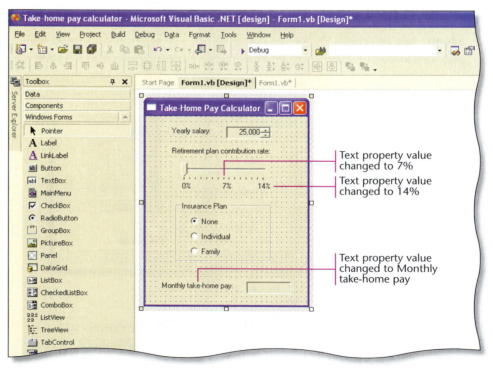

FIGURE 2-52

7. Click the Form1.vb [Design] tab. Run the application. Use relevant test data to verify that the modifications made to the project are correct. Use the modified application to determine the monthly take-home pay for each data set: (a) 30,000 yearly salary; 14% contribution to retirement plan; and the Family insurance plan; (b) 45,000 yearly salary; 13% contribution to retirement plan; and the Individual insurance plan. The monthly take-home pay for (a) is $1,416.25 and for (b) is $2,186.88.

8. Document the application by pressing the PRINT SCREEN key to capture a screen image of the form's user interface design and then print it using Paint. Use the Print command on the File menu to print the code for the form, Form1.vb.

2 Profit Margin Calculation

As an analyst for Ergo Office Chairs, you have been asked to update a simple profit margin calculator used by the accounting department. The application accepts a current inventory amount for a specific item, a unit cost for the item, and a margin used in pricing the item. The result produced is the total profit that can be expected from the total number of items in inventory. The application currently accepts a margin ranging from 20% to 40%. The president of the company has recently announced that all products must have a 30% to 45% margin. Additionally, the application currently limits the number of items on hand in inventory to 50. New requirements dictate that this inventory limit be increased to 75.

Perform the tasks on the next page to update the application as shown in Figure 2-53.

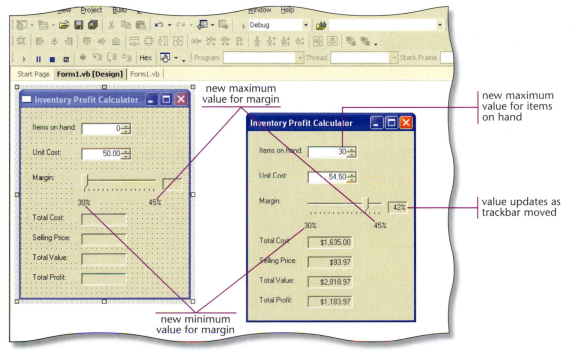

FIGURE 2-53

(continued)

2 Profit Margin Calculation *(continued)*

1. Start Visual Basic .NET and open the project, Ergo Office Chairs, from the Chapter2\Ergo Office Chairs folder on the Data Disk.

2. Click the 20% Label control. Change the Text property value from 20% to 30%.

3. Click the 40% Label control. Change the Text property value from 40% to 45%.

4. Click the Margin TrackBar control. Change the Minimum property value from 20 to 30. Change the Maximum property value from 40 to 45.

5. Click the Items on hand ListBox control. Change the Maximum property value from 50 to 75.

6. Navigate to the code window. Find the line of code that reads Private Sub CalculateTotalProfit(). Above this line, type the following line of code, substituting your own name and correct date where appropriate:

```
' Updated by: J. Quasney                    September 8, 2004
```

7. Locate the line of code that begins with Private Sub tbMarginScroll. Immediately below this line, type the following line of code:

```
txtMargin.Text = Convert.ToString(tbMargin.Value) & "%"
```

This line of code appends a percentage symbol to the value of the Margin TrackBar control and assigns the result to the Margin TextBox control next to the trackbar.

8. Save the project and then run the project to make certain no errors exist. If any errors are encountered, correct them, and save the project again. Run the project and enter the values shown in Figure 2-53 on the previous page. Verify that the results of your project match those shown in the figure.

9. Document the user interface design of the form using the PRINT SCREEN key on the keyboard and print it using the Windows Paint application. Document the form code by printing the code for the Form1.vb form.

3 Navigating the Help System

Perform the following tasks using a computer. After each step, use the Print command on the File menu to print the Help topic.

1. Start Visual Basic .NET. Click the Contents command on the Help menu. Navigate the Contents window through the following topic hierarchy: Visual Studio .NET; Developing with Visual Studio .NET; Working with Code, HTML, and Resource Files; Editing Code, HTML, and Text; Managing the Code Editor and View. Click the topic, Managing the Code Editor and View, to display the topic on a tab in the main work area.

2. Click the Index command on the Help menu. Type open project in the Look for box. Double-click the topic, Open Project dialog box, to display the topic on a tab in the main work area.

3. Click the Search command on the Help menu. Type trackbar in the Look for box and then click the Search button. Double-click the first result in the Search Results window to display the topic on a tab in the main work area (Figure 2-54).

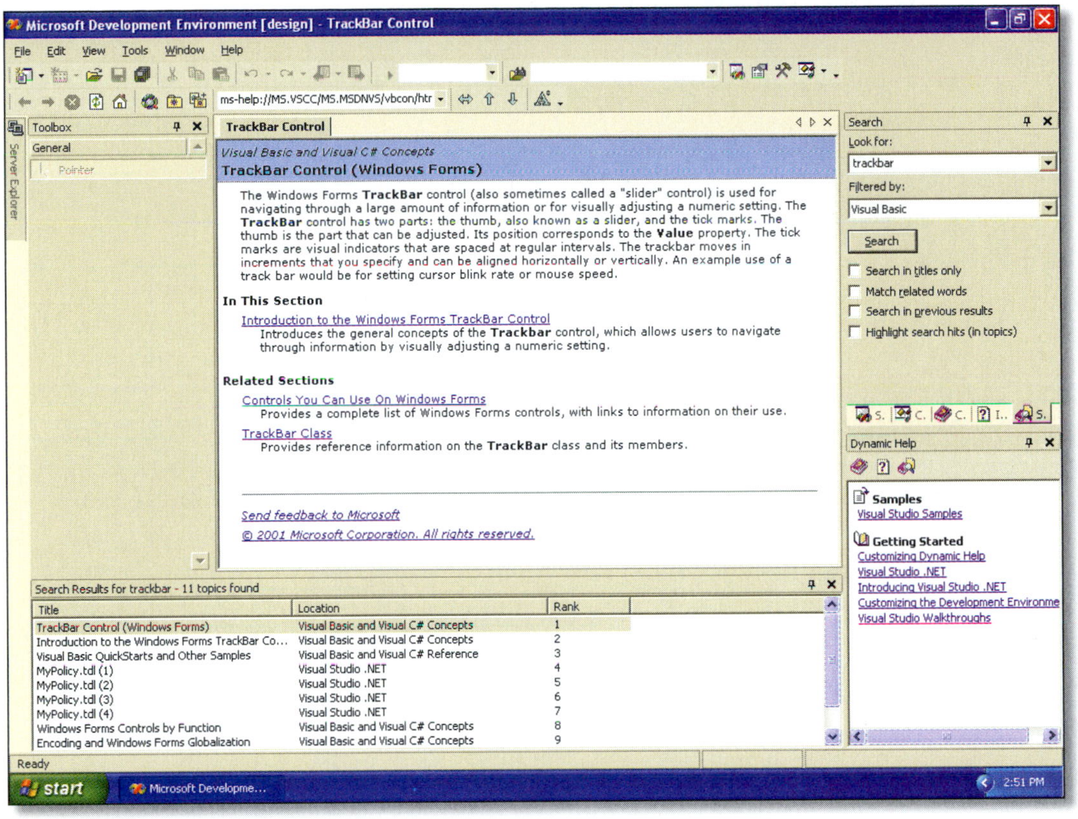

FIGURE 2-54

4. Use one of the methods discussed in this chapter to navigate to the Visual Basic Walkthroughs Help topic. Use the Print command on the File menu to print the Help topic. Scroll down through the topic and click the Creating a Simple Windows Form link. Print this topic.

5. Navigate to the Search window by clicking the Search tab at the bottom of the right Help window. Type Start Page in the Look for box. Click the Search in titles only check box. Click the Highlight search hits (in topics) check box. Click the Search button. When the results display in the Search Results window, double-click the Start Page topic to display the topic on a tab in the main work area.

4 Finding Help on the Visual Basic .NET Environment

Open Visual Basic .NET. While on the Start Page, navigate to the following two Help topics in the Dynamic Help window: Customizing the Development Environment and Visual Basic Sample Abstracts. Read and print each of the Help topics. Click the Help on Help command on the Help menu and then print the topic. Using the Help system, learn about the Microsoft Document Explorer and how to use it. Print the Help topics.

PROGRAMMING ASSIGNMENTS

5 Searching the Web

Using a Web search engine, such as Google, type the keywords VB.NET and IDE. Visit five Web pages that discuss configuring the Visual Basic .NET IDE. Print each Web page.

6 Future Value Calculation

Open the project, Jacks Trading Cards, from the Chapter2\Jacks Trading Cards folder on the Data Disk. The application calculates the possible future value of trading cards sold at Jack's Trading Cards based on the increase in value to date. Increase the maximum beginning price value from 25 to 50. Increase the maximum current price from 50 to 100. Change the interface to indicate that the application now calculates a future value result for 1 year in the future, as opposed to 6 months in the future. Change the code to calculate future value using the number 52 for the number of weeks (1 year), rather than 26 weeks (6 months). Document the application by printing the user interface design and the code for the Form1.vb form.

7 Modifying a User Interface

Open the project, Marias Gift Shop, from the Chapter2\Marias Gift Shop folder on the Data Disk. Maria uses this application to calculate how much a savings account or Certificate of Deposit (CD) at various banks might earn. Maria requests that you make a few changes to the application. She requests that rates vary from 2% to 7% (Text property value of the Label control), that the rate default to 5% rather than 2% (Value property of the TrackBar control), and that the principal default to 1000 rather than 0 (Text property value of the TextBox control). She would also like the result to display as currency (change Fixed to Currency in the code). Document the application by printing the user interface design and the code for the Form1.vb form.

8 Navigating the Start Page

The Visual Basic .NET Start Page contains several links on the left side of the page. Explore several of the items on the Start Page, such as What's New, Online Community, Headlines, and Downloads. These pages are Web pages maintained by Microsoft that display on the Start Page. Navigate the pages and print at least five different pages using the Print command on the File menu.

9 Visual Basic .NET Sample Applications

Visual Basic .NET includes two complete applications as samples. You will find many references to these samples in the Help system. The samples are called Duwamish and Fitch and Mather. Locate information about the Duwamish sample and print the Help page that shows a UML Sequence Diagram for creating a new customer account in the Duwamish Account Management system.

3

Building an Application in the Visual Basic .NET Environment

Objectives

You will have
mastered the material in
this chapter when you can:

- Design a Visual Basic .NET application
- Start a new Visual Basic .NET project
- Change the size of a form
- Change the property values of a form
- Add controls to a form
- Move and resize controls on a form
- Use the Label, TextBox, NumericUpDown, and Button controls
- Change the property values of controls
- Change the Name property to rename a control
- Write the code for a Click event procedure
- Display line numbers in the code window
- Use control properties in a method
- Document code with a comment header and comment statements

Introduction

As you have learned, Visual Basic .NET is a programming environment that allows you to develop, maintain, and execute applications and application components for the Windows operating system or any system that supports the .NET architecture. This chapter concentrates on using the Visual Basic .NET IDE to develop a new Visual Basic .NET application. After completing this chapter, you should be able to start a new Visual Basic .NET project and describe the components of a Visual Basic .NET project. You also will learn how to design a Windows application with a user-friendly interface and then implement and test the application. In the process, you will learn how to add controls to a form and then modify properties of the controls to fit the needs of the application. You also will understand how to write Visual Basic .NET code and document the code with comment statements. Finally, you will learn how to execute and test the Windows application.

Chapter Three — State Tax Computation

The Windows application developed in this chapter is the State Tax Computation application, which calculates the state tax payment for a taxpayer based on the taxpayer's income, number of dependents, and a standard state tax rate of 3% (Figure 3-1). To calculate a state tax payment using the State Tax Computation application, the user first enters the taxpayer's income in the Taxpayer's income input area. Next, the user enters the number of dependents the taxpayer can claim, between 0 and 10, in the Number of dependents input area. Once the data is entered, the user clicks the Compute Tax button and the application calculates the state tax payment by subtracting $600 for each dependent from the taxpayer's income and then multiplying the result by the standard state tax rate of 3%.

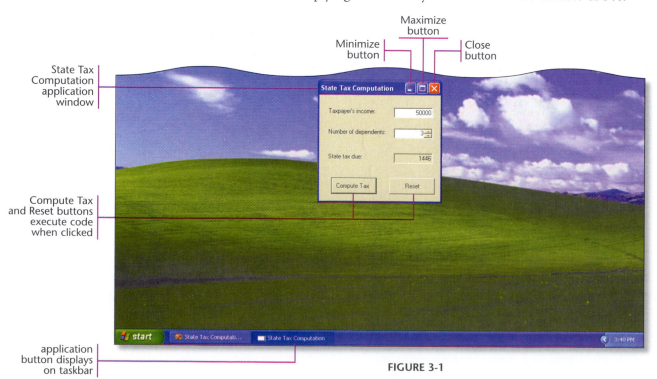

FIGURE 3-1

The calculation used by the State Tax Computation application to determine the state tax payment is represented by the following equation:

State Tax = 0.03 × (Income − (600 × Dependents))

The equation first multiplies the number of dependents (Dependents) by $600 and then subtracts the result of this calculation from the taxpayer's income in dollars (Income). The application then multiplies the result of that calculation by 0.03 (3%), to determine the state tax payment due (State Tax). After completing the calculation and determining the state tax payment, the application displays the state tax in the State tax due output area. When the user clicks the Reset button, the State Tax Computation application resets the input and output areas to their original values of 0.

As shown in Figure 3-1, the State Tax Computation application includes several of the common features of Windows applications. The application, for instance, occupies a window that the user can move on the desktop. The application window includes buttons that allow a user to minimize, maximize, or close the window. The application window also includes two buttons — the Compute Tax and Reset buttons — that a user can click to instruct the application to execute the code assigned to the button. Figure 3-2 shows the code the application executes when a user clicks the Compute Tax or Reset button.

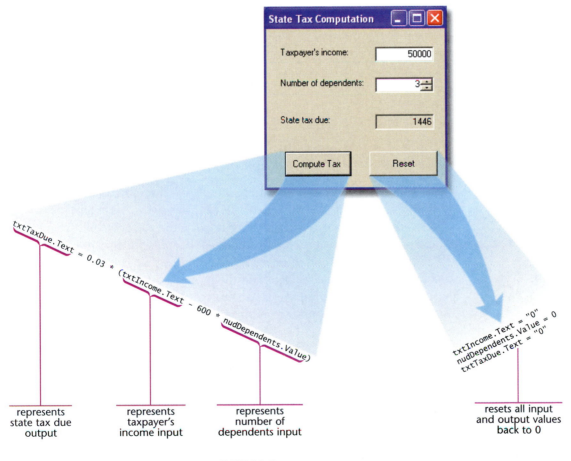

| represents state tax due output | represents taxpayer's income input | represents number of dependents input | resets all input and output values back to 0 |

FIGURE 3-2

Program Development

As you learned in Chapter 1, the tasks involved in developing an application follow the series of six iterative phases outlined in the development cycle. The development cycle for the State Tax Computation application consists of tasks that correspond to the six phases, as shown in .

Table 3-1 State Tax Computation Application Development Tasks

DEVELOPMENT PHASE	TASK NUMBER	TASK NAME	TASK
Analyze requirements	1	Analyze problem	Analyze the state tax computation problem.
Design solution	2	Design interface	Design the user interface for the application, including input areas, output areas, and form controls.
	3	Design program	Design the logic for the code and write pseudocode.
Validate design	4	Validate design	Prove that the solution produces correct results for the state tax computation program.
Implement design	5	Develop interface	Add user interface elements, such as input areas, output areas, and Button controls on a form.
	6	Write code	Write code to add event procedures for the buttons; add comment statements in code.
Test solution	7	Test	Test the application.
	8	Debug	Fix any problems with the application.
Document solution	9	Document	Print the program.

Analysis and Design

The first two phases in the development cycle — analysis and design — involve analyzing the problem the application is intended to solve and then designing a solution. Analysis is required to understand the problem the application should solve. Once the problem is understood, a developer can work with users to design a user-friendly interface for the application. The final stage of the design phase is to design the logic behind the program.

Figure 3-3 shows the requirements document that initiates the development cycle for the State Tax Computation application. The design requirements listed by the user are specific enough to allow for the development cycle to begin. The document specifies the reason for the request, the algorithm used to make the calculation, and the terminology that the user should see in the interface.

PROBLEM ANALYSIS   The problem that the State Tax Computation application should solve is the calculation of state tax due for a taxpayer based on the taxpayer's income, number of dependents, and a standard state tax rate

REQUEST FOR NEW APPLICATION

Date submitted:	August 28, 2003
Submitted by:	Jan Davies
Purpose:	The Personnel department often is asked to do a quick computation of a customer's state tax. Employees would save time and provide more accurate information if they had a stand-alone application at their disposal to perform the calculation.
Application title:	State Tax Computation
Algorithms:	State tax is computed as follows: *State Tax = 0.03 x (Income – (600 x Dependents))*
Notes:	1) Support personnel are accustomed to the following terminology: **Taxpayer's income** for Income in the above algorithm, **Number of dependents** for Dependents in the above algorithm, **State tax due** for State Tax in the above algorithm. 2) The application should allow the user to enter values for Taxpayer's income and Number of dependents, so that State tax due can be computed. 3) Because the taxpayer can only claim between zero and ten dependents, the application should limit the user's entry to only valid inputs of positive whole numbers ranging from zero to ten. 4) The application should also allow the user to reset all values on the screen to zero (0) so that another calculation can be performed. 5) The computation should be designated by the term, Compute. The reset of the values should be designated by the term, Reset.

Approvals

Approval Status:	X	Approved
		Rejected
Approved by:	Jessie Simms	
Date:	September 2, 2003	
Assigned to:	J. Quasney, Programmer	

FIGURE 3-3

of 3%. To complete the calculation and generate results, or output, for the user, the State Tax Computation application requires the user to input two values: Taxpayer's income and Number of dependents.

As you have learned, the application uses the equation

State Tax = $0.03 \times (\text{Income} - (600 \times \text{Dependents}))$

to calculate the state tax payment due by a taxpayer. The equation requires two inputs to complete one calculation and generate one output. The first input, Taxpayer's income, is represented by Income in the equation. The second input, Number of dependents, is represented by Dependents in the equation. The application uses these inputs to calculate, or process, the output, State tax due, which is represented by State Tax in the equation. Each element of the equation corresponds to an element in the code that displays below the Compute Tax button in Figure 3-2 on page VB 3.03.

As indicated in the requirements document, the application also must provide a way to reset input and output values back to 0, so that a user can calculate the state tax payment due for another taxpayer. To reset these values, the application uses the equations

Income = 0
Dependents = 0
State Tax = 0

to tell the application to set the inputs — Taxpayer's income (Income) and Number of dependents (Dependents) — and the output — State tax due (State Tax) — back to the original values of 0. Each element of the equation corresponds to an element in the code that displays below the Reset button in Figure 3-2 on page VB 3.03.

INTERFACE DESIGN   Once you have analyzed the problem and understand the needs, the next step is to design the user interface (Table 3-1 on page VB 3.04). A **user interface** (**UI**) is the way that a program accepts data and instructions from the user and presents results. A **graphical user interface** (**GUI**) provides visual cues such as a menu, a button, or a small picture, called an icon, to help the user enter data and give instructions to the computer. Many programmers design a user interface by creating hand drawings that show the various interface elements and how they will display to a user. Figure 3-4 shows an example of a hand drawing created during interface design for the State Tax Computation application. The title of the application and the text that displays in the input and output labels are specified in the requirements document (Figure 3-3 on the previous page).

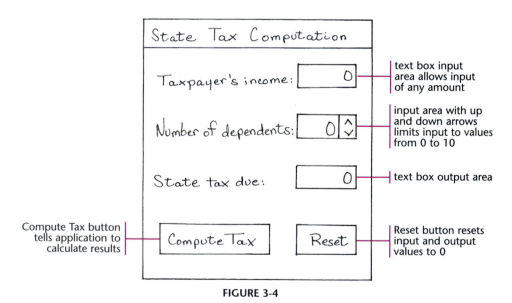

FIGURE 3-4

When designing a user interface in Visual Basic .NET, you must consider the inputs, processing, and outputs of data required by an application and then choose appropriate controls. In this application, the first input is the taxpayer's income amount. Because the taxpayer's income can be any amount, the user interface must allow the user to enter any number for the taxpayer's income. As shown in Figure 3-4, an input area with a text box is best for this kind of input, because it allows the user to enter any amount. The second input is the number of dependents. Because the taxpayer can claim only between 0 and 10 dependents, the user interface should limit the user's entry to only valid inputs of positive whole numbers ranging from 0 to 10. An input area with up and down arrows can limit a user's input to specified values in a range (Figure 3-4). As the programmer, you can determine the range, or boundaries, of the allowable entries in the input area. The user enters data in this input area in two ways. First, the user can use the UP ARROW or DOWN ARROW keys on the keyboard or use the mouse to click the up and down arrows in the input area to select any allowable value. Second, the user can type a number in the text box portion of the input area. If the value entered is out of the allowable range, Visual Basic .NET automatically changes the value to the closest allowable value.

Aesthetics versus Function

In designing a user interface, visual aesthetics should follow functional considerations. The function, or purpose, of a user interface is to provide a user with direct ways to accomplish tasks. Avoid the temptation to use flashy or confusing visual elements within the application, unless they will help a user more easily complete a task.

The output of the State Tax Computation application is a numeric value calculated as the result of the tax computation equation. A text box works well to display this type of output. The output area, however, should provide visual cues to a user to indicate that the area should not be used for input. Two simple and effective ways to indicate an output area are (1) modifying a property of the output area so that a user cannot input data in the control and (2) using a gray background for the output area.

Consistent Design Principles

Applications should follow basic graphic design principles and should be consistent visually and functionally.

Finally, a user of the application needs some way to instruct the application to calculate or process the output, based on the inputs that have been provided. Adding one or more buttons to a user interface allows a user to initiate an action by clicking the button, which causes the code assigned to the button to be executed. In the State Tax Computation application, clicking the Compute Tax button tells the application to perform the calculation to determine State tax due; clicking the Reset button resets the input and output values back to their original values of zero.

Real-World Experience

Use concepts and metaphors familiar to users to ensure the user interface parallels real-world experience.

PROGRAM DESIGN Once you have designed the interface, the next step is to design a program that creates the desired results. The two program tasks include (1) calculating the state tax payment due using the equation,

State Tax = 0.03 × (Income − (600 × Dependents))

and (2) resetting the input and output values back to 0, so the user can perform the calculation again using different input values. The user can execute these tasks by clicking the corresponding button on the user interface.

One way to design the program code to execute these two tasks is to use pseudocode. Figure 3-5 shows the pseudocode used to design the procedures needed to execute the two program tasks. The pseudocode is not Visual Basic .NET code, but rather an English description of how the code should behave. For small programming projects, you can write pseudocode by hand along with a logic diagram. The pseudocode for the algorithm comes from the requirements document (Figure 3-3 on page VB 3.05).

```
ComputeTax Button Click Event
        Tax = .03 X (Income – 600 X Dependents)
End

Reset Button Click Event
        Income = 0
        Dependents = 0
        TaxDue = 0
End
```

FIGURE 3-5

Having analyzed the problem, designed the interface, and designed the program, the analysis and design of the application is complete. As shown in Table 3-1 on page VB 3.04, the next task in the development cycle is to develop the user interface of the application using Visual Basic .NET. Before you can begin developing the user interface, you first must start Visual Basic .NET and start a new project.

Starting a New Project

As you have learned, a project is a collection of code and other files that usually encompasses one application or class. When you start Visual Basic .NET, you can choose to open an existing project or start a new project. When you choose to start a new project, you can choose which type of application or Windows component you want to create.

Visual Basic .NET allows you to select from a number of different project types and templates so you can develop many different types of applications. The State Tax Computation application is a Windows application with a Windows user interface for user input and output display. The application is based on the Windows Application template provided by Visual Basic .NET. The following steps start Visual Basic .NET and start a new project using the Windows Application template.

To Start a New Visual Basic .NET Project

1. Insert the Data Disk in drive A. See page xvi in the preface of this book for instructions for downloading the Data Disk or see your instructor for information about accessing the files required in this book.

2. Start Visual Basic .NET. When the Start Page displays, click the New Project button on the Start Page.

   The New Project dialog box displays. By default, the Visual Basic Projects project type and Windows Application template are selected. A default project name and location display in the Name box and Location box. The default location may differ on your computer (Figure 3-6).

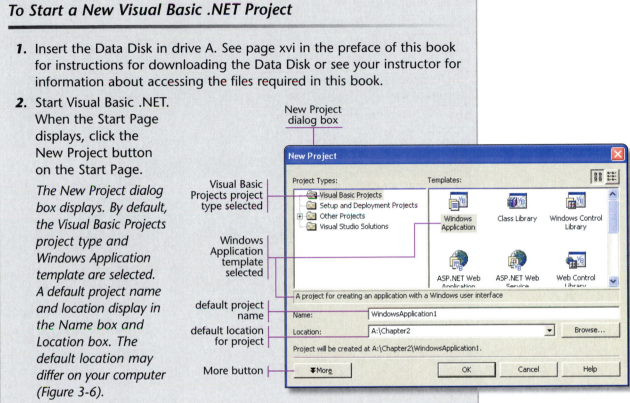

New Project dialog box

Visual Basic Projects project type selected

Windows Application template selected

default project name

default location for project

More button

FIGURE 3-6

3. Click the More button.

   The New Project dialog box expands to show more options (Figure 3-7).

default location where Visual Basic .NET will create project

dialog box expanded

Create directory for Solution check box

FIGURE 3-7

(continued)

4. Click the Create directory for Solution check box. Double-click the text, WindowsApplication1, in the Name box. Type State Tax Computation in the Name box.

The Create directory for Solution check box is checked, so Visual Basic .NET will create a subdirectory with the same name as the project when the project is created. The new project and solution names display in the Name box and the New Solution Name box, respectively. The message below the New Solution Name box displays the new project name and location (Figure 3-8).

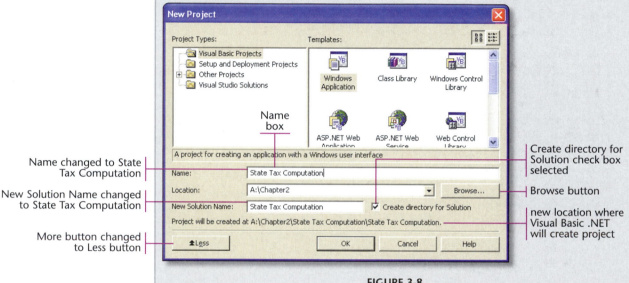

Name changed to State Tax Computation

New Solution Name changed to State Tax Computation

More button changed to Less button

Name box

Create directory for Solution check box selected

Browse button

new location where Visual Basic .NET will create project

FIGURE 3-8

5. Click the Browse button. If necessary, select 3½ Floppy (A:) in the Look in box. Double-click Chapter3 in the Look in list.

Visual Basic .NET opens the Project Location dialog box. A list of folders on the Data Disk in drive A displays in the Project Location dialog box. Chapter3 becomes the current folder in the Look in box (Figure 3-9).

Project Location dialog box

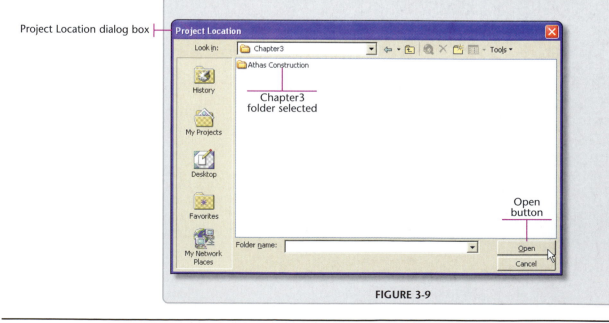

Chapter3 folder selected

Open button

FIGURE 3-9

6. Click the Open button.

The Location box and the message below the New Solution Name box change to display the Chapter3 folder as the location where Visual Basic .NET will create the project (Figure 3-10).

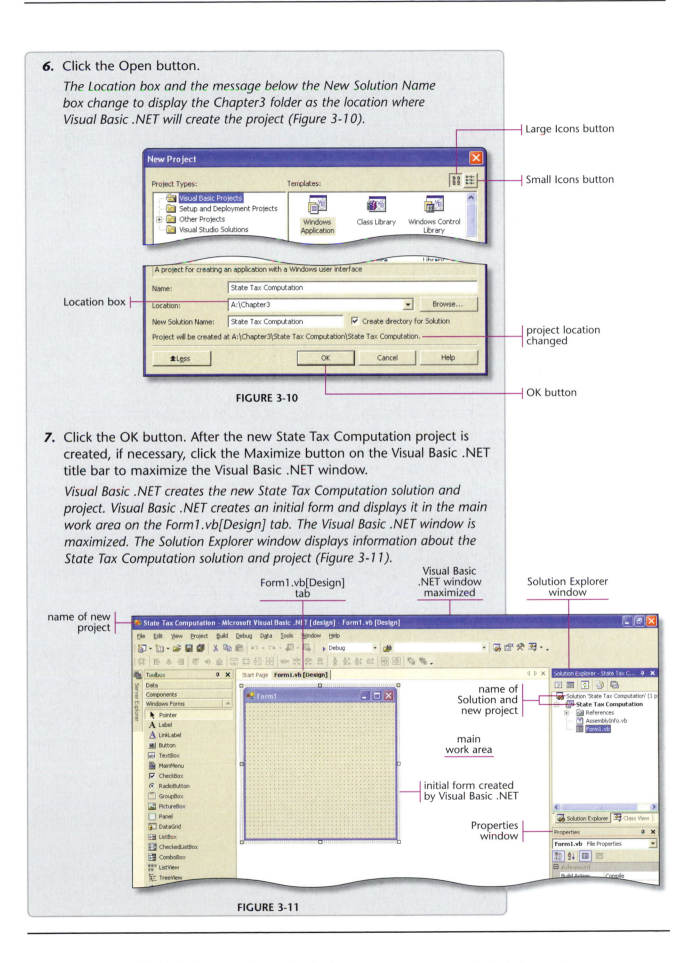

Large Icons button

Small Icons button

Location box

project location changed

OK button

FIGURE 3-10

7. Click the OK button. After the new State Tax Computation project is created, if necessary, click the Maximize button on the Visual Basic .NET title bar to maximize the Visual Basic .NET window.

Visual Basic .NET creates the new State Tax Computation solution and project. Visual Basic .NET creates an initial form and displays it in the main work area on the Form1.vb[Design] tab. The Visual Basic .NET window is maximized. The Solution Explorer window displays information about the State Tax Computation solution and project (Figure 3-11).

Form1.vb[Design] tab

Visual Basic .NET window maximized

Solution Explorer window

name of new project

name of Solution and new project

main work area

initial form created by Visual Basic .NET

Properties window

FIGURE 3-11

After Visual Basic .NET creates the new project, the solution and project name, State Tax Computation, displays in the Solution Explorer window (Figure 3-11 on the previous page). Form1.vb is selected in the Solution Explorer window to indicate that Form1.vb currently is active in the main work area. The Properties window displays information about Form1.vb.

Clicking the Create directory for Solutions check box in the New Project dialog box (Figure 3-8 on page VB 3.10) tells Visual Basic .NET to create a sub-directory with the same name as the project, in the project location. All of the files associated with the State Tax Computation project will be saved in this sub-directory, to separate them from other projects created in the Chapter3 folder.

The Large Icons button and Small Icons button (Figure 3-10 on the previous page) toggle how the Template area of the New Project dialog box displays. When the **Large Icons button** is selected, the template names display as large icons, as shown in Figure 3-10. When the **Small Icons button** is selected, the template names display in a list with smaller icons to their left.

Working with Form Properties for a Windows Application

A project can contain many forms. Visual Basic .NET always adds an initial form to a new Windows Application project. At run time, the form becomes the window in which the application displays. When you start a new project using the Windows Application template, Visual Basic .NET creates an initial form and displays it in the main work area on the Form1.vb[Design] tab, as shown in Figure 3-11 on the previous page. A **form** is an instance of the System.Windows.Forms.Form class in the .NET framework.

The first step in developing the user interface for the State Tax Computation application is to change several form properties, such as the size of and location where the application window displays on the desktop during run time. The hand drawing of the user interface created during interface design (Figure 3-4 on page VB 3.06) serves as a guide for setting the form properties and helps you develop a user interface that supports the inputs, processing, and outputs of data required by the application.

Changing the Size of a Form

During design time, you set the size of a form to define the size of the application window on the desktop during run time. When Visual Basic .NET creates the initial form, it sets the form to a default size.

> **Tip**
>
> **Form Sizing**
> As you start developing the user interface, you should adjust the form size to accommodate the input area, output area, and other user interface elements.

The following steps set the size of the State Tax Computation form, which currently has the file name, Form1.vb.

To Change the Size of a Form

1. Click the Form1 form in the main work area. Point to the center sizing handle on the form's right border.

The Form1 form is active, as indicated by the change in the color of the Form1 form title bar. The Properties window displays the form name in the Object box. The mouse pointer changes to a double two-headed arrow, indicating the form can be sized (Figure 3-12).

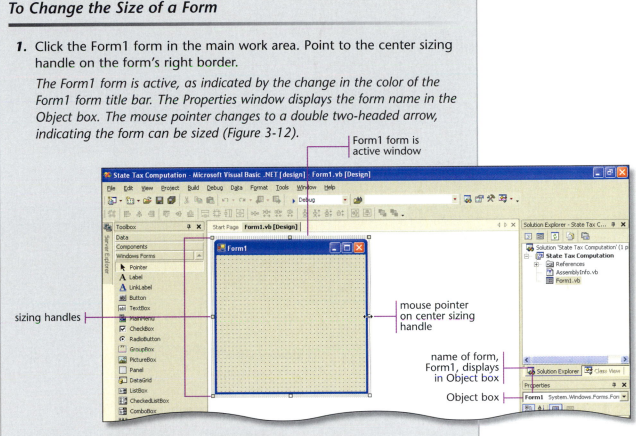

FIGURE 3-12

2. Drag the form's right border to the left to decrease the form width by approximately one-half inch.

The form's right border is moved approximately one-half inch to the left (Figure 3-13).

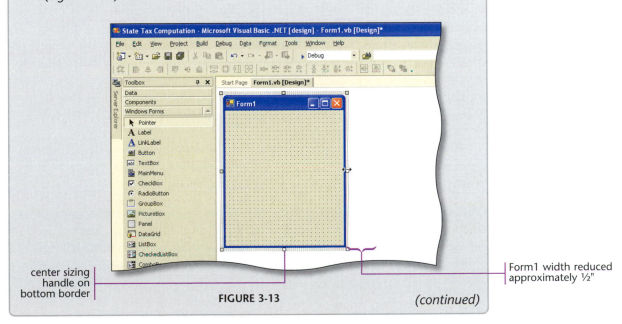

FIGURE 3-13

(continued)

> **3.** Point to the center sizing handle on the form's bottom border and then drag the form's bottom border up to decrease the form height approximately one-half inch.
>
> *The form's bottom border is moved up approximately one-half inch (Figure 3-14).*
>
>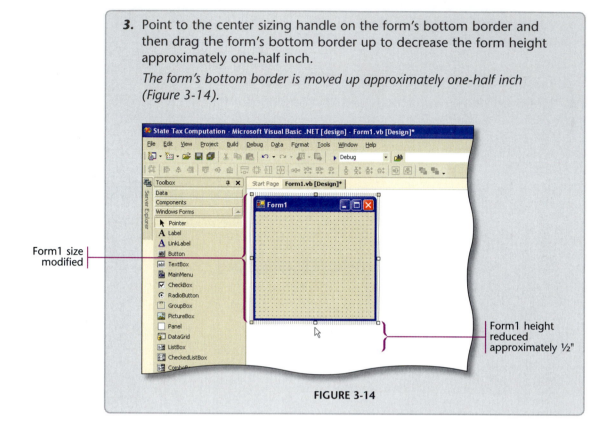
>
> **FIGURE 3-14**

You can adjust a form's size at any point during design time. In the preceding steps, you modified the width and height of the form by dragging the form's right and bottom borders. You also can drag the lower-right corner of the form to change its width and height at the same time.

Using the Property Window

As you learned in Chapter 2, a property is an attribute of an object or control, such as its background color or the text that displays with it. Width and Height are properties of a form. The form's **Width property** defines the width of the form in pixels; the **Height property** defines the height of the form in pixels. A **pixel** is a single point on a display monitor. A typical PC monitor contains approximately 96 pixels per inch. As you resize the form by dragging its borders, Visual Basic .NET automatically updates the Width and Height properties in the Properties window

As you have learned, the Properties window contains a list of attributes for the object currently selected in the main work area. As shown in Figure 3-15, the Properties window consists of the following elements.

OBJECT BOX The **Object box** displays the name of the currently selected object or control. An object can be a control or form in the main work area or any item selected in the Solution Explorer window, including a solution, project, or other file. Clicking the Object box arrow displays a list of objects associated with the current form in the main work area, including the form itself. You can select a different object by selecting an object in the list or by clicking the object in the main work area.

PROPERTIES LIST   The **Properties list** displays the set of properties for the object named in the Object box and the current value of those properties.

TOOLBAR   The **toolbar** in the Properties window includes buttons that allow you to change the display of the Properties list. The **Categorized button** displays properties grouped by category, such as Appearance or Behavior, in the Properties list. The Properties list displays in categorized view by default. The **Alphabetic button** displays properties alphabetically in the Properties list. As shown in Figure 3-15, the **Properties button** is selected, indicating that a list of properties currently displays in the Properties list. The **Property Pages button** is activated when a project or solution is selected in the Solution Explorer window. Clicking the Property Pages button opens a dialog box with options you can set for a solution or project. Depending on the tasks you are completing in the Visual Basic .NET IDE, the buttons on the Properties window toolbar sometimes may change.

DESCRIPTION PANE   The **description pane** at the bottom of the Properties window displays information about the property currently selected in the Properties list.

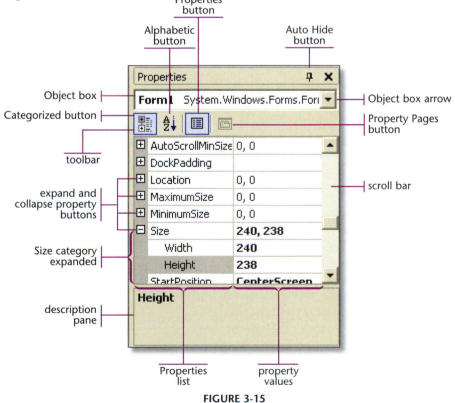

FIGURE 3-15

Because the Properties list for an object can include numerous properties, the Properties window includes a scroll bar that allows you to navigate the list. In categorized view, groups of properties are collapsed together for easier navigation through the Properties list. When a group of properties is collapsed, a plus (+) sign displays next to the group category name in the Properties list (Figure 3-15 on the previous page). Clicking the plus sign expands the group to display all of the properties in that group.

It is not necessary to set every property for each object you add to an interface because Visual Basic .NET assigns an initial value, called the **default value**, for each of the properties. Property values can be numbers, text, or a selection from a list. A property that determines a size of a control, for example, will have a property value that is a number. A property that displays a message on the screen will have a property value that is text. A property, such as a color with a few discrete values, will have a list of options for the property value. Clicking the property value arrow value displays the list of options from which you can select. For some properties, the property value has a button that opens a dialog box in which you can set property values. Clicking the button for the Font property value opens the Font dialog box, which allows you to set font face, style, color, and so on.

Setting Properties

As you develop the user interface for an application, you need to change only the property values for which you do not want to use the default values.

The commonly used properties of objects will be discussed as they are used in this book. When adding a new control to a form, you should navigate the Properties list to understand better the unique properties and property values for that control.

Changing StartPosition, Title, and FormBorderStyle Property Values

To develop the user interface of the State Tax Computation form, as shown in Figure 3-1 on page VB 3.02, you must modify several of the default form property values. The first form property to change is the StartPosition property. The **StartPosition property** of a form specifies the position where the application window displays on the Windows desktop when the application is run. The default value for the StartPosition property is **WindowsDefault**, which tells the .NET CLR to position the application window wherever Windows sees fit to display it on the screen. Changing the StartPosition property value from WindowsDefault to the value of **CenterScreen** sets the application window to display in the center of the user's screen.

Next, the title on the application window should convey the purpose or use of the application. The **Text property** of the form allows you to set the title that displays on the application window title bar at run time. The default value for the Text property is a generic name (Form1) that Visual Basic .NET assigns when creating the form. As specified by the project design, the Text property value must be changed to display State Tax Calculation on the application window title bar.

The third form property value to change is the FormBorderStyle property. The **FormBorderStyle property** controls the appearance of the border of a form. The FormBorderStyle property determines if a user can resize an application window at run time and how other objects on the form, such as the Minimize button, Maximize button, Control menu box, title bar, and Help button, behave or display. The FormBorderStyle property can take one of seven property values, as listed in Table 3-2.

Table 3-2 FormBorderStyle Property Values

CONTROL OR CHARACTERISTIC	FORMBORDERSTYLE PROPERTY VALUE						
	None	*FixedSingle*	*Fixed3D*	*FixedDialog*	*Sizable*	*FixedToolWindow*	*SizableToolWindow*
Minimize button	No	Available	Available	Available	Available	No	No
Maximize button	No	Available	Available	Available	Available	No	No
Control menu box	No	Yes	Yes	Yes	Yes	No	No
Title bar	No	Yes	Yes	Yes	Yes	Yes	Yes
Help button	No	Available	Available	Available	Available	No	No
Sizable	No	No	No	No	Yes	No	Yes

The default value for the FormBorderStyle property is Sizable. Using the **Sizable property value** displays the application window with borders the user can drag to resize the application window at run time. The State Tax Computation application window, like many Windows Application windows, should not be sizable. Allowing the user to resize the State Tax Computation application window would distort the display of the input and output areas and buttons, making the user interface difficult to use. To prevent a user from resizing the application window, set the FormBorderStyle property value to FixedDialog. Using the **FixedDialog property value** displays the application window in one size, with the appearance of a standard Windows dialog box.

The following steps change the StartPosition, Text, and FormBorderStyle property values of the State Tax Computation application window from the default values to the values discussed above.

To Change the StartPosition, Title, and FormBorderStyle Property Values of a Form

1. **Click the title bar of the Form1 form to select the form. Scroll the Properties list until the FormBorderStyle property displays.**

   The Form1 form is selected and the form name displays in the Object box in the Properties window (Figure 3-16).

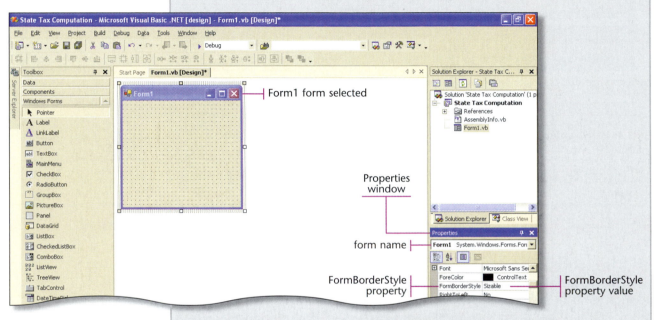

FIGURE 3-16

2. **Click the Sizable value next to the FormBorderStyle property. Click the FormBorderStyle box arrow next to the value, Sizable.**

   Clicking the FormBorderStyle box arrow displays a list of seven possible values for the FormBorderStyle property (Figure 3-17).

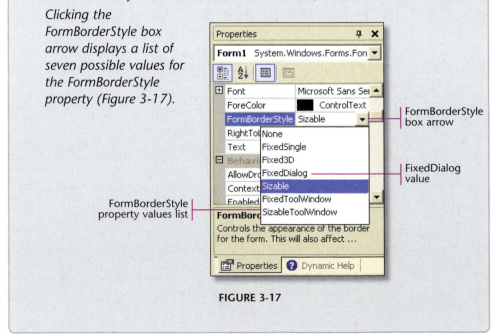

FIGURE 3-17

3. Click FixedDialog in the FormBorderStyle property values list.

The FormBorderStyle property value is set to FixedDialog. The Form1 form border changes to a slightly thinner border. The Form1 icon changes to indicate that the FormBorderStyle property value is FixedDialog (Figure 3-18).

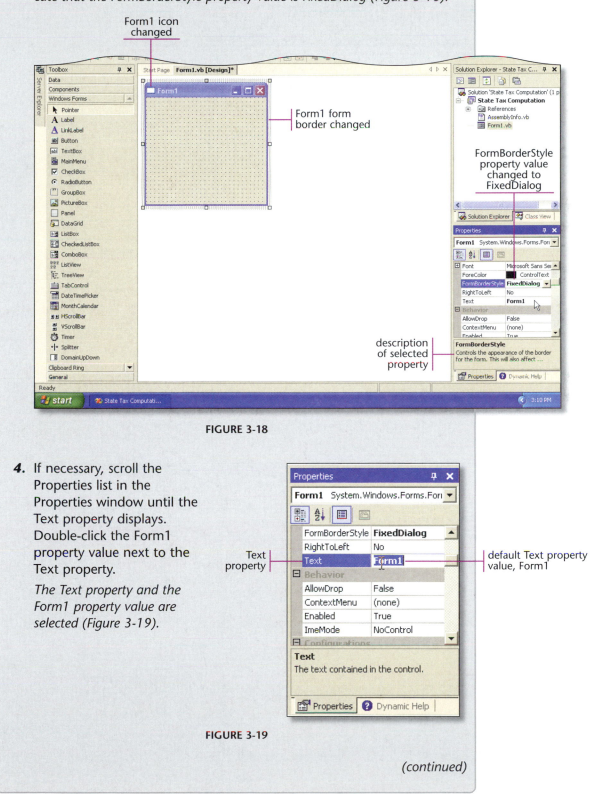

FIGURE 3-18

4. If necessary, scroll the Properties list in the Properties window until the Text property displays. Double-click the Form1 property value next to the Text property.

The Text property and the Form1 property value are selected (Figure 3-19).

FIGURE 3-19

(continued)

5. Type State Tax Computation as the Text property.

The Text property value is set to State Tax Computation although only a portion displays (Figure 3-20). The form title bar still displays the default property value, Form1.

form title bar displays default property value, Form1

Text property

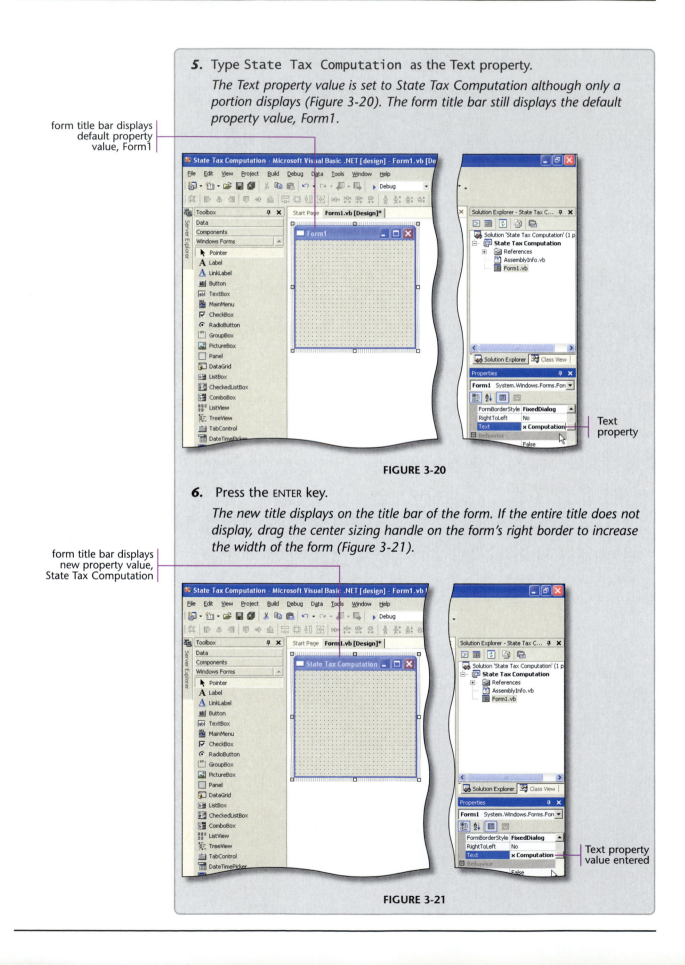

FIGURE 3-20

6. Press the ENTER key.

The new title displays on the title bar of the form. If the entire title does not display, drag the center sizing handle on the form's right border to increase the width of the form (Figure 3-21).

form title bar displays new property value, State Tax Computation

Text property value entered

FIGURE 3-21

7. Scroll the Properties list in the Properties window until the StartPosition property displays. Click the WindowsDefaultLocation value next to the StartPosition property. Click the StartPosition box arrow next to the value, WindowsDefaultLocation.

Clicking the StartPosition box arrow displays a list of five possible values for the StartPosition property (Figure 3-22).

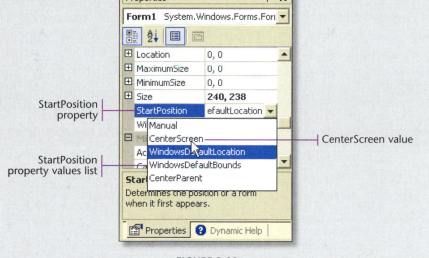

StartPosition property

StartPosition property values list

CenterScreen value

FIGURE 3-22

8. Click CenterScreen in the StartPosition property values list.

The StartPosition property value is set to CenterScreen (Figure 3-23). The CenterScreen property value indicates that the application window will display in the center of the screen during run time. During design time, no changes are visible on the form.

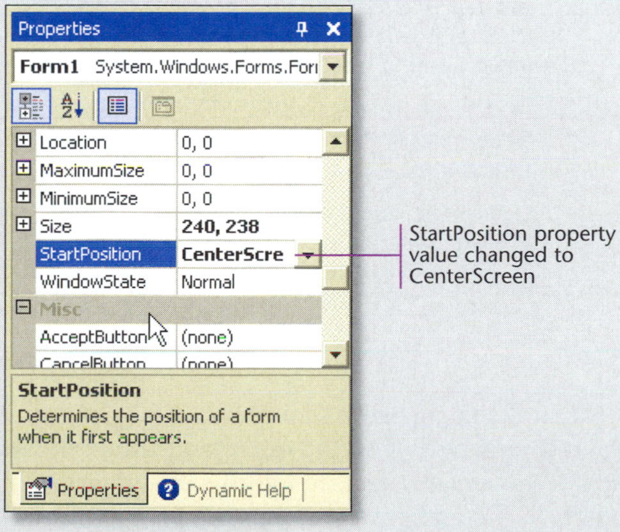

StartPosition property value changed to CenterScreen

FIGURE 3-23

During design time, the form remains sizable and displays in the upper-left corner of the main work area, regardless of the property values set for the FormBorderStyle and StartPosition properties. At run time, however, the property values will ensure that the form displays in the center of the screen and cannot be resized by the user.

Changing Additional Form Property Values

A form for a Windows Application project has numerous other properties and property values that allow you to customize the form to fit program requirements. Table 3-3 shows several commonly used form properties by category, with a brief description and a list of available property values. A bold property value indicates that this value is the default value for the property.

Table 3-3   Form Properties

CATEGORY	PROPERTY	DESCRIPTION	PROPERTY VALUES
Appearance	BackColor	Sets background color of application window	Any color selected from dialog box
	ForeColor	Sets default color for controls that are added to the form	Any color selected from dialog box
	FormBorderStyle	Dictates appearance of form border; whether the form is sizable; and how the Minimize and Maximize buttons, Control menu box, and Help button behave	None FixedSingle Fixed3D FixedDialog **Sizable** FixedToolWindow SizableToolWindow
	Text	Sets title to display on title bar of application window	Any value
Behavior	Enabled	Sets form to be usable during run time	**True** False
Layout	WindowState	Dictates how a window should display initially during run time	**Normal** Minimized Maximized
Window Style	ControlBox	Determines if a Windows control box should display on the form	**True** False
	Icon	Defines the icon that displays on the top-left corner of the window title bar and on the taskbar at run time	Any icon selected from a file via a dialog box

When designing a form, it is important to understand all of the form properties that are available so you can select the best options. The Visual Basic .NET Help system contains detailed information about all the form properties and property values and provides example uses for properties.

Working with Controls for a Windows Application

As you have learned, a form is an object in Visual Basic .NET. The State Tax Computation form includes four different types of controls, as shown in Figure 3-24. These controls and their functions include the following.

LABEL   A **Label control** is used to display text, such as Taxpayer's income, on a form. During run time, the person using the application cannot change the text displayed in a label.

TEXTBOX   A **TextBox control** is used to display text or allow users to enter text on a form. During run time, the contents of a TextBox control can be changed by the person using the application. A TextBox control frequently is used to allow a user to input values for processing by the application.

NUMERICUPDOWN   A **NumericUpDown control** is used to display or allow users to enter numbers on a form. During run time, the contents of a NumericUpDown control can be changed by the person using the application. Up and down arrows in the control allow the user to change the value displayed in the control; the user also can type a value in the control. The up and down arrows increment and decrement the displayed value within a predefined range. If the user enters a number outside of the range, the control changes the entered number to the closest allowable value within the predefined range.

BUTTON   A **Button control** is used during run time to initiate actions called events. A Button control usually is placed on the user interface to allow a user to indicate that the application should execute an action such as calculating a value, resetting values, or closing a window.

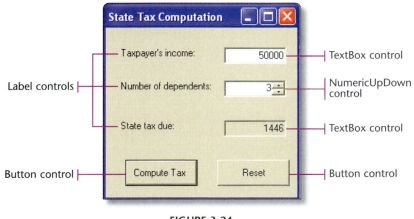

FIGURE 3-24

Adding Controls to a Form

You can add controls to a form using the Toolbox window, which displays on the left side of the Visual Basic .NET IDE (Figure 3-25 on the next page). The Toolbox window usually displays six tabs such as Windows Forms, Data, Components, and so on. The **Windows Forms tab**, which is selected by default, includes buttons that represent common controls used on a Windows form. By default, the Windows Forms sheet in the Toolbox window contains forty intrinsic controls. An **intrinsic control** is a control that is included on the Windows Forms sheet by default and cannot be removed. You can add additional controls to the Windows Forms sheet, by selecting from the thousands of additional controls available from Microsoft and third-party vendors. The remaining five tabs in the Toolbox window and specific controls and their functions are discussed as they are used in this book.

Adding Label Controls to a Form

The next step in developing the State Tax Computation application is to add the labels such as Taxpayer's income that are used to identify the input and output areas of the State Tax Computation window. You can add a control to a form using one of three methods: drawing, dragging, or double-clicking. The following steps show how to use the Toolbox window to add Label controls to the form by drawing.

To Add Label Controls to a Form by Drawing

1. If necessary, click the Windows Forms tab in the Toolbox window. Point to the Label button in the Toolbox window.

The Windows Forms sheet displays in the Toolbox window (Figure 3-25). The Label button adds a Label control to the form.

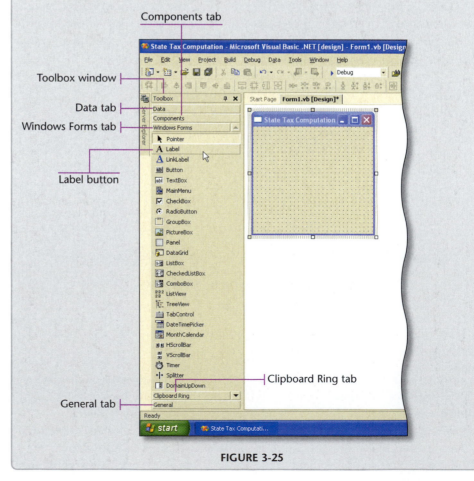

FIGURE 3-25

2. Click the Label button. Point to the upper-left corner of the form.

The Label button on the Windows Forms sheet is selected. When the mouse pointer is positioned over the form, the mouse pointer changes to cross hairs with a Label control indicator (Figure 3-26).

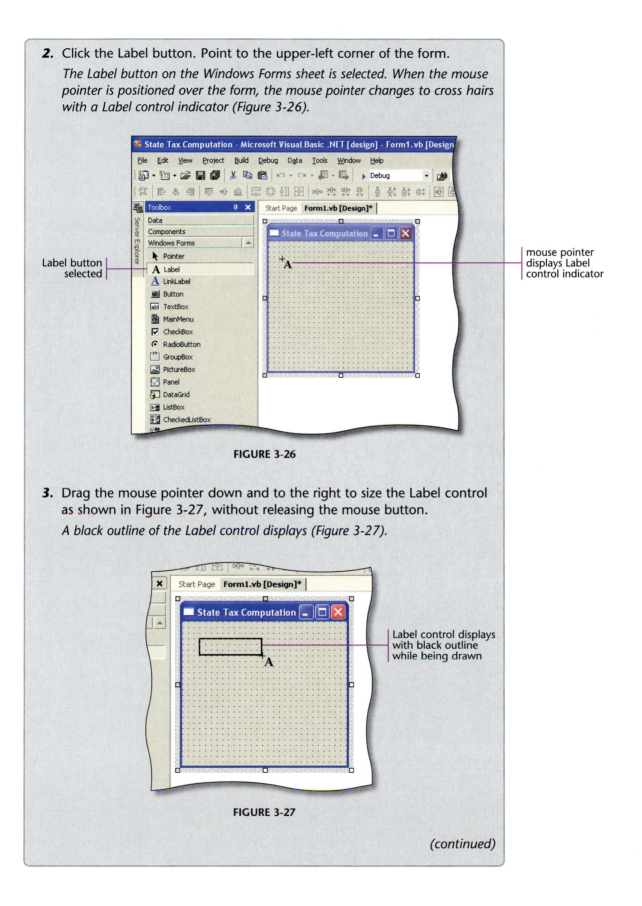

Label button selected

mouse pointer displays Label control indicator

FIGURE 3-26

3. Drag the mouse pointer down and to the right to size the Label control as shown in Figure 3-27, without releasing the mouse button.

A black outline of the Label control displays (Figure 3-27).

Label control displays with black outline while being drawn

FIGURE 3-27

(continued)

4. When the Label control outline is the desired size, release the mouse button.

The black outline of the Label control changes to a dotted gray border with sizing handles. The default Text property value of the Label control (Label1) displays in the control. The properties for the Label control display in the Properties window. The Pointer button is selected on the Windows Forms sheet, indicating that no controls are selected (Figure 3-28).

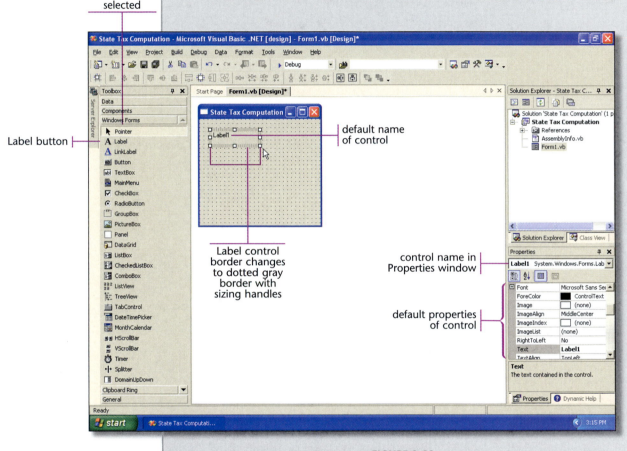

FIGURE 3-28

5. Click any blank area on the Form1 form.

The Label control no longer is selected and the Form1 form is selected (Figure 3-29).

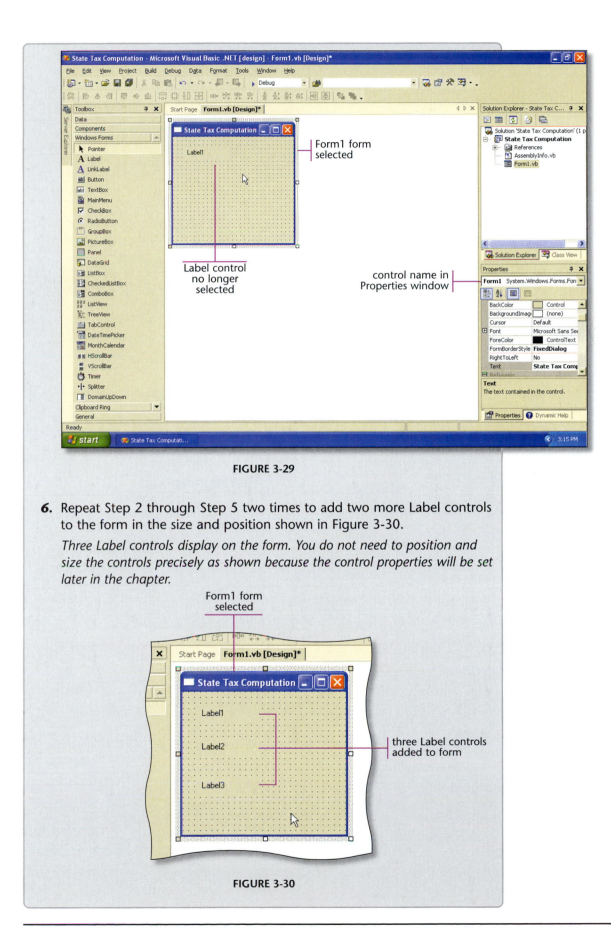

FIGURE 3-29

6. Repeat Step 2 through Step 5 two times to add two more Label controls to the form in the size and position shown in Figure 3-30.

Three Label controls display on the form. You do not need to position and size the controls precisely as shown because the control properties will be set later in the chapter.

FIGURE 3-30

Three Label controls that will provide text descriptions of the input and output areas of the application window are added to the form. When you are adding controls to a form, the dots on the background of the form, called the **positioning grid**, serve as anchors for aligning the controls. As you position or size a control on a form, the top, bottom, left, and right borders of the controls always align themselves, or **snap**, to the dots that display on a form. This functionality helps you align controls with greater precision.

Adding TextBox Controls to a Form

As you have learned, you can add a control to a form using one of three methods: drawing, dragging, or double-clicking. The following steps use the dragging method to add two TextBox controls to the Form1 form.

To Add TextBox Controls to a Form by Dragging

1. Point to the TextBox button in the Toolbox window (Figure 3-31).

The TextBox button adds a TextBox control to the form.

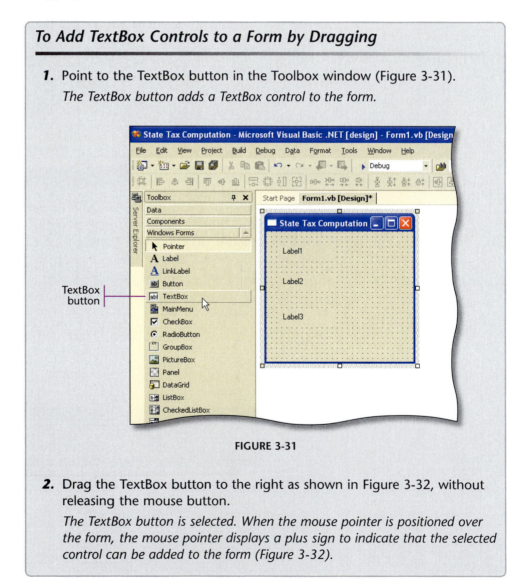

FIGURE 3-31

2. Drag the TextBox button to the right as shown in Figure 3-32, without releasing the mouse button.

The TextBox button is selected. When the mouse pointer is positioned over the form, the mouse pointer displays a plus sign to indicate that the selected control can be added to the form (Figure 3-32).

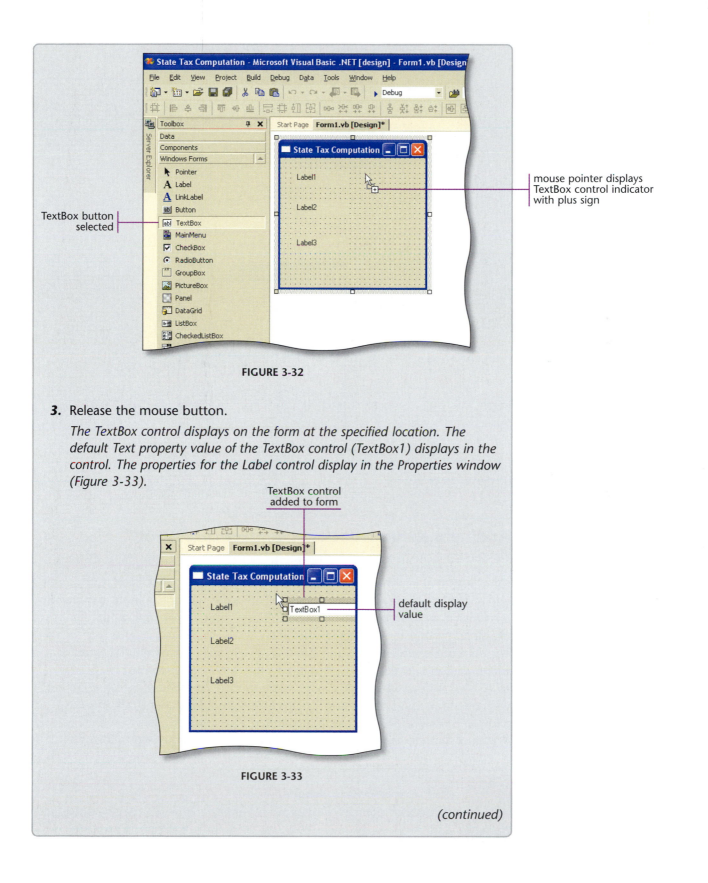

FIGURE 3-32

3. Release the mouse button.

The TextBox control displays on the form at the specified location. The default Text property value of the TextBox control (TextBox1) displays in the control. The properties for the Label control display in the Properties window (Figure 3-33).

FIGURE 3-33

(continued)

4. Repeat Step1 through Step 3 to add a second TextBox control to the form in the size and position shown in Figure 3-34. Click any blank area on the Form1 form.

Two TextBox controls display on the form (Figure 3-34). You do not need to position and size the controls precisely as shown because the control properties will be set later in the chapter. The TextBox control no longer is selected and the Form1 form is selected.

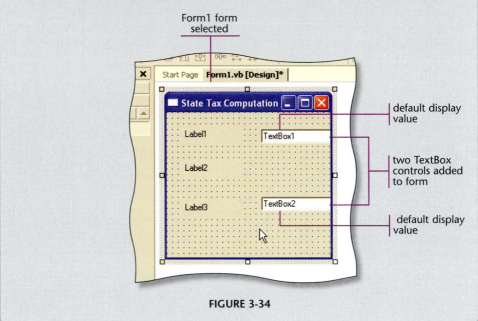

FIGURE 3-34

Adding a NumericUpDown Control to a Form

Two TextBox controls are added to the form, one for the Taxpayer's income input area and one to display State tax due in the output area. Next, you should add a NumericUpDown control. During run time, a user can input a value into a NumericUpDown control. In the State Tax Computation application, for example, the NumericUpDown control allows users to enter a value for Number of dependents. Up and down arrows in the control allow the user to increment and decrement the displayed value within a predefined range of 0 to 10. The user also can type a value in the control. If the user enters a number outside of the range, the control changes the entered number to the closest allowable value within the predefined range. The following steps use the dragging method to add a NumericUpDown control to the Form1 form.

NumericUpDown Ranges

If the user enters a number in a NumericUpDown control outside the range of the minimum and maximum allowed, the control automatically changes the entered number to the closest allowable value.

To Add a NumericUpDown Control to a Form by Dragging

1. Click the down scroll arrow in the Toolbox window until the NumericUpDown button displays on the Windows Forms sheet (Figure 3-35).

   The NumericUpDown button adds a NumericUpDown control to a form.

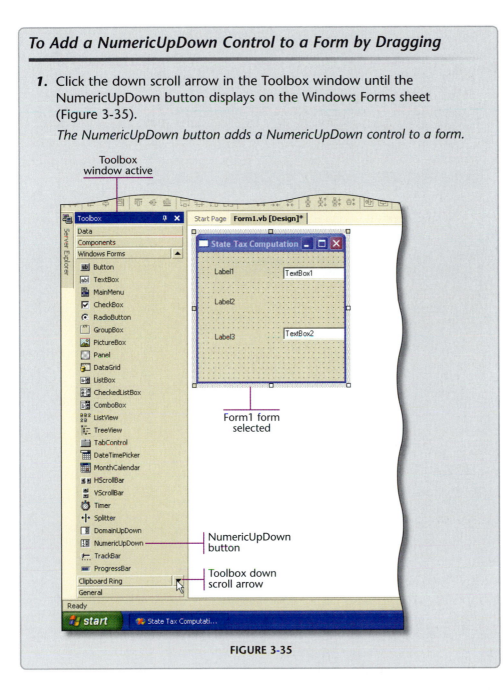

FIGURE 3-35

2. Drag the NumericUpDown button to the right of the Form1 form, as shown in Figure 3-36.

The NumericUpDown control displays at the specified location (Figure 3-36). You do not need to position and size the control precisely as shown, because the control properties will be set later in the chapter.

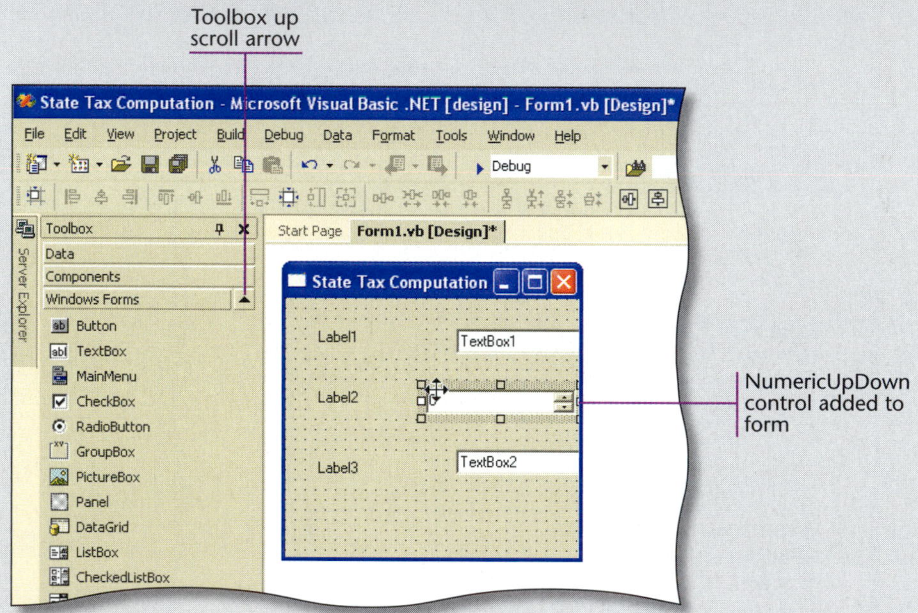

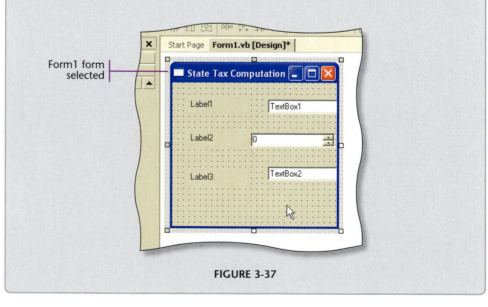

FIGURE 3-36

3. Click any blank area on the Form1 form.

The NumericUpDown control no longer is selected and the Form1 form is selected (Figure 3-37). The NumericUpDown control displays a default value of 0.

FIGURE 3-37

Adding Button Controls to a Form

The final two controls to add to the form are the two buttons used for the Compute Tax and Reset buttons on the application window. As you have learned, you can add a control to a form by double-clicking the control button on the Windows Forms sheet in the Toolbox window. The following steps use the double-clicking method to add two Button controls to the Form1 form.

To Add Button Controls to a Form by Double-Clicking

1. If necessary, click the up scroll arrow in the Toolbox window to display the Button button on the Windows Forms sheet. Point to the Button button.

The Button button adds a Button control to a form.

2. Double-click the Button button.

Visual Basic .NET adds a Button control to the top-left corner of the form (Figure 3-38).

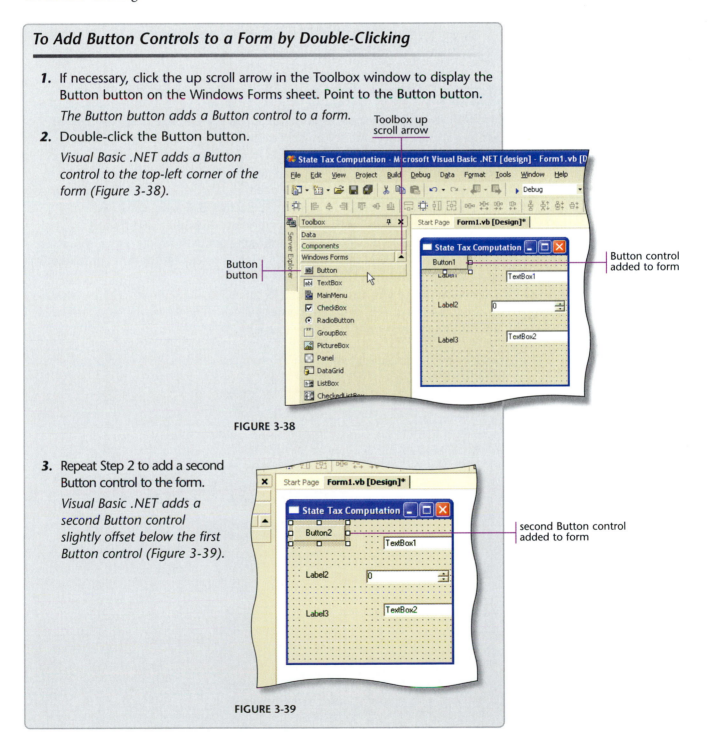

FIGURE 3-38

3. Repeat Step 2 to add a second Button control to the form.

Visual Basic .NET adds a second Button control slightly offset below the first Button control (Figure 3-39).

FIGURE 3-39

Whether you use the drawing, dragging, or double-clicking method to add a control to a form depends on your preference and the type of control you are adding to the form. As shown in the preceding steps, double-clicking a control button on the Windows Forms sheet adds a default-sized control to the upper-left corner of the form. If another control already is located at the upper-left corner of the form, double-clicking a control button adds the new control above and slightly offset from the previous control. If you add a control by double-clicking a control button on the Windows Forms sheet, you will need to move the control from the upper-left corner of the form, and frequently, you will want to change the control's size from the default.

Moving Controls on a Form

With all of the controls added to the form, you can move the controls to position them as they should display on the user interface in the application window. When working with forms, you may find it is faster to add all of the required controls to the form and then position them correctly on the form. If you position individual controls before adding all of the controls, you may have to reposition those controls to accommodate any additional controls.

The user interface design created earlier in the chapter (Figure 3-4 on page VB 3.06) serves as a guide for positioning controls on the form. To develop the user interface specified in the design of the project, the Button controls must be moved from the upper-left corner of the form.

You can move a control on a form by dragging the control to a new location or by setting properties in the Properties window. The following steps move the two Button controls on the form by dragging.

To Move Controls on a Form

1. Point to the center of the Button2 control, being sure not to point to a sizing handle.

The mouse pointer changes to a double two-headed arrow (Figure 3-40).

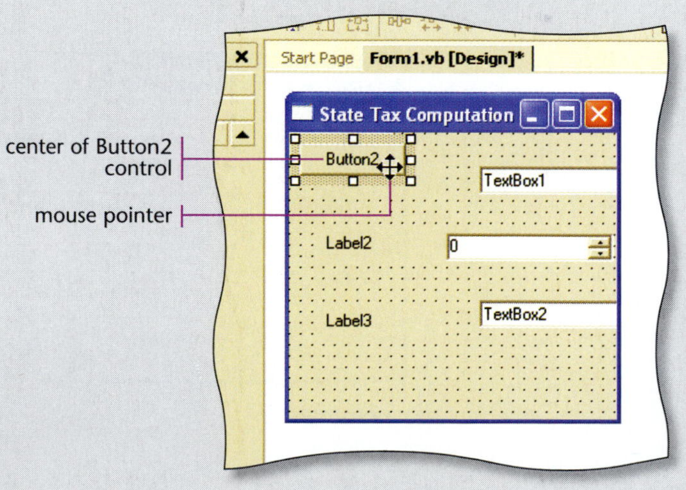

FIGURE 3-40

2. Drag the Button2 control to the bottom right of the form, as shown in Figure 3-41.

The Button2 control displays in the specified location. The outline of the Button2 control changes to a solid gray border with sizing handles (Figure 3-41).

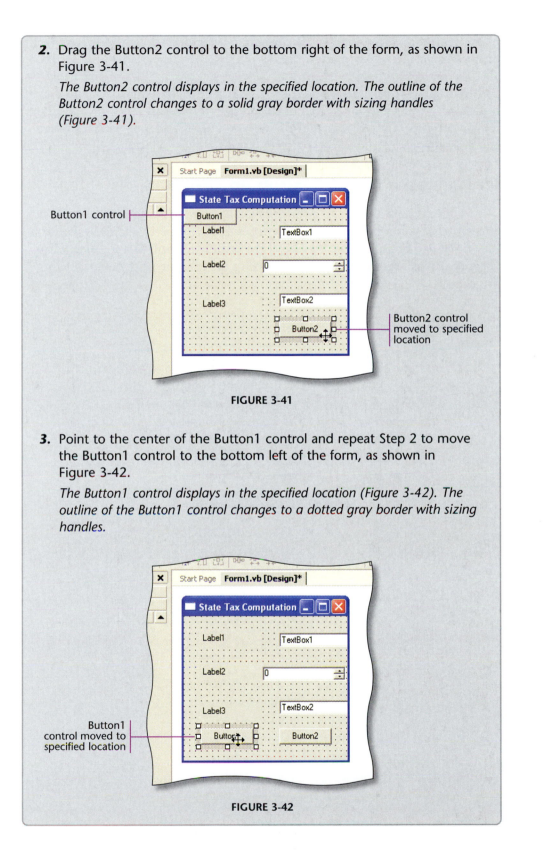

FIGURE 3-41

3. Point to the center of the Button1 control and repeat Step 2 to move the Button1 control to the bottom left of the form, as shown in Figure 3-42.

The Button1 control displays in the specified location (Figure 3-42). The outline of the Button1 control changes to a dotted gray border with sizing handles.

FIGURE 3-42

The location of a control on the form in design time determines where the control displays in the application window at the beginning of run time. The **Top property** and **Left property** are two properties that determine the location of the control at design time and the beginning of run time. Dragging a control on a form changes the property values of the control's Top and Left properties. The Top and Left property values determine, or set, the number of pixels that the control displays from the top and left sides of the form at design time and the beginning of run time. A control does not have to remain in its original location during run time. Changing a control's location during run time will be covered in a later chapter.

Changing the Size of Controls on a Form

You can change the size of a control by dragging the sizing handles on the border of the control or by setting properties in the Properties window. Perform the following steps to change the size of the Button controls to a size that will allow the button text to display as specified in the user interface design for the project.

To Change the Size of Controls on a Form

1. If necessary, click the Button1 control. Point to the bottom-right corner sizing handle on the border of the Button1 control.

Sizing handles display on the border around the Button1 button control. The mouse pointer changes to a diagonal two-headed arrow (Figure 3-43).

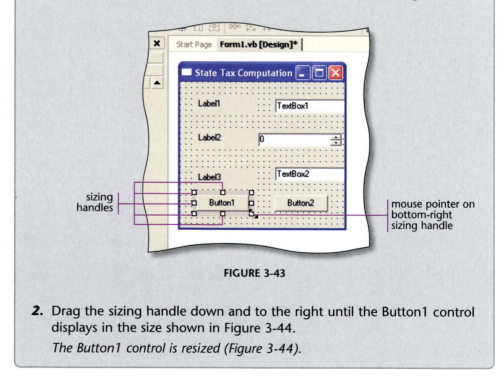

FIGURE 3-43

2. Drag the sizing handle down and to the right until the Button1 control displays in the size shown in Figure 3-44.

The Button1 control is resized (Figure 3-44).

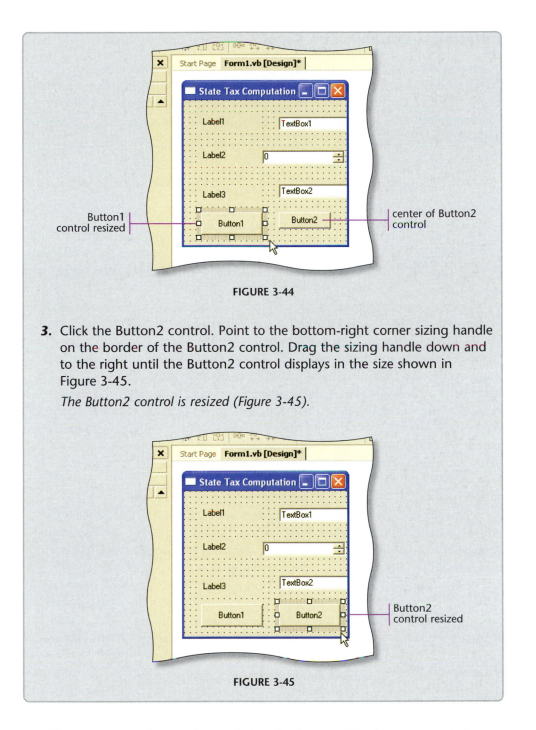

FIGURE 3-44

3. Click the Button2 control. Point to the bottom-right corner sizing handle on the border of the Button2 control. Drag the sizing handle down and to the right until the Button2 control displays in the size shown in Figure 3-45.

The Button2 control is resized (Figure 3-45).

FIGURE 3-45

The steps to set the location and size of a form and the locations and sizes of Button controls on a form are similar. This similarity is due to the fact that a Visual Basic .NET form is a type of control, just as Button, TextBox, and Label, are controls.

Deleting a Control on a Form

If you click the wrong control button on the Windows Forms sheet in the Toolbox or want to modify the controls used on a form, you can delete a control from a form at any point during design time. To delete a control, click the control to select it and then press the DELETE key. You also can right-click the control and then click Delete on the shortcut menu.

TextBox, Label, NumericUpDown, and Button Control Properties

TextBox, Label, NumericUpDown, and Button controls often are used in a Windows application. These controls are easy for users to understand, and they provide most of the input and output areas needed for an application's user interface.

To finish developing the user interface of the State Tax Computation application, you must change the default property values of the TextBox, Label, Button, and NumericUpDown controls. The property values for each control will be changed to position and size the controls correctly on the form and to define how users interact with the controls during run time. During run time, for instance, if a user wants to change a value in a specific input area, the user typically clicks the control used for that input area to select it. When a user selects a control, the control is said to have **focus** and Visual Basic .NET places the insertion point in the control or displays a dotted rectangle around the control on the form. A user also can use the TAB key on the keyboard to select, or set, the focus on a specific control. Using the TAB key to set the focus on a control is called **tabbing**.

The **TabIndex property** determines the order in which Visual Basic .NET sets the focus on controls when a user presses the TAB key. When the application window first displays at run time, Visual Basic .NET will set the initial focus on the control with the lowest value for the TabIndex property.

In the State Tax Computation application window, the TextBox control used as the input area for Taxpayer's income should have initial focus. Subsequent tabbing should set the focus on the Number of dependents NumericUpDown control, the Compute Tax Button control, and, finally, the Reset Button control. Once the last control in the TabIndex sequence is reached, pressing the TAB key will restart the sequence and set the focus on the Taxpayer's income TextBox control. If you want Visual Basic .NET to skip a control during tabbing, you can change the value of its **TabStop property** from True to False.

Common Properties of Controls

Many of the controls used in developing a Windows application share common properties. The Form, TextBox, and Label controls, for example, all have Text, Size, and Location properties. TextBox, Label, and NumericUpDown controls use the TabStop and TabIndex properties. Table 3-4 lists some of the more common properties for controls. Entries listed in bold in the table are the default property values. Appendix C contains a complete summary of the properties, events, and methods for controls introduced in this book.

Table 3-4 Common Properties of Controls

CATEGORY	PROPERTY	DESCRIPTION	PROPERTY VALUES
Appearance	BackColor	Sets the background color of the control	Select a color from a pop-up dialog box.
	Cursor	Defines which mouse pointer (cursor) displays when user moves the mouse over the control	Select a mouse pointer from a list of more than 20 mouse pointers.
	Font	Defines the text font to use if text displays in the control	Select a font style from a pop-up dialog box.
	ForeColor	Changes the foreground color, usually of the text that displays on the control	Select a color from a pop-up dialog box.
Behavior	Enabled	If True, control is usable at run time; if False, a user cannot change control value and control may display grayed out	**True** False
	TabStop	Determines whether the TAB key sets focus on the control during run time	**True** False
	TabIndex	Determines the order in which the TAB key navigates to the control	Any positive whole number
	Visible	If True, control displays at run time; if False, control does not display	**True** False
Data	Tag	Defines data to be stored with the control (data does not display to user)	Any text
Design	Locked	Ensures that a control cannot be moved during design time; prevents inadvertently moving the control once it is positioned	True **False**
	Name	Provides a descriptive, unique identifier for the control	Any text
	Size	Indicates height and width of the control in pixels	Two positive whole numbers, separated by a comma
	Location	Indicates distance from the top and left border of the form in pixels	Two positive whole numbers, separated by a comma

Although the properties in Table 3-4 are common among many different controls, the properties can cause different effects. Properties such as Size and Location, for example, have the same effect for each control. Other properties, such as Enabled and Font, cause different effects for different controls.

TextBox Control Properties

A TextBox control has many properties used to define how the control displays on the form and how the user interacts with the control during run time. The Height property, Width property, and **Location property** define the position and size of the TextBox control in the application window. The **ReadOnly property** determines whether or not the user can input data into the TextBox control at run time. The ReadOnly property value can be either True or False. The default value is False, meaning that users can input data into the TextBox control. Table 3-5 lists several of the properties associated with the TextBox control, with a brief description and a list of available property values. Entries listed in bold in the table are the default property values.

Table 3-5   *TextBox Control Properties*

CATEGORY	PROPERTY	DESCRIPTION	PROPERTY VALUES
Appearance	BorderStyle	Determines how the border of the TextBox control displays	None FixedSingle **Fixed3D**
	Text	Sets the text that displays inside the control	Any text with a character length up to the value specified in the MaxLength property
	TextAlign	Determines if text in the control displays left-aligned, right-aligned, or centered	**Left** Right Center
Behavior	AutoSize	Indicates whether the height of the control automatically changes when the font size in the control is changed	**True** False
	MaxLength	Sets the maximum number of characters a user can input into the text control	Any positive whole number from 0 through **32767**
	Multiline	Determines if text in the control displays on more than one line	True **False**
	ReadOnly	If True, a user cannot type or edit text in control during run time; if False, user can type and edit text in control	True **False**
	WordWrap	If MultiLine is True, text in control wraps to the next line when the text is longer than the width of the control	**True** False

Several of the properties of the two TextBox controls added to the form must be changed from the default values, according to the design of the application. Table 3-6 lists the properties and values for the two TextBox controls that require changes.

Table 3-6 *TextBox Control Property Values for the State Tax Computation Application*

CONTROL	PROPERTY	PROPERTY VALUE	EFFECT
TextBox1	Text	0	Sets 0 to display as the initial value in the control at run time
	Location: X	144	Indicates distance from left border of the form in pixels
	Location: Y	24	Indicates distance from top border of the form in pixels
	Size: Width	76	Sets the width of the control in pixels
	Size: Height	20	Sets the height of the control in pixels
	TextAlign	Right	Sets text to display right-aligned on the control
TextBox2	Text	0	Sets 0 to display as initial value in the control at run time
	TabStop	False	Indicates that TAB key should not set focus on the control when user navigates the window by tabbing during run time
	Location: X	144	Indicates distance from left border of the form in pixels
	Location: Y	112	Indicates distance from top border of the form in pixels
	Size: Width	76	Sets the width of the control
	Size: Height	20	Sets the height of the control
	ReadOnly	True	Prohibits user from entering data in control; sets background color to display as gray
	TextAlign	Right	Sets text to display right-aligned in the control

As defined in the user interface design for the State Tax Computation application, the first TextBox control, TextBox1, should allow a user to input a value for Taxpayer's income. The second TextBox control, TextBox2, should display the output value for State tax due. As shown in Figure 3-45 on page VB 3.37, the two TextBox controls currently display the default Text property values of TextBox1 and TextBox2. As listed in Table 3-6, the Text property values are changed to display zero (0) as the initial value at run time. Because it displays an output value, the TabStop property is set to False to indicate that TAB key should not set focus on the control when a user navigates the window by tabbing during run time.

The steps on the next page set the property values for the two TextBox controls, as listed in Table 3-6.

To Change Properties of TextBox Controls

1. Click the TextBox1 control. If necessary, scroll the Properties list until the Text property displays. Double-click the Text property value.

Sizing handles display around the TextBox1 control. The control name (TextBox1) displays in the Object box of the Properties window. The Text property displays in the Appearance property category in the Properties list, and the current Text property value, TextBox1, is selected (Figure 3-46).

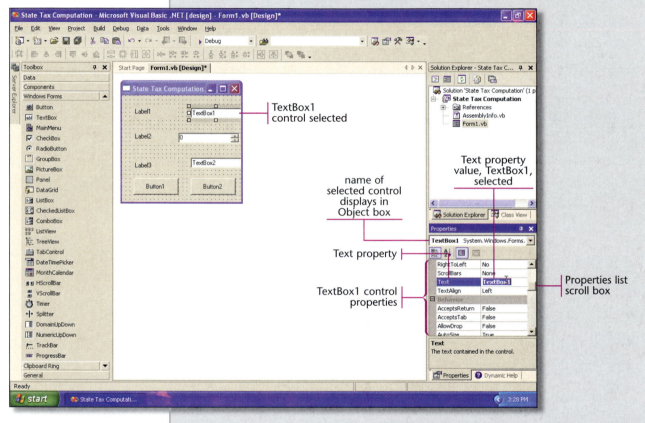

FIGURE 3-46

2. Type 0 as the new value, as indicated in Table 3-6, and then press the ENTER key.

The new Text property value, 0, displays in the Properties window and in the TextBox control on the form (Figure 3-47). You can use the BACKSPACE key or the LEFT ARROW and DELETE keys to correct mistakes made while typing.

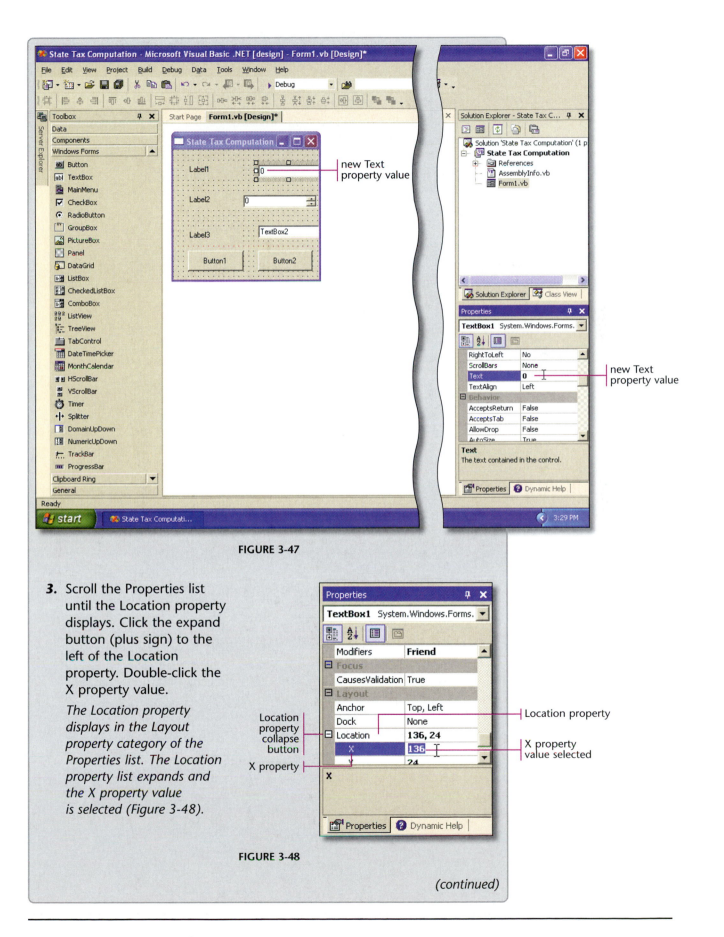

FIGURE 3-47

3. Scroll the Properties list until the Location property displays. Click the expand button (plus sign) to the left of the Location property. Double-click the X property value.

The Location property displays in the Layout property category of the Properties list. The Location property list expands and the X property value is selected (Figure 3-48).

FIGURE 3-48

(continued)

4. Type 144 as the X property value, as indicated in Table 3-6, and then press the ENTER key.

The TextBox control displays in the location indicated by the new X property value (Figure 3-49). The value updates in both the Location property and the X property, so that the X property value displays when the Location property is collapsed.

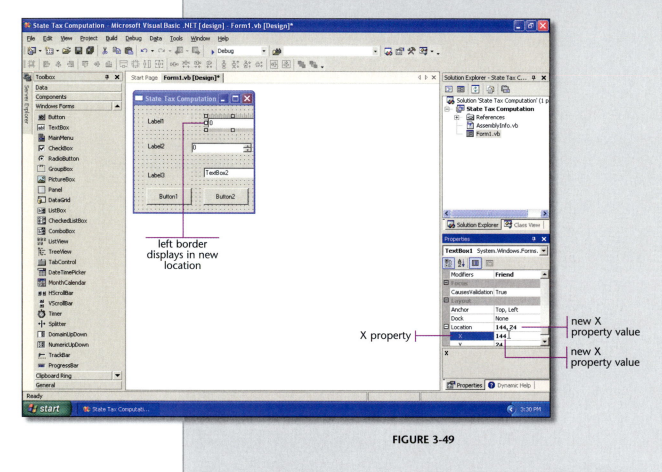

FIGURE 3-49

5. Repeat Steps 3 and 4 to change the Location: Y, Size: Width, and Size: Height, and TextAlign property values for the TextBox1 control, as shown in Table 3-6.

The TextBox1 control displays in the correct location with the size, value, and alignment as defined in the user interface design (Figure 3-50).

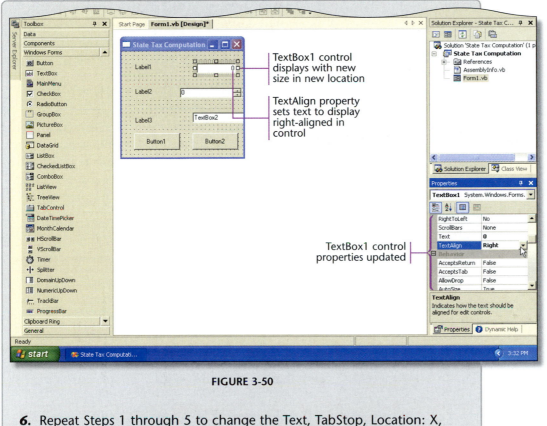

FIGURE 3-50

6. Repeat Steps 1 through 5 to change the Text, TabStop, Location: X, Location: Y, Size: Width, Size: Height, ReadOnly, and TextAlign property values for the TextBox2 control.

7. Select the Form1 form by clicking an empty area of the form that does not contain any other controls.

The Form1 form is selected (Figure 3-51). The TextBox2 control displays in the correct location with the size, value, and alignment as defined in the user interface design.

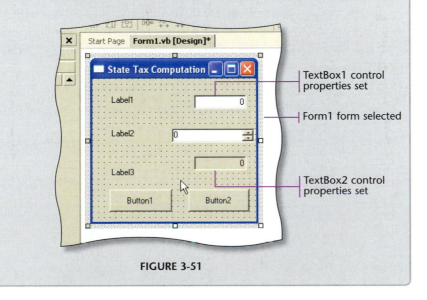

FIGURE 3-51

As shown in the preceding steps, the Properties window allows you to change the appearance of the TextBox controls by changing property values. By following the same basic steps, you can use the Properties window to change property values for most controls during design time.

Label Control Properties

As you have learned, a Label control such as Label1 is used to display text on a form. During run time, the person using the application cannot change the text in a label. The important properties for a Label control include the Location, Size, Font, and Text properties. Table 3-7 lists several of the properties associated with the Label control, with a brief description and a list of available property values.

Table 3-7   Label Control Properties

CATEGORY	PROPERTY	DESCRIPTION	PROPERTY VALUES
Appearance	FlatStyle	Determines the 3D appearance of the control	Flat Popup **Standard** System
	Image	Sets an image to display on the visible portion of the Label control, along with the Text	Select a picture from the hard drive using a dialog box.
	ImageAlign	If the Image property is set, determines where the image displays	Select a location from a pop-up graphical display map.
	Text	Defines the visible text that displays on the control	Any text with any character length

Several of the properties of the three Label controls added to the form must be changed from the default values, according to the design of the application. Table 3-8 shows the properties and values for the three Label controls that require changes.

Table 3-8   Label Control Property Values for the State Tax Computation Application

CONTROL	PROPERTY	VALUE	EFFECT
Label1	Text	Taxpayer's income:	Sets Taxpayer's income: to display as the initial value in the control at run time
	Location: X	16	Indicates distance from left border of the form in pixels
	Location: Y	24	Indicates distance from top border of the form in pixels

Table 3-8 *Label Control Property Values for the State Tax Computation Application (continued)*

CONTROL	PROPERTY	VALUE	EFFECT
	Size: Width	104	Sets the width of the control in pixels
	Size: Height	16	Sets the height of the control in pixels
Label2	Text	Number of dependents:	Sets Number of dependents: to display as the initial value in the control at run time
	Location: X	16	Indicates distance from left border of the form in pixels
	Location: Y	64	Indicates distance from top border of the form in pixels
	Size: Width	128	Sets the width of the control in pixels
	Size: Height	16	Sets the height of the control in pixels
Label3	Text	State tax due:	Sets State tax due: to display as the initial value in the control at run time
	Location: X	16	Indicates distance from left border of the form in pixels
	Location: Y	112	Indicates distance from top border of the form in pixels
	Size: Width	88	Sets the width of the control in pixels
	Size: Height	16	Sets the height of the control in pixels

The user interface design for the State Tax Computation application specifies that the Label controls should display to the left of the NumericUpDown and TextBox controls to provide descriptions of the controls. As shown in Figure 3-51 on page VB 3.45, the three Label controls currently display the default Text property values of Label1, Label2, and Label3. Table 3-8 lists the new Text property values that must be entered so the controls display descriptions of the NumericUpDown and TextBox controls. The property values also must be changed to set the location and size of each Label control.

The steps on the next page set the property values for the three Label controls, as listed in Table 3-8.

To Change Properties of Label Controls

1. Click the Label1 control. Scroll the Properties list until the Text property displays and then double-click the Text property.

   Sizing handles display around the Label1 control. The control name (Label1) displays in the Object box of the Properties window. The Text property is highlighted in the Properties list. The current Text property value, Label1, is selected.

2. Type Taxpayer's income: as the new Text property, as indicated in Table 3-8 on the previous page and then press the ENTER key.

   The new Text property value, Taxpayer's income:, displays in the Properties window and in the Label control on the form (Figure 3-52). You can use the BACKSPACE key or the LEFT ARROW and DELETE keys to correct mistakes made while typing.

new Text property value

name of selected control, Label1, displays in Object box

Text property

new Text property value

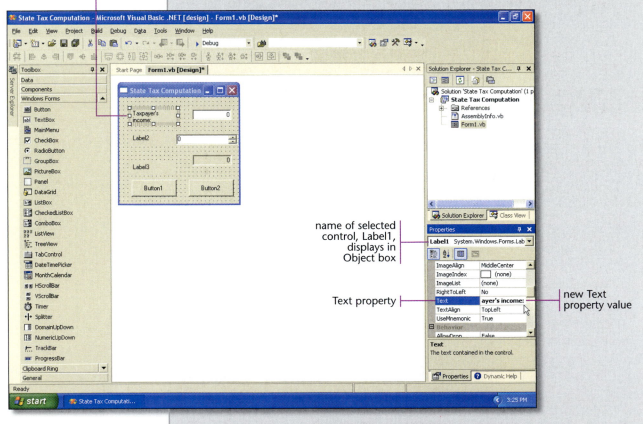

FIGURE 3-52

3. Scroll the Properties list until the Location property displays. Click the expand button (plus sign) to the left of the Location property and then double-click the X property value.

   The Location property displays in the Layout property category of the Properties list. The Location property expands and the X property value is selected (Figure 3-53).

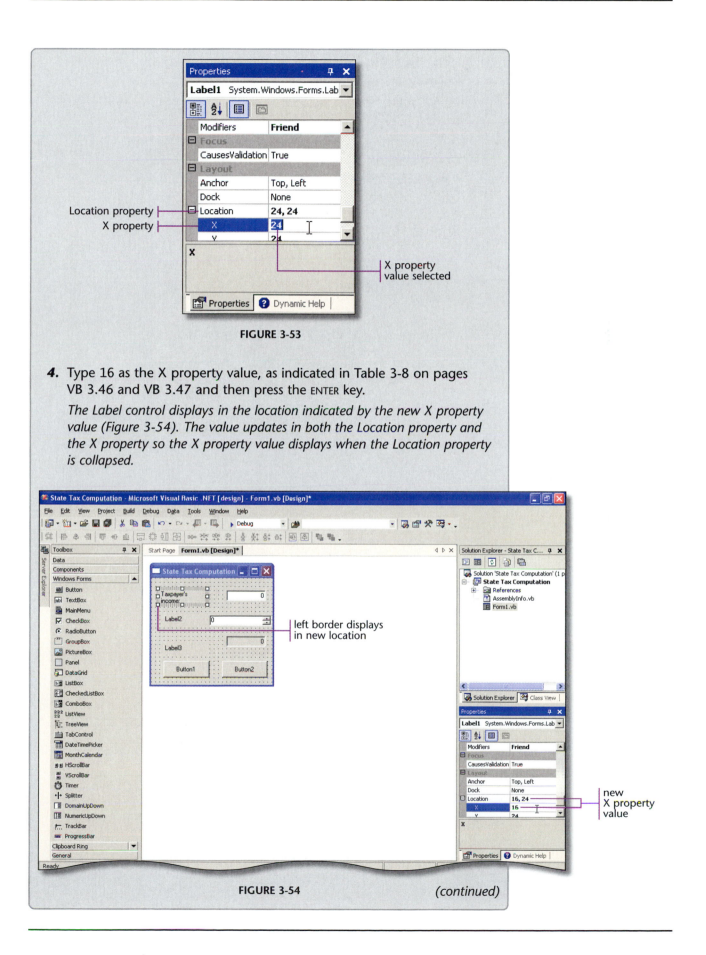

FIGURE 3-53

4. Type 16 as the X property value, as indicated in Table 3-8 on pages VB 3.46 and VB 3.47 and then press the ENTER key.

The Label control displays in the location indicated by the new X property value (Figure 3-54). The value updates in both the Location property and the X property so the X property value displays when the Location property is collapsed.

FIGURE 3-54

(continued)

5. Repeat Steps 3 and 4 to change the remaining property values for the Label1 control, as shown in Table 3-8 on pages VB 3.46 and VB 3.47.

The Label1 control displays in the correct location with the size as defined in the user interface design (Figure 3-55).

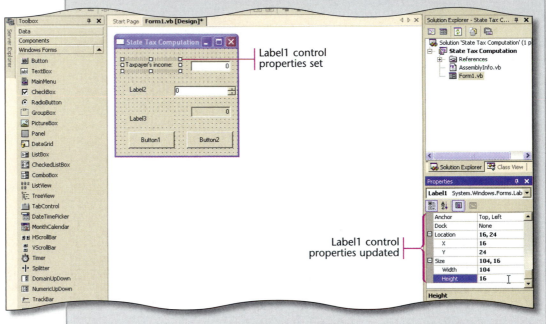

FIGURE 3-55

6. Repeat Steps 1 through 4 for the Label2 and Label3 controls.

7. Select the Form1 form by clicking an empty area of the form that does not contain any other controls.

The Form1 form is selected (Figure 3-56). The Label1, Label2, and Label3 controls display in the correct location with the size and text defined in the user interface design.

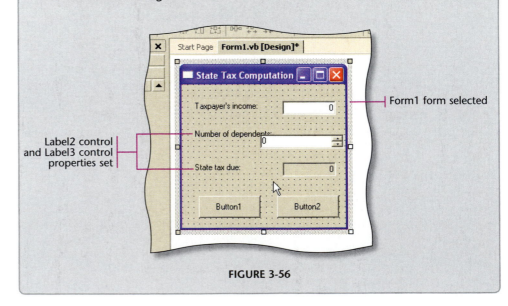

FIGURE 3-56

As shown in Figure 3-56, the Label controls now display on the form as they should display to a user using the State Tax Computation application.

NumericUpDown Control Properties

A NumericUpDown control allows the user to change an input value by typing it on the keyboard, using the UP ARROW or DOWN ARROW keys on the keyboard, or using the mouse to click the up and down arrows. The **Value property** defines the current value displayed in the control. The **Minimum property** and **Maximum property** determine the range of allowable values. If the user enters a number outside of the range set by the Minimum and Maximum property values, the control automatically changes the entered number to the closest allowable value. The property values for the Value, Minimum, and Maximum properties can be integer or decimal values, depending on the value of the **DecimalPlaces property**. The DecimalPlaces property defaults to 0, to indicate that only integer values are accepted as input. Table 3-9 lists several of the properties associated with the NumericUpDown control, with a brief description and a list of available property values.

Table 3-9   *NumericUpDown Control Properties*

CATEGORY	PROPERTY	DESCRIPTION	PROPERTY VALUES
Appearance	BorderStyle	Determines how the border of the control displays	None FixedSingle **Fixed3D**
	TextAlign	Defines if text in the control displays left-aligned, right-aligned, or centered	**Left** Right Center
	UpDownAlign	Determines if the up and down arrows on the control display on left or right side of the control	Left **Right**
	Value	Sets the value that displays in the control	Any value within the range set by the Minimum and Maximum property values
Behavior	InterceptArrowKeys	If True, a user can use the UP ARROW and DOWN ARROW keys to change the value in control; if False, the user cannot	**True** False
Data	DecimalPlaces	Defines numbers of decimal places that display in the value in the control	Any whole number from **0** to 99
	Increment	Defines amount to add or subtract from the displayed value each time user clicks the up or down arrow on control	Any positive number
	Maximum	Determines the highest allowable value in the control; if user enters a higher value, the value is set automatically to the Maximum value	Any number

(continued)

Table 3-9 NumericUpDown Control Properties (continued)

CATEGORY	PROPERTY	DESCRIPTION	PROPERTY VALUES
Data	Minimum	Determines the lowest allowable value in the control; if user enters a lower value, the value is set automatically to the Maximum value	Any number
	ThousandsSeparator	Determines if a Thousands separator character is used in the value, when appropriate; if True, the value displays with a Thousands separator character set on user's system; if False, no Thousands separator character displays	True **False**

Several of the properties of the NumericUpDown control must be changed from the default values, according to the application requirements. Table 3-10 shows the properties and values of the NumericUpDown control that require changes.

Table 3-10 NumericUpDown Control Property Values for the State Tax Computation Application

CONTROL	PROPERTY	VALUE	EFFECT
NumericUpDown1	Value	0	Sets 0 to display as the initial value in the control at run time
	Location: X	144	Indicates distance from left border of the form in pixels
	Location: Y	64	Indicates distance from top border of the form in pixels
	Size: Width	76	Sets the width of the control in pixels
	Size: Height	20	Sets the height of the control in pixels
	Minimum	0	Defines the lowest value allowed in the control
	Maximum	10	Defines the highest value allowed in the control
	TextAlign	Right	Sets text to display right-aligned in the control

As defined in the user interface design for the State Tax Computation application, the NumericUpDown control should accept only values for Number of dependents from 0 through 10 and the value should display right-aligned in the control. The property values also must be changed to set the location and size of the NumericUpDown control. The following steps set the property values of the NumericUpDown1 control, as listed in Table 3-10.

To Change Properties of a NumericUpDown Control

1. Click the NumericUpDown1 control.

2. Scroll the Properties list until the Location property displays.

3. Click the expand button (plus sign) to the left of the Location property.

4. Double-click the X property value.

5. Type 144 as the X property value, as indicated in Table 3-10, and then press the ENTER key.

6. Repeat Steps 1 through 5 to change the remaining property values for the NumericUpDown1 control, as shown in Table 3-10.

7. Click any blank area of the Form1 form.

The Form1 form is selected (Figure 3-57). The NumericUpDown1 control displays in the correct location with size, value, minimum, maximum, and alignment as defined in the user interface design.

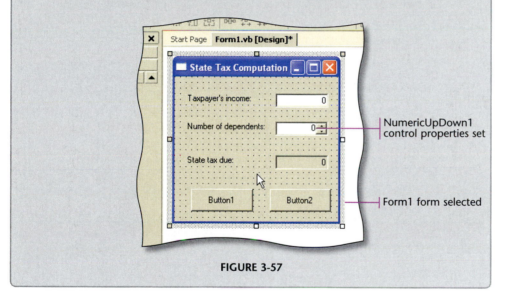

FIGURE 3-57

Button Control Properties

Adding one or more buttons to a user interface allows a user to initiate an action by clicking the button, which causes the code associated with the button to be executed. A Button control, for example, can instruct the application to calculate or process an output, based on inputs that have been provided. In the case of the State Tax Computation application, Button controls allow a user to tell the application to perform the computation or to reset the data on the form. Table 3-11 on the next page lists several of the properties associated with the Button control, with a brief description and a list of available property values.

Table 3-11   Button Control Properties

CATEGORY	PROPERTY	DESCRIPTION	PROPERTY VALUES
Appearance	FlatStyle	Determines the 3D appearance of the control	Flat Popup **Standard** System
	Image	Sets an image to display on the visible portion of the Label control, along with the Text	Select a picture from the hard drive using a dialog box.
	ImageAlign	If Image property is set, determines where the image displays	Select a location from a pop-up graphical display map.
	TextAlign	Determines where the Text should display on the button	Select one of nine locations from a pop-up graphical display map.

The Location and Size properties of the two Button controls already have been changed to position and size the buttons correctly on the form. The only other property change required is to change the Text property value to define the text that displays on the button face. Table 3-12 shows the properties and values of the Button1 and Button2 controls that require changes.

Table 3-12   Button Control Property Values for the State Tax Computation Application

CONTROL	PROPERTY	VALUE	EFFECT
Button1	Text	Compute Tax	Sets the text that displays on the button face to Compute Tax
Button2	Text	Reset	Sets the text that displays on the button face to Reset

The following steps set the property values of the Button1 and Button2 controls, as listed in Table 3-12.

To Change Properties of Button Controls

1. Click the Button1 control.
2. Scroll the Properties list until the Text property displays.
3. Double-click the Text property value.
4. Type Compute Tax as the Text property value, as indicated in Table 3-12, and then press the ENTER key.

5. Repeat Steps 1 through 4 to change the Text property value for the Button2 control, as shown in Table 3-12.

6. Click any blank area of the Form1 form.

The Form1 form is selected (Figure 3-58). The Button1 and Button2 controls display with the Text property values defined in the user interface design.

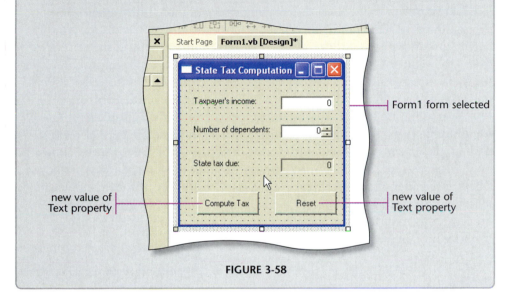

FIGURE 3-58

All of the controls have been added to the form and changed to reflect the desired user interface design. The user interface for the State Tax Computation application is complete. The TextBox, Label, NumericUpDown, and Button controls now display on the form as they should display in the application window at run time.

Changing the Name Property of Controls

As you have learned, Visual Basic .NET assigns unique default names to controls, such as Form1, Label1, Label2, TextBox1, and Button1. The **Name property** of a control reflects its name. Each control has its own unique default name to distinguish it from another instance of the same class of objects; Visual Basic .NET also adds a number to each default control name to ensure that the control name is unique. For example, because the form in the State Tax Computation application includes more than one TextBox control, Visual Basic .NET names the first TextBox control, TextBox1, and the second TextBox control, TextBox2.

It is useful to change the default name of a control to provide a more descriptive name. In general, you should rename controls that will have one or more properties changed at run time, such as controls used for input and output. You also should rename forms, which are a type of control. This is particularly true for Visual Basic .NET projects that include multiple forms. Because the State Tax Computation program includes only one form, it is not necessary to rename the form. You also do not need to rename controls that are used for static display, such as the Label controls in the State Tax Computation application.

Although Visual Basic .NET may initially set the text that displays in the control to match the name of the control, the text in a control and the name of the control are defined by two different properties and property values. For example, the text that displays on the Compute Tax button is set by the Text property; the name of the Button control, Button1, is set by the Name property.

Renaming controls is not a requirement of programming in Visual Basic .NET, but rather a convention that makes programs more understandable by programmers. When naming forms and controls, it is beneficial to follow a standardized **naming convention**, which is an agreed upon method for naming controls so the control can be identified easily in code. Companies or programming teams often maintain standards for the names of controls to ensure that everyone on the programming team understands the purpose of the controls.

When defining standards for naming forms and controls, you can follow some simple rules. First, the control name should indicate the type of control. Second, the control name should describe the purpose of the control. Following these rules, you can create naming conventions that use a three-letter prefix and a descriptive identifier as the name of the control. All forms, for example, would have the prefix of frm followed by a descriptive identifier. Using this convention, the Form1 form in the State Tax Computation application would be named frmStateTaxComputation.

Naming Forms

In a project with multiple forms, all forms in an application should be assigned an appropriate name other than the default name. When naming a form, use a prefix of frm followed by a descriptive identifier.

When creating naming standards for other controls, such as a TextBox, Label, NumericUpDown, or Button control, again you can use a three-letter prefix and a descriptive identifier as the name of the control. Each type of control would have a unique prefix, such as txt for a TextBox control and lbl for a Label control.

Naming Controls

A descriptive name should be used when naming a control used for input or output. A control that will not be changed during run time, such as a Label control, does not necessarily need a name. When naming a control, use a unique three-character prefix together with a descriptive identifier. The following three-character prefixes can be used for TextBox, Label, NumericUpDown, and Button controls:

txt – TextBox controls

lbl – Label controls

nud – NumericUpDown controls

btn – Button controls

Table 3-13 shows how these naming conventions apply to the input and output controls on the form in the State Tax Computation application.

Table 3-13   *Control Names for the State Tax Computation Application*

CURRENT CONTROL NAME PROPERTY VALUE	NEW NAME PROPERTY VALUE
TextBox1	txtIncome
TextBox2	txtTaxDue
NumericUpDown1	nudDependents
Button1	btnCompute
Button2	btnReset

The following steps change the Name property values of these controls to set the Name property values to the names listed in Table 3-13.

To Change the Name Property of Controls

1. Click the TextBox1 control.
2. Scroll the Properties list until the Name property displays in the Properties window.
3. Double click the Name property value.
4. Type `txtIncome` as the new Name property value for the TextBox1 control, as indicated in Table 3-13.
5. Repeat Steps 1 through 4 to set the Name property values for the TextBox2, NumericUpDown1, Button1, and Button2 controls.
6. Click any blank area on the Form1 form to select it.

   The Name property value of each control is set to the values indicated in Table 3-13. The form and controls show no visible change.

The steps followed to change the Name property value of a control are the same as those followed to change any other property value for a control. It is important to name controls correctly while creating the interface and before writing any code. Otherwise, if you refer to any of the control names in code and then change the name of a control, the name change may not be reflected automatically in your code and will cause unintended results.

Tip

Setting Control Names
Be certain to name your controls while designing the interface and before writing any code.

With the control names set, the required changes to the control properties for the State Tax Computation application are complete. The next step in developing the application is to write the code that executes when the user clicks the Compute and Reset buttons.

TextBox and NumericUpDown Control Methods

You began the development of the State Tax Computation application by developing the user interface, which consisted of a form and controls. You then set the properties of the controls. The final step in developing the State Tax Computation application is to write the code, or *actions,* that will occur in the application in response to specific events. Visual Basic .NET has its own language, which are the words and symbols used to write the code.

Events are messages sent to an object such as a control when the application runs. As you have learned, Visual Basic .NET controls are objects; just as a method is a message sent to an object, an event procedure is a message sent to a control. Events can be initiated when a user completes a task, such as clicking or dragging a control. Events also can be initiated by the application itself. Events trigger **event procedures**, which are groups of code statements, sometimes simply called code. **Code statements** are instructions to the computer written at design time for the computer to execute at run time.

In Visual Basic .NET, certain controls are capable of recognizing events. For example, most types of Visual Basic .NET controls that display in the application window recognize the **Click event**, which is an event initiated when the user clicks the left mouse button. Button controls are one type of control that can recognize the Click event. A control's name is used to associate an event with a specific control on a form, in order to tell Visual Basic .NET that an event initiated by that control should trigger the event procedure or code statements. For example, when the user clicks the left mouse button with the mouse pointer positioned on a specific Button control, such as btnCompute, the code in the btnCompute_Click event procedure executes.

A program that behaves as just described is called **event driven**. Code in event-driven programs executes only when a certain event, such as clicking a button, triggers the code to execute. Windows applications built using Visual Basic .NET are event driven.

Assignment Statements

Many times, the actions that you want to occur in the application in response to events can be expressed as changes in property values of controls on the form. The generalized code statement used to change the value of a control property is

controlname.propertyname = propertyvalue

where controlname is the name of the control, propertyname is the name of the property to change, and propertyvalue is the new value to which the property value should be changed. This type of code statement is known as an **assignment statement**, which is a code statement that changes the value of a variable or property of an object or control. Variables will be discussed in

Chapter 4. The assignment statement tells the application to set the control property on the left side of the statement to the property value on the right side of the statement. In the State Tax Computation application, for example, you can use an assignment statement to change the Text property of a TextBox control at run time so it displays the State tax due in the output area. Table 3-15 shows the general form of the assignment statement. Appendix D summarizes all of the general forms of statements introduced in this book.

Table 3-14 **Assignment Statement**	
General form:	1. Object = newvalue 2. Object.Property = newvalue
Purpose:	To change the value of the object or object property on the left side of the equal sign to the value on the right side of the equal sign.
Examples:	1. `Button1.Text = "Compute Tax"` 2. `txtTaxDue.Text = 0.03 * (txtIncome.Text - 600 * nudDependents.Value)` 3. `i = 0`

Comment Statements

Programmers often add comments within their code statements as a form of **internal documentation**. A **comment** is text added within an event procedure that explains how the code in the event procedure works or why it was written. Comments are not executed in event procedures and are ignored by the .NET CLR. Comments are included only for informational purposes for you or for other programmers. Each comment line must begin with an apostrophe (') or the letters **REM**. The following general rules apply to the placement of comments in code statements.

Tip

Comment Placement

Use comments to remind yourself and other programmers of the purpose of code. Use comments in the following three ways:

1. Place a comment that identifies the file and its purpose at the top of every class or file that contains code. This type of comment typically is called a **comment header**.

2. Place a comment at the top of every event procedure or function.

3. Place comments near portions of code that need clarification or serve an important purpose.

The general form of a comment statement is shown in Table 3-15.

Table 3-15 **Comment Statement**

General form:	1. ' comment 2. REM comment
Purpose:	To insert explanatory comments in a program as internal documentation.
Examples:	1. ' Payroll: Overtime hour calculation ' Programmer: J. Quasney ' Date: September 23, 2003 ' Purpose: This project calculates total overtime pay for ' each department for a given time period. 2. REM Compute the overtime hours

---

In the code used for the State Tax Computation application, a comment header identifies the application, programmer, date, and purpose for the State Tax Computation application. Figure 3-59 shows the comment header. Visual Basic .NET automatically generates the line numbers shown in Figure 3-59 when the code is entered in the code window.

```
136     ' Chapter 3:    State Tax Computation
137     ' Programmer:   J. Quasney
138     ' Date:         September 2, 2003
139     ' Purpose:      This project calculates state income tax due based
140     '               on income level and number of dependents.
```

FIGURE 3-59

The code shown in Figure 3-59 includes **tab characters**, which are used to indent items on each line and are produced by pressing the TAB key. For example, in line 136, the tab character exists after the 3: and before the words, State Tax Computation.

Writing Code in the Code Window

During program design, you used pseudocode to design the program code to execute two tasks in the State Tax Computation application: computing state tax due when a user clicks the Compute Tax button and setting all values to 0 when a user clicks the Reset button (Figure 3-5 on page VB 3.08). The event procedure that is triggered when the user clicks the Compute Tax button, which is named btnComputeTax, is the btnCompute_Click event procedure. The btnCompute_Click event procedure calculates the State tax due based on a Taxpayer's income and Number of dependents entered by the user and then displays the result in the State tax due text box. The btnCompute_Click event procedure also includes a single comment statement to provide an explanation of the code. Figure 3-60 shows the code that needs to be entered to add the btnComputeTax_Click event procedure. The code is the Visual Basic .NET language for the pseudocode in Figure 3-5 on page VB 3.08.

```
142                 ' Calculate tax and display the result in the txtTaxDue text box
143                 txtTaxDue.Text = 0.03 * (txtIncome.Text - 600 * nudDependents.Value)
```

FIGURE 3-60

As shown in Line 143 of Figure 3-60, the code uses an assignment statement to assign the value of the calculation by changing the Text property of the txtTaxDue TextBox control. The right side of the assignment statement contains the equation used to calculate the state tax payment due by a taxpayer. The Taxpayer's income is referenced in the statement by using the Text property of the txtIncome TextBox control. The Number of dependents is referenced by using the Value property of the nudDependents NumericUpDown control. Both of these values are entered by the user at run time via the controls in the State Tax Computation application window. For example, the Text property of the txtIncome TextBox control is referenced by the code, txtIncome.Text.

Tip

Referencing Control Properties

In code, a reference to control properties is made by typing the name of the control followed by a period, and then the property name.

The code in Figure 3-59 and Figure 3-60 contains **line numbers** on the left side of each line. Visual Basic .NET automatically numbers all lines of code, regardless of whether you entered the lines or Visual Basic .NET generated the lines automatically. Visual Basic .NET includes an option to display line numbers in the code window. The default setting for this option is not to display line numbers. Programmers often display and print line numbers with code to facilitate communication when discussing the code. The remainder of this book will utilize line numbers when discussing, displaying, and printing code.

In Visual Basic .NET, the code window includes a built-in technology called Intellisense to help you write code. **Intellisense** anticipates your needs during coding and displays prompts to assist you in coding. As you type in the code window, Intellisense assists you by helping to complete words as you type, displaying appropriate list boxes from which you can select events, properties, or methods, and highlighting typographical or syntax errors in your code. A **syntax error** is an error caused by code statements that violate one of the structure or syntax rules of the Visual Basic .NET language. For example, the assignment statement requires an object or property on the left of the equal sign and a valid object or property value on the right side of the equal sign. If you do not include one of the required elements on either side of the equal sign, then you have created code with a syntax error.

As you write code in the code window, using proper spacing and indenting code will make the code more readable. The TAB key often is used to align code properly. Using blank spaces is also acceptable, but more cumbersome to enter. Companies or programming teams usually maintain their own set of coding standards that instruct programmers how code should be indented or aligned in the code window. In this book, the TAB key is used to indent code.

The following steps turn on the display of line numbers and insert the comment header and the code for the btnCompute_Click event procedure.

To Show Line Numbers and Write Code for a Comment Header and the btnCompute_Click Event Procedure

1. Click Tools on the menu bar and then click Options. When the Options dialog box displays, click the Text Editor folder in the Options list.

2. If necessary, click the Basic folder below the Text Editor folder in the Options list. When the Basic options display, click Line numbers in the Display area.

    The Options dialog box displays. The Text Editor folder and Basic subfolder are open in the Options list, and the Line numbers check box is selected in the Display area (Figure 3-61). The Options list consists of categories of options for working in the Visual Basic .NET IDE. The Basic options on the right side of the dialog box include the Line numbers check box that turns on line numbers.

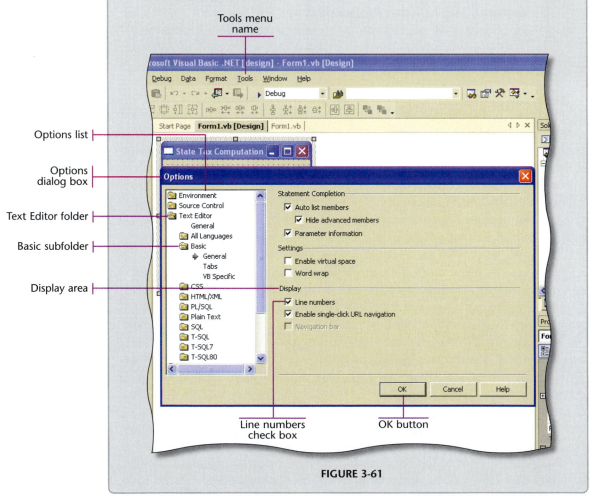

FIGURE 3-61

3. Click the OK button.

4. Double-click the Compute Tax button on the Form1 form in the main work area.

The code window opens in the main work area (Figure 3-62). The name of the current form, Form1, displays in the Object box in the Code window. The Click event is the default event for Button controls, so Visual Basic .NET automatically creates a Click event procedure when you double-click the button on the form. The event procedure name displays in the Procedure box. Visual Basic .NET inserts two lines of code for the Click event procedure, lines 137 and 139, as well as other code that is collapsed in the code region at line 4. The insertion point is placed inside the btnCompute_Click event procedure. Line numbers display on the left side of the code window.

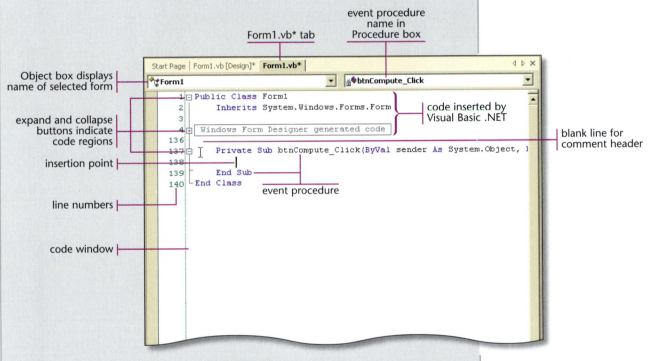

FIGURE 3-62

5. Click the left side of the blank line above the word, Private, on line 137. Type the five comment header lines exactly as illustrated in Figure 3-59 on page VB 3.60. Do not type the line numbers. You can insert your own name as the programmer. Press the TAB key at the start of each line to indent each line of code properly as shown in the table. Press the TAB key after typing each colon to indent the text as illustrated in Figure 3-59. You may need to press the TAB key more than once after typing each colon to create the correct indentation. Press the ENTER key after each of the first four lines. Do not press the ENTER key after the last line.

When you click above the word, Private, the Procedure box changes to display Declarations. The code window displays the comment header for the State Tax Computation application (Figure 3-63 on the next page).

(continued)

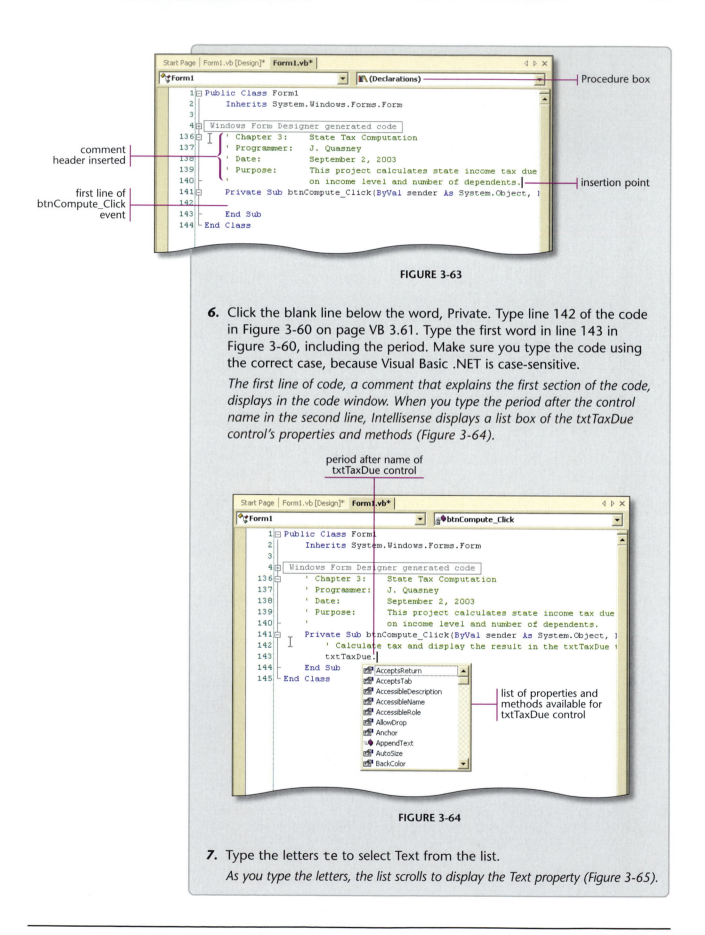

FIGURE 3-63

6. Click the blank line below the word, Private. Type line 142 of the code in Figure 3-60 on page VB 3.61. Type the first word in line 143 in Figure 3-60, including the period. Make sure you type the code using the correct case, because Visual Basic .NET is case-sensitive.

The first line of code, a comment that explains the first section of the code, displays in the code window. When you type the period after the control name in the second line, Intellisense displays a list box of the txtTaxDue control's properties and methods (Figure 3-64).

FIGURE 3-64

7. Type the letters te to select Text from the list.

As you type the letters, the list scrolls to display the Text property (Figure 3-65).

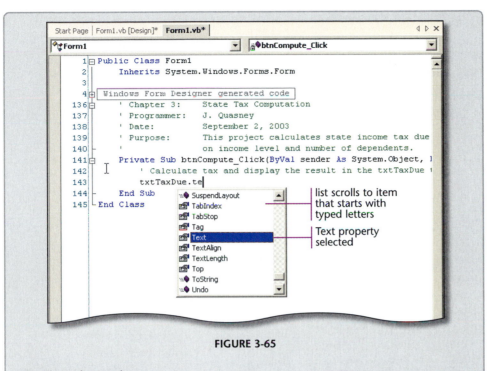

FIGURE 3-65

8. Press the TAB key.

Intellisense inserts the word, Text, in the code after the period (Figure 3-66). When working in the code window, the TAB key is used to enter a selection from the list.

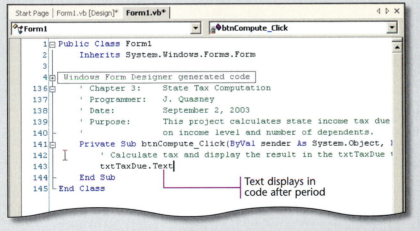

FIGURE 3-66

9. Type the remaining code in Line 143 in Figure 3-60 on page VB 3.61. Do not press the ENTER key after typing the code.

The code window scrolls horizontally as you type text that extends past the right edge of the window. The code will calculate the state income tax and then use the assignment statement to assign the result of the calculation to the Text property of the txtTaxDue TextBox control. The complete btnCompute_Click event procedure displays in the code window (Figure 3-67 on the next page).

(continued)

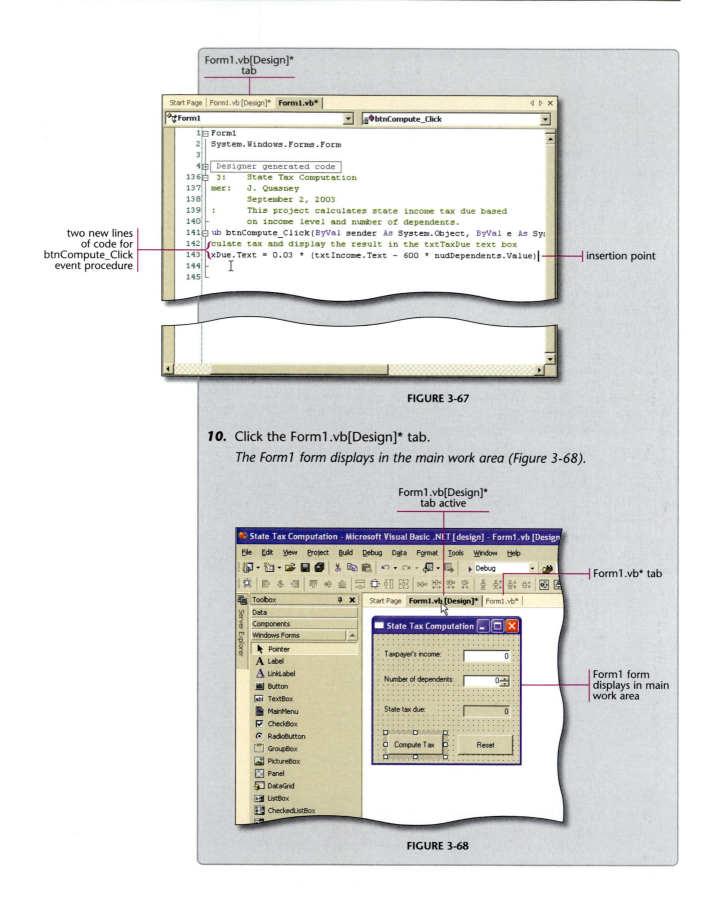

FIGURE 3-67

10. Click the Form1.vb[Design]* tab.

The Form1 form displays in the main work area (Figure 3-68).

FIGURE 3-68

The preceding steps showed how to write code for the btnCompute_Click event procedure for the btnComputeTax button. The code executes when the user clicks the Compute Tax button during run time. Steps 6 through 8 demonstrate the capabilities of the Intellisense system built into the Visual Basic .NET IDE. As shown in these steps, Intellisense assists coding by anticipating and displaying a list of properties, objects, and methods that are spelled similarly to the text you are typing.

As shown in Figure 3-62 on page VB 3.63, when the code window first opens, Visual Basic .NET places the insertion point inside the btnCompute_Click event procedure. The Click event is the default event for Button controls, so Visual Basic .NET automatically creates that event procedure when you double-click the button on the form.

Line numbers display in Figure 3-62, after the Line numbers option is set in the Options dialog box. Line numbers will continue to display and print in the code until the option is turned off. The option will remain set even after quitting and restarting Visual Basic .NET. If you are working in a computer lab, you may have to turn on the Line numbers option if it is not turned on.

As shown in the code window, an event procedure begins with the line that contains the text, Private Sub, and ends with the line that contains the text, End Sub. The line that starts with Private Sub is called the **event procedure declaration**. Because event procedures are methods for controls, the word, **Private**, indicates that this is a private method for the object. The word, **Sub**, which is short for Subroutine, indicates the beginning of a method. The next part of the event procedure declaration, btnCompute_Click, is the name of the event procedure. Finally, parameters to the event procedure are listed at the end of the event procedure declaration. Parameters are covered in more detail in Chapter 5. The line that includes the text, **End Sub**, indicates the end of the event procedure.

As indicated in the design of the application, the btnReset button must assign a value of 0 to the input and output controls in the application when clicked by a user. The btnReset_Click event procedure is assigned to the btnReset button so that it executes when the btnReset button is clicked.

As shown in Figure 3-69, the three assignment statements in lines 148 through 150 set the property values of the controls when the event procedure executes.

```
147        ' Set all input and output display values to 0
148        txtIncome.Text = "0"
149        nudDependents.Value = 0
150        txtTaxDue.Text = "0"
```

FIGURE 3-69

Line 148 sets the Text property value of the txtIncome TextBox control to the value of "0" (zero). Because Text boxes display alphanumeric characters, not numeric values, double quotation marks are used around the value to tell Visual Basic .NET to treat the 0 as a character, rather than a numeric value. Line 149 sets the Value property value of the nudDependents NumericUpDown control to 0, its minimum value. Because the Value property is a numeric property, it does not require the double quotation marks around the 0. Line 150 sets the Text property value of the txtTaxDue output TextBox control to a value of 0. Again, the 0 is in double quotation marks, meaning that Visual Basic .NET should treat the value as a character, not a numeric value.

The following steps insert the code for the btnReset_Click event procedure.

To Write Code for the btnReset_Click Event Procedure

1. Double-click the Reset button on the Form1 form in the main work area.

The code window opens in the main work area (Figure 3-70). Visual Basic .NET creates the btnReset_Click event procedure and places the insertion point inside the btnReset_Click event procedure. The event procedure name displays in the Procedure box.

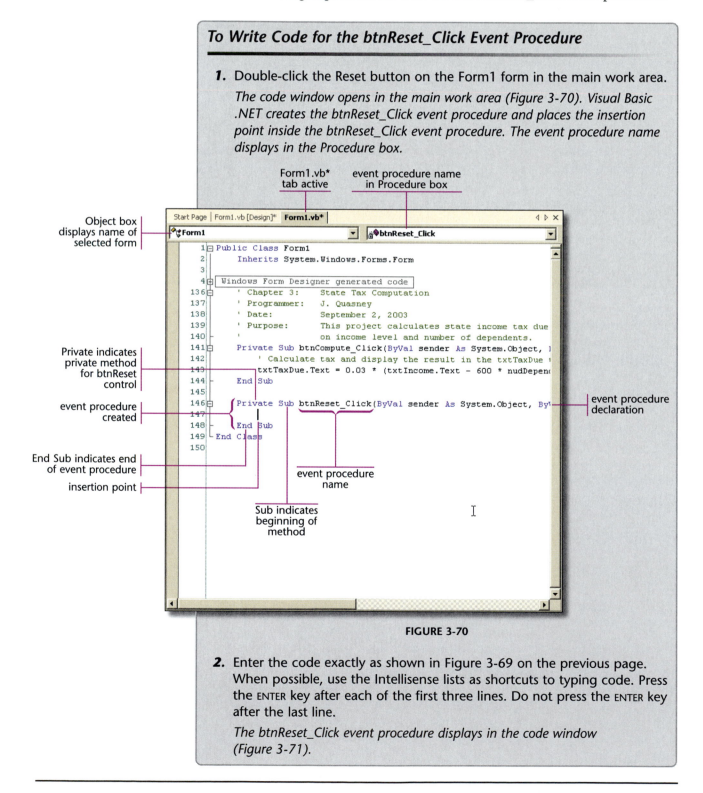

FIGURE 3-70

2. Enter the code exactly as shown in Figure 3-69 on the previous page. When possible, use the Intellisense lists as shortcuts to typing code. Press the ENTER key after each of the first three lines. Do not press the ENTER key after the last line.

The btnReset_Click event procedure displays in the code window (Figure 3-71).

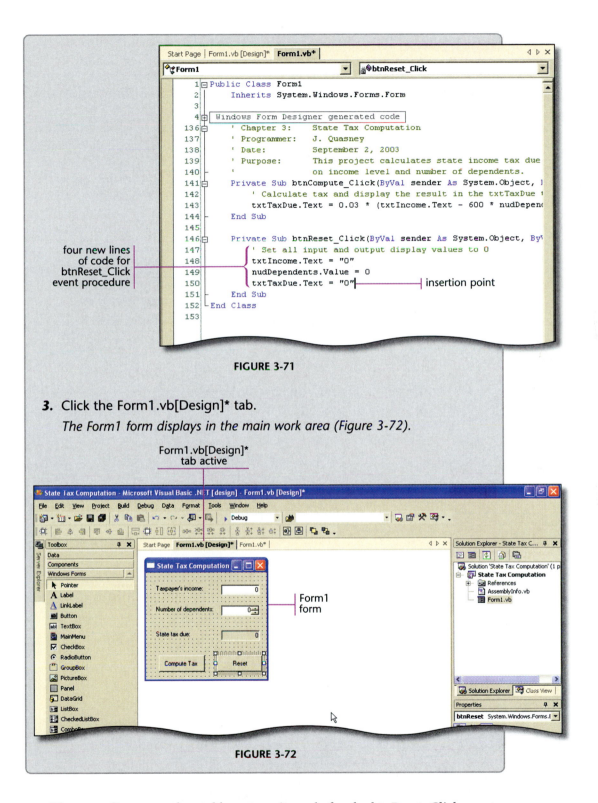

FIGURE 3-71

3. **Click the Form1.vb[Design]* tab.**

The Form1 form displays in the main work area (Figure 3-72).

FIGURE 3-72

The preceding steps showed how to write code for the btnReset_Click event procedure for the btnReset button. The code for the State Tax Computation application is now complete, with code written to include comments that clarify the purpose of the project and the meaning of the code and two Click event procedures that are triggered when a user clicks either the Compute Tax or Reset button in the State Tax Computation application.

Saving and Testing the Application

Before testing a new Visual Basic .NET project or quitting Visual Basic .NET, you should save your work. You also should save your project periodically while you work on it and before you run it for the first time. Visual Basic .NET will save your project automatically when you run it. During the process of developing a project, however, you should save your work at regular intervals. As you learned in Chapter 2, a Visual Basic .NET project is saved as a set of files. The following steps to save the form and project files for the State Tax Computation project on the Data Disk in drive A and then run the application to test the code.

To Save and Test a Project

1. Click the Save All button on the Standard toolbar.

The asterisk next to Form1.vb [Design] on the window title bar and the main work area tab no longer display, indicating that the project has been saved. Because the project was created and saved initially on the Data Disk in drive A, Visual Basic .NET automatically saves the project on the Data Disk in drive A.

2. Click the Start button on the Visual Basic .NET Standard toolbar.

Visual Basic .NET opens the Output window temporarily and displays messages as the application starts. The State Tax Computation application window displays, and Visual Basic .NET sets the focus to the first text box. The application button displays on the Windows taskbar (Figure 3-73).

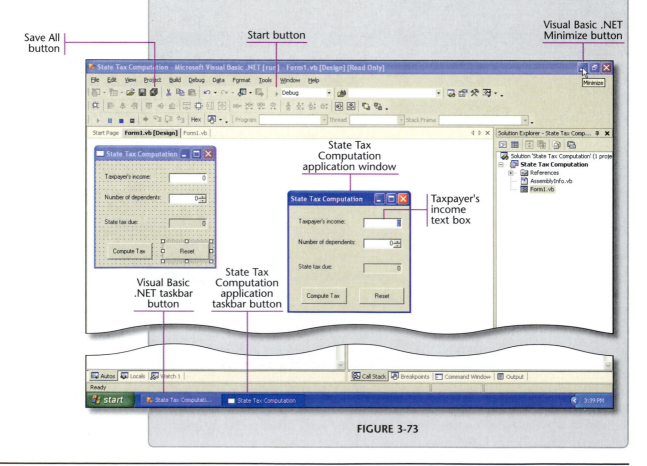

FIGURE 3-73

3. Click the Minimize button on the Visual Basic .NET title bar. Type 50000 in the Taxpayer's income text box and then point to the Number of dependents NumericUpDown box up arrow.

The Visual Basic .NET IDE is minimized. The State Tax Computation application runs in a window separate from the Visual Basic .NET application. The State Tax Computation application window displays as shown in Figure 3-74. The value, 50000, will be used as the input value for Taxpayer's income.

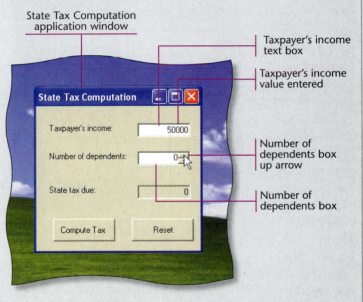

State Tax Computation
application window

Taxpayer's income
text box

Taxpayer's income
value entered

Number of
dependents box
up arrow

Number of
dependents box

FIGURE 3-74

4. Click the Number of dependents box up arrow until the number 3 displays.

The State Tax Computation application window displays as shown in Figure 3-75. The value, 3, will be used as the input value for Number of dependents.

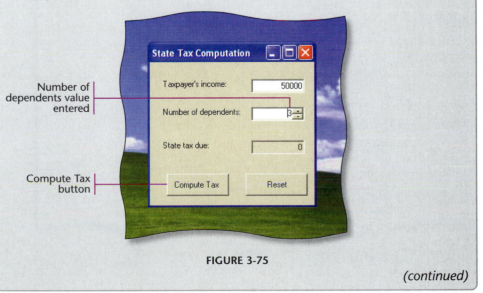

Number of
dependents value
entered

Compute Tax
button

FIGURE 3-75

(continued)

5. Click the Compute Tax button.

The State Tax Computation application calculates the State tax due based on the values input to the application. The resulting output value, 1446, displays in the State tax due text box (Figure 3-76). The result indicates that a taxpayer with a yearly income of $50,000 and 3 dependents owes a state tax of $1,446.

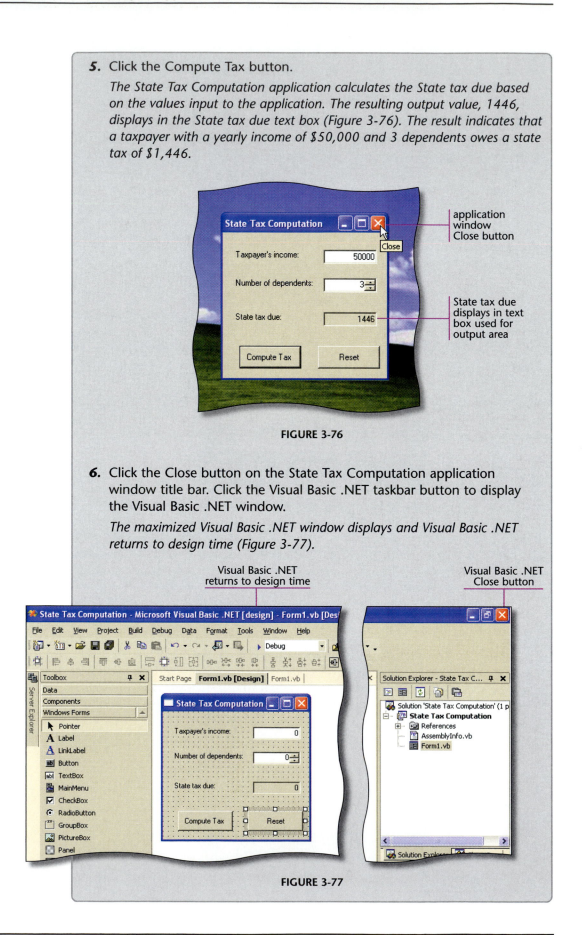

FIGURE 3-76

6. Click the Close button on the State Tax Computation application window title bar. Click the Visual Basic .NET taskbar button to display the Visual Basic .NET window.

The maximized Visual Basic .NET window displays and Visual Basic .NET returns to design time (Figure 3-77).

FIGURE 3-77

To test the State Tax Computation application fully, you should run the application again, trying different values for the Taxpayer's income and Number of dependents. As you enter the values and run the application, perform the calculation at the top of page VB 3.03 by hand and compare the results with the results of the program. You also should test the application by entering more than 10 dependents or a negative number for the number of dependents. If you enter more than 10 dependents or a negative number for the number of dependents, the NumericUpDown control should automatically change the value to the closest allowed value, either 0 or 10.

To test the Reset button, you should click it to test that the Reset button sets the three values in the application window to 0. Finally, you should test that you do not need to restart the application each time you want to perform another tax calculation. Instead, you should be able to click the Reset button each time you want to try another set of input values.

If your application does not run as expected, check your code and the property values set for the controls to make sure they match the specifications in this chapter. Other things to test include:

- Checking for incorrect spelling in text on Label controls
- Checking alignment and size of Label, TextBox, NumericUpDown, and Button controls
- Ensuring that the application window displays centered in the Windows environment
- Checking the application window to be sure it is not sizable
- Ensuring that tabbing using the TAB key on the keyboard properly moves the insertion point to the next control

Continue debugging the application by updating the property values and code to match the steps in this chapter until the application operates as designed.

Documenting the Application and Quitting Visual Basic .NET

The development process for the State Tax Computation application is complete. After finishing the development tasks on a project, the final step of the development cycle is to document the application. When you have completed working with Visual Basic .NET, you should quit the Visual Basic .NET system. The steps on the next page document the application and quit Visual Basic .NET. Line numbers are printed on the code listing.

To Document the Application and Quit Visual Basic .NET

1. If necessary, close the Output window. Click the Form1.vb[Design] tab, and then follow the steps on page VB 2.34 in Chapter 2 using the PRINT SCREEN key to print a record of the user interface design of the State Tax Computation form.

   The State Tax Computation form is printed (Figure 3-78).

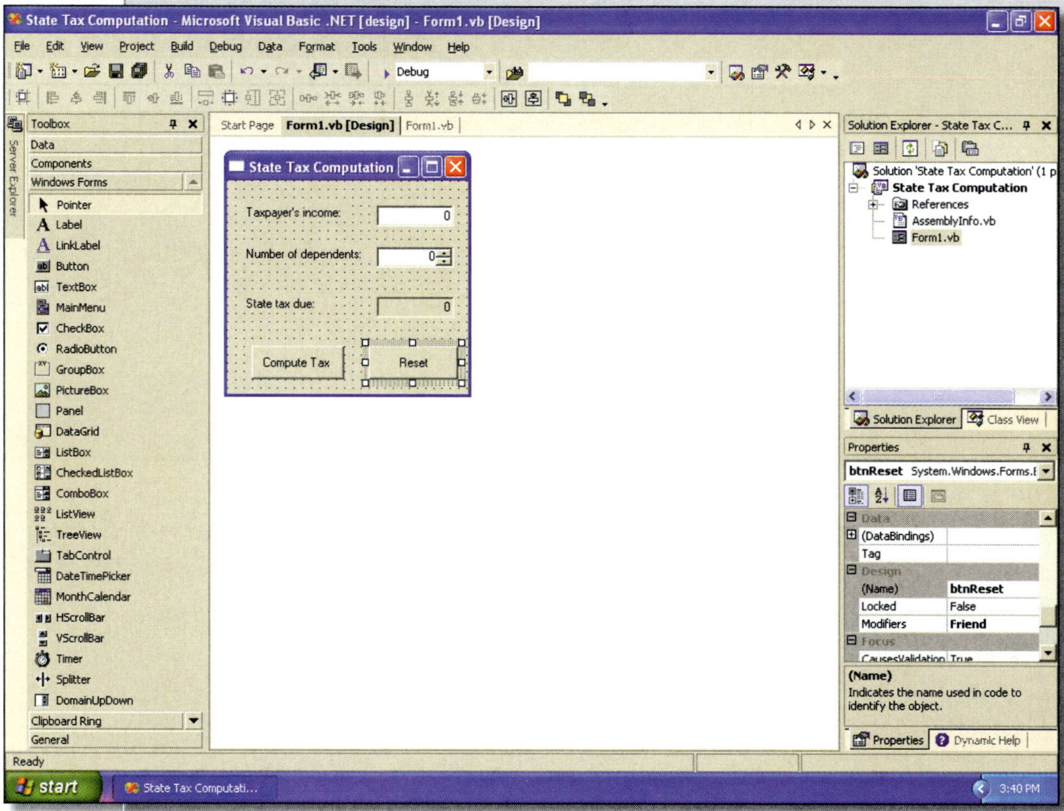

FIGURE 3-78

2. Click the Form1.vb tab. Click File on the menu bar and then click Page Setup.

3. When the Page Setup dialog box displays, click Line numbers and then click the OK button.

4. Follow the steps on page VB 2.40 in Chapter 2 using the Print command on the File menu to print a record of the code of the State Tax Computation form.

   The State Tax Computation code is printed (Figure 3-79).

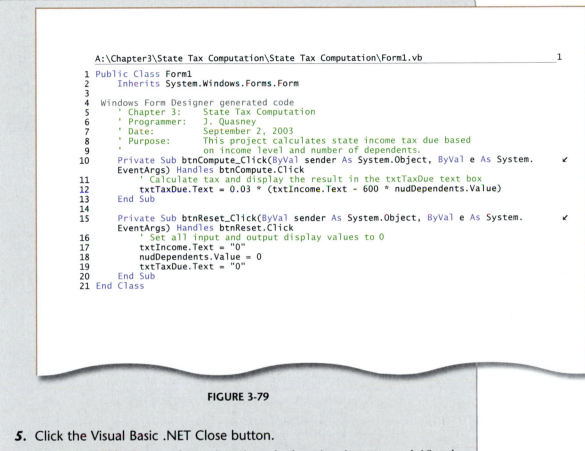

```
A:\Chapter3\State Tax Computation\State Tax Computation\Form1.vb                    1
1  Public Class Form1
2      Inherits System.Windows.Forms.Form
3
4  Windows Form Designer generated code
5      ' Chapter 3:      State Tax Computation
6      ' Programmer:     J. Quasney
7      ' Date:           September 2, 2003
8      ' Purpose:        This project calculates state income tax due based
9      '                 on income level and number of dependents.
10     Private Sub btnCompute_Click(ByVal sender As System.Object, ByVal e As System.    ⤶
       EventArgs) Handles btnCompute.Click
11         ' Calculate tax and display the result in the txtTaxDue text box
12         txtTaxDue.Text = 0.03 * (txtIncome.Text - 600 * nudDependents.Value)
13     End Sub
14
15     Private Sub btnReset_Click(ByVal sender As System.Object, ByVal e As System.    ⤶
       EventArgs) Handles btnReset.Click
16         ' Set all input and output display values to 0
17         txtIncome.Text = "0"
18         nudDependents.Value = 0
19         txtTaxDue.Text = "0"
20     End Sub
21 End Class
```

FIGURE 3-79

5. Click the Visual Basic .NET Close button.

If you made changes to the project since the last time it was saved, Visual Basic .NET displays the Microsoft Visual Basic .NET dialog box. If you click the Yes button, you can resave your project and quit. If you click the No button, you will quit without saving changes. Clicking the Cancel button will close the dialog box.

Chapter Summary

In this chapter, you learned how to develop a Visual Basic .NET application, from the initial analysis and design of the user interface and program through development, testing, and documentation. In the process, you learned how to start a new project in Visual Basic .NET, develop a user interface on a form, and add Label, TextBox, NumericUpDown, and Button controls to a form. You learned common properties for forms and controls and learned how to change the appearance and behavior of forms and controls by setting property values for properties such as StartPosition, Text, Location, Size, TextAlign, Maximum, and Minimum. You also learned how to properly name forms and controls. You then learned how to write code for two Click event procedures and include comments to document the purpose of the code. You learned how line numbers assist programmers and how to display them in the code window. Finally, you saved and tested the application to ensure that it met the program requirements defined during the design phase.

What You Should Know

Having completed this chapter, you now should be able to perform the tasks shown in Table 3-16.

Table 3-16   Chapter 3 What You Should Know

TASK NUMBER	TASK	PAGE
1	Start a New Visual Basic .NET Project	VB 3.09
2	Change the Size of a Form	VB 3.13
3	Change the StartPosition, Title, and FormBorderStyle Property Values of a Form	VB 3.18
4	Add Label Controls to a Form by Drawing	VB 3.24
5	Add TextBox Controls to a Form by Dragging	VB 3.28
6	Add a NumericUpDown Control to a Form by Dragging	VB 3.31
7	Add Button Controls to a Form by Double-Clicking	VB 3.33
8	Move Controls on a Form	VB 3.34
9	Change the Size of Controls on a Form	VB 3.36
10	Change Properties of TextBox Controls	VB 3.42
11	Change Properties of Label Controls	VB 3.48
12	Change Properties of a NumericUpDown Control	VB 3.53
13	Change Properties of Button Controls	VB 3.54
14	Change the Name Property of Controls	VB 3.57
15	Show Line Numbers and Write Code for a Comment Header and the btnCompute_Click Event Procedure	VB 3.62
16	Write Code for the btnReset_Click Event Procedure	VB 3.68
17	Save and Test a Project	VB 3.70
18	Document the Application and Quit Visual Basic .NET	VB 3.74

Key Terms

Alphabetic button *(VB 3.15)*
assignment statement *(VB 3.58)*
Button control *(VB 3.23)*
Categorized button *(VB 3.15)*
CenterScreen *(VB 3.16)*
Click event *(VB 3.58)*
code statements *(VB 3.58)*
comment *(VB 3.59)*
comment header *(VB 3.59)*
DecimalPlaces property *(VB 3.51)*
default value *(VB 3.16)*
description pane *(VB 3.15)*
End Sub *(VB 3.67)*
events *(VB 3.58)*
event driven *(VB 3.58)*
event procedure declaration *(VB 3.62)*
event procedures *(VB 3.58)*
FixedDialog property value *(VB 3.17)*
focus *(VB 3.38)*
form *(VB 3.12)*
FormBorderStyle property *(VB 3.17)*
graphical user interface (GUI)
    (VB 3.06)
Height property *(VB 3.14)*
icon *(VB 3.06)*
Intellisense *(VB 3.61)*
internal documentation *(VB 3.59)*
intrinsic control *(VB 3.24)*
Label control *(VB 3.23)*
Large Icons button *(VB 3.12)*
Left property *(VB 3.35)*
line numbers *(VB 3.61)*
Location property *(VB 3.40)*

Maximum property *(VB 3.51)*
Minimum property *(VB 3.51)*
Name property *(VB 3.55)*
naming convention *(VB 3.56)*
NumericUpDown control *(VB 3.23)*
Object box *(VB 3.14)*
pixel *(VB 3.14)*
positioning grid *(VB 3.28)*
Private *(VB 3.67)*
Properties button *(VB 3.15)*
Properties list *(VB 3.15)*
Property Pages button *(VB 3.15)*
ReadOnly property *(VB 3.40)*
REM *(VB 3.59)*
Sizable property valve *(VB 3.17)*
Small Icons button *(VB 3.12)*
snap *(VB 3.28)*
StartPosition property *(VB 3.16)*
Sub *(VB 3.67)*
syntax error *(VB 3.61)*
tab characters *(VB 3.60)*
tabbing *(VB 3.38)*
TabIndex property *(VB 3.38)*
TabStop property *(VB 3.38)*
Text property *(VB 3.16)*
TextBox control *(VB 3.23*
toolbar *(VB 3.15)*
Top property *(VB 3.35)*
user interface (UI) *(VB 3.06)*
Value property *(VB 3.51)*
Width property *(VB 3.14)*
WindowsDefault *(VB 3.16)*
Windows Forms tab *(VB 3.23)*

KEY TERMS

Homework Assignments

Label the Figure

Identify the elements shown in Figure 3-80.

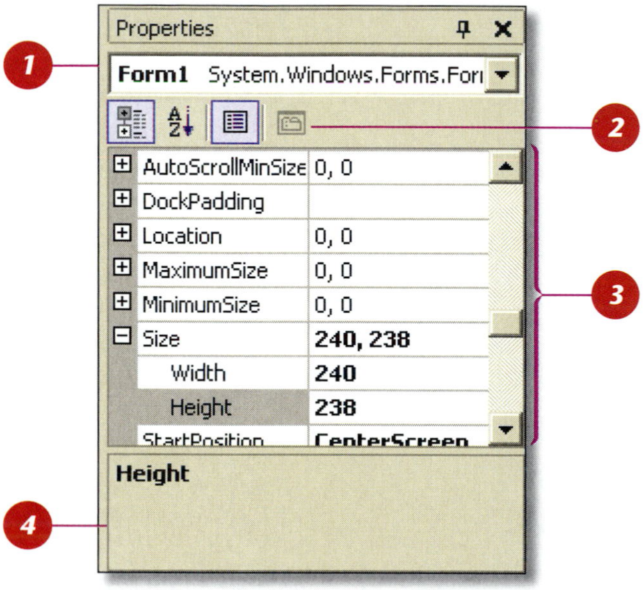

FIGURE 3-80

1. _____   2. _____   3. _____   4. _____

Short Answer

1. When you create a new project, Visual Basic .NET always creates _____ form(s).

2. Briefly describe the following form properties: Text, FormBorderStyle, and Fixed Dialog.

3. A _____ control is used to display text on a form. A _____ control is frequently used as a way for the user to input information into the application. A _____ control is used during run time to initiate actions called events. By default, the _____ in the Toolbox window contains 40 intrinsic controls.

4. List the steps to delete a control from a form.

5. If you add three Label controls, three TextBox controls, and two Button controls to an empty form, what will be their default names? It is good programming practice to change the names of the controls you plan to reference in your code. Identify the property you use to change the name of a control, the window you use to change it, and the recommended prefixes for naming the following controls: TextBox; Label; NumericUpDown; and Button.

6. Assume you have a TextBox control on a form named txtVolume and you want to assign it the product of three other text boxes on the form named txtLength, txtWidth, and txtHeight. Write the assignment code statement.

7. Each comment line must begin with a(n) _____ or the letters _____.

8. If you want to assign the value zero (0) to a TextBox control, then write the zero as _____. If you want to assign the value zero (0) to a NumericUpDown control, then write the zero as _____.

9. Write assignment code statements for the following:
   a. Assign txtAnswer1 the value 3
   b. Assign txtAnswer2 the value of txtAnswer1 less 2
   c. Assign txtAnswer3 the product of txtAnswer1 and txtAnswer2
   d. Triple the value of txtAnswer3
   e. Assign txtAnswer4 the quotient of txtAnswer3 divided by txtAnswer2
   f. Increment txtAnswer5 by 1
   g. Decrement txtAnswer6 by 3
   h. Cube the value of txtAnswer7

Learn It Online

Start your browser and visit scsite.com/vbnet/exs. Follow the instructions in the exercises below.

1. **Chapter Reinforcement TF, MC, and SA**   Click the True/False, Multiple Choice, and Short Answer link below Chapter 3. Print and then answer the questions.

2. **Practice Test**   Click the Practice Test link below Chapter 3. Answer each question, enter your first and last name at the bottom of the page, and then click the Grade Test button. When the graded practice test displays on your screen, click Print on the File menu to print a hard copy. Continue to take practice tests until you score 80% or better. Hand in a printout of the final practice test.

3. **Crossword Puzzle Challenge**   Click the Crossword Puzzle Challenge link below Chapter 3. Read the instructions, and then enter your first and last name. Click the Play button. Work the crossword puzzle. When you are finished, click the Submit button. When the crossword puzzle redisplays, click the Print button.

4. **Tips and Tricks**   Click the Tips and Tricks link below Chapter 3. Click a topic that pertains to Chapter 3. Right-click the information and then click Print on the shortcut menu. Construct a brief example of what the information relates to in Visual Basic .NET to confirm you understand how to use the tip or trick. Hand in the example and printed information.

5. **Newsgroups**   Click the Newsgroups link below Chapter 3. Click a topic that pertains to Chapter 3. Print three comments.

6. **Expanding Your Horizons**   Click the Articles for Visual Basic .NET below Chapter 3. Click a topic that pertains to Chapter 3. Print the information. Construct a brief example of what the information relates to in Visual Basic .NET to confirm you understand the contents of the article. Hand in the example and printed information.

7. **Search Sleuth**   Select three key terms from the Key Terms section of this chapter and then use the Google search engine at google.com (or any major search engine) to display and print two Web pages for each key term.

Debugging Assignment

Start Visual Basic .NET and open the project, Athas Construction, from the Chapter3/Athas Construction folder on the Data Disk. See page xvi in the preface of this book for instructions for downloading the Data Disk or see your instructor for information about accessing the files required in this book. The Athas Construction application consists of several controls, including a TextBox control used to input Board Length, a NumericUpDown control used to input Number of boards, a second TextBox control used to display the output value for Total square feet, and three Label controls that provide descriptive labels for the TextBox and NumericUpDown controls. The application also includes two Button controls. Clicking the first Button control (Calculate) should compute the Total square feet based on the input for Board Length and Number of boards. The Total square feet is equal to the input length times the number of boards, which are one foot-wide pieces of flooring. Clicking the second Button control (Reset) should reset the values of the input and output controls to 0.

1. Fix any typographical or display problems on the form and the controls on the form. Make sure the controls line up in a visually appealing manner. Check that the TabIndex properties for the TextBox, NumericUpDown, and Button controls are logical. Check the StartPosition property value to ensure that the application will display in the center of the screen when the application starts.

2. Run the project and enter 10 for the Board Length and 5 for the Number of boards. Click the Calculate button on the lower left to check the resulting output. Note any errors in the processing and close the running application.

3. Double-click the Calculate Button control on the lower left of the form and fix any errors you found with the code. Run the project again and test the changes you just made.

4. With the application still running, click the Reset button on the lower right of the window and check its functionality. Note any errors in the processing and exit the running application.

5. Double-click the Reset Button control on the lower right of the form and fix any errors you found with this button. Insert a new line in the comment header indicating that you fixed bugs in the code.

6. Run the project and enter 10 for the length and 5 for the number of boards. Click the Calculate button. The window should display as shown in Figure 3-81.

7. Print the form and all of the code for the project.

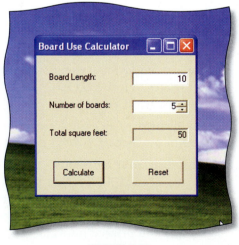

FIGURE 3-81

Programming Assignments

1 Designing a Visual Basic .NET Application

At Pacific Realty, real estate agents receive a commission rate that ranges from 1% (.01) to 7% (.07) on home sales in increments of .1% (.001), depending on the home sale price. Design an application that accepts the home sale price and a commission rate as inputs. The application should calculate and display the resulting commission and allow the user to reset the input and output values. The formula for calculating the commission is:

Commission = SalesPrice × CommissionRate

Perform the following tasks to design two solutions to the problem.

1. On paper, design a suitable user interface for the application. Be as specific as possible in naming controls and specifying their functions.

2. List all properties and property values for the form and any controls that the application requires. You need only to list those properties that must be changed from their default values.

3. On paper, write pseudocode for any events that need to be coded, based on your design in step 1.

4. Desk-check your design by testing your application on paper. Draw a three-column table with the two input values in columns 1 and 2, and the output value in column 3. Create three rows that contain various input values for the home sale price and commission rate. Test your program design by substituting the values in columns 1 and 2 into your pseudocode. Write the results in column 3. Double-check the values against the formula in the instructions to make certain the pseudocode properly solves the problem.

5. Create an alternate design to the solution, using at least one different control in the interface design. Repeat steps 1 through 4 for this alternate design.

2 Employee Payroll Calculation

You want to develop an application that computes an employee's weekly pay based on a standard salary plus overtime pay. Overtime pay is computed as 5% of weekly pay multiplied by the number of overtime hours worked.

Build an application with a user interface that resembles the one shown in Figure 3-82.

1. Design the application on paper based on the methods you learned in this chapter.

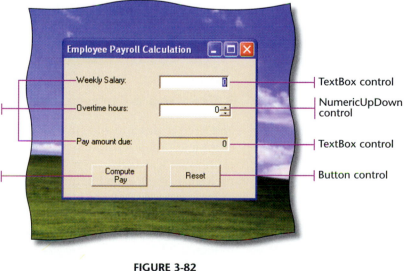

FIGURE 3-82

(continued)

2 Employee Payroll Calculation (*continued*)

2. Start a new project in Visual Basic .NET using the Windows Application template. Create the application in the Chapter3 folder of the Data Disk and name the project, Employee Payroll Calculation.

3. Add three Label controls, two TextBox controls, a NumericUpDown control, and two Button controls to the form.

4. Position, align, and size the controls appropriately, as shown in Figure 3-82 on the previous page.

5. Change the form's Text property value to Employee Payroll Calculation, the FormBorderStyle property value to FixedDialog, and the StartPosition property value to CenterScreen.

6. Change the Text property value of the Label and Button controls as follows:

Label1 control	`Weekly Salary:`
Label2 control	`Overtime hours:`
Label3 control	`Pay amount due:`
Button1 control	`Convert`
Button2 control	`Reset`

7. Change the property values of the TextBox and NumericUpDown controls to set the initial display value to 0. Change the Name properties of the input and output controls to assign appropriate control names. Modify the TabStop, TabIndex, and ReadOnly properties, as necessary. The NumericUpDown control should have a Maximum value of 100, a Minimum value of 0, and an Increment value of 1.

8. Open the code window for the Compute Pay Button control and enter the code to make the computation. Insert appropriate comments for the project and the event procedure. The appropriate formula is PayAmount = Weekly Salary + .05 × Weekly Salary × Overtime Hours.

9. Return to the Form1.vb form and then open the code window for the Reset button control. Enter code in the event procedure that resets the input and output controls to display 0. Return to the Form1.vb form.

10. Save the project and then run the application to make certain no errors exist. If any errors are encountered, correct them, and save the form and the project again.

11. Print the form and all of the code for the project.

3 Creating a Currency Converter

You need to develop an application that can display the value of U.S. dollars in euros and pounds, based on changing currency exchange rates. Create an application that will allow a user to enter an amount in U.S. dollars and then calculate the values in euros and pounds. The exchange rates should default to the values shown in Figure 3-83, and the user should be able to vary the rates from .5 to 3 in increments of .01.

Perform the following tasks to build an application similar to the one shown in Figure 3-83.

1. Design the application on paper based on the methods you learned in this chapter.

2. Start a new Windows Application project in Visual Basic .NET. Create the application in the Chapter3 folder of the Data Disk and name the project, Currency Converter.

3. Set the title to display on the title bar of the form to Currency Converter.

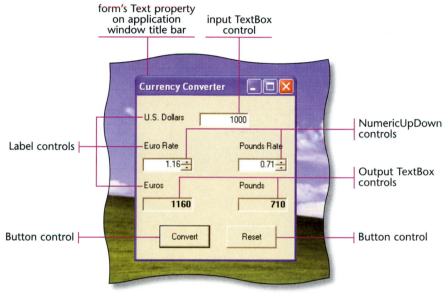

FIGURE 3-83

4. Place Label controls on the form to display the words U.S. Dollars, Euro Rate, Pounds Rate, Euros, and Pounds.

5. Set the form to be centered on the desktop when the application runs and do not allow the user to size the window during run time. (*Hint*: Use the StartPosition and FormBorderStyle properties.)

6. Add one TextBox control for input, two TextBox controls for output, and two NumericUpDown controls for input. Add two Button controls.

7. Set the Name property for all input, output, and Button controls. Set a Minimum, Maximum, and Increment for the NumericUpDown control. Set the DecimalPlaces property on the NumericUpDown controls to 2. Set defaults of 0 for the TextBox controls, 1.16 for the euro NumericUpDown control exchange rate, and .71 for the pounds NumericUpDown control exchange rate. Set the Text property of each Button control, as indicated in Figure 3-83. If necessary, set the text in the TextBox and NumericUpDown controls to display right-aligned. Modify the TabStop, TabIndex, and ReadOnly properties as necessary.

8. Write the code to display the result of calculations in the output TextBox controls. The calculation for each result is the amount in U.S. dollars multiplied by the exchange rate. Make sure the Reset button sets the exchange rates to the default, rather than 0. Be sure to add a comment header and appropriate comments to your code.

9. Save the project and then run the application to make certain no errors exist. If any errors are encountered, correct them, and save the form and the project again.

10. Print the form and all of the code for the project.

4 Maturity Calculator

You are planning to invest money and would like to know what your investment will be worth within a specified period. You have decided to develop an application similar to the one shown in Figure 3-84 that will allow entry of different amounts, different annual interest rates, and different number of years. This will aid you in determining how much you would like to invest. When a button is clicked, the application displays the maturity value of the investment based on quarterly compounding.

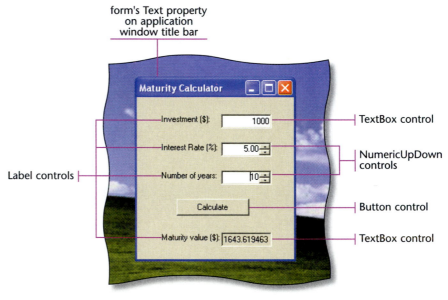

FIGURE 3-84

Perform the following tasks to build the application.

1. Design the application on paper based on the methods you learned in this chapter.

2. Open a new Windows Application project in Visual Basic .NET. Create the application in the Chapter3 folder of the Data Disk and name the project, Maturity Calculator.

3. Change the form title to Maturity Calculator. Set the form to be centered in the application window during run time and do not allow the user to size the form at run time.

4. Add four Label controls, two TextBox controls, two NumericUpDown controls, and one Button control to the form.

5. Position and size the controls as shown in Figure 3-84. Set the Text property of all the Label controls as shown in Figure 3-84.

6. Set the Text properties of the input and output TextBox controls to 0. Make the numbers appear right-justified in the boxes.

7. For the Interest Rate (%) NumericUpDown control, set the DecimalPlaces property to 2, set the range of allowed values from 3 to 8, set the increment to allow the user to increment the value by .01, and right-justify the value in the control.

8. For the Number of years NumericUpDown control, set the range of allowed values from 2 to 30, set the increment to allow the user to increment the value by 1, and right-justify the value in the control.

9. Make the Maturity value ($) output TextBox control read-only by setting its ReadOnly property to True.

10. Set TabStop and TabIndex properties appropriately for input controls and the Button control.

11. Rename the input and output controls using the following names: txtInvestment, nudInterestRate, nudYears, btnCalculate, and txtValue.

12. Write the Click event for the Button control. *Hint:* For the btnCalculate button Click event, type the following code statement:

```
txtValue.Text = txtInvestment.Text * (1 + nudInterestRate.Value / 400) ^ (4 * nudYears.Value)
```

13. Save the project and then run the application to make certain no errors exist. If any errors are encountered, correct them, and save the form and the project again.

14. Print the form and all of the code for the project.

5 Miles per Gallon Computation

The supervisor of Maria's Limousine maintenance department has asked you to develop an application to help prevent maintenance problems. At the end of each shift, drivers submit mileage and the amount of gas used for the day's trips. The supervisor would like you to develop an application that will take this information and compute the miles per gallon for the limousine for the shift. She can then take the information and compare it with historical values to see if the data is within an acceptable range.

6 Sales Tax Computation

Stan's Subs would like an application that calculates the sales tax for the front counter employees. The application should let the employee enter the amount of the customer's order and then calculate a 4% sales tax. When the employee clicks the Calculate button, the application should display the amount of the customer's order, the tax, and the total of the customer's order and tax added together.

7 Metric Conversion

As a part-time worker at McIntyre's Hardware store, you have been asked to use your Visual Basic .NET skills to assist with some routine calculations. Your first project is to develop an application for the Paint department to convert liters to pints and gallons. Use the knowledge gained in this chapter to develop an application to perform this calculation.

8 Calories Computation

Union Cafeteria has asked you to develop an application for determining the calorie count in an entrée. Based on the ingredients, the chef knows total number of grams of protein, fat, and carbohydrates for a recipe. There are four calories in a gram of protein, four calories in a gram of carbohydrates, and nine calories in a gram of fat. Create an application that will take the number of grams of each and then display the total calories when the user clicks a Compute Calories button.

9 Computing an Average

An instructor has asked you to develop a Visual Basic .NET application that takes four test scores and computes an average. The scores can range from 50 to 100. Use NumericUpDown controls to input the scores, and a ReadOnly TextBox control to display the result. As the value changes in the NumericUpDown control, change the average using the OnChange event of the NumericUpDown control. Use Visual Basic .NET Help for more information about the OnChange event. Include only one button for allowing scores to be reset to their default value of 100.

10 Rule-of-Thumb Calculation

Your friend is a tailor and performs rule-of-thumb calculations of various types to compute measurements of male customers. These rules are: Neck Size = 3 × (Weight / Waistline), Hat Size = (3 × Weight) / (2.125 × Waistline), and Shoe Size = 50 × (Waistline / Weight). He has asked you to create an application that will accept the required inputs, perform the various calculations, and output the results. Use the / (forward slash) to indicate arithmetic division in the code.

11 Computing Financial Ratios

As an intern at a financial services company, you have been asked to develop an application that computes several fundamental financial ratios based on readily available financial data. Ratios are the result of one financial value divided by another financial value. The equations for the required ratios are: Price earnings ratio = Market price per share / Earnings per share, Dividend payout ratio = Dividends per share / Earnings per share, and Dividend yield ratio = Dividends per share / Market price per share. The three inputs required are Market price per share, Earnings per share, and Dividends per share. Develop an application that accepts the necessary inputs, and then displays the ratios. Use the / (forward slash) to indicate arithmetic division in the code. Include a Reset button to set the values back to 0 in the window. Use at least one TextBox and at least one NumericUpDown control in the application.

4

Working with Variables, Constants, Data Types, and Expressions

Objectives

You will have
mastered the material in
this chapter when you can:

- Use the RadioButton and GroupBox controls
- Use the Layout toolbar to size and align controls
- Set a default button on a form
- Lock controls on a form
- Declare variables and constants
- Use variables and constants within code
- Describe Visual Basic .NET data types
- Convert between data types
- Code a form Load event procedure
- Use the Option Strict statement
- Use arithmetic expressions
- Describe the order of operator precedence in code
- Use the Pmt function
- Use the Format$ function

Introduction

Visual Basic .NET provides a variety of tools and constructs, such as controls, data types, and code structures, to help Visual Basic .NET programmers build Windows-based applications quickly and easily. This chapter concentrates on using these tools and constructs to develop the Windows application shown in Figure 4-1. The application uses two new controls: the GroupBox and the RadioButton. You will learn about the different types of variables and constants in Visual Basic .NET. You also will learn how to write code that performs mathematical operations. Finally, you will use some of the built-in functions that are supplied by Visual Basic .NET.

Chapter Four — Calculating Automobile Loan Payments

The Windows application developed in this chapter is the Automobile Loan Calculator, which calculates a customer's monthly automobile loan payment based on a loan amount, interest rate, and the term, or length, of the loan (Figure 4-1). To calculate a monthly payment, the user first enters the customer's desired loan amount in the Loan amount box. Next, the user selects an interest rate using the Current interest rate (%) box and then clicks an option button in the Years in loan area to select the term for the loan.

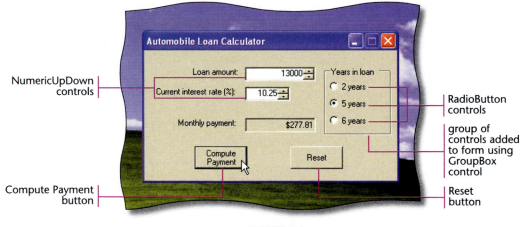

FIGURE 4-1

When the user clicks the Compute Payment button, the application first converts the user input data into values it can use in an equation. The application then computes and displays the monthly loan payment in the Monthly payment text box. The dealership currently extends loan amounts between $0 and $25,000, inclusive.

The calculation used to compute the monthly payment is represented by the following formula:

MonthlyPayment = (InterestRate × (1 + InterestRate) ^ NumberofPayments) / ((1 + InterestRate) ^ NumberofPayments − 1) × LoanAmount where NumberofPayments is the number of months that the customer will have the loan, or 12 times the number selected in the Years in loan area. InterestRate is a monthly rate, which is determined by dividing the yearly Current interest rate by 12. The ^ symbol indicates that a number should be raised to a power using an exponent. For example, x^2 means x^2 and (1 + InterestRate) ^ NumberofPayments means $(1 + \text{InterestRate})^{\text{NumberofPayments}}$. When the user clicks the Reset button, the Loan amount is set to 0, the Current interest rate (%) is set to 5.00, the Years in loan is set to 5 years, and the Monthly payment is set to $0.00.

Program Development

The development cycle for the Automobile Loan Calculator application consists of tasks that correspond to the six development cycle phases, as shown in Table 4-1.

Table 4-1 Automobile Loan Calculator Application Development Tasks

DEVELOPMENT PHASE	TASK NUMBER	TASK NAME	TASK
Analyze requirements	1	Analyze problem	Analyze the automobile loan calculator problem.
Design solution	2	Design interface	Design the user interface for the application, including input areas, output areas, and form controls.
	3	Design program	Design the logic for the code and write pseudocode.
Validate design	4	Validate design	Prove that the solution produces correct results for the automobile loan calculator program.
Implement design	5	Develop interface	Add user interface elements, such as input areas, output areas, and Button controls on a form.
	6	Write code	Write code to add event procedures for the buttons; add comment statements in code.
Test solution	7	Test	Test the application.
	8	Debug	Fix any problems with the application.
Document solution	9	Document	Print the program.

Analysis and Design

Figure 4-2 on the next page shows the requirements document that initiates the development cycle for the Automobile Loan Calculator application. The document shows the algorithm used to compute a monthly payment based on a loan amount, monthly interest rate, and the number of monthly payments to pay back the loan.

REQUEST FOR NEW APPLICATION

Date submitted:	September 15, 2004
Submitted by:	Steven Wang
Purpose:	Sales representatives often are asked to make quick estimates of monthly payments for customers who may take out a loan for an automobile purchase. Sales representatives would like an easy-to-use application that calculates monthly payments based on the loan amount, interest rate, and length of loan.
Application title:	Automobile Loan Calculator
Algorithms:	A monthly payment is calculated as follows: *MonthlyPayment = (InterestRate x (1 + InterestRate) ^ NumberofPayments) / ((1 + InterestRate) ^ NumberofPayments – 1) x LoanAmount* The *InterestRate* is a monthly interest rate (annual rate / 12). The *NumberofPayments* is the number of years for the loan x 12.
Notes:	1) Sales representatives are accustomed to the following terminology: ***Loan amount***, ***Current interest rate***, and ***Monthly payment.*** 2) The application should allow the user to enter values for the loan amount, current interest rate, and length of loan in years so the monthly payment can be computed. Loan amounts typically are incremented by amounts of $1000. Interest rates typically are incremented by values of .05%. 3) The general loan program only allows loans to be 2 years, 5 years, or 6 years. 4) At this time, users can obtain loans for a minimum amount of $0 and a maximum of $25,000, inclusive. This may change every few months, however. 5) The application also should allow the user to reset values for Loan amount and Monthly payment to zero (0) so that another calculation can be performed. Years in loan should be set to 5, which is the most common length of a loan. The interest rate should be reset to 5.0% because interest rates do not go below this in our general loan program. 6) The computation should be designated by the term, Compute Payment. The reset of the values should be designated by the term, Reset.

Approvals

Approval Status:	X	Approved
		Rejected
Approved by:	Lillian Bukiet	
Date:	September 17, 2004	
Assigned to:	J. Quasney, Programmer	

FIGURE 4-2

PROBLEM ANALYSIS The problem that the Automobile Loan Calculator application should solve is the calculation of a monthly payment for a customer based on the loan amount requested by the customer, the current interest rate, and the length of the loan. To complete the calculation and generate results, or output, for the user, the Automobile Loan Calculator application requires the user to input three values: Loan amount, Current interest rate, and Years in loan.

As stated in the formula of the requirements document in Figure 4-2, the application uses the following formula:

$$\text{MonthlyPayment} = (\text{InterestRate} \times (1 + \text{InterestRate}) \wedge \text{NumberofPayments}) \, / \\ ((1 + \text{InterestRate}) \wedge \text{NumberofPayments} - 1) \times \text{LoanAmount}$$

to calculate the customer's monthly loan payment. The formula requires three inputs to complete one calculation and generate one output. The first input, loan amount, is represented by LoanAmount in the formula. The second input, Current interest rate, is a yearly interest rate. This input is divided by 12 to determine the monthly interest rate. The monthly interest rate is represented by InterestRate in the formula. The third input, Years in loan, is multiplied by 12 and represented by NumberofPayments in the formula. The application uses these inputs to calculate the output, monthly payment, which is represented by MonthlyPayment in the formula.

As indicated in the requirements document, the application also must provide a way to reset input and output values back to initial values, so that a user can calculate the monthly payment for another loan scenario. To reset these values, the application uses the formulas

LoanAmount = 0
Rate = 5
NumberofYears = 5
MonthlyPayment = $0.00

to tell the application to set the inputs — Loan amount (LoanAmount), Current interest rate (Rate), and Number of years (NumberofYears) and the output — Monthly payment (MonthlyPayment), back to the original values. Each element of the formula corresponds to an element in the requirements document.

INTERFACE DESIGN   The requirements for the application specify several input and output controls that should fit easily on a small form. The loan amount and interest rate inputs meet the criteria for a NumericUpDown control. As you learned in Chapter 3, a NumericUpDown control is used to display or allow users to enter numbers on a form. The up and down arrows increment and decrement the displayed value within a predefined range. If the user enters a number outside of the range, the control changes the number to the closest allowable value within the predefined range. As defined in the requirements document (Figure 4-2), the NumericUpDown control used to enter Loan amount should be set to increment or decrement by $1,000. The maximum value allowed in the NumericUpDown control — in this case, $25,000 — will be set by an event procedure that assigns a maximum value to the Maximum property of the Loan amount NumericUpDown control (Figure 4-3 on the next page). The NumericUpDown control used to enter Current interest rate will be set to increment or decrement by .05 with a minimum value of 5.00% and a maximum value of 15.00%. The output value meets the requirements for a read-only TextBox control. The output value in the TextBox control should be formatted as currency.

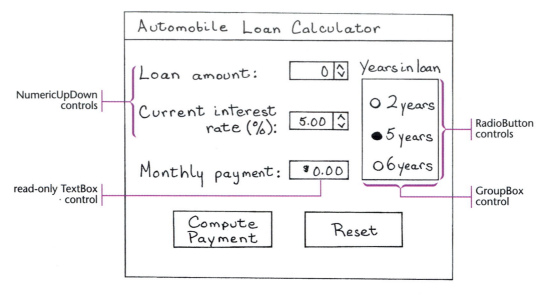

FIGURE 4-3

The application also must give users a way to select one of three options for the number of years for a loan. RadioButton controls, which are commonly called option buttons, allow a user to select one of several mutually exclusive, predefined values. The option buttons on the form are drawn with a box around them to indicate that they are grouped together. In the Automobile Loan Calculator application, three option buttons are grouped together as choices for Years in loan. To meet the specifications in the requirements document, the user can select 2 years, 5 years, or 6 years — the three types of loans allowed in the general loan program. The two actions listed in the requirements document — compute and reset — are designated by two Button controls at the bottom of the form.

PROGRAM DESIGN   The two program tasks include (1) calculating the monthly loan payment using the formula

MonthlyPayment = (InterestRate × (1 + InterestRate) ^ NumberofPayments) /
((1 + InterestRate) ^ NumberofPayments – 1) × LoanAmount

and (2) resetting the input and output values back to their original values, so the user can perform the calculation again using different input values. The user can execute these tasks by clicking the Compute Payment button or the Reset button on the user interface.

Figure 4-4 shows the pseudocode that represents the logic of the requirements. Table 4-2 outlines the event procedures defined in the pseudocode, along with the events that trigger the procedures and the actions performed by each.

Visual Basic .NET includes several built-in coding shortcuts, called functions. Some of these functions perform common financial calculations without the need to code a formula. The Visual Basic .NET Pmt function performs the same calculation shown in the pseudocode for the Compute Payment Click Event. The built-in functions remove some of the complexity of the code. They also reduce the probability of making a mistake when coding a complex formula. When the Compute Payment Click Event is coded, the Pmt function will be used to perform the calculation shown in the pseudocode.

Form Load Event
      LoanAmount.Maximum = MaximumLoanAllowed
End

Reset Button Click
      LoanAmount = 0
      InterestRate = 5%
      YearsInLoan = 5
      MonthlyPayment = 0
End

2-Years Click Event
      NumberOfPayments = 24
End

5-Years Click Event
      NumberOfPayments = 60
End

6-Years Click Event
      NumberOfPayments = 72
End

Compute Payment Click Event
      MonthlyPayment = (InterestRate X (1 + InterestRate) ^ NumberOfPayments) / ((1 + InterestRate) ^ NumberOfPayments – 1) X LoanAmount
      Display MonthlyPayment
End

FIGURE 4-4

Table 4-2   Automobile Loan Calculator Event Procedures

EVENT PROCEDURE	EVENT	ACTION PERFORMED
Form Load	Form load event executes when user starts the application	Sets the maximum value allowed in the Loan amount NumericUpDown control
Reset Button Click	Click event executes when user clicks the Reset button	Resets the input and output values to original states
2-Years Click	Click event executes when user clicks the corresponding 2 years option button	Sets the NumberofPayments to 24 months (2 years, 12 months per year)
5-Years Click	Click event executes when user clicks the corresponding 5 years option button	Sets the NumberofPayments to 60 months (5 years, 12 months per year)
6-Years Click	Click event executes when user clicks the corresponding 6 years option button	Sets the NumberofPayments to 72 months (6 years, 12 months per year)
Compute Payment Click	Click event executes when user clicks the Compute Payment button	Performs the calculation in the requirements document to calculate and then display the monthly payment

VALIDATE DESIGN   You can validate the program design by stepping through the requirements and making sure that the design addresses each requirement. The formula in the Algorithms section of the requirements document is handled in the design by the Computer Payment Click event (Figure 4-4 on the previous page). The items in the first note in the Notes section are shown as requested on the storyboard (Figure 4-3 on page VB 4.06). The requirements in the second and third notes also are handled on the storyboard by appropriate controls. The requirement in the fourth note is handled in the Form Load Event in the pseudocode by assigning a maximum value to the Maximum property of the Loan amount NumericUpDown control. The requirements of the fifth and sixth notes are met by the two buttons and the associated pseudocode.

As shown in Table 4-1 on page VB 4.03, after validating the program design, the next phase in the development cycle is to develop the user interface of the application using Visual Basic .NET.

Starting the Project and Creating the User Interface

The Automobile Loan Calculator application is a Windows application with a graphical user interface for user input and output display. The application is based on the Windows Application template provided by Visual Basic .NET. The following steps start Visual Basic .NET and start a new project using the Windows Application template.

To Start Visual Basic .NET and Start a New Project

1. Start Visual Basic .NET. When the Start Page displays, click the New Project button on the Start Page.

2. When the New Project dialog box displays, if necessary, click Create directory for Solution. Double-click the text, WindowsApplication1, in the Name box. Type Automobile Loan Calculator in the Name box.

The new project name displays in the Name box, and the solution name displays in the New Solution Name box. Because the Create directory for Solution check box is selected, Visual Basic .NET will create a subdirectory with the same name as the project when it creates the project.

3. Click the Browse button. If necessary, click 3½ Floppy (A:) in the Look in box. Click Chapter4 and then click the Open button.

4. Click the OK button. After the new Automobile Loan Calculator project is created, if necessary, click the Maximize button on the Visual Basic .NET window title bar to maximize the Visual Basic .NET window. If necessary, close the Output window.

Visual Basic .NET creates the new Automobile Loan Calculator solution and project. Visual Basic .NET creates an initial form and displays it in the main work area.

After Visual Basic .NET creates the new project, the solution and project name, Automobile Loan Calculator, display in the Solution Explorer window. Form1.vb is selected in the Solution Explorer window to indicate that the Form1.vb tab is selected in the main work area. The Properties window displays information about Form1.vb.

Setting Form Properties and Adding Controls

The next step is to set the properties of the Form1 form and add controls to the form to create the user interface. Several of the property values of the Form1 form must be changed. Table 4-3 lists the Form1 form property value changes that need to be made.

Table 4-3   Form1 Form Property Values for the Automobile Loan Calculator Application

PROPERTY	VALUE	EFFECT
Size: Width	360	Sets the width of the form in pixels
Size: Height	216	Sets the height of the form in pixels
FormBorderStyle	FixedDialog	Disallows resizing of the window at run time
StartPosition	CenterScreen	Causes the form to display in the center of the user's screen at the start of run time
MaximizeBox	False	Disables the Maximize button on the window's title bar at run time
Text	Automobile Loan Calculator	Sets the value of the window on the title bar

The user interface design also specifies that the Form1 form should include the following controls: three Label controls, two NumericUpDown controls, one TextBox control, two Button controls, a GroupBox control, and three RadioButton controls. Perform the steps on the next page to add the Label, NumericUpDown, TextBox, and Button controls by drawing them on the form.

To Set Form Properties and Add Controls

1. Select Form1 in the main work area. Set the properties of Form1 as specified in Table 4-3 on the previous page.

The form displays as shown in Figure 4-5. The Maximize button on the form title bar is inactive. The form is properly sized and the form title is set.

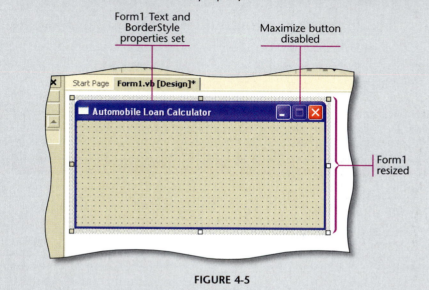

FIGURE 4-5

2. Add three Label controls, two NumericUpDown controls, one TextBox control, and two Button controls by selecting the appropriate control in the Toolbox window and drawing the control on Form1, as shown in Figure 4-6. These controls will be positioned precisely later in this chapter.

Three Label controls, two NumericUpDown controls, one TextBox control, and two Button controls display on the form (Figure 4-6).

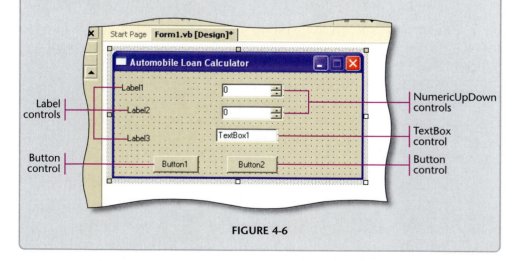

FIGURE 4-6

Adding a GroupBox Control to a Form

A **GroupBox control** is used as a container for other controls, as shown in Figure 4-1 on page VB 4.02. A **container control** serves as a holding area for other controls, indicating that the controls within the container are somehow related. In this application, the GroupBox control will serve as a container control for the three RadioButton controls.

When you draw the GroupBox control, the center of the GroupBox control displays with a positioning grid inside of it on the form so you can draw and position other controls inside the GroupBox control.

To Add a GroupBox Control to a Form

1. Add the GroupBox control by clicking the GroupBox button in the Toolbox window and drawing the GroupBox1 control on Form1, as shown in Figure 4-7.

The GroupBox1 control contains a positioning grid and has a thin border to indicate its size and location. The control name, GroupBox1, displays on top of the control (Figure 4-7).

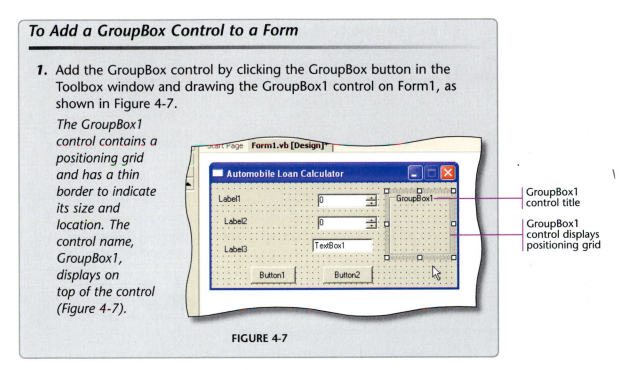

FIGURE 4-7

As shown in Figure 4-7, the default GroupBox control name, GroupBox1, displays on top of the control. You can change the control name by changing the value of the Text property to indicate the function of the controls it contains. The center of the GroupBox control contains a positioning grid so other controls can be drawn and positioned inside the GroupBox control. In the case of the GroupBox1 control, the RadioButton controls that indicate the length of the loan in years will be drawn and positioned inside the control (Figure 4-1 on page VB 4.02). When you add controls by drawing them inside a GroupBox control, dragging the GroupBox control to a new position also repositions the controls contained inside the GroupBox control.

Using Container Controls

Container controls are used to serve as a holding area for other controls, indicating that the controls within the container are related.

Adding RadioButton Controls to Create a Group of Controls

The **RadioButton control** presents a set of choices, such as the number of years in a loan (Figure 4-1 on page VB 4.02). RadioButton controls are placed in **groups** that permit the user to make only one selection from a group of RadioButton controls, such as the number of years. For a RadioButton to be part of a group, it must be added directly inside the GroupBox control that serves as a container.

RadioButton Control

Use the RadioButton control to present a set of choices from which a user is permitted to make only one selection.

Adding a RadioButton Control to a Group

For a RadioButton to be part of a group, you must add it directly inside the GroupBox control that serves as a container.

The Automobile Loan Calculator offers three options for the number of years in a loan (2, 5, or 6). Perform the following steps to create a group of three RadioButton controls within the GroupBox1 control.

To Add RadioButton Controls to Create a Group of Controls

1. Drag the RadioButton button from the Toolbox window to the top of the GroupBox1 control. Be sure to release the mouse button while the mouse pointer is positioned within the borders of the GroupBox1 control.

A RadioButton control is added inside the GroupBox1 control (Figure 4-8).

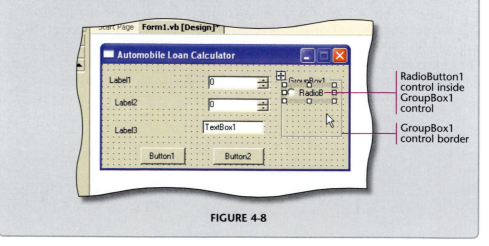

FIGURE 4-8

2. Repeat Step 1 two more times to place two more RadioButton controls inside the GroupBox1 control. Position the controls as shown in Figure 4-9.

The three RadioButton controls form a group of controls inside the GroupBox1 control (Figure 4-9).

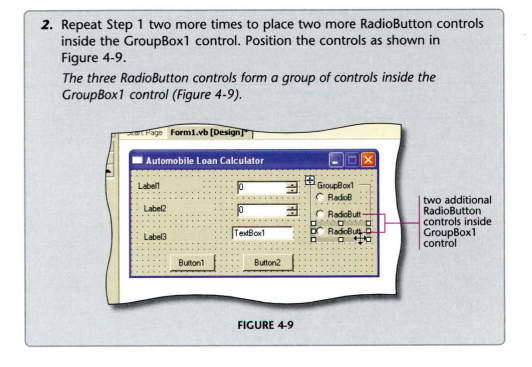

FIGURE 4-9

The RadioButton controls were added to the form inside the GroupBox control in order to form a RadioButton group. When several RadioButton controls display in a group, only one of the RadioButton controls can be checked at any time. You do not need to write code to enforce this rule. The controls automatically enforce this rule. You can create multiple groups of RadioButton controls by adding additional container controls to the form for each RadioButton group. If the RadioButton controls on a form are not placed inside one or more container controls, all of the RadioButton controls function as one group and only one can be selected at a time.

Changing Control Properties

Several of the items listed in the requirements document for the Automobile Loan Calculator application (Figure 4-2 on page VB 4.04) require you to change the default property values for the controls. Table 4-4 on the next page lists property values for the Label, NumericUpDown, TextBox, and Button controls that must be set to meet these requirements.

Table 4-4 *Control Property Values for the Automobile Loan Calculator Application*

CONTROL	PROPERTY	VALUE	EFFECT
Label1	Text	Loan amount:	Sets Loan amount: to display as the initial value in the control at run time
	TextAlign	TopRight	Causes the text in the label to align to the right side of the control
·Label2	Text	Current interest rate (%):	Sets Current interest rate (%): to display as the initial value in the control at run time
	TextAlign	TopRight	Causes the text in the label to align to the right side of the control
Label3	Text	Monthly payment:	Sets Monthly payment: to display as the initial value in the control at run time
	TextAlign	TopRight	Causes the text in the label to align to the right side of the control
NumericUpDown1	Name	nudLoanAmount	Changes control's name to a descriptive name
	Increment	1000	Causes the value in the control to increment or decrement by 1,000 when the up or down arrows are clicked
	TabIndex	0	Causes this control to be the first control on the form to receive focus
	TextAlign	Right	Sets text to display right-aligned in the control
NumericUpDown2	Name	nudRate	Changes control's name to a descriptive name
	DecimalPlaces	2	Sets the number of decimal places of the value to display in the control
	Increment	.05	Causes the value in the control to increment or decrement by .05 when the up or down arrows are clicked
	Maximum	15	Defines the highest value allowed in the control
	Minimum	5	Defines the lowest value allowed in the control
	TabIndex	1	Causes this control to be the second control on the form to receive focus
	TextAlign	Right	Sets text to display right-aligned in the control
	Value	5	Sets 5 to display as the initial value in the control at run time
TextBox1	Name	txtMonthlyPayment	Changes control's name to a descriptive name
	ReadOnly	True	Disallows the user from entering a value in the control at run time
	Text	$0.00	Sets $0.00 to display as the initial value in the control at run time
	TextAlign	Right	Sets text to display right-aligned in the control
Button1	Text	Compute Payment	Sets the text that displays on the button face to Compute Payment
	TabIndex	3	Causes this control to be the fourth control on the form to receive focus

Table 4-4   Control Property Values for the Automobile Loan Calculator Application (continued)

CONTROL	PROPERTY	VALUE	EFFECT
	Name	btnComputePayment	Changes control's name to a descriptive name
Button2	Text	Reset	Sets the text that displays on the button face to Reset
	TabIndex	4	Causes this control to be the fifth control on the form to receive focus
	Name	btnReset	Changes control's name to a descriptive name

The following step sets the property values of the Label controls, NumericUpDown controls, TextBox control, and Button controls on the Form1 form. Size and Position properties will be set later in this chapter.

To Change Properties of Controls

1. Change the property values of the three Label controls, two NumericUpDown controls, one TextBox control, and two Button controls, as listed in Table 4-4.

The controls display on Form1 as shown in Figure 4-10.

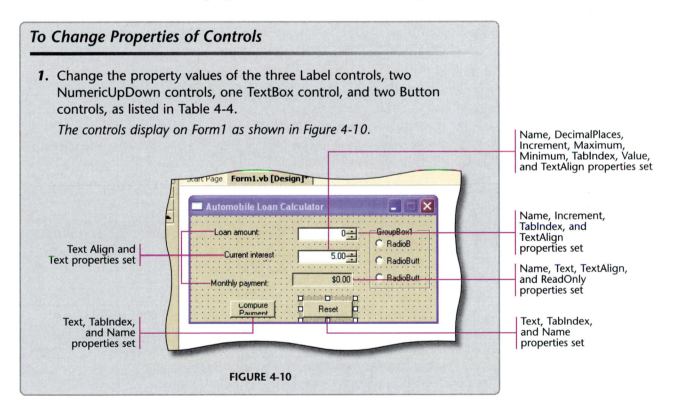

FIGURE 4-10

Recall that the NumericUpDown control allows the user to change the value displayed in the control by clicking the arrows or typing a value in the control. With the Increment property value for the nudLoanAmount control to 1000, the application will only allow a user to enter a Loan amount in increments of $1,000 dollars, by clicking the up and down arrows or typing a value. The DecimalPlaces and Value property values set for the nudRate control ensure that the Current interest rate (%) displays to the user with two decimal places and an initial value of 5.00. The values set for the Increment, Maximum, and Minimum properties only allow a user to input a Current interest rate (%) in increments of .05%, with a minimum value of 5.00% and a maximum value of 15.00%.

NumericUpDown Control
Use the NumericUpDown control to allow the user to enter numbers on a form by clicking the up and down arrows or by typing.

GroupBox Control Properties

The GroupBox control is used as a container for other controls. The GroupBox control has several properties that relate to its appearance.

- A GroupBox control can have only a rectangular shape.
- A GroupBox control can have a label, indicated by its Text property value.
- When RadioButton controls are added inside a GroupBox control, only one can be selected during run time.

In general, you do not name GroupBox controls because they seldom are referenced in code. If you do name a GroupBox control, however, use the grp prefix in the name. Table 4-5 lists the common properties of the GroupBox control.

Naming GroupBox Controls
When naming GroupBox controls, use the grp prefix for the name.

Table 4-5   *GroupBox Control Properties*

CATEGORY	PROPERTY	DESCRIPTION	PROPERTY VALUES
Appearance	FlatStyle	Determines the 3D appearance of the control	Flat Popup **Standard** System
	Text	Indicates the label to display on the upper-left edge of the control	Any value, or set blank if no label is desired.
Design	GridSize: Width and Gridsize: Height	Determines the size of the positioning grid within the control	Width and Height properties can be any positive whole number (**8, 8**).

Table 4-6 lists the two GroupBox control property values — Text and TabIndex — that must be changed for the Automobile Loan Calculator application.

Table 4-6 *GroupBox Control Property Values for the Automobile Loan*
Calculator Application

CONTROL	PROPERTY	VALUE	EFFECT
GroupBox1	Text	Years in loan	Sets the caption of the control on the top-left side of the control
	TabIndex	2	Causes the first RadioButton in the GroupBox to be the third control on the form to receive focus

The following steps set the property values for the GroupBox control, as listed in Table 4-6.

To Change the Properties of a GroupBox Control

1. Click inside the GroupBox1 control, but not on one of the RadioButton controls in the GroupBox1 control. If the RadioButton controls obscure the inside of the GroupBox1 control, click the border of the GroupBox1 control to select it.

The GroupBox1 control is selected (Figure 4-11).

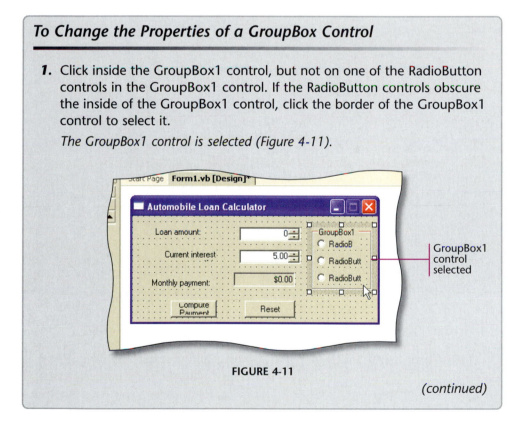

FIGURE 4-11

(continued)

2. Change the property values for the GroupBox1 control, as listed in Table 4-6.

The Text property of the GroupBox1 controls displays on top of the GroupBox1 control (Figure 4-12).

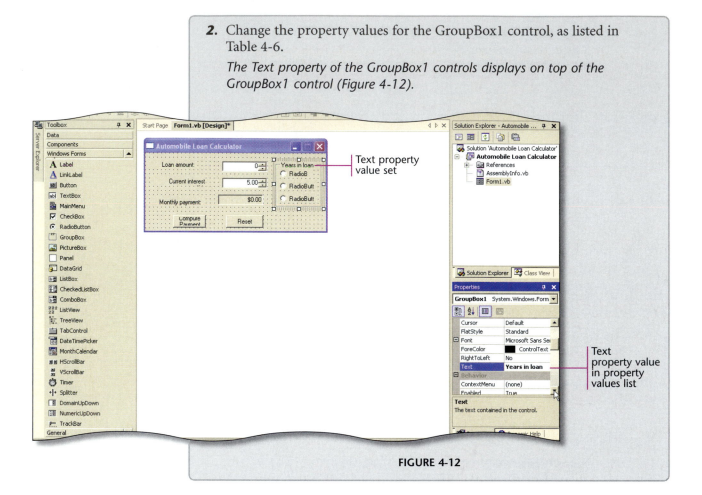

FIGURE 4-12

The GroupBox control now displays with a Years in loan label that describes the function of the RadioButton controls it contains. The next step is to set the properties of the RadioButton controls contained inside the GroupBox1 control.

RadioButton Control Properties

As you have learned, only one RadioButton control in a group of RadioButton controls may be selected at a time during run time or design time. The **Checked property** value determines which RadioButton control is selected. The Checked property can have the value of True or False. The True value indicates that the RadioButton control is selected, or checked; the False value indicates that the RadioButton control is not selected. The RadioButton control also has a property, CheckAlign, whose value defines on which side of the control the option button displays. When naming a RadioButton control using the Name property value, use the rad prefix in the name to indicate a RadioButton control. Table 4-7 lists the common RadioButton control properties.

Naming RadioButton Controls
When naming RadioButton controls, use the rad prefix for the name.

Table 4-7   RadioButton Control Properties

CATEGORY	PROPERTY	DESCRIPTION	PROPERTY VALUES
Appearance	CheckAlign	Determines the location of the check box inside the control map	Select a location from a pop-up graphical display. (**MiddleLeft**)
	Checked	Determines whether the RadioButton is selected (checked) or not	True **False**
	FlatStyle	Determines the 3D appearance of the control	Flat Popup **Standard** System
	Image	Sets an image to display on the visible portion of the Label control, along with the Text	Select a picture from the hard disk using a dialog box.
	ImageAlign	If the Image property is set, determines where the image displays	Select a location from a pop-up graphical display map. (**MiddleCenter**)
	Text	Defines the visible text that displays on the control	Any text with any character length.
Behavior	AutoCheck	Causes the RadioButton to change state automatically (value of Checked property) when clicked	**True** False

The requirements for the Automobile Loan Calculator application require that the Text property values for the three RadioButton controls are 2 years, 5 years, and 6 years, respectively (Table 4-8). The requirements document also specifies that 5 years is the default number of years for a loan, which means the RadioButton2 control (5 years) should be set to display initially as checked during run time.

Table 4-8   RadioButton Control Property Values for the Automobile Loan Calculator Application

CONTROL	PROPERTY	VALUE	EFFECT
RadioButton1	Name	radTwoYears	Changes control's name to a descriptive name
	TabIndex	0	Causes focus on this control first when the GroupBox1 control receives focus
	Text	2 years	Sets the value of the label next to the check box
RadioButton2	Name	radFiveYears	Changes control's name to a descriptive name
	TabIndex	1	Second control to receive focus after the TAB key is pressed in the GroupBox1 control
	Text	5 years	Sets the value of the label next to the check box
RadioButton3	Name	radSixYears	Changes control's name to a descriptive name
	TabIndex	2	Third control to receive focus after the TAB key is pressed in the GroupBox1 control
	Text	6 years	Sets the value of the label next to the check box

The following steps set the property values for the three RadioButton controls, as listed in Table 4-8 on the previous page.

To Change the Properties of RadioButton Controls

1. Select the RadioButton1 control. Change the property values for the RadioButton1 control, as listed in Table 4-8.

The Name, TabIndex, and Text property values of the control are set. The Text property, 2 years, displays in the control. The new name of the control is radTwoYears (Figure 4-13).

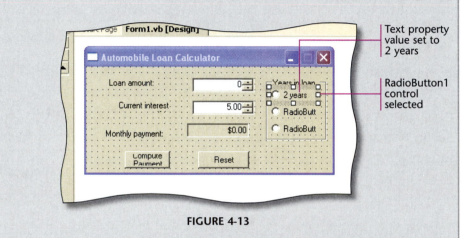

FIGURE 4-13

2. Select the RadioButton2 control. Change the property values for the RadioButton2 control, as listed in Table 4-8. Select the Checked property in the Properties window and then click the Checked property down arrow in the property values list.

The Name, TabIndex, and Text property values of the control are set. The Text property, 5 years, displays in the control. The new name of the control is radFiveYears. The Checked property is selected in the Properties window and the two possible Checked property values, True and False, display in the property values list (Figure 4-14).

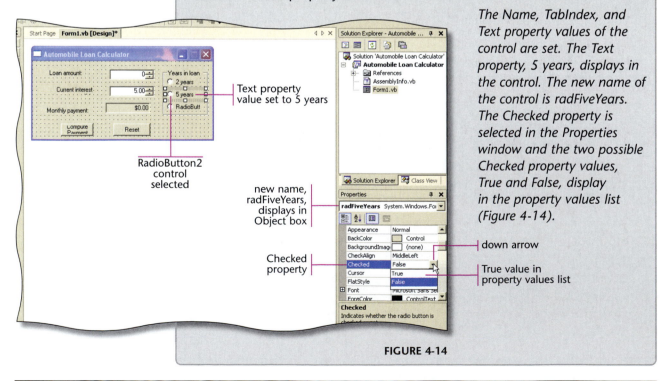

FIGURE 4-14

3. Click True in the Checked property values list.

The Checked property value is set to True, which sets the radFiveYears control to display as selected at run time (Figure 4-15). The filled circle in the radFiveYears control indicates that the control is selected.

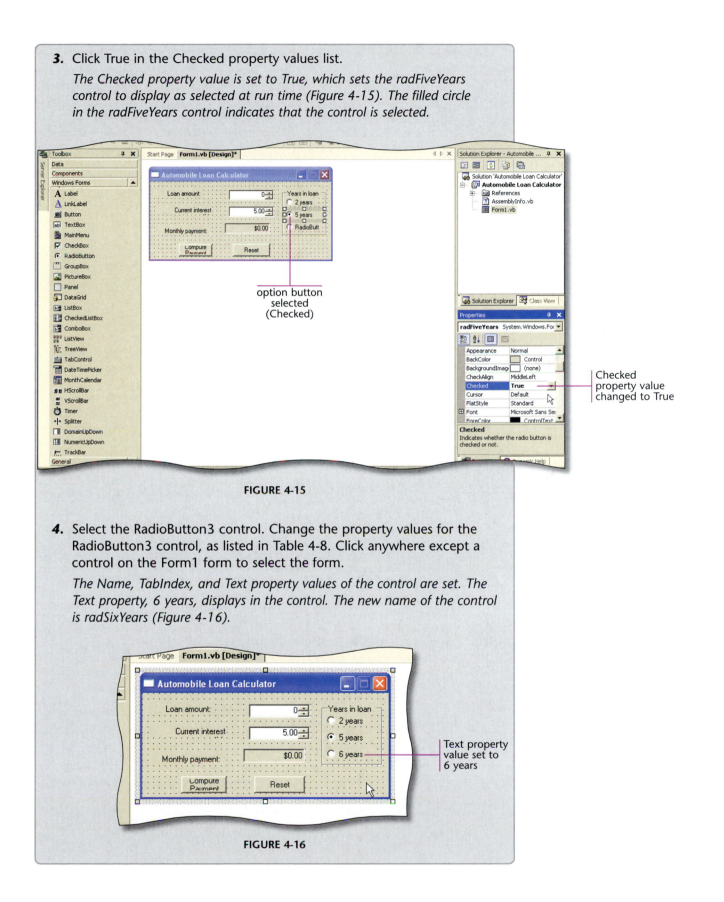

FIGURE 4-15

4. Select the RadioButton3 control. Change the property values for the RadioButton3 control, as listed in Table 4-8. Click anywhere except a control on the Form1 form to select the form.

The Name, TabIndex, and Text property values of the control are set. The Text property, 6 years, displays in the control. The new name of the control is radSixYears (Figure 4-16).

FIGURE 4-16

As soon as the Checked property value of the radFiveYears control is changed to True, the 5 years option button displays selected in the GroupBox1 control. With the exception of the size and position properties, all properties are now set for the form and controls. To complete the user interface, the next step is to size and position the controls correctly.

Using the Layout Toolbar

The Layout toolbar contains tools that allow you to adjust the alignment, spacing, and size of any group of controls on a form. The Layout toolbar includes buttons that map to all of the commands available on the Format menu. The Layout toolbar simplifies the task of changing Size and Position property values by allowing you to adjust two or more controls automatically until they are properly aligned, spaced, or sized.

Tip

Layout Toolbar
The Layout toolbar simplifies the task of changing Size and Position property values by allowing you to adjust two or more controls automatically until they are properly aligned, spaced, or sized.

Selecting Multiple Controls and Using the Align Rights Button

Before using the buttons on the Layout toolbar, you first select two or more controls on a form. You select two or more controls on a form by selecting the first control, holding down the CTRL key on the keyboard, and then selecting additional controls without releasing the CTRL key. When selecting multiple controls, Visual Basic .NET makes the sizing handles of the last control you select black.

Tip

Selecting Multiple Controls
You select two or more controls on a form by selecting the first control, holding down the CTRL key on the keyboard, and then selecting additional controls without releasing the CTRL key.

The following steps select the three Label controls used to label the NumericUpDown controls and the TextBox control and then align the right side of the three controls so that the right side of all three Label controls are vertically aligned.

To Select Multiple Controls and Use the Align Rights Button

1. Select the Label2 control, which has the Text property value of Current interest rate (%):.

The Label2 control is selected (Figure 4-17).

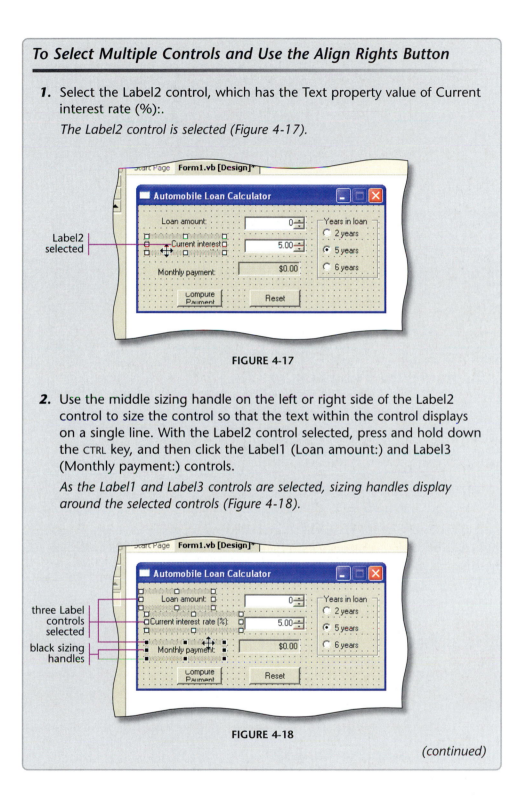

FIGURE 4-17

2. Use the middle sizing handle on the left or right side of the Label2 control to size the control so that the text within the control displays on a single line. With the Label2 control selected, press and hold down the CTRL key, and then click the Label1 (Loan amount:) and Label3 (Monthly payment:) controls.

As the Label1 and Label3 controls are selected, sizing handles display around the selected controls (Figure 4-18).

FIGURE 4-18

(continued)

3. Click the Align Rights button on the Layout toolbar and then click the Make Vertical Spacing Equal button on the Layout toolbar. If necessary, click one of the controls and move all of the controls together to align them as shown in Figure 4-19.

The right borders of the three Label controls are aligned (Figure 4-19). The controls are set to have equal vertical spacing.

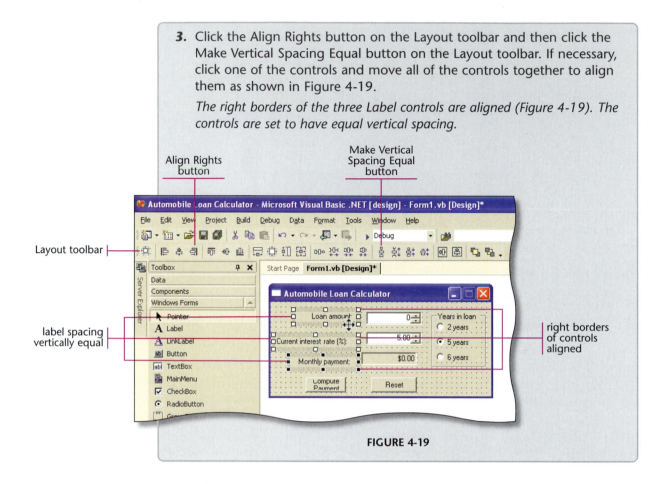

FIGURE 4-19

Clicking the Align Rights button changes the Position: Left property of the selected controls, so that the right sides of all of the controls are aligned with the right side of the last control you selected. The last control you select serves as the basis for aligning any additional controls you had already selected. This rule applies for all of the buttons on the Layout toolbar.

Sizing and Aligning Multiple Controls

When you select multiple controls and size and align the controls using the Layout toolbar, the last control you select serves as the basis for aligning the controls you subsequently select.

Sizing and Aligning Controls

When multiple controls used for input or output display in a column, it is good practice to size and align the controls together. You can use the Make Same Size button and Align Lefts button in conjunction to perform this task quickly. The following step sizes and aligns the input and output controls in the center of the form.

To Size and Align Input and Output Controls

1. Select the nudLoanAmount, nudRate, and txtMonthlyPayment controls by selecting one of the controls, holding down the CTRL key, and then selecting the other controls one at a time. Select the control which is best sized and positioned last, so that the other controls are sized and positioned based on that control. Click the Make Same Size button on the Layout toolbar and then click the Align Lefts button on the Layout toolbar. If the controls do not display as shown in Figure 4-20, then change the Height and Width property values in the property values list to 20 and 100, respectively, while the three controls are still selected.

The input and output controls are properly sized and aligned (Figure 4-20).

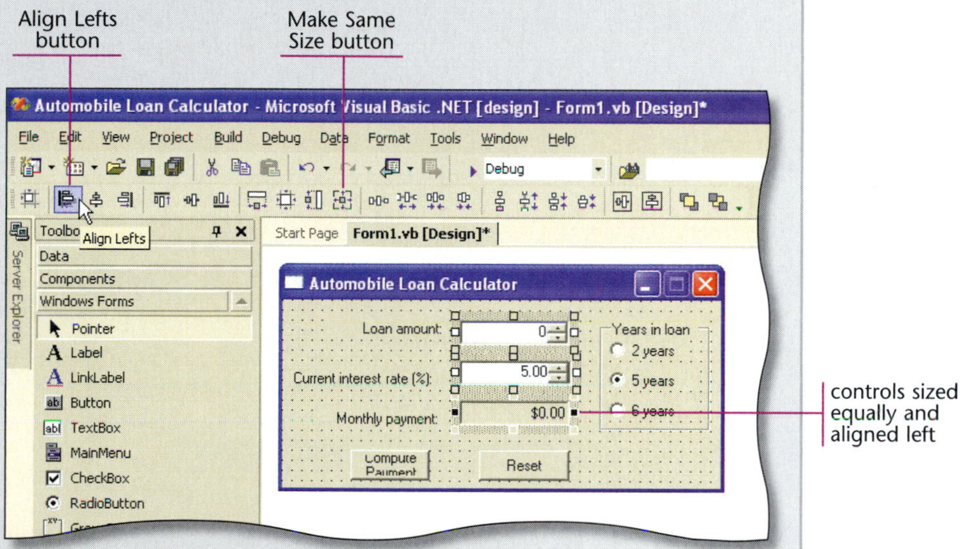

FIGURE 4-20

As you have learned, the last control you select serves as the basis for sizing and aligning all of the other controls. If none of the controls is the size or alignment you want to have for all of the controls, use the sizing handles to size a control properly and then move the control to the proper alignment. Once the control has the proper size and alignment, you can select the other controls and then select the properly sized one last. You then can use the Make Same Size button to size the controls and the Align Lefts or Align Rights button to align the controls.

Sizing and Aligning Button Controls

A good user interface design often requires that Button controls are centered on a form. The step on the next page sizes and aligns the Button controls at the bottom of the Form1 form and centers both buttons together horizontally.

To Size and Align Button Controls

1. Click anywhere on the Form1 form. Select the btnComputePayment and btnReset controls by selecting one of the controls, holding down the CTRL key, and then selecting the other control. If necessary, size and position one control first, and then make certain to select this control last. Click the Make Same Size button on the Layout toolbar and then click the Align Tops button on the Layout toolbar. If the controls do not display as shown in Figure 4-21, then change the Height and Width property values in the property values list to 32 and 75, respectively, while the two controls are still selected. Click the Increase Horizontal Spacing button on the Layout toolbar several times until the buttons are separated as shown in Figure 4-21. Click the Center Horizontally button on the Layout toolbar.

The Button controls are properly sized and aligned and are centered horizontally on the form (Figure 4-21).

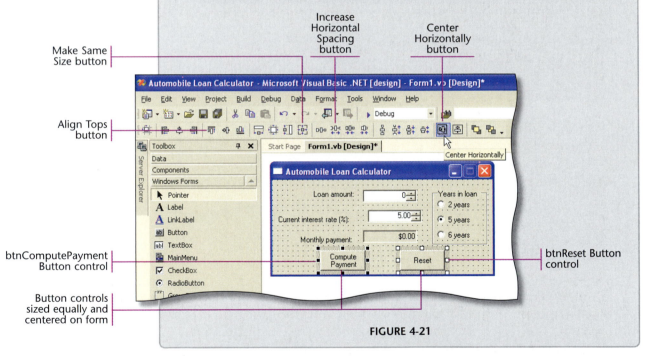

FIGURE 4-21

Each time you click the Increase Horizontal Spacing button on the Layout toolbar, Visual Basic .NET increases the horizontal spacing between the buttons. To undo this operation or decrease the spacing between the controls, click the Decrease Horizontal Spacing button. You can center a control on a form vertically or horizontally using the Center Vertically or Center Horizontally button on the Layout toolbar.

Sizing and Aligning Controls in a Group

Controls in a group, such as the RadioButton controls contained inside a GroupBox control, must be sized and aligned as a group. If you select a control that is in a group and then another control not in the same group, the buttons on the Layout toolbar have no effect on the alignment of the controls. The RadioButton controls in the GroupBox control should have their left sides aligned and should be equally spaced vertically. The following steps size and align the RadioButton controls in a group.

To Size and Align Controls in a Group

1. Select the radTwoYears, radFiveYears, and radSixYears controls by selecting one of the controls, holding down the CTRL key, and then selecting the other controls. Click the Make Same Size button on the Layout toolbar. Click the Make Vertical Spacing Equal button on the Layout toolbar. Make certain that the last control you select has been properly aligned and sized.

   The RadioButton controls are sized properly and equally spaced vertically (Figure 4-22).

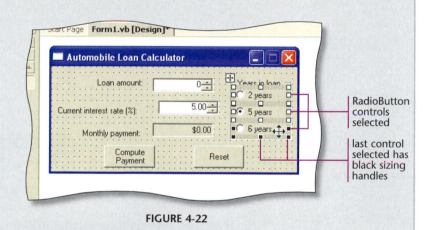

FIGURE 4-22

2. Click the Align Lefts button on the Layout toolbar. If the controls do not display as shown in Figure 4-23, then change the Height and Width property values in the property values list to 24 and 80, respectively, while all the controls are still selected.

   The RadioButton controls are properly sized and aligned as shown in Figure 4-23.

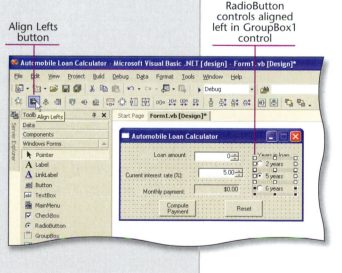

FIGURE 4-23

The Make Vertical Spacing Equal button allows you to make the space between the tops and bottoms of two or more controls the same. The Make Horizontal Spacing Equal button does the same for the left and right sides of two or more controls.

Aligning the Tops of Controls

The final step in sizing and aligning the controls is to align the tops of the controls. The following steps use the Align Tops button to align the tops of the controls, using the top of the nudLoanAmount control as the basis for alignment.

To Align the Tops of Controls

1. Select the nudLoanAmount control. With the nudLoanAmount control selected, hold down the CTRL key and then select the Label1 control and the GroupBox1 control. Click the Align Tops button on the Layout Toolbar.

   The tops of the Label1, nudLoanAmount, and GroupBox1 controls are properly sized and aligned (Figure 4-24).

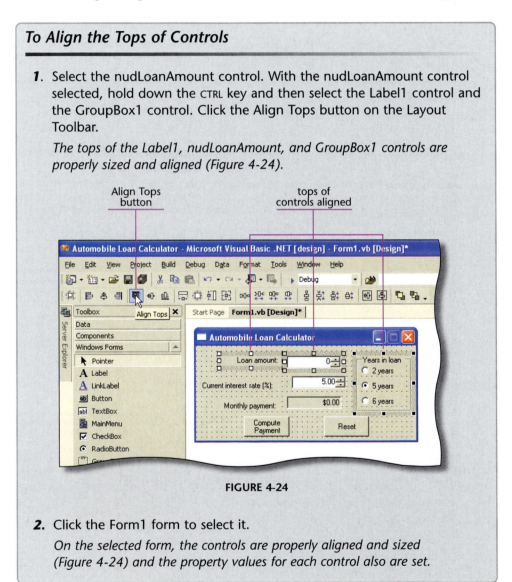

FIGURE 4-24

2. Click the Form1 form to select it.

   On the selected form, the controls are properly aligned and sized (Figure 4-24) and the property values for each control also are set.

By choosing groups of controls selectively and using the functionality of the buttons on the Layout toolbar, you can size and align the controls on a form to achieve a polished and symmetrical appearance. Depending on how controls are initially added to a form, the steps to align and size the controls using the Layout toolbar can differ.

Now that the controls on the form are aligned properly, they should have the Size and Position property values shown in Table 4-9. The step below uses the Properties window to confirm that the controls use the size and position as shown in Table 4-9 to match the controls shown in Figure 4-25. The width of the nudRate control should not be the same as the other input and output controls, so you must set its width using the Properties window.

Table 4-9   Size and Position Property Values for Controls in the Automobile Loan Calculator Application

CONTROL	LOCATION: X (LEFT)	LOCATION: Y (TOP)	WIDTH	HEIGHT
Label1	40	24	100	23
Label2	8	52	136	23
Label3	40	96	100	23
nudLoanAmount	144	24	100	20
nudRate	144	52	64	20
txtMonthlyPayment	144	96	100	20
btnComputePayment	72	136	75	32
btnReset	208	136	75	32
GroupBox1	256	24	96	96
radTwoYears	8	16	80	24
radFiveYears	8	40	80	24
radSixYears	8	64	80	24

To Verify the Size and Position of Controls

1. Select each control and use the Properties window to verify that the Location: X, Location: Y, Height, and Width property values are set to the values listed in Table 4-9. Make certain to change the Width property of the nudRate control by setting the Width property in the property list.

   The input and output controls are properly sized and aligned (Figure 4-25).

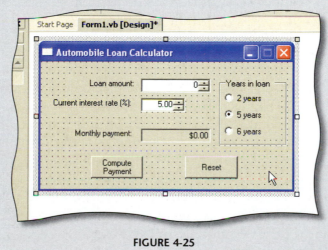

FIGURE 4-25

As shown in the previous steps, the order in which you perform some tasks when laying out a form impacts decisions you make about setting property values. For example, you should set the Text property value of a Label control before setting its Size property value, because the Size property value may need to be increased to accommodate more text.

Setting a Default Button on a Form and Locking Controls

At least two other properties and user interface design changes are best left until the bulk of the work on the form is complete and most controls are added and their properties are set. Such changes include setting the default button on a form so it is selected when a user presses the ENTER key and locking the controls on a form to ensure that controls cannot be moved accidentally during design time.

Setting the Default Button on a Form

Often, the user interface design of a form specifies one particular button on the form that executes the central task that the form was designed to accomplish. The Compute Payment button in the Automobile Loan Calculator application, for example, executes the central task of computing a monthly loan payment. In such instances, you should set that button to be the default button for a form. A **default button** on a form is specified by the **AcceptButton property**, which tells the application that pressing the ENTER key on the form is equivalent to clicking the button specified in the AcceptButton property. When the user presses the ENTER key or clicks the default button on a form that has the AcceptButton property set, the Click event procedure of the button specified by the AcceptButton executes.

Tip

AcceptButton Property
One button on a form can be set to be the default button. The AcceptButton property of a form specifies this button. When the user presses the ENTER key or clicks the default button on a form that has the AcceptButton property set, the Click event procedure of the button specified by the AcceptButton property executes.

As noted above, the default button for the Form1 form is the Compute Payment button, so the AcceptButton property must be set to this button's name. The following steps set the AcceptButton property of Form1 to the name of the Compute Payment Button control, btnComputePayment.

To Set the Default Button on a Form

1. With the Form1 form selected, select the AcceptButton property in the Properties window. Click the AcceptButton down arrow in the property values list.

The three possible values of the AcceptButton property display in the property values list. The last two values are names of the two Button controls on Form1 (Figure 4-26).

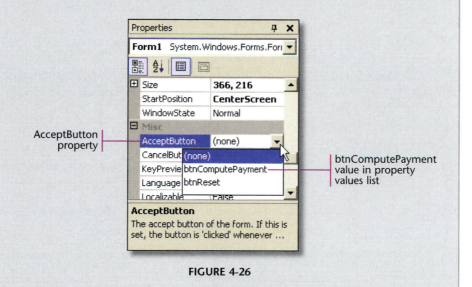

FIGURE 4-26

2. Click btnComputePayment in the AcceptButton property values list.

The AcceptButton property value is set to btnComputePayment (Figure 4-27). The AcceptButton property value indicates which button's Click event procedure executes when the user presses the ENTER key while using the application during run time. A black border displays around the btnComputePayment control on Form1.

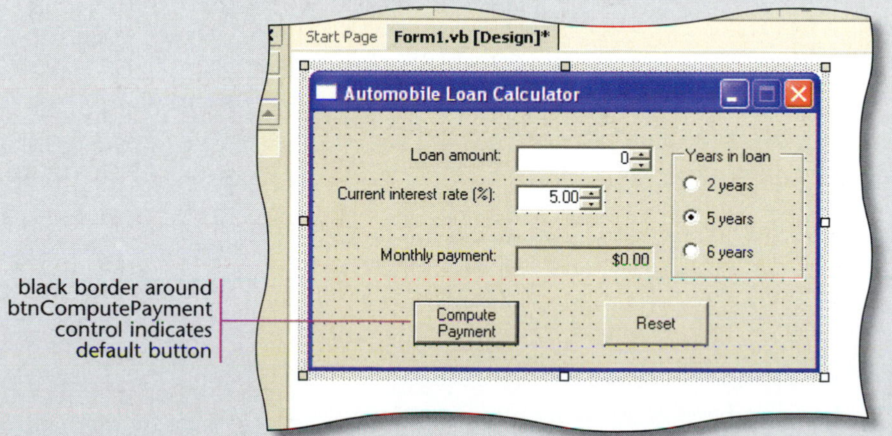

FIGURE 4-27

The Compute Payment button is now set as the default button based on the AcceptButton property. When the user presses the ENTER key while the window or any control on the window has focus during run time, the btnComputePayment_Click event procedure executes. The modifications to the controls on the Form1 form — including the size, alignment, position, tab order, and other properties — are now complete.

Locking Controls on a Form

After completing the layout of controls a form, Visual Basic .NET allows you to lock controls on a form. **Locking controls** disallows the ability to move controls or modify control sizes on a form during design time. Locking prevents the accidental moving or resizing of controls on a form. With Visual Basic .NET, you can either lock individual controls or all the controls on a form, including the form itself.

> **Tip**
>
> **Locking Controls**
> Locking controls disallows the ability to move controls or modify control sizes on a form during design time. Locking prevents the accidental moving or resizing of controls on a form.

The following steps lock the Form1 control and all of the controls on the Form1 form.

To Lock Controls on a Form

---

1. If necessary, select Form1. Click Format on the menu bar.
   The Format menu displays (Figure 4-28).

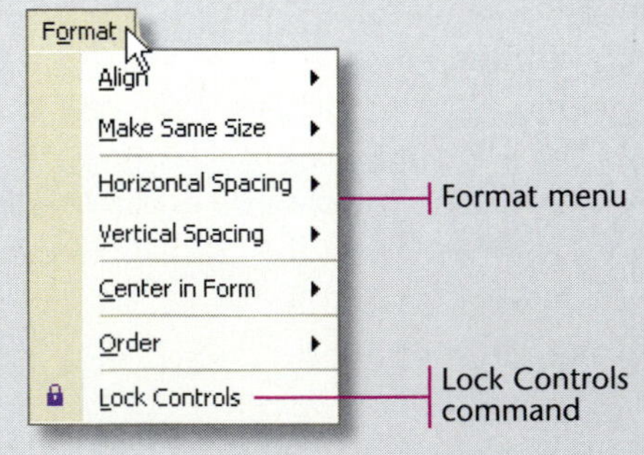

FIGURE 4-28

2. Click Lock Controls on the Format menu.
   The sizing handles on Form1 no longer display and a black border appears around the form, indicating that the form and the controls on the form are locked (Figure 4-29). While the form and controls are locked, they cannot be resized or moved.

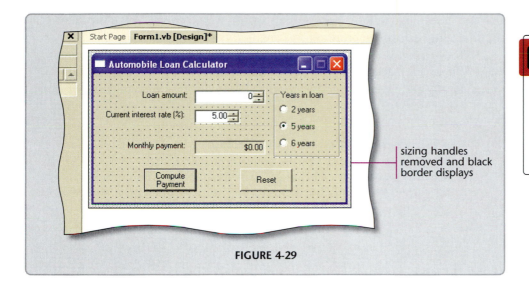

sizing handles
removed and black
border displays

FIGURE 4-29

OTHER WAYS

1. Right-click anywhere on form, click Lock Controls on shortcut menu
2. Press ALT+O, L

After the form and controls are locked, sizing handles no longer display when you select the form, because the form cannot be resized. Similarly, if you select a control on the form, sizing handles will not display.

To lock an individual control, select the control and then click the Lock Controls command on the Format menu. To lock two or more controls, use the CTRL key to select additional controls, and then click the Lock Controls command on the Format menu.

To unlock a form or controls, you select the form or individual control and then click Lock Controls again on the Format menu. A lock icon next to the Lock Controls command on the Format menu indicates the current status of the selected form or control. With the form and controls locked, the user interface for the Automobile Loan Calculator application is now complete.

Declaring Constants and Variables

With the user interface complete, the next step is to write the code, or actions, that will occur within the application in response to specific events in the Automobile Loan Calculator application. As indicated in the program design, the code for the Automobile Loan Calculator requires six event procedures. One event procedure is needed for each of the two Button controls on the form, and one event procedure is needed for each of the three RadioButton controls. A sixth event procedure is needed to execute when the application starts, to set the maximum value allowed for the loan amount in the nudLoanAmount control. The maximum value allowed for the loan amount is stored in the code, so that the value can be changed in the code easily as the program requirements change over time.

A **value**, such as 150, 0.03, 8.14, "yes", "no", or the value allowed for the loan amount for the nudLoanAmount control, is a number or string that programmers use in the code. Variable and constants are used in code statements to store temporary values used by other code statements. A **variable** represents a location in computer memory that can change values as the code executes. Similarly, a **constant** represents a location in computer memory, but its value cannot change during execution of the code. Constants often are used to define values that are used many times in an application and were defined in the program requirements before the program was created.

When you want to use a constant in code, you first must declare the constant. When you **declare** a constant, you tell Visual Basic .NET the name and data type of the constant you want to use, along with the value of the constant.

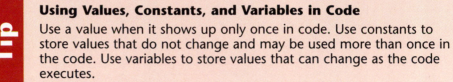

Tip

Using Values, Constants, and Variables in Code
Use a value when it shows up only once in code. Use constants to store values that do not change and may be used more than once in the code. Use variables to store values that can change as the code executes.

Data Types

The **data type** of a variable or constant determines what kind of data the variable or constant can store, such as numeric or character. For example, the maximum value allowed for a loan amount is a numeric value. As shown in Table 4-10, Visual Basic .NET supports several data types for text (character) values, such as character and string, and several types for numeric values, such as decimal and integer.

Table 4-10   Visual Basic .NET Data Types

CATEGORY	DATA TYPE	DESCRIPTION	RANGE
Character	**Char**	16-bit (2 bytes) character	1 16-bit character
	String	Sequence of 0 or more 16-bit characters	0 to 2,000,000,000 16-bit characters
Integral	**Short**	16-bit integer value	-32,768 to 32,767
	Integer	32-bit (4 bytes) integer value	-2147483648 to 2147483647
	Long	64-bit (8 bytes) integer value	-9,223,372,036,854,775,808 to 9,223,372,036,854,775,807
	Byte	8-bit (1 byte) unsigned integer value	0 to 255
Nonintegral	**Decimal**	128-bit (16 bytes) fixed point	1.0e-28 to 7.9e28
	Single	32-bit floating point	+-1.5e-45 to +-3.4e38
	Double	64-bit floating point	+-5.0e-324 to +-1.7e308
Miscellaneous	**Boolean**	32-bit value	True or **False**
	Date	64-bit signed integer – each increment represents 100 nanoseconds elapsed since the beginning of January 1 in the year 1	January 1, 0001:00:00:00 to December 31, 9999:23:59:59
	Object	32-bit number that represents the location of the object in memory	Any object

Recall from Chapter 1 that an intermediate .NET system, known as the Common Language Runtime (CLR), takes control of the application and runs the application under the operating system. The CLR is the environment that executes Visual Basic .NET programs. The CLR also determines the data types that are allowed in Visual Basic .NET. Each data type corresponds to a data type in the CLR.

As shown in Table 4-10, each data type takes up a certain number of bytes in memory when the variable or constant is used. As you write the code for an application, you choose the data type for variables and constants in code. In general, you should try to use the data type that takes up the smallest amount of memory. In addition, where possible, you should try to use integral data types that represent whole numbers, such as 1, 5, and 1000, because arithmetic operations are fastest with whole numbers. If a variable or constant will not contain a decimal amount, use an integral data type. If a variable or constant might contain a decimal, use a nonintegral data type.

Tip

Choosing Data Types

Try to use the data type that takes up the smallest amount of memory.

Declaring Constants

As previously discussed, when you want to use a constant in code, you first must declare the constant by telling Visual Basic .NET the name, data type, and value of the constant. Using a constant in code ensures that, if the value stated in the requirements changes in the future, you only have to change the value in one place in the code. Using a constant also makes the value's purpose more clear because the value is given a meaningful name.

The following rules apply when choosing names for constants.

1. The name must begin with a letter, although the name can begin with an underscore as long as another valid character also is used in the name.
2. The name can be up to 16,383 characters in length.
3. The name cannot contain punctuation or blank spaces.

When naming constants, this book uses a naming convention that gives the constant a descriptive name but does not indicate the data type of the constant.

To declare a constant, you use the **Const keyword**. Table 4-11 on the next page shows the general form of a constant declaration statement. When declaring a constant, the general form of the constant declaration statement indicates that a data type is not needed. Good coding practice, however, dictates that a constant or variable always be declared with a data type. Declaring a data type (1) makes the code more readable to others and (2) eliminates the time-consuming process of having Visual Basic .NET determine the data type during run time. Code is more efficient and foolproof if all constants and variables are defined explicitly with a data type.

Table 4-11	*Constant Declaration Statement*
General forms:	1. Const name As type = value 2. Const name = value
Purpose:	The **constant declaration statement** declares a constant that cannot change during the execution of code. The name of the constant can be used in code to represent the value assigned to the constant. The use of a constant allows you to change the value in only one place in the code in the future if the value stated in the requirements changes.
Examples:	1. Const MaxVolume as Integer = 11 2. Const CurrencyString as String = "Dollars" 3. Const DrumCapacity = 1500.13

Declaring Constants and Variables 1
Although it is not generally required, good coding practice dictates that a constant or variable always be declared with a data type.

Declaring Constants and Variables 2
Code is more efficient and foolproof if all constants and variables are defined explicitly with a data type.

Figure 4-30 shows the code necessary to declare the constant needed in the Automobile Loan Calculator application. The constant, MaximumLoanAllowed, reflects the current maximum amount that the dealership will loan a customer. The code also contains the comment header for the form.

```
189    ' Chapter 4:      Automobile Loan Calculator
190    ' Programmer:     Jeff Quasney
191    ' Date:           September 22, 2004
192    ' Purpose:        This project calculates the monthly payment for
193    '                 a loan based on loan amount, interest rate, and
194    '                 length of the loan.
195    Const MaximumLoanAllowed As Integer = 25000
```

FIGURE 4-30

The following steps add the comment header and constant declaration statement to the Form1.vb form. The constant is not declared in any event procedure. By declaring the constant outside of any event procedure, the constant can be used in any event procedure within the form.

To Declare a Constant

1. Double-click the Form1 form in an area that does not contain a control. When the code window displays, click line 189.

The code window opens in the main work area (Figure 4-31). Visual Basic .NET creates the Form1_Load event procedure. The insertion point is on line 189.

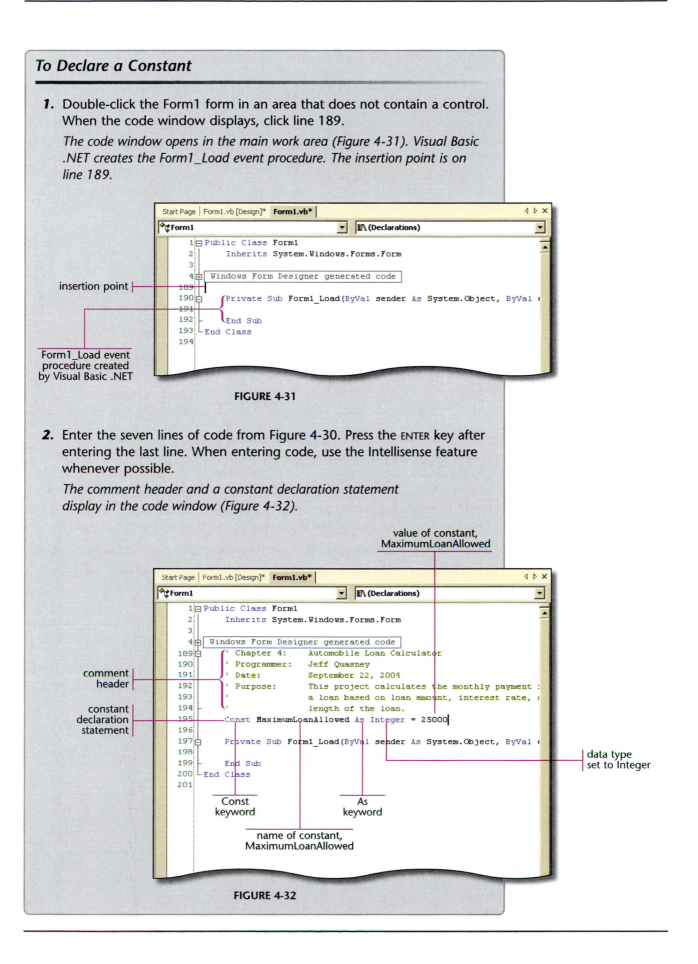

insertion point

Form1_Load event procedure created by Visual Basic .NET

FIGURE 4-31

2. Enter the seven lines of code from Figure 4-30. Press the ENTER key after entering the last line. When entering code, use the Intellisense feature whenever possible.

The comment header and a constant declaration statement display in the code window (Figure 4-32).

value of constant, MaximumLoanAllowed

comment header

constant declaration statement

data type set to Integer

Const keyword

As keyword

name of constant, MaximumLoanAllowed

FIGURE 4-32

Coding a Form Load Event Procedure

Like any other control, forms include event procedures. As previously noted, the Automobile Loan Calculator application includes an event procedure that executes when the application starts and the form loads. This event procedure sets the maximum value allowed for the loan amount in the nudLoanAmount control. The form event procedure that executes whenever the form initially displays to the user is a **form Load event**. The code you write for the Load event is code that you want to execute before the CLR allows the user to take any action on the form, such as entering data. You can see the list of Form events available for a form by selecting the item, (Base Class Events), in the Object box in the code window and then displaying the list of event procedures by clicking the Procedure box arrow.

Form Load Event

The form Load event executes for a form whenever the form initially displays to the user. The code you write for the Load event is code that you want to execute before the CLR allows the user to take any action on the form, such as entering data.

The Automobile Loan Calculator application calls for assigning the nudLoanAmount.Maximum property the value of the constant, MaximumLoanAllowed, when the form first loads. A constant may be used in an assignment statement, but it can only be on the right side of an assignment statement. Figure 4-33 shows the assignment statement needed to set the property value nudLoanAmount.Maximum to the constant, MaximumLoanAmount.

```
198        ' Set the maximum value of the Loan amount NumericUpDown control
199        nudLoanAmount.Maximum = MaximumLoanAllowed
```

FIGURE 4-33

The line of code after the comment in Figure 4-33 sets the Maximum property of the nudLoanAmount to equal the value of the MaximumLoanAmount constant, 25000. The assignment statement is added to the Form1_Load event procedure, so that the property is set when the user starts the application and before the user is able to enter any data into the controls on the form. As shown in the previous steps, you start coding the Form1_Load event by double-clicking any area on the form that does not contain a control.

The following step adds the comment and assignment statements in Figure 4-33 to the Form1_Load event of Form1.

To Code a Form Load Event Procedure

1. Click line 198 in the Form1_Load event procedure and then enter the two lines of code from Figure 4-33. Do not press the ENTER key after entering the second line.

The comment line and assignment statement display in the code window as lines 198 and 199 (Figure 4-34). Because the statement is part of the Form1_Load event procedure, the assignment statement will execute when the user starts the application.

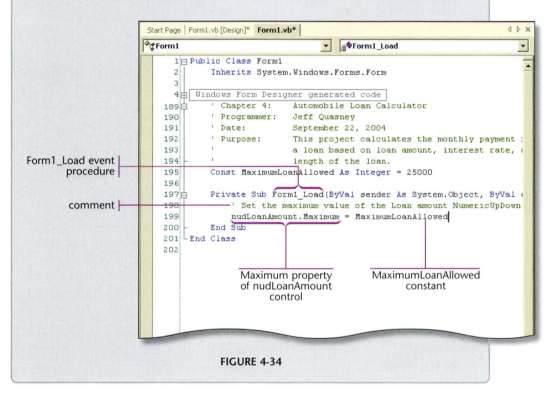

FIGURE 4-34

The Form1_Load event procedure can be used to set any or all of the properties of the Form1 form or controls. The reason that the nudLoanAmount.Maximum property is set in the procedure is that the requirements document for the application (Figure 4-2 on page VB 4.04) states that the value is likely to change in the future. By explicitly assigning this value in the code, the code only needs to be changed in one place if the value changes.

Setting the Reset Button Properties

As outlined in the program requirements, when the user clicks the Reset button during run time, four controls must be reset to their default property values. In the Automobile Loan Calculator application, the btnReset_Click event procedure is assigned to the btnReset control so that it executes when the btnReset button is clicked. The btnReset_Click event procedure is used to set the Value property value of the nudLoanAmount control to 0, the Value property value of the nudRate control to 5, the Checked property value of the radFiveYears control to True, and the Text property value of the txtMonthlyPayment control to $0.00. Figure 4-35 shows comments and four lines of code used to code the btnReset_Click event procedure that resets the controls on the form to their default values.

```
203        ' Reset Loan Amount and Monthly payment to zero. Reset
204        ' the interest rate to 5%, and select five years for the
205        ' length of the loan
206        nudLoanAmount.Value = 0
207        nudRate.Value = 5
208        radFiveYears.Checked = True
209        txtMonthlyPayment.Text = "$0.00"
```

FIGURE 4-35

The following step inserts the code for the btnReset_Click event procedure.

To Code the btnReset_Click Event Procedure

1. Click the Form1.vb[Design] tab and then double-click the btnReset control. When the code window displays, enter the seven lines of code from Figure 4-35. Do not press the ENTER key after entering the last line.

The code window opens in the main work area (Figure 4-36). Visual Basic .NET creates the btnReset_Click event procedure, and the insertion point is positioned on line 203 in the procedure. The comment lines and assignment statements display in the code window as lines 203 through 209. The assignment statement will execute when the user clicks the Reset button during run time.

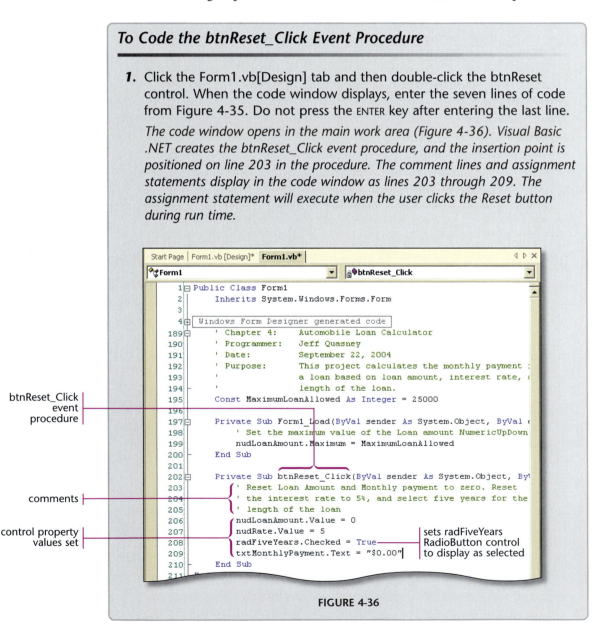

FIGURE 4-36

The code for the btnReset_Click event procedure is now complete. When a user clicks the Reset button during run time, the code will set the control property values as indicated in lines 206 through 209. The code in line 208, which sets the Checked property value of the radFiveYears RadioButton control to True, performs the same action as if the user clicked the 5 years option button in the Years in loan area of the form.

Using the Option Strict Statement

When you use an assignment statement, Visual Basic .NET does not require you to use the same data type on both sides of the assignment. Visual Basic .NET converts the variables or constants to the proper data type so it can make a valid assignment. This conversion process, however, can cause problems with code and makes code more unreadable for others. For example, if you leave the data conversions to Visual Basic .NET, you may try assigning an Integer variable with a value of 50,000 to a variable declared as a Short. In this case, the Integer value exceeds the maximum value that can fit in a Short variable. This condition causes a run time error to occur and the CLR halts the program.

The **Option Strict statement** can be used to instruct Visual Basic .NET to force you to ensure that all assignment statements use the same data type on both sides of the assignment. Option Strict also forces you to declare a data type for all variables and constants explicitly. Table 4-12 shows the general form of an Option Strict statement.

Table 4-12	*Option Strict Statement*
General forms:	1. Option Strict On 2. Option Strict Off
Purpose:	When set to On, the Option Strict statement requires all constants and variable to be declared with a data type and requires assignment statements to have the same data type on each side of the assignment.
Examples:	1. Option Strict On 2. Option Strict Off

By default, Option Strict is set to Off, which means that Visual Basic .NET does not require a data type to be the same on each side of an assignment and that you do not need to declare a data type for each variable. For the remainder of this book, Option Strict will be set to On, meaning that you must declare a data type for all constants and variables and you must use the same data type on each side of an assignment statement.

If you use an Option Strict statement, the statement must be the first line of code entered in the code window. Figure 4-37 shows the Option Strict statement included in the code window.

```
1 Option Strict On
```

FIGURE 4-37

The following step inserts the code for an Option Strict statement that sets Option Strict setting to On.

To Code an Option Strict Statement

1. Click to the left of the keyword, Public, and to the right of the collapse button on line 1. Press the ENTER key, position the insertion point at the beginning of line 1, and then type the code Option Strict On as shown in Figure 4-37 on the previous page. Do not press the ENTER key after entering the code.

The Option Strict On statement displays as the first line of code (Figure 4-38). All lines of code are moved down and renumbered.

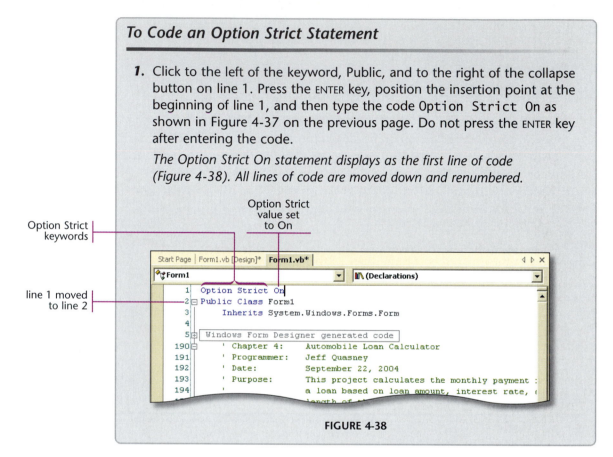

FIGURE 4-38

When the Option Strict statement is entered on the first line, all other lines of code are moved down and renumbered. The Option Strict On statement causes Visual Basic .NET to require that all assignment statements use the same data type on both sides of the equal sign and that a data type is declared for all constants and variables.

Declaring Global Variables

As with constants, variables also are used in code statements to store temporary values used by other code statements. Unlike a constant, which does not change as the code executes, a variable represents a location in computer memory that can change values as the code executes. If you want to use a variable in code, you first must declare the variable by telling Visual Basic .NET the name, data type, and value of the variable.

The rules for naming variables are the same as the rules for naming constants: the name must begin with a letter, although the name can begin with an underscore as long as another valid character also is used in the name, the name can be up to 16,383 characters in length, and cannot contain punctuation or blank spaces. Table 4-13 shows the prefixes used for naming variables in this book, based on the data type of the variable.

Table 4-13 Naming Convention for Variables

DATA TYPE	PREFIX
Short	shr
Integer	int
Long	lng
Byte	byt
Decimal	dec
Single	sng
Double	dbl
Char	chr
String	str
Boolean	bln
Date	dtm
Object	obj

To declare a variable, you use the **Dim statement**. Table 4-14 shows the general form of a Dim statement.

Table 4-14 Dim Statement (simple)

General form:	1. Dim variablename As datatype = initialvalue 2. Dim variablename As datatype 3. Dim variablename
Purpose:	The Dim statement declares a variable.
Examples:	1. `Dim intScore As integer = 0` 2. `Dim strName As String` 3. `Dim lngInStock`

Visual Basic .NET allows you to declare a variable either in a procedure or in the area of code outside of a procedure, in the general area of a class. Variables and constants have an attribute called scope. **Scope** refers to a variable or constant's accessibility and is defined by the placement of the variable declaration in the code. Depending on where a variable is declared, the scope of the variable can be limited so it is not usable everywhere in a project's code. The MaximumLoanAmount constant declared earlier in this chapter was declared in the general area of the form and has scope that is global to the form. The MaximumLoanAmount is a global constant. Variables typically are declared at the start of an event procedure, using the general forms in Table 4-14. A variable declared within an event procedure only has scope within that procedure and is considered a **local variable**. A declaration made outside of a specific event procedure and in the general area of the code, such as the constant declaration statement on line 195 in Figure 4-30 on page VB 4.36, has scope for all of the procedures in the form and is considered a **global variable**.

When the user clicks a RadioButton control in the Automobile Loan Calculator application to specify the number of years in the loan, the CheckChanged event procedure of the RadioButton control executes. By placing an assignment to a global variable in the CheckChanged event procedure of each RadioButton control, you can tell Visual Basic .NET to update the global variable with the correct number of months in the loan whenever the user clicks a RadioButton control. Even after the event procedure has finished executing, the variable retains the newly assigned value. The name of this variable will be gdblMonths. The variable is named with a preceding character, g, to indicate that it is a global variable using the short data type.

Naming Global Variables

Append the letter g in front of the properly formed variable name when naming global variables. After the g, use a prefix to indicate data type and then add a descriptive word or words.

Figure 4-39 shows the declaration of the global variable, gdblMonths. The global variable is assigned an initial value of 60, which is the number of months in the 5 years loan, which serves as a default length of a loan. Just as with the global constant, MaximumLoanAllowed, the global variable, gdblMonths, is declared in the general section of the code. The coding standard used in this book requires that global variables be declared after the comment header for the code file and before any constant declarations.

```
196        Dim gdblMonths As Double = 60.0
```

FIGURE 4-39

Global Variable Placement

Place global variables after the comment header in the code, but before any constant declarations.

The following step inserts the code to declare a global variable for the Automobile Loan Calculator application.

To Declare a Global Variable

1. Click the end of line 195 and then press the ENTER key. Enter the line of code from Figure 4-39 and do not press the ENTER key.

The declaration for the global variable, gdblMonths, displays in the code window as line 196 (Figure 4-40). The declaration for the global variable is entered below the comment header and above the constant declaration statement.

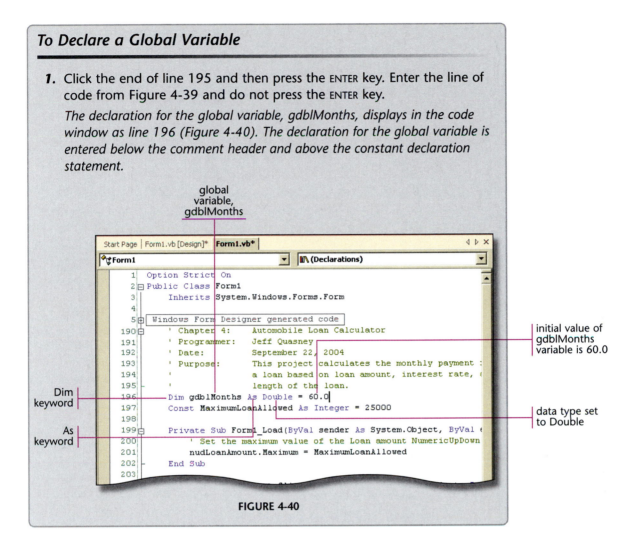

FIGURE 4-40

The gdblMonths variable now contains the number of months that corresponds to the default number of years in a loan.

Coding the Event Procedures for the RadioButton Controls

The next step in developing the Automobile Loan Calculator application is to code the event procedures for the RadioButton controls, so that the gdblMonths variable is set to the correct number of months, 24 (2 years), 60 (5 years), or 72 (6 years) depending on which RadioButton the user clicks.

The event procedure that executes when the user clicks a RadioButton is the CheckChanged event procedure. Figure 4-41 shows the code for the radTwoYears_CheckChanged event procedure. The value assigned to the gdblMonths global variable is 24.0, which is the number of months in two years.

```
215        gdblMonths = 24.0
```

FIGURE 4-41

Figure 4-42 shows the code for the radFiveYears_CheckChanged event procedure. The value assigned to the gdblMonths global variable is 60.0, which is the number of months in five years.

```
219                    gdblMonths = 60.0
```

FIGURE 4-42

Figure 4-43 shows the code for the radSixYears_CheckChanged event procedure. The value assigned to the gdblMonths global variable is 72.0, which is the number of months in six years.

```
223                    gdblMonths = 72.0
```

FIGURE 4-43

The following steps insert the code for the three event procedures that execute when the corresponding RadioButton control is clicked. The code in each event procedure sets the gdblMonths global variable to the correct number of months whenever the user clicks one of the RadioButton controls.

To Code the CheckChanged Event Procedures for RadioButton Controls

1. Click the Form1.vb[Design] tab and then double-click the radTwoYears control. When the code window displays, enter the code on line 215 of Figure 4-41 on the previous page. Do not press the ENTER key after entering the line of code.

    The assignment statement displays in the code window on line 215 (Figure 4-44). The value assigned to the gdblMonths global variable is 24.0, the number of months in two years.

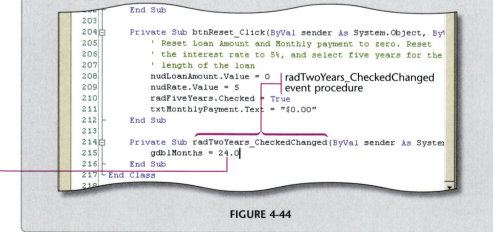

FIGURE 4-44

2. Click the Form1.vb[Design] tab and then double-click the radFiveYears control. When the code window displays, enter the code on line 219 from Figure 4-42. Do not press the ENTER key after entering the line of code.

The assignment statement displays in the code window on line 219 (Figure 4-45). The value assigned to the gdblMonths global variable is 60.0, the number of months in five years.

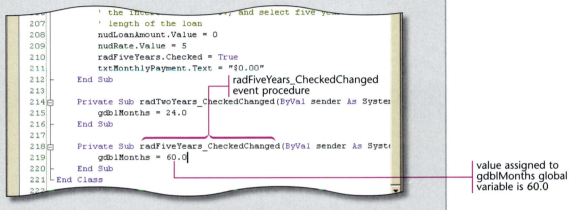

FIGURE 4-45

3. Click the Form1.vb[Design] tab and then double-click the radSixYears control. When the code window displays, enter the code on line 223 from Figure 4-43. Do not press the ENTER key after entering the line of code.

The assignment statement displays in the code window as lines 223 (Figure 4-46) The value assigned to the gdblMonths global variable is 72.0, the number of months in six years.

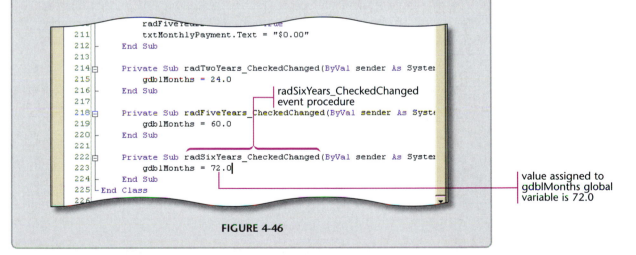

FIGURE 4-46

The code in the previous steps declared, initialized, and modified the gdblMonths variable, which is used as the number of months for the calculation of the monthly loan payment.

Declaring Local Variables

The next step is to declare the local variables needed to complete the loan amount calculation. Recall that a local variable declared within an event procedure only has scope within that procedure. In the Automobile Loan Calculator application, the btnComputePayment_Click event procedure performs the calculation described in the requirements document. Five local variables are necessary to perform the calculation. Table 4-15 describes the variables needed for the calculation, their data types, and their use. Each of these local variables will be declared within the btnComputePayment_Click event procedure

Table 4-15   Local Variables in the btnComputePayment_Click Event Procedure

NAME	DATA TYPE	PURPOSE
dblRate	Double	The actual interest rate used in the final payment calculation
dblMonths	Double	The number of months for the length of the loan
dblPayment	Double	The final calculated monthly payment amount
dblLoanAmount	Double	The numeric value of the loan amount requested
strPayment	String	A string representation of the monthly payment used for display to the user

Figure 4-47 shows the comments used to describe the btnComputeLoan_Click event procedure and the Dim statements used to declare the local variables listed in Table 4-14 on page VB 4.43. Line 231 shows three variables — dblRate, dblMonths, dblPayment — all declared with a data type of Double. The three variables are declared with a data type of Double because the line of code that performs the calculation shown later in the chapter requires Double values. Line 232 shows two variables — dblLoanAmount and strPayment — declared as Double and String data types, respectively.

```
227         ' Validate inputs and compute the monthly payment using
228         ' the inputs. Determine the interest rate to be used
229         ' based on the input rate divided by 12.0. Display the
230         ' result in the txtMonthlyPayment Textbox.
231         Dim dblRate, dblMonths, dblPayment As Double
232         Dim dblLoanAmount As Double, strPayment As String
```

FIGURE 4-47

The following step inserts the comments and code to start the btnComputePayment_Click event procedure and declares the local variables within the event procedure.

To Declare Local Variables

1. Click the Form1.vb[Design] tab and then double-click the btnComputePayment control. When the code window displays, enter the six lines of code from Figure 4-47. Do not press the ENTER key after entering the last line.

The comment lines and local variable declarations display in the code window as lines 227 through 232 (Figure 4-48).

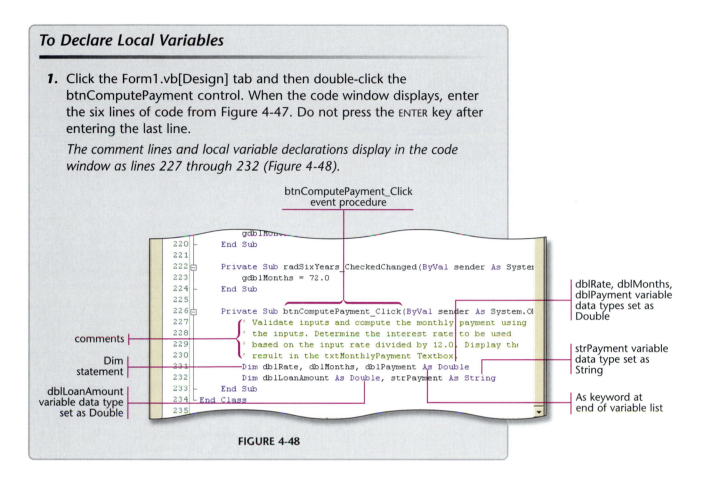

btnComputePayment_Click event procedure

dblRate, dblMonths, dblPayment variable data types set as Double

strPayment variable data type set as String

As keyword at end of variable list

comments

Dim statement

dblLoanAmount variable data type set as Double

```
220    End Sub
221
222    Private Sub radSixYears_CheckedChanged(ByVal sender As Syster
223        gdblMonths = 72.0
224    End Sub
225
226    Private Sub btnComputePayment_Click(ByVal sender As System.Ol
227        ' Validate inputs and compute the monthly payment using
228        ' the inputs. Determine the interest rate to be used
229        ' based on the input rate divided by 12.0. Display the
230        ' result in the txtMonthlyPayment Textbox.
231        Dim dblRate, dblMonths, dblPayment As Double
232        Dim dblLoanAmount As Double, strPayment As String
233    End Sub
234    End Class
235
```

FIGURE 4-48

The code declares the variables within the btnComputePayment_Click event procedure. Therefore, these local variables may be used only within this event procedure. If you tried to refer to the variables in another event procedure, Visual Basic .NET would indicate a syntax error.

Converting Data Types

Because Option Strict is On, the btnComputePayment_Click event procedure must ensure that all data being used in the calculation has the same data type before making the calculation. One of the values used in the calculation, however, nudLoanAmount, uses a different data type. The Value property of the nudLoanAmount control has a Decimal data type.

To set the value to the correct data type, the Value property of the nudLoanAmount control must be converted from a Decimal data type to a Double data type. This is accomplished by converting the Value property of the nudLoanAmount to a Double data type, and then assigning the result to the dblLoanAmount variable, which is declared with a Double data type.

Visual Basic .NET includes several methods that allow you to convert the value of a variable or constant to another data type, and then use the result in a statement. For example, the **Convert.ToDouble() method** converts the value of a variable to a Double data type. The Visual Basic .NET online Help documentation includes additional explanations of the various methods available for data conversions. You place the item you want to convert inside the parentheses. The items within parentheses that are supplied to a function, method, or event are called arguments. **Arguments** are values that are passed to the function, method, or event and are used by the function, method, or event to perform its operation.

Table 4-16 shows some examples of the results of using data type conversion methods.

Figure 4-49 shows the assignment statement that uses the Convert.ToDouble() method to convert the Value property of the nudLoanAmount control to a Double data type, and then assign the result to the dblLoanAmount variable.

Table 4-16 Data Type Conversion Examples	
STATEMENT	**RESULT**
Convert.ToString(498.72)	"498.72"
Convert.ToInteger(498.72)	499
Convert.ToBoolean(498.72)	True
Convert.ToDouble(498)	498.0

```
234            dblLoanAmount = Convert.ToDouble(nudLoanAmount.Value)
```

FIGURE 4-49

The following step inserts the code for the assignment statement that converts a Decimal data type to a Double data type, and then assigns the result to a local variable in the btnComputePayment_Click event procedure.

To Code an Assignment Statement to Convert a Data Type

1. Press the ENTER key twice. Enter the line of code from Figure 4-49 and do not press the ENTER key.

Line 234 displays in the code window (Figure 4-50). This assignment statement uses the Convert.ToDouble() method to convert the nudLoanAmount.Value property to a Double data type and assign the result to the dblLoanAmount variable.

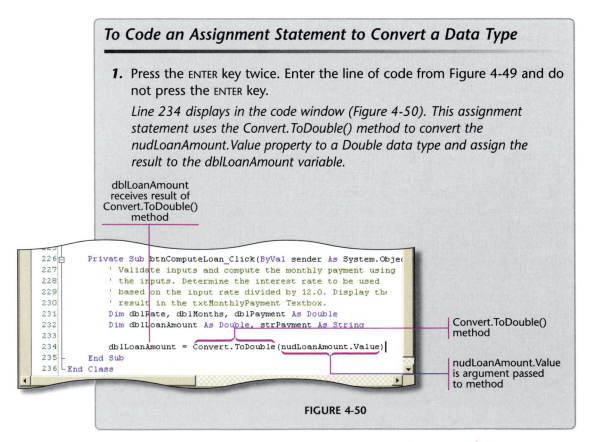

dblLoanAmount receives result of Convert.ToDouble() method

Convert.ToDouble() method

nudLoanAmount.Value is argument passed to method

FIGURE 4-50

The assignment statement converts the value of the nudLoanAmount.Value property to a Double data type, and then assigns this value to the dblLoanAmount variable. Once converted and stored in the local variable, dblLoanAmount, this value can be used in other code statements in the btnComputePayment_Click event procedure that require the Double data type.

Numeric Expressions and Operator Precedence

An **expression** can perform a calculation, manipulate characters, call a function, or test data. A **numeric expression** is any expression that can be evaluated as a number. A numeric expression can include values, variables, and constants, as well as certain control properties. The data type of any value in an arithmetic expression must be one of the numeric data types from Table 4-10 on page VB 4.34. A numeric expression cannot contain string variables, string constants, or objects.

The values, variables, constants, and control properties in a numeric expression often are separated from each other by parentheses and arithmetic operators. An **arithmetic operator** is used to manipulate two or more numeric values. Commonly used arithmetic operators are the plus sign (+) used to sum two numbers and the asterisk (*) used to multiply two numbers. Table 4-17 shows seven arithmetic operators listed in the order of operator precedence. **Order of operator precedence** is a predetermined order that defines the sequence in which operators are evaluated and resolved when several operations occur in an expression.

Table 4-17   Arithmetic Operators

ARITHMETIC OPERATOR	MEANING
^	Used to raise a number to the power of an exponent
*	Used to multiply two numbers
/	Used to divide two numbers and return a decimal result
\	Used to divide two numbers and return an integer result
Mod	Used to divide two numbers and return only the remainder
+	Used to sum two numbers
–	Used to find the difference between two numbers or to indicate the negative value of a numeric expression

The process of raising a number to the power of an exponent is called exponentiation. For example, $4 \wedge 2$ is the same as 4^2 and is equal to 16, and $3 \wedge 4$ is the same as 3^4 and is equal to 81. In programming, the asterisk (*) is used to indicate multiplication and the forward slash (/) indicates division. Therefore, 8 * 4 is equal to 32, and 8 / 4 is equal to 2. For addition and subtraction, the traditional + and – signs are used.

Two arithmetic operators that may be unfamiliar to you are the backslash (\)
and Mod, both of which are used to indicate a division operation. The backslash
operator instructs Visual Basic .NET first to round the dividend and the divisor
to integers (whole numbers) and then truncate any decimal portion of the
quotient. For example, 5 \ 3 is equal to 1, and 6.8 \ 3.2 is equal to 2.

The **Mod operator** (also called the **modulo operator**) is used to divide two
numbers and then return the remainder of the division operation as an integer.
For example, 34 Mod 6 is equal to 4 because 34 divided by 6 is 5 with a remainder of 4. Also, 23 Mod 12 is equal to 11 because 23 divided by 12 is 1 with a
remainder of 11.

A programmer must be concerned with both the form and evaluation of an
expression. It is necessary to consider the purpose of the expression, as well as
the rules for forming a valid expression, before you start to write expressions in
Visual Basic .NET statements with confidence.

Forming Valid Numeric Expressions

The definition of a numeric expression dictates the manner in which a
numeric expression can be validly formed. For example, the following statement
formed to assign A twice the value of B is invalid:

A = 2B ' Invalid statement

Visual Basic .NET will reject the statement because a constant and a variable
within the same expression must be separated by an arithmetic operator. The
statement can be written validly as follows:

A = 2 * B

It also is invalid to use a string variable or string constant in a numeric
expression. The following are invalid numeric expressions:

6 + "DEBIT" / C
"25" / B + "X" − 19

Evaluation of Numeric Expressions

As you form complex numeric expressions involving several arithmetic
operations, it is important to consider the order in which Visual Basic .NET
will evaluate the expression. For example, if you entered the statement:

A = 8 / 4 / 2

would the expression assign a value of 1 or 4 to A? The answer depends on how
Visual Basic .NET evaluates the expression. If Visual Basic .NET completes the
operation, 8 / 4, first and only then 2 / 2, the expression yields the value 1. If
Visual Basic .NET completes the second operation, 4 / 2, first and only then
8 / 2, it yields 4.

Visual Basic .NET follows the normal algebraic rules to evaluate an expression. The normal algebraic rules that define the order in which the operations
are evaluated are as follows: Unless parentheses dictate otherwise, reading from
left to right in a numeric expression, all exponentiations are performed first,

then all multiplications and/or divisions, then all integer divisions, then all modulo arithmetic, and finally, all additions and/or subtractions. Following these algebraic rules, Visual Basic .NET would evaluate the expression 8 / 4 / 2 to yield a value of 1.

Tip

Order of Operator Precedence

Unless parentheses dictate otherwise, reading from left to right in a numeric expression, all exponentiations are performed first, then all multiplications and/or divisions, then all integer divisions, then all modulo arithmetic, and finally, all additions and/or subtractions.

This order of operator precedence, which defines the order in which operators are evaluated, is sometimes called the rules of precedence, or the hierarchy of operations. The meaning of these rules can be made clear with some examples.

For example, the expression 18 / 3 ^ 2 + 4 * 2 is evaluated as follows:

$$
\begin{aligned}
18 / 3 \wedge 2 + 4 * 2 &= 18 / 9 + 4 * 2 \\
&= 2 + 4 * 2 \\
&= 2 + 8 \\
&= 10
\end{aligned}
$$

If you have trouble following the logic behind this evaluation, use the following technique. Whenever a numeric expression is to be evaluated, read, or scan, the expression from left to right five different times and apply the order of operator precedence rules outlined above each time you read the expression. On the first scan, every time you encounter an ^ operator, you perform exponentiation. In this example, 3 is raised to the power of 2, yielding 9.

On the second scan, moving from left to right again, every time you encounter the operators, * and /, perform multiplication and division. Hence, 18 is divided by 9, yielding 2, and 4 and 2 are multiplied, yielding 8.

On the third scan, from left to right, perform all integer division. On the fourth scan, from left to right, perform all modulo arithmetic. This example includes no integer division or modulo arithmetic so no operations are performed.

On the fifth scan, moving again from left to right, every time you encounter the operators, + and −, perform addition and subtraction. In this example, 2 and 8 are added to form 10.

The following expression includes all seven arithmetic operators and yields a value of 2. This particular expression assumes that Option Strict is set to Off, because a value, 4.8, with the Double data type, a Nonintegral data type, is used in an arithmetic expression that uses only integers.

$$
\begin{aligned}
3 * 9 \text{ Mod } 2 \wedge 2 + 5 \setminus 4.8 / 2 - 3 &= 3 * 9 \text{ Mod } 4 + 5 \setminus 4.8 / 2 - 3 \quad \text{<-end of first scan} \\
&= 27 \text{ Mod } 4 + 5 \setminus 2.4 - 3 \quad \text{<-end of second scan} \\
&= 27 \text{ Mod } 4 + 2 - 3 \quad \text{<-end of third scan} \\
&= 3 + 2 - 3 \quad \text{<-end of fourth scan} \\
&= 2 \quad \text{<-end of fifth scan}
\end{aligned}
$$

The expression below yields the value of –2.73, as follows:

$$2 - 3 * 4 / 5 \wedge 2 + 5 / 4 * 3 - 2 \wedge 3 = 2 - 3 * 4 / 25 + 5 / 4 * 3 - 8 \quad \text{<-end of first scan}$$
$$= 2 - 0.48 + 3.75 - 8 \qquad \text{<-end of second scan}$$
$$= -2.73 \qquad \text{<-end of third scan}$$

When operations of the same precedence are encountered, the normal rules of precedence apply. For example,

A – B – C is interpreted as (A – B) – C
A / B / C is interpreted as (A / B) / C
A ∧ B ∧ C is interpreted as (A ∧ B) ∧ C
A \ B \ C is interpreted as (A \ B) \ C
A Mod B Mod C is interpreted as (A Mod B) Mod C

Using Parentheses in Numeric Expressions

Parentheses may be used to change the order of operations. In Visual Basic .NET, parentheses normally are used to avoid ambiguity and to group terms in a numeric expression. The order in which the operations in an expression containing parentheses are evaluated can be stated as follows: when parentheses are inserted into an expression, the part of the expression within the parentheses is evaluated first, and then the remaining expression is evaluated according to the normal rules of operator precedence.

Use of Parentheses in a Numeric Expression
When parentheses are inserted into an expression, the part of the expression within the parentheses is evaluated first, and then the remaining expression is evaluated according to the normal rules of operator precedence.

If the first example was rewritten with parentheses, as $(18 / 3) \wedge 2 + 4 * 2$, then it would be evaluated in the following manner:

$$(18 / 3) \wedge 2 + 4 * 2 = 6 \wedge 2 + 4 * 2$$
$$= 36 + 4 * 2$$
$$= 36 + 8$$
$$= 44$$

Evaluating expressions with parentheses should be done as follows: Make five scans from left to right within each pair of parentheses, and only after doing this, make the standard five passes over the entire numeric expression.

Evaluating Expressions with Parentheses
Make five scans from left to right within each pair of parentheses, and only after doing this, make the standard five passes over the entire numeric expression.

The expression below yields the value of 1.41, as follows:

$$(2 - 3 * 4 / 5) \wedge 2 + 5 / (4 * 3 - 2 \wedge 3) = (2 - 3 * 4 / 5) \wedge 2 + 5 / (4 * 3 - 8)$$
$$= (2 - 2.4) \wedge 2 + 5 / (12 - 8)$$
$$= (-0.4) \wedge 2 + 5 / 4$$
$$= 0.16 + 5 / 4$$
$$= 0.16 + 1.25$$
$$= 1.41$$

When coding a numeric expression, use parentheses freely when in doubt as to the valid form and evaluation of a numeric expression. For example, if you want Visual Basic .NET to divide 8 * D by 3 ^ P, the expression may correctly be written as 8 * D / 3 ^ P, but you also may write it as follows:

$$(8 * D) / (3 \wedge P)$$

> **Tip**
>
> **Use of Parentheses when Coding Expressions**
> When coding a numeric expression, use parentheses freely when in doubt as to the valid form and evaluation of a numeric expression. Adding parentheses helps to provide clarity when you are evaluating an expression.

For more complex expressions, Visual Basic .NET allows parentheses to be contained within other parentheses. When this occurs, the parentheses are said to be **nested**. In this case, Visual Basic .NET evaluates the innermost parenthetical expression first, and then goes on to the outermost parenthetical expression. Thus, 18 / 3 ^ 2 + (3 * (2 + 5)) is broken down in the following manner:

$$18 / 3 \wedge 2 + (3 * (2 + 5)) = 18 / 3 \wedge 2 + (3 * 7)$$
$$= 18 / 3 \wedge 2 + 21$$
$$= 18 / 9 + 21$$
$$= 2 + 21$$
$$= 23$$

Table 4-18 gives examples of the Visual Basic .NET equivalent of some algebraic statements and the equivalent Visual Basic .NET assignment statements.

Table 4-18   Algebraic Statements and Equivalent Assignment Statements

ALGEBRAIC STATEMENTS	EQUIVALENT VISUAL BASIC .NET ASSIGNMENT STATEMENTS
$H = \sqrt{X^2 + Y^2}$	`H = (X ^ 2 + Y ^ 2) ^ 0.5`
$S = AL^P K^{1-P}$	`S = A * L ^ P * K ^ (1 - P)`
$Q = \dfrac{-b + \sqrt{b^2 - 4ac}}{2a}$	`Q = (-B + (B ^ 2 - 4 * A * C) ^ 0.5) / (2 * A)`
$A = F\left[\dfrac{r}{(1+r)^n - 1}\right]$	`A = F * (R / (((1 + R) ^ N) - 1))`
$P = \sqrt[3]{(x-p)^2 + y^2}$	`P = ((X - P) ^ 2 + Y ^ 2) ^ (1 / 3)`
$Z = \dfrac{ab}{x + \sqrt{x^2 - a^2}}$	`Z = A * B / (X + (X ^ 2 - A ^ 2) ^ 0.5)`

When coding expressions, be sure to avoid two common errors. First, check that you have surrounded the correct part of an expression with parentheses. Second, check that you have balanced the parentheses, by checking that the expression has as many close parentheses as open parentheses.

Construction of Error-Free Numeric Expressions

If you have written a numeric expression observing the order of operator precedence, Visual Basic .NET can translate the expression without generating any error messages. This is no guarantee, however, that Visual Basic .NET actually will be able to evaluate it. In other words, although a numeric expression may be formed in a valid fashion, Visual Basic .NET may not be able to evaluate it because of the numbers involved. In situations where error conditions arise during execution, Visual Basic .NET will halt the program and display a dialog box informing you of the error.

Applying the following rules when coding expressions should help you avoid such hazards:

1. Do not attempt to divide by 0.
2. Do not attempt to determine the square root of a negative value.
3. Do not attempt to raise a negative value to a nonintegral value.
4. Do not attempt to compute a value that is greater than the largest permissible value or less than the smallest permissible nonzero value for the data type.

Table 4-19 illustrates some examples of the combinations to be avoided in numeric expressions written in a Visual Basic .NET program.

Table 4-19 *Invalid Numeric Expressions*

ERROR	EXAMPLES

Division by 0	1. Z = 2 * 8
	   A = 16
	   B = A - Z
	   C = A / B
	2. W = X / 0

Negative number raised to Nonintegral value	Value = -25 Result = Value ^ (1 / 2)
Number too large	Dim Value As Single Value = 999999 ^ 500

Coding an Expression to Calculate a Monthly Interest Rate

The formula used to compute the monthly payment requires that a monthly interest rate be used. In the Automobile Loan Calculator application, the user enters the current annual interest rate, which is expressed as a percentage. Therefore, the rate entered by the user must be divided by 100, and then divided by 12 in order to calculate the monthly rate to use in the final calculation. Figure 4-51 shows the numeric expression needed to calculate the monthly rate.

```
236          ' Set the true interest rate based on the input rate
237          ' divided by 12.0.
238          dblRate = (Convert.ToDouble(nudRate.Value) / 100.0) / 12.0
```

FIGURE 4-51

Line 238 first converts the Value property, which has the Decimal data type, of the nudRate control to the data type of Double. The result then is divided by 100.0. The result of that calculation then is divided by 12.0. Because Option Strict is On, all values in the expression must be of the same data type. The decimal place (.0) thus is added to the values 100 and 12 to make them 100.0 and 12.0, values of the Double data type. If the values 100 and 12 are used, Visual Basic .NET interprets the values as integers of the Short data type and will display an error message at run time. The following step inserts the code for an expression to calculate the monthly rate for use in the btnComputePayment_Click event procedure.

To Code an Expression to Calculate a Monthly Interest Rate

1. Press the ENTER key twice. Enter the lines of code from Figure 4-51 and do not press the ENTER key.

Lines 236 through 238 display in the code window (Figure 4-52). The assignment statement in line 238 calculates a monthly interest rate and then assigns the value to the dblRate variable.

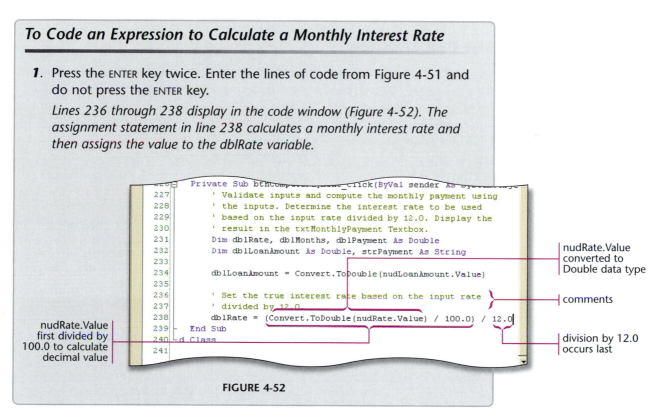

FIGURE 4-52

After line 238 executes, the dblRate variable contains a monthly interest rate expressed as a decimal value.

The next step is to use the variables, dblRate, gdblMonths, and dblLoanAmount to calculate the monthly payment.

Intrinsic Functions

Visual Basic .NET includes built-in functions, or **intrinsic functions,** that you can use in your code. For a complete list and descriptions of all these Visual Basic .NET functions, search online Help using the phrase, run-time library members. The Visual Basic .NET **run-time library** is divided into several categories, such as financial and date and time functions. These functions are not part of the .NET Framework class library discussed in Chapter 1, and are available only when coding Visual Basic .NET programs. Appendix E contains an overview of common .NET Framework class library classes. The fact that these intrinsic functions are not part of the .NET Framework class library is what makes them different from methods, such as Convert.ToDouble(), used earlier in this chapter. Intrinsic functions are accessible to Visual Basic .NET only. They are not available in other .NET languages. Visual Basic .NET includes intrinsic functions largely for backward compatibility with older versions of Visual Basic. In Visual Basic .NET, classes in the .NET Framework class library duplicate most functionality of intrinsic functions. The intrinsic financial functions, however, which are very useful, are not duplicated in the framework.

The Pmt Function

As indicated in the program design on page VB 4.06, the actual computation for the monthly payment is performed by one of Visual Basic .NET's financial functions, the Pmt function. The **Pmt function** is in the financial category of the run-time library functions. The Pmt function returns the payment for a loan based on periodic, constant payments and a constant interest rate. The Pmt function performs the work of the calculation described in the requirements document. The function is used in a code statement in the following manner:

Pmt(rate, nper, pv, fv, due)

As shown, the Pmt function accepts five arguments. The five arguments within the Pmt function are described in Table 4-20.

Table 4-20   Arguments Passed to the Pmt Function

ARGUMENT	DESCRIPTION
rate	Interest rate per period. For example, if you get a car loan at an annual percentage rate of 9 percent and make monthly payments, the rate per period is 0.09/12, or .0075.
nper	Total number of payment periods in the loan. For example, if you make monthly payments on a five year car loan, your loan has a total of 5 * 12 (or 60) payment periods.
pv	Present value that a series of payments to be made in the future is worth now (to the lender). For example, if you borrow $10,000 to buy a car, its pv is –10,000.
fv (optional)	Future value or cash balance you want after you have made the final payment. The future value of a loan is 0.
due (optional)	Number indicating when payments are due. Use 0 if payments are due at the end of the period, and use 1 if the payments are due at the beginning of the period.

Table 4-21 lists the other Visual Basic .NET intrinsic financial functions, their arguments, and their purpose.

Table 4-21 **Intrinsic Financial Functions**

FUNCTION	ARGUMENTS	PURPOSE
Ddb()	cost salvage life period factor (optional)	Calculates the depreciation of an asset for a specific period using the double-declining balance method or some other method you specify by changing the factor argument.
Fv()	rate nper pmt pv (optional) due (optional)	Calculates the future value of an annuity based on periodic, fixed payments and a fixed interest rate.
Ipmt()	rate per nper pv fv (optional) due (optional)	Calculates the interest payment for a given period of an annuity based on periodic, fixed payments and a fixed interest rate.
Irr()	valuearray() guess (optional)	Calculates the internal rate of return for a series of periodic cash flows. The series of cash flows is placed in the valuearray() argument.
Mirr()	valuearray() financerate reinvestrate	Calculates the modified internal rate of return for a series of periodic cash flows. The series of cash flows is placed in the valuearray() argument.
Nper()	rate pmt pv fv (optional) due (optional)	Calculates the number of periods for an annuity based on periodic, fixed payments and a fixed interest rate.
Npv()	rate valuearray()	Calculates the net present value of an investment based on a series of periodic cash flows and a discount rate. The series of cash flows is placed in the valuearray() argument.
Ppmt()	rate per nper pv fv (optional) due (optional)	Calculates the principal payment for a given period of an annuity based on periodic, fixed payments and a fixed interest rate.
Pv()	rate nper pmt fv (optional) due (optional)	Calculates the present value of an annuity based on periodic, fixed payments to be paid in the future and a fixed interest rate.

(continued)

Table 4-21   Intrinsic Financial Functions *(continued)*

FUNCTION	ARGUMENTS	PURPOSE
Rate()	nper pmt pv fv (optional) due (optional) guess (optional)	Calculates the interest rate per period for an annuity.
Sln()	cost salvage life	Calculates the straight-line depreciation of an asset for a single period.
Syd()	cost salvage life period	Calculates the sum-of-years digits representation of an asset for a specified period.

In the btnComputePayment_Click event procedure, the dblRate variable contains the monthly interest rate (rate), the dblMonths variable contains the number of months (nper), and the dblLoanAmount variable contains the value of the loan (pv). As indicated in Table 4-20 on page VB 4.58, for a loan, the Pmt function requires a negative value for the present value (pv) argument, because a payment is considered a debit (negative value) and the specifications call for displaying the payment as a positive number. The negative value of a variable is indicated by placing a minus sign (–) before the variable name.

Using a Negative Value

The negative value of a variable is indicated by placing a minus sign (–) before the variable name.

Figure 4-53 shows the code required to call the Pmt function and assign the result of the function to the dblPayment variable. Functions return a value and the value returned has a data type, just as any value does in code. Therefore, because Option Strict is set to On, the data type of the resulting value of the Pmt function, which is a Double, must match the data type of the variable it is assigned to, dblPayment.

```
240        ' Calculate the monthly payment using the .NET PMT
241        ' function. Format the result as currency and then
242        ' display the result in the txtMonthlyPayment Textbox.
243        dblPayment = Pmt(dblRate, gdblMonths, -dblLoanAmount)
```

FIGURE 4-53

The following step illustrates using the Pmt function.

To Use the Pmt Function

1. Press the ENTER key twice. Enter the lines of code from Figure 4-53 and do not press the ENTER key.

Lines 240 through 243 display in the code window (Figure 4-54). The assignment statement calls the Pmt function to calculate the monthly payment and assigns the result to the dblPayment variable.

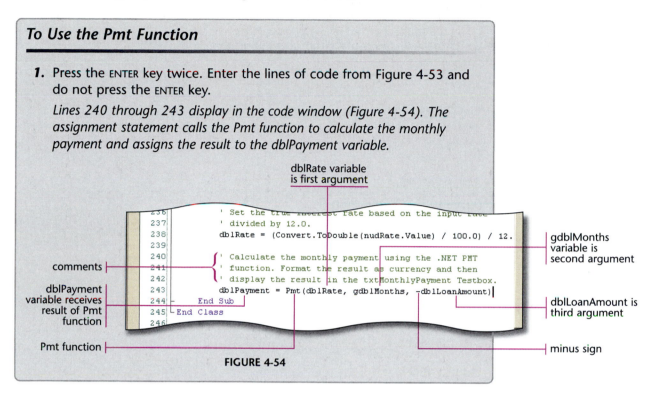

FIGURE 4-54

Figure 4-54 shows the Pmt function and the three arguments passed to it. The minus sign before the dblLoanAmount variable tells the Pmt function to calculate a payment on a loan. The result of the Pmt function is assigned to the dblPayment variable.

The Format$ Function

The statements in Figure 4-55 format the result of the Pmt function as dollars and cents and place the value in the txtMonthlyPayment TextBox control.

```
244          strPayment = Format$(dblPayment, "Currency")
245          txtMonthlyPayment.Text = strPayment
```

FIGURE 4-55

strPayment is a string variable declared at the top of the event procedure. The **Format$ function** is an intrinsic function that takes the first item in parentheses, dblPayment, and formats it as specified by the second item in the parentheses, "Currency". Currency is a predefined format name, which means Visual Basic .NET will display the value dblPayment in a more readable fashion in the Monthly payment text box. The Format$ function returns a value with a String data type. Table 4-22 on the next page summarizes the more frequently used predefined formats for the Format$ function in Visual Basic .NET. The last column in the table shows the result of formatting the value, 12345.678.

Tip

Using the Format$ Function

Use the Format$ function to make displayed numeric results more visually appealing and understandable to the user.

Table 4-22   Common Formats for the Format$ Function

FORMAT	DESCRIPTION	RESULT OF FORMATTING 12345.678
General Number, G, g	Displays the number as is	12345.678
Currency, C, c	Displays the number with a dollar sign, a thousands separator, and two digits to the right of the decimal; negative numbers display in parentheses	$12,345.68
Fixed, F, f	Displays at least one digit to the left and two digits to the right of the decimal separator	12345.68
Standard, N, n	Displays the number with a thousands separator; if appropriate, displays two digits to the right of the decimal	12,345.68
Percent, P, p	Displays the number multiplied by 100 with a % sign	1,234,567.80%
Scientific, E, e	Uses standard scientific notation	1.234568e+004
True/False	Displays False if the number is 0; otherwise, displays True	True
On/Off	Displays Off if the number is 0; otherwise, displays On	On
Yes/No	Displays No if the number is 0; otherwise, displays Yes	Yes

The following step enters the code shown in Figure 4-55 on the previous page in the btnComputePayment_Click event procedure.

To Use the Format$ Function

1. Press the ENTER key. Enter the lines of code from Figure 4-55 and do not press the ENTER key.

Lines 244 and 245 display in the code window (Figure 4-56). The first statement formats the dblPayment variable as currency and assigns the resulting string to the strPayment variable. Line 245 assigns the strPayment string variable to the Text property of the txtMonthlyPayment TextBox control.

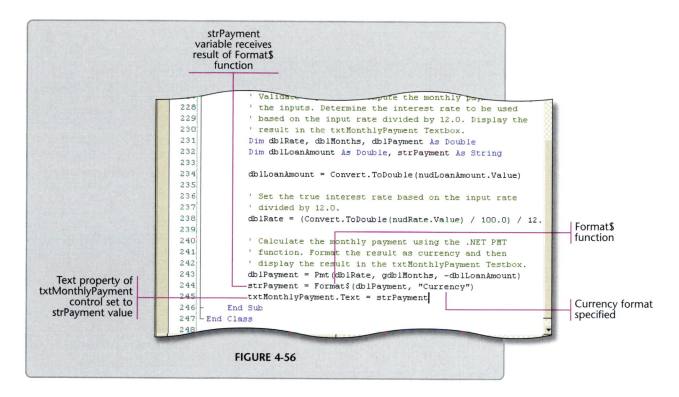

strPayment
variable receives
result of Format$
function

Format$
function

Text property of
txtMonthlyPayment
control set to
strPayment value

Currency format
specified

```
228    ' Validate ... compute the monthly pay...
229    ' the inputs. Determine the interest rate to be used
230    ' based on the input rate divided by 12.0. Display the
231    ' result in the txtMonthlyPayment Textbox.
       Dim dblRate, dblMonths, dblPayment As Double
232    Dim dblLoanAmount As Double, strPayment As String
233
234    dblLoanAmount = Convert.ToDouble(nudLoanAmount.Value)
235
236    ' Set the true interest rate based on the input rate
237    ' divided by 12.0.
238    dblRate = (Convert.ToDouble(nudRate.Value) / 100.0) / 12.
239
240    ' Calculate the monthly payment using the .NET PMT
241    ' function. Format the result as currency and then
242    ' display the result in the txtMonthlyPayment Testbox.
243    dblPayment = Pmt(dblRate, gdblMonths, -dblLoanAmount)
244    strPayment = Format$(dblPayment, "Currency")
245    txtMonthlyPayment.Text = strPayment
246        End Sub
247  End Class
248
```

FIGURE 4-56

The preceding steps showed how to use the Format$ function to change the appearance of the output value, dblPayment. The Format$ function converts the value of the dblPayment variable to a string and then applies the Currency format to the result. The formatted string is assigned to the Text property of the txtMonthlyPayment control, meaning that the result is displayed to the user.

The coding phase for the Automobile Loan Calculator application is now complete and the application can be tested.

Saving, Testing, and Documenting the Project

The following steps save the form and project files for the Automobile Loan Calculator project on the Data Disk in drive A and then run the application to test the code.

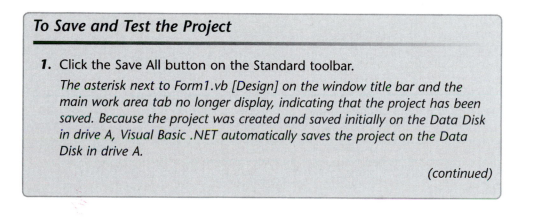

To Save and Test the Project

1. Click the Save All button on the Standard toolbar.

The asterisk next to Form1.vb [Design] on the window title bar and the main work area tab no longer display, indicating that the project has been saved. Because the project was created and saved initially on the Data Disk in drive A, Visual Basic .NET automatically saves the project on the Data Disk in drive A.

(continued)

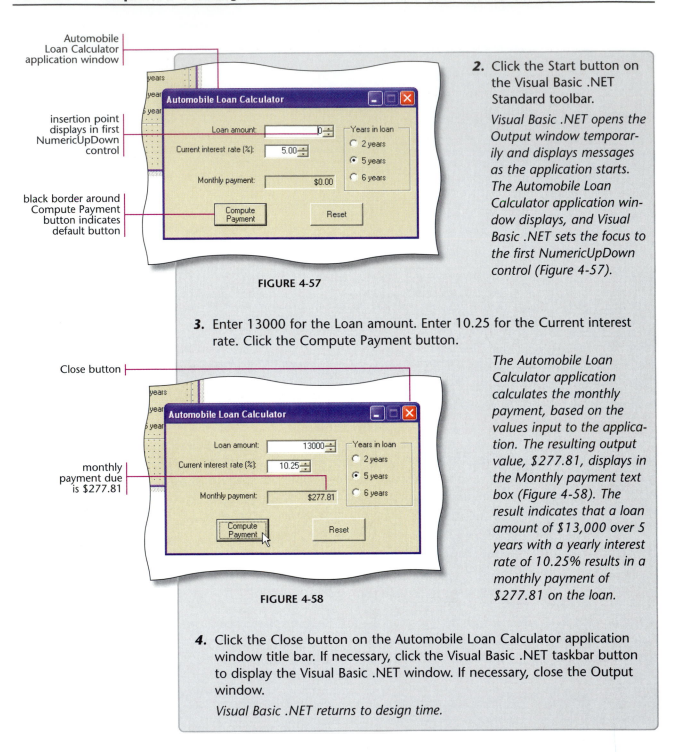

Automobile
Loan Calculator
application window

insertion point
displays in first
NumericUpDown
control

black border around
Compute Payment
button indicates
default button

FIGURE 4-57

2. Click the Start button on the Visual Basic .NET Standard toolbar.

Visual Basic .NET opens the Output window temporarily and displays messages as the application starts. The Automobile Loan Calculator application window displays, and Visual Basic .NET sets the focus to the first NumericUpDown control (Figure 4-57).

3. Enter 13000 for the Loan amount. Enter 10.25 for the Current interest rate. Click the Compute Payment button.

Close button

monthly
payment due
is $277.81

The Automobile Loan Calculator application calculates the monthly payment, based on the values input to the application. The resulting output value, $277.81, displays in the Monthly payment text box (Figure 4-58). The result indicates that a loan amount of $13,000 over 5 years with a yearly interest rate of 10.25% results in a monthly payment of $277.81 on the loan.

FIGURE 4-58

4. Click the Close button on the Automobile Loan Calculator application window title bar. If necessary, click the Visual Basic .NET taskbar button to display the Visual Basic .NET window. If necessary, close the Output window.

Visual Basic .NET returns to design time.

When testing the application, it is important to test the boundary conditions stated in the requirements. In the Automobile Loan Calculator application, the requirements state the boundary condition for the maximum loan amount to be $25,000. Therefore, you should test the value of 25000 for the Loan amount and some value higher than 25000 to make certain that the program behaves correctly.

Testing an Application

When testing an application, make certain that all rules are tested for their minimum and maximum values. Also, test any special cases that are specified in the requirements document.

Once you have tested the data validation rules for minimum and maximum values, the testing process for the Automobile Loan Calculator application is complete. The final step of the development cycle is to document the application. The following steps document the application and quit Visual Basic .NET. Line numbers are printed on the code listing.

To Document the Application and Quit Visual Basic .NET

1. If necessary, close the Output window. Click the Form1.vb [Design] tab, and then follow the steps on page VB 2.34 of Chapter 2 using the PRINT SCREEN key to print a record of the user interface design of the Automobile Loan Calculator form.

A record of the user interface design of the Automobile Loan Calculator application is printed (Figure 4-59).

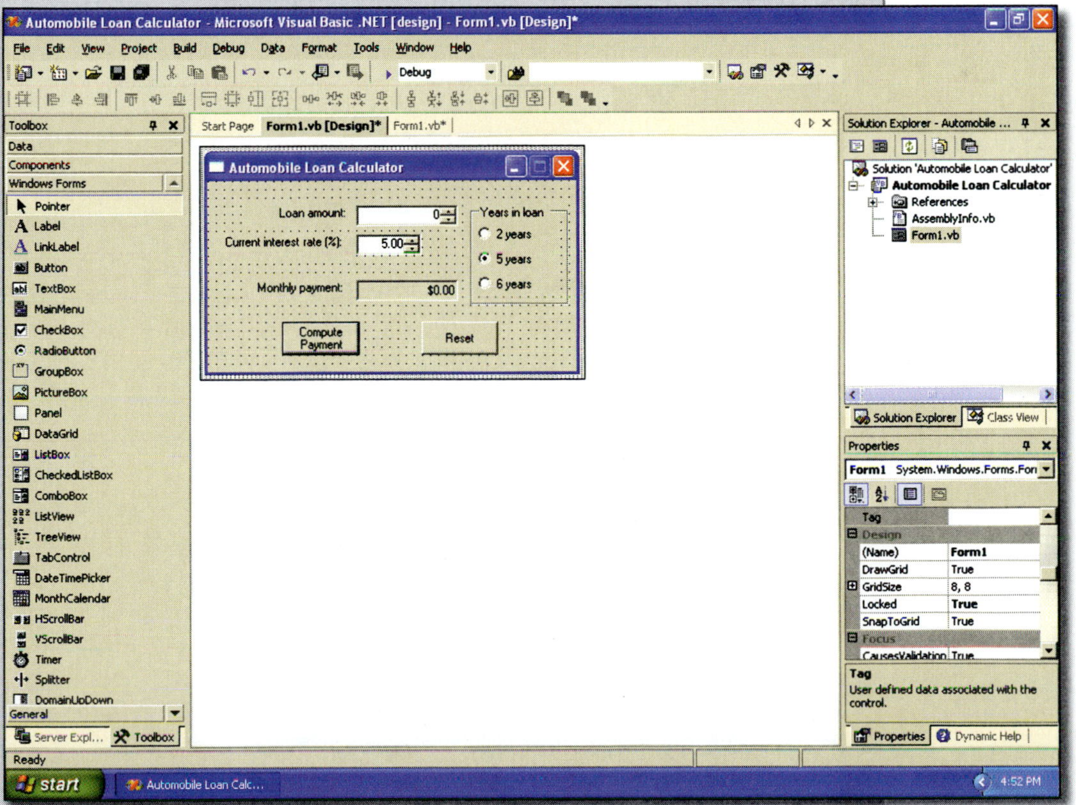

FIGURE 4-59

(continued)

2. Click the Form1.vb tab. Click File on the menu bar and then click Page Setup.

3. When the Page Setup dialog box displays, if necessary, click Line numbers and then click the OK button.

4. Follow the steps on page VB 2.40 of Chapter 2 using the Print command on the File menu to print a record of the code for the Automobile Loan Calculator application.

   A record of the Automobile Loan Calculator application code is printed (Figure 4-60).

```
A:\Chapter4\Automobile Loan Calculator\Automobile Loan Calculator\Form1.vb                    1
 1 Option Strict On
 2 Public Class Form1
 3     Inherits System.Windows.Forms.Form
 4
 5 Windows Form Designer generated code
 6     ' Chapter 4:      Automobile Loan Calculator
 7     ' Programmer:     Jeff Quasney
 8     ' Date:           September 22, 2004
 9     ' Purpose:        This project calculates the monthly payment for
10     '                 a loan based on loan amount, interest rate, and
11     '                 length of the loan.
12     Dim gdblMonths As Double = 60.0
13     Const MaximumLoanAllowed As Integer = 25000
14
15     Private Sub Form1_Load(ByVal sender As System.Object, ByVal e As System.EventArgs) ↵
       Handles MyBase.Load
16         ' Set the maximum value of the Loan amount NumericUpDown control
17         nudLoanAmount.Maximum = MaximumLoanAllowed
18     End Sub
19
20     Private Sub btnReset_Click(ByVal sender As System.Object, ByVal e As System.       ↵
       EventArgs) Handles btnReset.Click
21         ' Reset Loan Amount and Monthly payment to zero. Reset
22         ' the interest rate to 5%, and select five years for the
23         ' length of the loan
24         nudLoanAmount.Value = 0
25         nudRate.Value = 5
26         radFiveYears.Checked = True
27         txtMonthlyPayment.Text = "$0.00"
28     End Sub
29
30     Private Sub radTwoYears_CheckedChanged(ByVal sender As System.Object, ByVal e As   ↵
       System.EventArgs) Handles radTwoYears.CheckedChanged
31         gdblMonths = 24.0
32     End Sub
33
34     Private Sub radFiveYears_CheckedChanged(ByVal sender As System.Object, ByVal e As  ↵
       System.EventArgs) Handles radFiveYears.CheckedChanged
35         gdblMonths = 60.0
36     End Sub
37
38     Private Sub radSixYears_CheckedChanged(ByVal sender As System.Object, ByVal e As   ↵
       System.EventArgs) Handles radSixYears.CheckedChanged
39         gdblMonths = 72.0
40     End Sub
41
42     Private Sub btnComputePayment_Click(ByVal sender As System.Object, ByVal e As      ↵
       System.EventArgs) Handles btnComputePayment.Click
43         ' Validate inputs and compute the monthly payment using
44         ' the inputs. Determine the interest rate to be used
45         ' based on the input rate divided by 12.0. Display the
46         ' result in the txtMonthlyPayment Textbox.
47         Dim dblRate, dblMonths, dblPayment As Double
48         Dim dblLoanAmount As Double, strPayment As String
49
50         dblLoanAmount = Convert.ToDouble(nudLoanAmount.Value)
51
52         ' Set the true interest rate based on the input rate
53         ' divided by 12.0.
54         dblRate = (Convert.ToDouble(nudRate.Value) / 100.0) / 12.0
55
56         ' Calculate the monthly payment using the .NET PMT
57         ' function. Format the result as currency and then
58         ' display the result in the txtMonthlyPayment Textbox.
59         dblPayment = Pmt(dblRate, gdblMonths, -dblLoanAmount)
60         strPayment = Format$(dblPayment, "Currency")
61         txtMonthlyPayment.Text = strPayment
62     End Sub
63 End Class
64
```

FIGURE 4-60

5. Click the Visual Basic .NET Close button.

If you made changes to the project since the last time it was saved, Visual Basic .NET displays the Microsoft Visual Basic .NET dialog box. If you click the Yes button, you can save your project and quit. If you click the No button, you will quit without saving changes. Clicking the Cancel button will close the dialog box.

Chapter Summary

In this chapter, you learned how to use two new controls: the GroupBox control and the RadioButton control. You learned how to use the Layout toolbar to align and size controls quickly. You then learned how to set a default button on a form and lock a form and its controls, so that they could not be moved or resized accidently. You learned how to declare variables and constants and how data types are used. You also learned how to code mathematical expressions and the order of operator precedence. Finally, you learned how to use instrinsic functions, such as Pmt and Format$, and pass parameters to functions.

What You Should Know

Having completed this chapter, you now should be able to perform the tasks shown in Table 4-23.

Table 4-23   Chapter 4 What You Should Know

TASK NUMBER	TASK	PAGE
1	Start Visual Basic .NET and Start a New Project	VB 4.08
2	Set Form Properties and Add Controls	VB 4.10
3	Add a GroupBox Control to a Form	VB 4.11
4	Add RadioButton Controls to Create a Group of Controls	VB 4.12
5	Change the Properties of Controls	VB 4.15
6	Change the Properties of a GroupBox Control	VB 4.17
7	Change the Properties of RadioButton Controls	VB 4.20
8	Select Multiple Controls and Use the Align Rights Button	VB 4.23
9	Size and Align Input and Output Controls	VB 4.25
10	Size and Align Button Controls	VB 4.26
11	Size and Align Controls in a Group	VB 4.27
12	Align the Tops of Controls	VB 4.28
13	Verify the Size and Position of Controls	VB 4.29
14	Set the Default Button on a Form	VB 4.31
15	Lock Controls on a Form	VB 4.32
16	Declare a Constant	VB 4.37
17	Code a Form Load Event Procedure	VB 4.39
18	Code the btnReset_Click Event Procedure	VB 4.40
19	Code an Option Strict Statement	VB 4.42
20	Declare a Global Variable	VB 4.45
21	Code the CheckChanged Event Procedures for RadioButton Controls	VB 4.46
22	Declare Local Variables	VB 4.49
23	Code an Assignment Statement to Convert a Data Type	VB 4.50
24	Code an Expression to Calculate a Monthly Interest Rate	VB 4.57
25	Use the Pmt Function	VB 4.61
26	Use the Format$ Function	VB 4.62
27	Save and Test the Project	VB 4.63
28	Document the Application and Quit Visual Basic .NET	VB 4.65

Key Terms

AcceptButton property *(VB 4.30)*
argument *(VB 4.50)*
arithmetic operator *(VB 4.51)*
Boolean *(VB 4.34)*
Byte *(VB 4.34)*
Char *(VB 4.34)*
Checked property *(VB 4.18)*
Const keyword *(VB 4.35)*
constant *(VB 4.33)*
constant declaration statement
 (VB 4.36)
container control *(VB 4.11)*
Convert.ToDouble() method
 (VB 4.49)
data type *(VB 4.34)*
Date *(VB 4.34)*
Decimal *(VB 4.34)*
declare *(VB 4.34)*
default button *(VB 4.30)*
Dim statement *(VB 4.43)*
Double *(VB 4.34)*
expression *(VB 4.51)*
form Load event *(VB 4.38)*
Format$ function *(VB 4.61)*

global variable *(VB 4.44)*
groups *(VB 4.12)*
GroupBox control *(VB 4.11)*
Integer *(VB 4.34)*
intrinsic function *(VB 4.58)*
local variable *(VB 4.44)*
locking controls *(VB 4.32)*
Long *(VB 4.34)*
Mod operator *(VB 4.52)*
modulo operator *(VB 4.52)*
nested *(VB 4.55)*
numeric expression *(VB 4.51)*
Object *(VB 4.34)*
Option Strict statement *(VB 4.41)*
order of operator precedence
 (VB 4.51)
Pmt function *(VB 4.58)*
RadioButton control *(VB 4.12)*
run-time library *(VB 4.58)*
scope *(VB 4.43)*
Short *(VB 4.34)*
Single *(VB 4.34)*
String *(VB 4.34)*
value *(VB 4.33)*
variable *(VB 4.33)*

Homework Assignments

Short Answer

1. Which arithmetic operation is performed first in the following numeric expressions?
   a. 8 / 6 * 4
   b. intCount + intCount1 – intX
   c. 8 * (intInventoryAmount + 3)
   d. (X * (3 / Y)) ^ 6 + Z ^ (2 ^ 2) + 8 Mod 5
   e. dblPrice / dblInventory + dblTax
   f. (B ^ 2 – 4 * A * C) / (2 * A)

2. Evaluate each of the following:
   a. 4 * 5 * 3 / 6 – 6 ^ 2 / 12
   b. (3 ^ 4) + 7 * 4
   c. 7 * 5 / 2 + 9 Mod 3 + 3

3. Calculate the numeric value for each of the following valid numeric expressions if A = 3.0, C = 5.0, W = 3.0, T = 3.0, X = 1.0, and Y = 2.0.
   a. $(C - A * 3) + 8.1$
   b. $(A / (C + 1) * 4 - 5) / 2 + (4 \text{ Mod } 3 \setminus 3)$
   c. $50.0 / (X * Y) \wedge W$
   d. $X + 7.0 * Y * W / 3.0 - 7.0 / (T - X / Y) + W \wedge T$

4. Repeat the above assignment for the case of A = 2.0, C = 3.0, W = 4.0, T = 4.0, X = 2.0, and Y = 2.0.

5. Which of the following are invalid variable names in Visual Basic .NET? Why?
   a. X
   b. PriCe
   c. Const
   d. R.3
   e. 531
   f. Dim
   g. _Sng
   h. A-Z
   i .Q9
   j. _Integer

6. Write a valid statement for each of the following algebraic statements. Use appropriate variable names.
   a. $q = (d + e)^{1/3}$
   b. $d = (A^2)^{3.2}$
   c. $Y = a_1x + a_2x^2 + a_3x^3 + a_4x^4$
   d. $v = 100 - (2/3)^{100 - B}$

7. If necessary, insert parentheses so that each numeric expression results in the value indicated on the right side of the arrow.
   a. $8 / 2 + 2 + 12 \longrightarrow 14$
   b. $8 \wedge 2 - 1 \longrightarrow 8$
   c. $3.0 / 2.0 + 0.5 + 3.0 \wedge 1.0 \longrightarrow 5.0$
   d. $12.0 \text{ Mod } 5.0 \setminus 2.0 + 1.0 \wedge 2.0 + 1.0 * 2.0 * 3.0 / 4.0 - 3.0 / 2.0 \longrightarrow 0.5$
   e. $12 - 2 - 3 - 1 - 4 \longrightarrow 10$
   f. $7 * 3 + 4 \wedge 2 - 3 / 13 \longrightarrow 22$
   g. $3 * 2 - 3 * 4 * 2 + 3 \longrightarrow -60$
   h. $3 * 6 - 3 + 2 + 6 * 4 - 4 / 2 \wedge 1 \longrightarrow 33$

8. Consider the valid code below. What is displayed in the txtResult TextBox control when the code is executed?
   a. Dim A As Double = 2.0
      Dim B as Double = 3.0
      Dim D as Double
      D = (A ^ 4.0 / A * B) – (8 .0* B / 4.0)
      D = D + 1.0
      txtResult.Text = D

   b. Dim A As Double = 2.0
      Dim B As Double = 3.0
      Dim E1, E2, E3 As Double
      B = 4.0

```
El = A * B
E3 = 4.0 + 1.0
E2 = E2 / E3
A  = El + E2
txtResult.Text = D
```

9. What does the following code display in the Value1 and Value2 TextBox controls?

   dblAverage1 = 4.0 + 5.0 + 6.0 + 7.0 + 8.0 / 5.0

   dblAverage2 = (4.0 + 5.0 + 6.0 + 7.0 + 8.0) / 5.0

   txtValue1.Text = dblAverage1

   txtValue2.Text = dblAverage2

10. The _____ control is used as a container for other controls.

11. List the defaults for the following RadioButton controls.

    a. CheckAlign _____   b. Checked   _____   c. FlatStyle _____

    d. ImageAlign _____   e. AutoCheck _____

12. The _____ toolbar contains tools that allow you to adjust the alignment spacing and size of any group of controls on a form.

13. Use the _____ key to select two or more controls at the same time.

14. When the user presses the ENTER key during run time and the form has the name of a Button control assigned as the _____ property, the Click event procedure assigned to the button executes.

15. _____ disallows the ability to modify controls on a form during design time.

16. _____ are numbers or strings that programmers will never change in the code. _____ represent a location in memory which can change values as the code executes. _____ represents a location in memory, but its value cannot change during execution of the code.

17. The _____ determines what kind of data the variables or constants can store.

18. A variable or constant name must begin with a(n) _____ and can be up to _____ characters in length.

19. The _____ statement is used to instruct Visual Basic .NET to force the programmer to make certain all assignments occur with the same type on both sides of the assignment and that all variables are explicitly declared.

20. The _____ function converts the value of a numeric argument to a Double data type.

21. To display a positive payment, append a _____ to the front of the present value argument in the Pmt function.

22. The _____ function is used to format a value so that it displays in a meaningful form.

Learn It Online

Start your browser and visit scsite.com/vbnet/exs. Follow the instructions in the exercises below.

1. **Chapter Reinforcement TF, MC, and SA** Click the True/False, Multiple Choice, and Short Answer link below Chapter 4. Print and then answer the questions.

2. **Practice Test** Click the Practice Test link below Chapter 4. Answer each question, enter your first and last name at the bottom of the page, and then click the Grade Test button. When the graded practice test displays on your screen, click Print on the File menu to print a hard copy. Continue to take practice tests until you score 80% or better. Hand in a printout of the final practice test.

3. **Crossword Puzzle Challenge** Click the Crossword Puzzle Challenge link below Chapter 4. Read the instructions, and then enter your first and last name. Click the Play button. Complete the crossword puzzle. When you are finished, click the Submit button. When the crossword puzzle redisplays, click the Print button.

4. **Tips and Tricks** Click the Tips and Tricks link below Chapter 4. Click a topic that pertains to Chapter 4. Right-click the information and then click Print on the shortcut menu. Construct a brief example of what the information relates to in Visual Basic .NET to confirm you understand how to use the tip or trick. Hand in the example and printed information.

5. **Newsgroups** Click the Newsgroups link below Chapter 4. Click a topic that pertains to Chapter 4. Print three comments.

6. **Expanding Your Horizons** Click the Articles for Visual Basic .NET below Chapter 4. Click a topic that pertains to Chapter 4. Print the information. Construct a brief example of what the information relates to in Visual Basic .NET to confirm you understand the contents of the article. Hand in the example and printed information.

7. **Search Sleuth** Select three key terms from the Key Terms section of this chapter and then use the Google search engine at google.com (or any major search engine) to display and print two Web pages for each key term.

Debugging Assignment

Start Visual Basic .NET and open the project, Kona's Coffee Supply, from the Chapter4\Konas Coffee Supply folder on the Data Disk. See the inside back cover for instructions for downloading the Visual Basic .NET Data Disk or see your instructor for information on accessing the files required for this book. The project consists of a form that calculates the price of an order based on a quantity ordered, item price, and customer type. The calculate button calculates the total price for the order and then displays the result in a text box. Preferred customers and New customers receive a 4% discount. Delinquent customers pay an additional 5% on any order.

The Kona's Coffee Supply project contains bugs in the user interface and in the program code. Follow the steps below to debug the project.

1. Use the Layout toolbar to size and align controls that are not sized or aligned correctly. The Label controls should be right-aligned. The NumericUpDown controls and TextBox control should be left-aligned and sized the same. The Button controls should be centered on the form together and should be the same size.

2. The uppermost RadioButton control is not inside the GroupBox control container. Delete the control and add a new RadioButton control with correct properties in the appropriate location. Be sure not to lose the code associated with the control's event procedure.

3. The Compute Total button is not the default button. Make the Compute Total button the default button for the form.

4. Format the total as Currency in the code using the Format$ function.

5. A bug in the computation causes Delinquent customers to receive a 5% discount instead of a 5% penalty. Fix this bug.

6. Save the project and then run the project to test for any additional bugs. Enter 2500 for the quantity, 15.75 as the price, and select a Customer type of New. The application should display as shown in Figure 4-61 with a total of $37,800.00.

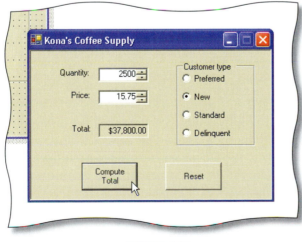

FIGURE 4-61

7. Document the form code for the Form1.vb form. Circle the lines of code you modified on the code printout.

Programming Assignments

1 Understanding Code Statements

Carefully read each of the following descriptions. Write code statements to accomplish specific tasks. Record your answers on a separate sheet of paper. Number your answers to correspond to the code descriptions.

1. Write a code statement that will display the characters, Salutations, in a Label control with a name of lblGreeting.

2. Write a code statement that will clear a TextBox control with the name of txtBlank.

3. Write a code statement that will create a variable called total. The variable should have a data type of Short.

4. When a RadioButton control with a name of radGreeting is checked, write a code statement that displays, Salutations, in a Label control with a name of lblGreeting; otherwise, when a second RadioButton control is checked the code statement should display, Farewell, in the same Label control.

2 Present Value Function

Start Visual Basic .NET. Open the project, Lottery Projection from the Chapter 4/Lottery Projection folder on the Data Disk. This application calculates the present value of payments received over a given number of years assuming a certain interest rate can be achieved in an investment in the same time frame. The calculation can be used to compare receiving a lump-sum lottery payment for a lottery winner versus receiving a certain number of payments over several years.

Perform the following tasks to complete the application.

1. Unlock the controls on the form.

2. Add the three RadioButton controls to the GroupBox1 control with the following labels:

```
10 yearly payments
20 yearly payments
25 yearly payments
```

Make 20 yearly payments the default. Use the Layout toolbar to size and align all of the controls on the form.

3. Set appropriate Name and Text properties for each of the new controls.

4. Open the code window by double-clicking the btnComputePV button and add code similar to the code below. This code will add a global variable in the general section of the Form1.vb code file to hold the number of years of payments selected by the user. Add appropriate comments to your code. Be sure to enter the Option Strict On code line as line 1 of the code.

```
Dim gdblYears As Double = 10.0
```

In the btnComputePV_Click event procedure, add code to declare variables that you will use in the event procedure as follows:

```
Dim dblAmount, dblPV As Double, strPV As String
```

5. After the code added in step 4, insert the following code to convert the Yearly payment amounts value to the data type Double and assign the result to the dblAmount variable.

```
dblAmount = Convert.ToDouble(txtAmount.Text)
```

6. Add the code to perform the calculation of the present value of the payments. The present value function, PV, accepts three inputs: the interest rate, the number of payments, and the amount of the payments. The interest rate is calculated from the Value property of the nudRate control. The number of payments is based on the item selected in the RadioButton group. Insert the following code after the code entered in step 5:

```
dblRate = Convert.ToDouble(nudRate.Value)
dblPV = PV(dblRate, gdblYears, -dblAmount)
```

7. To format the output value and display it on the form, insert code similar to the following code after the code inserted in step 6:

```
strPV = Format$(dblPV, "Currency")
txtPV.Text = strPV
```

8. Lock the controls on the form and then save the project.

9. Run the project and correct any errors. If changes have been made, save the project again. The application window should display as shown in Figure 4-62 at run time.

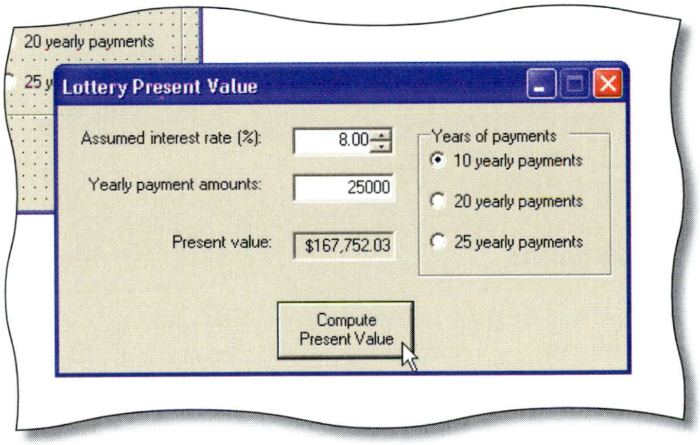

FIGURE 4-62

3 Production Lot Size Calculation

When a company manufactures several products, the management must decide how many units of one product should be produced before switching the manufacturing system over to produce another product. The number of units of a certain product to produce before switching to another product is called the lot size. Costs are associated both with having a number of units in inventory (CarryingCost) and with switching manufacturing to another product (SetupCost). If a company must produce a certain quantity of a product in a given year (UnitsPerYear), it must determine how many to produce at each production run in order to meet that quantity, keep inventory costs low, and

(continued)

3 Production Lot Size Calculation *(continued)*

keep the cost of switching the manufacturing system low. The production lot size tells the company how many units of a product to produce before changing the manufacturing over to another product.

The production lot size (ProductionLotSize) is calculated as follows:

ProductionLotSize = ((2 × UnitsPerYear × SetupCost) / CarryingCost) ^ .5

Design and write a program that calculates the production lot size based on a number of units to produce each year, a setup cost, and an inventory cost to carry a unit in inventory for a year. Use NumericUpDown controls for the three input values. Limit the UnitsPerYear between 500 and 15,000, the SetupCost between $150 and $500, and the CarryingCost between $1 and $5. The completed application should display as shown in Figure 4-63.

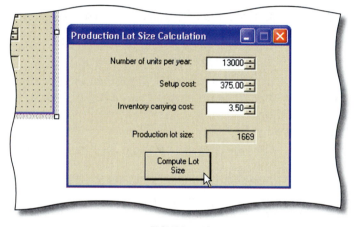

FIGURE 4-63

4 Modulus Operator

Write a program that will display the number of dollars and cents in two output TextBox controls based on user numeric input. For instance, if the user inputs 543, the program will display 5 in the Dollars output TextBox control and 43 in the Cents output TextBox control. For this program, use integer arithmetic and avoid using decimal variables and values. If necessary, review the integer remainder modular operator, Mod, introduced in this chapter. The completed application should display as shown in Figure 4-64.

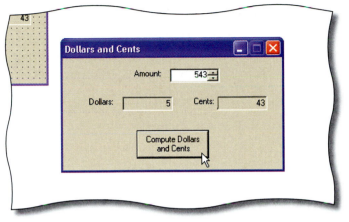

FIGURE 4-64

5 Using RadioButton Controls and Global Variables

Design and develop a project to assign a letter grade to a student's assignment based on a test score and other criteria. Use a NumericUpDown control to allow the instructor's assistant to enter a test score between 0 and 100. Use a group of RadioButton controls to determine the grade on Extra Credit Problem #1 – None, Average (3 point bonus), or Above average (5 point bonus). Use a second group of RadioButton controls to select whether a student handed in the assignment on time, with the default being On time. The other choices are 1 to 2 days late (5 point penalty) and more than 2 days late (automatic score of 0). Display the final total grade in a read-only TextBox control. Use global variables to keep track of which RadioButton control is checked before determining the final grade. Display the result in a message box with a user-friendly message. The completed application should display as shown in Figure 4-65.

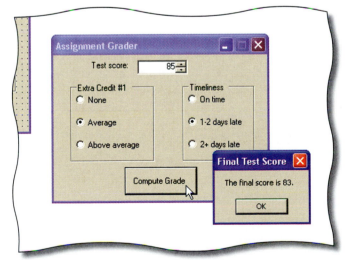

FIGURE 4-65

6 English to Metric Conversion

Design and develop a project to convert an English measurement in miles, yards, feet, and inches to a metric measurement in kilometers, meters, and centimeters. Use the following formula to change the English measurement to inches:

Total Inches = 63,360 × Miles + 36 × Yards + 12 × Feet + Inches

Use the following formula to determine the equivalent meters:

Meters = Total Inches / 39.37

Declare constants for all numeric values in the two formulas above. The variable used to represent the number of meters and the numeric constant 39.37 must be declared as the data type Double. The constants and data types in the first formula should be declared as integers. Convert the Total Inches in the second formula to a Double data type before using it in the calculation. Set Option Strict to On in your code.

(*Hint:* After the number of meters has been determined, the maximum number of kilometers can be computed from: Kilometers = Meters\ 1,000. Next, the remaining meters can be determined from: Remaining Meters = Meters – 1,000 * Kilometers. The number of integer meters in Remaining Meters then can be determined from: Integer Meters = Convert.ToInt32(Remaining Meters). Continue with the same technique to compute the number of centimeters.)

Use the following test data to test your program: 2 miles, 5 yards, 2 feet, and 7 inches. The result should be 3 kilometers, 224 meters, and 5.38 centimeters. The completed application should display as shown in Figure 4-66.

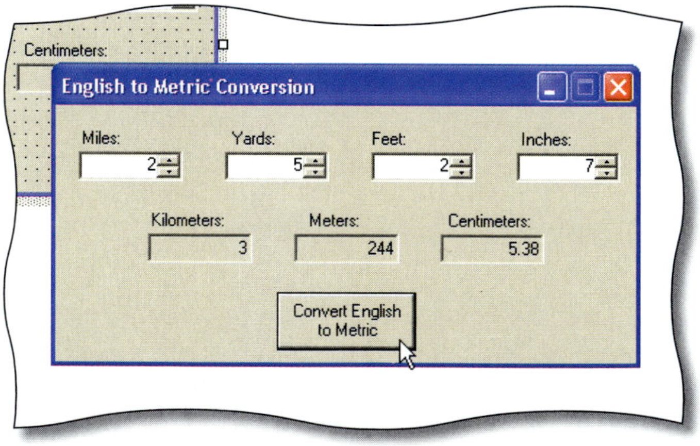

FIGURE 4-66

7 Multiple Groups of RadioButton Controls

You recently were hired at Stark Machines to build applications for its accounting department. One of your first assignments is to design and develop a Windows application to calculate employee yearly raises. You have decided that the yearly salary must be entered in a NumericUpDown control with a range of 10000 to 75000 for the salary. Use RadioButton controls to select the raise percentage rates of 8% for sales, 10% for labor, or 5% for management. The number of years from 1 to 35 can be selected using a NumericUpDown control. Use a second RadioButton control group to designate whether an employee has worked more than 15 years, in which case the employee is entitled to an additional 2% raise.

8 Slope and Intercept Calculation

Using the concepts presented in this chapter, design and write a program that accepts two sets of (X, Y) coordinates, (X1, Y1) and (X2, Y2), and then calculates and displays the slope and Y intercept of the line that intersects the two coordinates. Use NumericUpDown controls to limit the coordinates to integer values between 0 and 20.

9 Using Events and Expressions

Write a Windows application for a self-service printing center that sells self-service copies at 4 cents per page, computer time at $3.00 per ten minutes, and computer laser printing at 9 cents per page. Use NumericUpDown controls to input quantities of each item. Next to each quantity, include a read-only TextBox control that displays the price of the quantity multiplied by the price per unit listed above. Update each TextBox control when the ValueChanged event of each NumericUpDown control executes. When the Textbox control is updated, its TextChanged event will execute. In each of the three TextBox control's TextChanged event, include code that calculates the total in all three TextBox controls and then updates a fourth TextBox control at the bottom of the form with the total. Be sure to initialize all of the controls on the form correctly. The form should not contain any Button controls, only the controls mentioned above.

10 Writing an Expression for a Monthly Payment

Write a valid Visual Basic .NET expression for the Automobile Loan Payment formula in the project developed in this chapter. If you developed the Automobile Loan Payment application in this chapter, place the expression in your code as a substitute for the use of the Pmt function. Be sure to use any data type conversions necessary to conform to the restrictions of the Option Strict On statement. Test the change to be sure that you obtain the same results as the Pmt function.

A

Flowcharting, Pseudocode, and the Unified Modeling Language (UML)

Appendix A explains how to prepare, use, and read program flowcharts, pseudocode, and basic Unified Modeling Language (UML) diagrams. Chapter 1 includes an introduction to flowcharting and flowchart symbols beginning on page VB 1.14. Pseudocode is introduced on page VB 1.16, and the UML is discussed briefly on page VB 1.20.

Guidelines for Preparation of Flowcharts

Before the flowchart can be drawn, a thorough analysis of the problem, the input data, and the desired output results must be performed. The program logic required to solve the problem also must be determined. On the basis of this analysis, a **general flowchart** illustrating the main path of the logic can be sketched. This flowchart can be refined until the overall program logic is fully determined. This general flowchart is used to make one or more **detailed flowcharts** of the various branches of and detours from the main path of the program logic. After each detailed flowchart has been freed of logical errors and other undesirable features, such as unnecessary steps, the actual coding of the program in a computer language can be undertaken.

Straight-Line Flowcharts

Figure A-1 illustrates a general, straight-line flowchart. A **straight-line flowchart** is one in which the symbols are arranged sequentially, without any deviations or looping, until the terminal symbol that represents the end of the flowchart is reached. Once the operation indicated in any one symbol has been performed, that operation is never repeated.

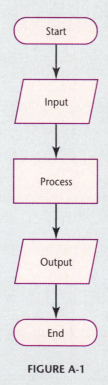

FIGURE A-1

Flowcharts with Looping

A general flowchart that illustrates an iterative, or repeating, process known as **looping** is shown in Figure A-2. The logic illustrated by this flowchart is in three major parts: initialization, process, and wrap-up. A flowline exits from the bottom symbol in Figure A-2 and enters above the diamond-shaped decision symbol that determines whether the loop is to be executed again. This flowline forms part of a loop inside which some operations are executed repeatedly until specified conditions are satisfied. This flowchart shows the input, process, and output pattern; it also uses a decision symbol that shows where the decision is made to continue or stop the looping process.

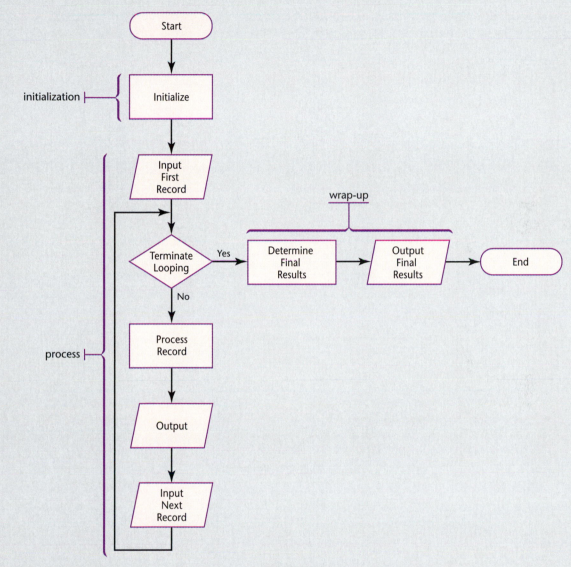

FIGURE A-2

Figure A-2 contains three braces that show the initialization, process, and wrap-up operations. For example, setting the program counters to 0 may represent an initialization operation and displaying the values of counters may represent a wrap-up operation.

Like the straight-line flowchart, a flowchart with looping need not have all the symbols shown in Figure A-2, or a flowchart can have many more symbols. For example, the process symbol within the loop in Figure A-2, when applied to a particular problem, may expand to include branching forward to bypass a process or backward to redo a process. It also is possible that through the use of decision symbols, the process symbol in Figure A-2 could be expanded to include several loops, some of which might be independent from each other and some of which might be within other loops.

A flowchart shows a process that is carried out. Flowcharts are flexible; they can show any logical process no matter how complex it may be, and they can show it in whatever detail is needed.

The two flowcharts illustrated in Figure A-3 represent the same program that accepts and then displays a record. Then the program loops back to the accepting operation and repeats the sequence, accepting and displaying any number of records. A connector symbol, represented by a circle with a letter or number in it (in this case, A), indicates the continuation of the looping process.

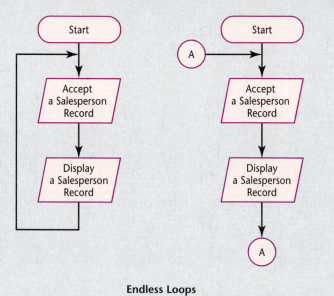

Endless Loops

FIGURE A-3

Although the flowcharts in Figure A-3 illustrate two ways a loop can be represented, the particular loop that is shown is an **endless loop**, also called an **infinite loop**. This type of loop should be avoided when constructing programs. In order to make a program finite, you must define it so it will terminate when specified conditions are satisfied.

Figure A-4 illustrates the use of a counter that terminates the looping process. Note that the counter is first set to 0 in the initialization step. After an account is read and a message is printed, the counter is incremented by 1 and tested to find whether it is now equal to 15. If the value of the counter is not 15, the looping process continues. If the value of the counter is 15, the looping process terminates.

For the flowchart used in Figure A-4, the exact number of accounts to be processed must be known beforehand. In practice, this will not always be the case because the number of accounts may vary from one run to the next.

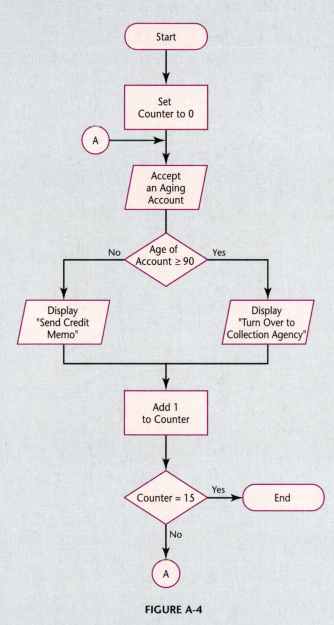

FIGURE A-4

A way to solve this type of problem is shown in Figure A-5, which illustrates the use of an end-of-file test to terminate the looping process. The value –999999 has been chosen to be the last account number. This kind of value sometimes is known as the **sentinel value** because it guards against continuing past the end-of-file. Also, the numeric item chosen for the last value cannot possibly be confused with a valid item because it is outside the range of the account numbers. Programs using an end-of-file test, such as the one shown in Figure A-5, are far more flexible and less limited than programs that do not, such as those illustrated in Figures A-3 and A-4 on pages VB A.04 and VB A.05.

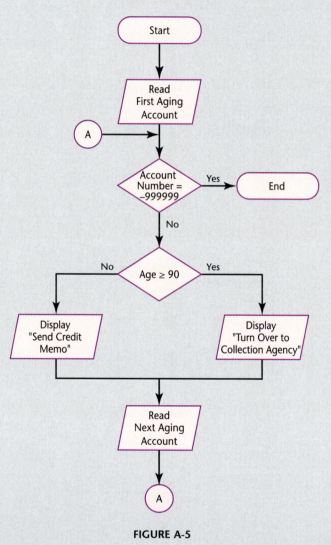

FIGURE A-5

Another flowchart with a loop is shown in Figure A-6. Figure A-6 illustrates the concept of counting. The flowchart incorporates the end-of-file test.

Simple computer programs do not require complex flowcharts and sometimes do not require flowcharts at all. As programs become more complex with many different paths of execution, however, a flowchart not only is useful but usually is a prerequisite for successful analysis and coding. Indeed, developing the problem solution by arranging and rearranging the flowchart symbols can lead to a more efficient solution.

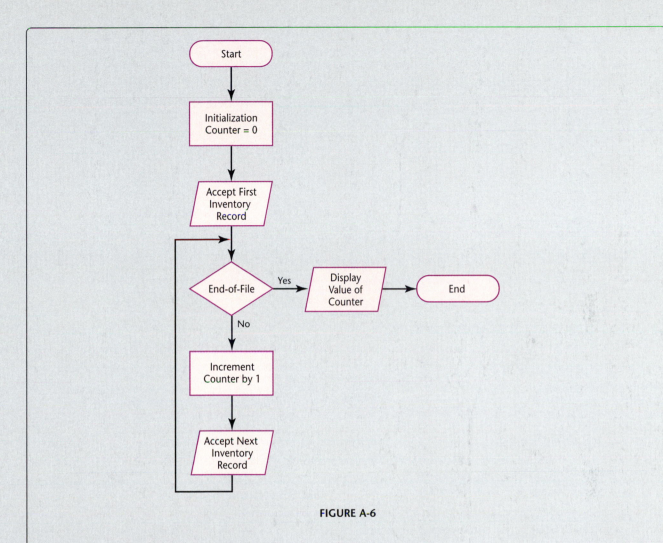

FIGURE A-6

Control Structures

The logic of almost any procedure or method can be constructed from the following three basic logic structures:

1. Sequence
2. If…Then…Else or Selection
3. Do While or Repetition

The following are two common extensions to these logic structures:

Do Until

Select Case (an extension of the If…Then…Else logic structure)

The **Sequence structure** is used to show one action or one action followed by another, as illustrated in Figures A-7a and A-7b. Every flowchart in this book includes this control structure.

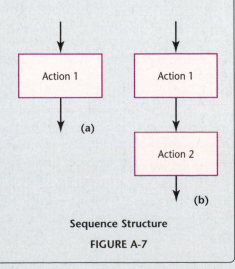

Sequence Structure

FIGURE A-7

The **If...Then...Else structure** represents a two-way decision made in the logic of the program. The decision is made on the basis of a condition that must be satisfied. If the condition is not satisfied, the program logic executes one action. If the condition is satisfied, the program logic executes a different action. This type of logic structure is shown in Figures A-8a and A-8b. The flowcharts presented in Figures A-4 and A-5 on pages VB A.05 and VB A.06 include this logic structure. The If…Then…Else structure also can result in a decision to take no action, as shown in Figure A-8b.

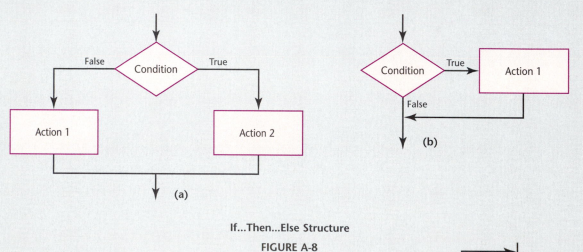

If...Then...Else Structure

FIGURE A-8

The **Do While structure** is the logic structure most commonly used to create a process that will repeat as long as the condition is true. The Do While structure is illustrated in Figure A-9 and has been used earlier in Figures A-2, A-5, and A-6. In a Do While structure, the decision to perform the action within the structure is at the top of the loop; as a result, the action will not occur if the condition is never satisfied.

The **Do Until structure** (Figure A-10) also is used for creating a process that will be repeated. The major differences between the Do Until and the Do While structures are that (1) the action within the structure of a Do Until always will be executed at least once, (2) the decision to perform the action within the structure is at the bottom of the Do Until loop, and (3) the Do Until loop exits when the condition is true.

Figure A-10 illustrates the Do Until structure, and the flowchart presented in Figure A-4 on page VB A.05 includes a Do Until structure.

The **Select Case structure** is similar to the If…Then…Else structure except that it provides more than two alternatives. Figure A-11 illustrates the Select Case structure.

A logical solution to a programming problem can be developed through the use of just these five logic structures. The program will be easy to read, easy to modify, and reliable; most important of all, the program will do what it is intended to do.

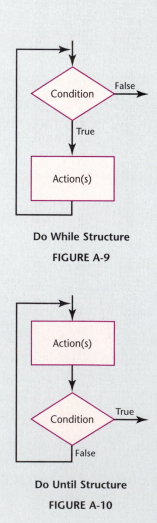

Do While Structure

FIGURE A-9

Do Until Structure

FIGURE A-10

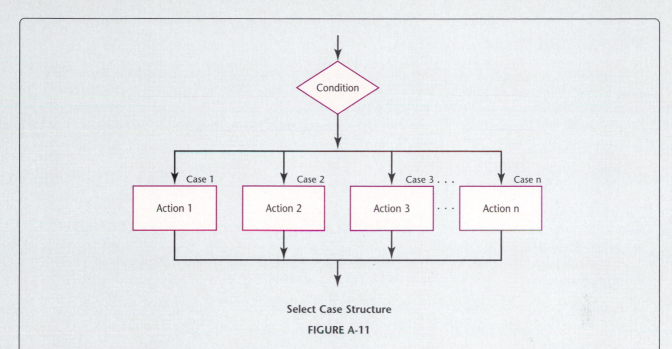

Select Case Structure

FIGURE A-11

Flowcharting Tips

The following recommendations can help make flowcharts more efficient and easier for others to understand. These suggestions assume that the input, processing, and output of the problem are defined properly in a requirements document.

1. Sketch a general flowchart and the necessary detail flowcharts before coding the problem. Repeat this step until you are satisfied with your flowcharts.

2. Use the control structures described on pages VB A.07 and VB A.08.

3. Put yourself in the position of the reader, keeping in mind that the purpose of the flowchart is to improve the reader's understanding of the solution to the problem.

4. Show the flow of processing from top to bottom and from left to right. When in doubt, use arrowheads as required to indicate the direction of flow.

5. Draw the flowchart so that it is neat and clear. Use the connector symbols to avoid excessively long flowlines.

6. Choose labels for each symbol that explain the function of the symbols in a clear and precise manner.

7. Avoid endless loops; construct loops so they will be terminated when specific conditions are satisfied.

The reason that flowcharts are so important is simple: the difficulties in programming lie mostly in the realm of logic, not in the syntax and semantics of the computer language. In other words, most computer errors are mistakes in logic, and a flowchart aids in detecting these types of mistakes.

Pseudocode

Pseudocode is a program design technique that uses natural English and resembles Visual Basic .NET code. It is an intermediate notation that allows the logic of a program to be formulated without diagrams or charts. Pseudocode resembles Visual Basic .NET in that specific operations can be expressed as commands that the program will execute. The following three examples illustrate pseudocode:

Accept Employee Record
MaleCounter = MaleCounter +1
Display Employee Record

What makes pseudocode appealing to many programmers is that it has no formal syntax, which allows programmers to concentrate on the design of the program rather than on the peculiarities of the programming language's syntax.

Although pseudocode has no formal rules, the following guidelines are commonly accepted by most programmers:

1. Begin the pseudocode with a program, procedure, or method title statement.

      Monthly Sales Analysis Report Procedure

2. End the pseudocode with a terminal program statement.

      End

3. Begin each statement on a new line. Use simple and short imperative sentences that contain a single transitive verb and a single object.

      Accept EmployeeNumber
      Subtract 10 From Quantity

4. Express assignments as a formula or as an English-like statement.

      WithholdingTax = 0. 20 × (GrossPay − 38.46 × Dependents)

   or

      Compute WithholdingTax

5. To avoid errors in the design, avoid using logic structures not available in the programming language being used.

6. For the If…Then…Else structure, use the following conventions:
   a. Indent the true and false tasks.
   b. Use End If as the structure terminator.
   c. Vertically align the If, Else, and End If statements.

These conventions for the If…Then…Else structure are illustrated in Figures A-12 and A-13.

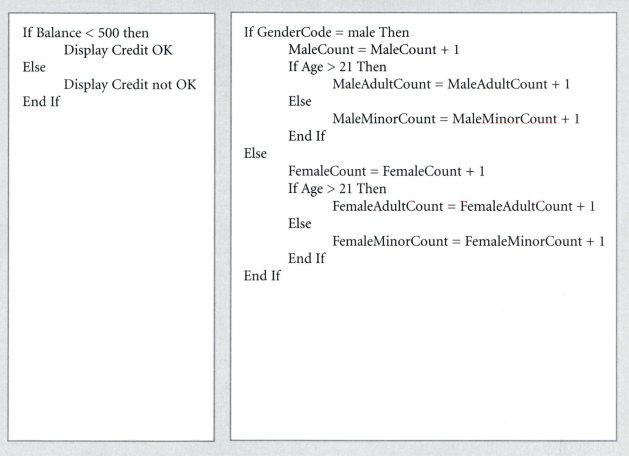

If Balance < 500 then
        Display Credit OK
Else
        Display Credit not OK
End If

If GenderCode = male Then
        MaleCount = MaleCount + 1
        If Age > 21 Then
                MaleAdultCount = MaleAdultCount + 1
        Else
                MaleMinorCount = MaleMinorCount + 1
        End If
Else
        FemaleCount = FemaleCount + 1
        If Age > 21 Then
                FemaleAdultCount = FemaleAdultCount + 1
        Else
                FemaleMinorCount = FemaleMinorCount + 1
        End If
End If

FIGURE A-12   FIGURE A-13

7. For the Do While structure, use the following conventions:
   a. If the structure represents a counter-controlled loop, begin the structure with Do.
   b. If the structure does not represent a counter-controlled loop, begin the structure with Do While.
   c. Specify the condition on the Do While or Do line.
   d. Use End Do as the last statement of the structure.
   e. Align the Do While or Do and the End Do vertically.
   f. Indent the statements within the loop.

The conventions for the Do While structure are illustrated in Figures A-14 and A-15 on the next page.

8. For the Do Until structure, use the following conventions:
   a. Begin the structure with Do Until.
   b. Specify the condition on the Do Until line.
   c. Use End Do as the last statement of the structure.
   d. Align the Do Until and the End Do vertically.
   e. Indent the statements within the loop.

```
SumFirst100Integers Procedure
        Sum = 0
        Do Integer = 1 to 100
                Sum = Sum + Integer
        End Do
        Display sum
End
```

FIGURE A-14

```
EmployeeFileList Procedure
        Display report and column headings
        EmployeeCount = 0
        Accept first Employee record
        Do While Not End-of-File
                Add 1 to EmployeeCount
                Display Employee record
                Accept next Employee record
        End Do
        Display EmployeeCount
End
```

FIGURE A-15

The conventions for the Do Until structure are illustrated in Figure A-16.

```
SumFirst100Integers Procedure
        Sum = 0
        Integer = 1
        Do Until Integer >100
                Sum = Sum + Integer
                Integer = Integer + 1
        End Do
        Display Sum
End
```

FIGURE A-16

9. For the Select Case structure, use the following conventions:
   a. Begin the structure with Select Case, followed by the variable to be tested.
   b. Use End Case as the structure terminator.
   c. Align Select Case and End Case vertically.
   d. Indent each alternative.
   e. Begin each alternative with Case, followed by the value of the variable that equates to the alternative.
   f. Indent the action of each alternative.

These conventions are illustrated in Figure A-17.

```
Select Case CustomerCode
        Case 100
                High-RiskCustomerCount = High-RiskCustomerCount + 1
        Case 200
                LowRiskCustomerCount = LowRiskCustomerCount + 1
        Case 300
                RegularCustomerCount = RegularCustomerCount + 1
        Case 400
                SpecialCustomerCount = SpecialCustomerCount + 1
End Case
```

FIGURE A-17

For an additional example of pseudocode, see Figure 1-14 in Chapter 1 on page VB 1.16.

The Unified Modeling Language (UML)

Just as flowcharts describe algorithms, object-oriented design (OOD) has a standard method to depict, or diagram, concepts for design purposes. The Unified Modeling Language (UML) is a notation used to describe object behaviors and interaction. The UML is a graphical language used to represent how a system behaves or should behave. The UML is a relatively new language, having been developed in the 1990s from a number of competing object-oriented design tools.

In OOD, each class can have one or more lower levels, called **subclasses**, or one or more higher levels, called **base classes**, or **superclasses**. For example, a class for Secretaries is a subclass of the Employee class. Person is a base class or superclass of Employee. The relationship among the classes, subclasses, and base classes is called the **hierarchy**. A **high-level class diagram** is a UML diagram used to show the hierarchical relationships among classes (Figure A-18).

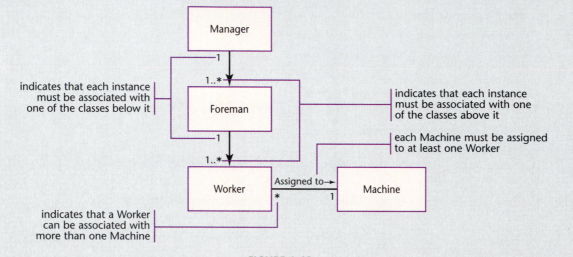

FIGURE A-18

Associations describe the manner in which instances of a class, or objects, are related. For example, two instances of a Worker class can have the association of being coworkers. This type of association is **bidirectional**, meaning each instance is associated with the other. Some associations are **unidirectional**, which means only one class is associated with the other. For example, a Worker instance can be assigned to operate an injection molder machine, which is an instance of the class Machines. The Worker is associated with the injection molder instance because a Worker must know how to operate the injection molder, but the injection molder does not have any information about or relationship to the Worker. In this way, the association between the Worker and Machine class is unidirectional.

The high-level class diagram shown in Figure A-18 depicts a hierarchy in which an instance of the Manager class can have several instances of the Foreman class associated with it; each instance of the Foreman class can have several workers associated with it; and each instance of the Worker class can be assigned to exactly one machine. Each class is represented by a box with the class name inside the box. Relationships are designated by lines between the classes.

The 1 below the Manager class indicates that each Manager class must have at least one Foreman class associated with it; the 1 below the Foreman class indicates that each Foreman class must have at least one Worker class associated with it. The 1..* above the Foreman class indicates that each Foreman class must be associated with at least one Manager class above it; the 1..* above the Worker class indicates that each Worker class must be associated with at least one Foreman class above it. The Assigned to label indicates that each Worker class is assigned to one Machine class. The 1 next to the Machine class indicates that each Machine class must be assigned at least one Worker class. The * next to the Worker class indicates that a worker can be associated with more than one Machine class.

Object-oriented programming (OOP) and OOD use many unique terms to describe program elements. In object-oriented terminology, the data stored about an object is called an attribute or property. An **attribute** or **property** is an identifying characteristic of individual objects, such as a name, weight, or color. An **operation** is an activity that reads or manipulates the data of an object. In OOD, an operation is a type of service. In OOP, the code that may be executed to perform a service is called a **method**.

A **detailed class diagram** is used to provide a visual representation of an object, its attributes, and its methods (Figure A-19 and Figure A-20). Figure A-19 shows the general form of a detailed class diagram. Figure A-20 shows a specific example of a detailed class diagram for the Foreman class. The Foreman class contains six attributes and five methods. The rules of the UML prescribe that each attribute and method begin with lowercase letters and that each method name is followed by parentheses. The parentheses indicate that the methods are procedures in the class. A detailed class diagram also can have additional notations.

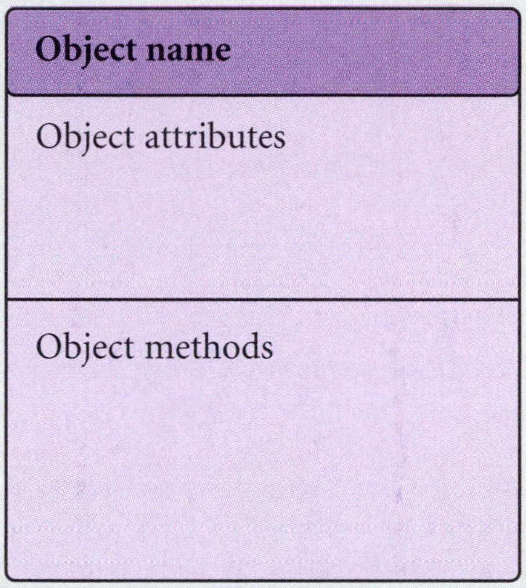

Object name
Object attributes
Object methods

FIGURE A-19

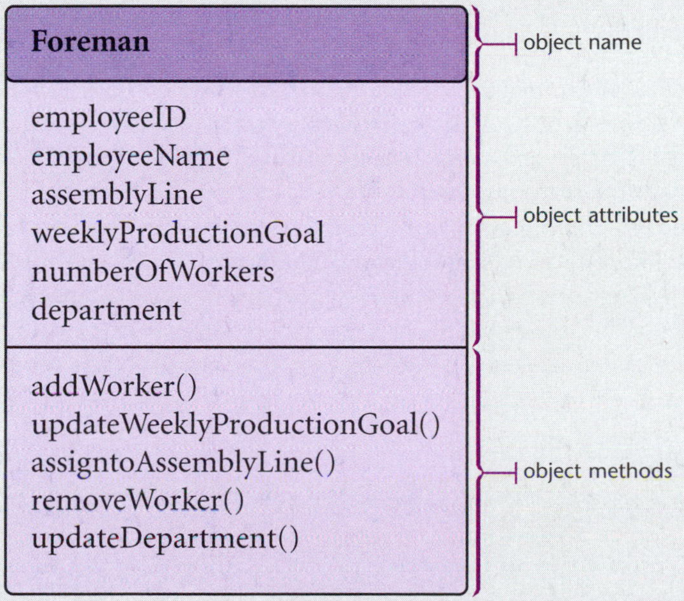

Foreman	object name
employeeID employeeName assemblyLine weeklyProductionGoal numberOfWorkers department	object attributes
addWorker() updateWeeklyProductionGoal() assigntoAssemblyLine() removeWorker() updateDepartment()	object methods

FIGURE A-20

Messages and Events

Message sending is a key component of object-oriented design because it describes how objects work together. For an object to do something, it must be sent a message. The **message** must have two parts: (1) the name of the object to which the message is being sent; and (2) the name of the operation that will be performed by the object. As you have learned, an operation is an activity that reads or manipulates the data of an object. An operation also can send additional messages while it performs its task.

Messages are sent through an interface to the object. Just as a user interface allows a program to accept data and instructions from the user, the **interface** is the way that an object receives messages.

As an example, suppose each time an assembly-line worker turns on a machine (an object), the machine tracks how many times it has been turned on by incrementing a counter. To turn on the machine, the worker presses a button on a panel to send a message to the machine. The button on the panel is the interface to the on method of the machine, and pressing the button is the event that sends a message to execute the on method. When the on method executes, part of its operation is to increment the numberTimesOn counter, which is an attribute of the machine. Suppose that the shop also uses an automated system to operate its machines. Machines can be turned on remotely using a computer. The interface that the computer uses to turn on the machine is different from the one the worker uses. The on method that executes on the machine, however, remains the same and the on method still increments the numberTimesOn counter attribute when it executes.

In OOD terminology, the operation, increment counter, is a service and the message, turn machine on, is called a **request for service**. Remember that in OOP terminology, the service is called a method and the message is what is sent when an event, such as a user pressing the on button, occurs. **Sequence diagrams** are used to represent the relationships among events and objects. In a sequence diagram, messages or events are shown as lines with arrows, classes are shown across the top in rectangles, and class names are underlined and prefaced by a colon (Figure A-21). As you read the sequence diagram, time progresses from top to bottom and the time the object is active is shown by vertical rectangles.

Figure A-21 illustrates a sequence diagram for a Foreman assigning a Worker to a Machine. The Foreman object in the first column interacts with other objects through the Foreman Interface. The Foreman sends a message through the Foreman Interface to find a Worker based on the worker's name. Next, the Foreman finds a Machine to assign the Worker based on the worker's skill. Finally, the assignment is made.

As shown in Figure A-21, nothing happens in a system unless a message is sent when an event occurs. At the conclusion of an operation, the system again will do nothing until another event occurs. This relationship of events causing operations is a key feature of OOP, and programs that are constructed in this way are said to be **event driven**.

The UML is a powerful tool because it can be used to describe any item, process, or concept in the real or imagined world. Its usefulness goes well beyond the programming world. People working in different disciplines or working in different industries can communicate concepts using the UML in a standard and well-understood manner. Another feature of the UML is that many types of diagrams provide different views of the same system, or object, in addition to the ones shown here. Different views of the same system are useful depending on a person's or object's role in the system.

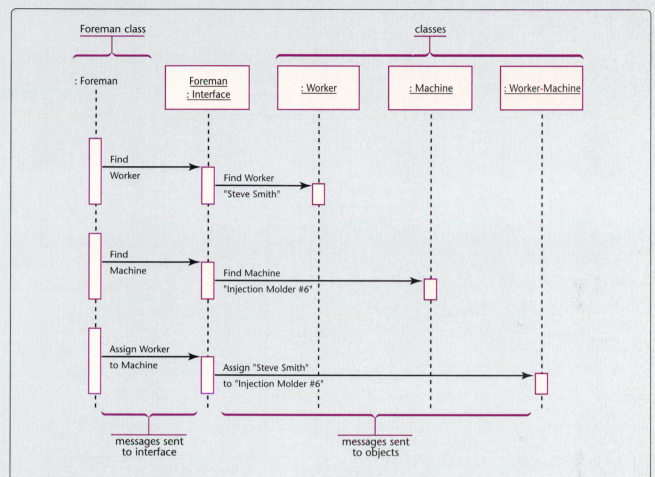

FIGURE A-21

HOMEWORK ASSIGNMENTS

1. In the flowchart in Figure A-22, what are the value of I and the value of J at the instant just after the statement J = J + 1 is executed for the fifth time? The value of I and J after the statement I = I + 2 is executed the tenth time? (A statement such as J = J + 1 is valid and is read as *the new value of J equals the old value of J plus one* or, equivalently, *the value of J is to be replaced by the value of J plus one*.)

2. Consider the section of a flowchart shown in Figure A-23. It assumes that an absent-minded person is going to work. This individual usually has the car keys but occasionally forgets them. Does the flowchart section in Figure A-23 incorporate the most efficient method of representing the actions to be taken? If not, redraw the flowchart portion given in Figure A-23.

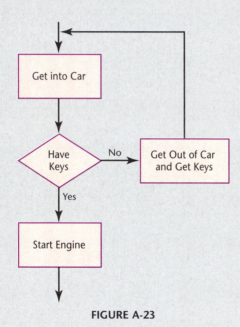

FIGURE A-23

3. In Figure A-24, the flowchart for a small program, what values of I and of J are printed when the output symbol is executed for the fiftieth time?

4. An opaque urn contains three diamonds, four rubies, and two pearls. Construct a flowchart that describes the following events: Take a gem from the urn. If it is a diamond, lay it aside. If it is not a diamond, return it to the urn. Continue in this fashion until all the diamonds have been removed. After all the diamonds have been removed, repeat the same procedure until all the rubies have been removed. After all the rubies have been removed, continue in the same fashion until all the pearls have been removed.

5. In the flowchart represented by Figure A-25, what is the value of I and the value of J at the instant the terminal symbol with the word End is reached?

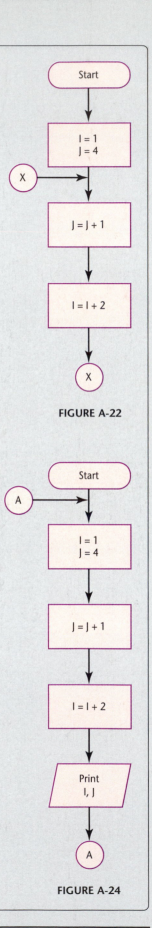

FIGURE A-22

FIGURE A-24

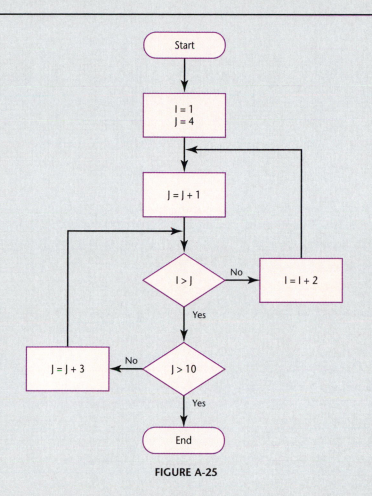

FIGURE A-25

6. Draw one flowchart, and only one, that will cause the mechanical mouse to go through any of the four mazes shown in Figure A-26. At the beginning, a user will place the mouse on the entry side of the maze, in front of the entry point, facing up toward the maze. The instruction Move to next cell will put the mouse inside the maze. Each maze has four cells. After that, the job is to move from cell to cell until the mouse emerges on the exit side. If the mouse is instructed to *Move to next cell* when a wall is in front of it, it will hit the wall and fall apart. Obviously, the mouse must be instructed to test whether it is *Facing a wall* before any *Move*. The physical movements and logical tests the mechanical mouse can complete are listed below Figure A-26.

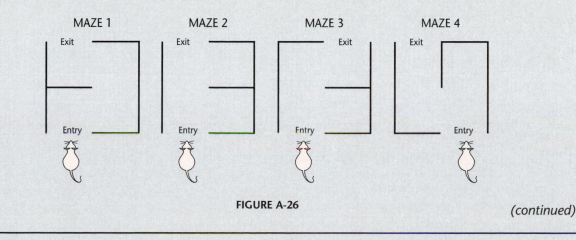

FIGURE A-26

(continued)

HOMEWORK ASSIGNMENTS

6. (continued)

  a. Physical movement:

    (1) Move to next cell. (The mouse will move in the direction it is facing.)

    (2) Turn right.

    (3) Turn left.

    (4) Turn around 180 degrees. (All turns are made in place, without moving to another cell.)

    (5) Halt.

  b. Logic:

    (1) Facing a wall? (Through this test, the mouse determines whether a wall is immediately in front of it, that is, on the border of the cell it is occupying and in the direction it is facing.)

    (2) Outside the maze?

    (3) On the entry side?

    (4) On the exit side?

7. Develop a detailed class diagram for an electric dishwasher. List at least eight attributes, including number of racks, model, and color. List at least six methods, including addDishes() and addDetergent().

8. Develop a high-level class diagram that shows the relationships among a manufacturer's inventory of finished products in its warehouses. The company has many warehouses that are managed by the inventory control supervisor. Each warehouse contains many bins of products. Each bin contains one product type.

9. Develop a sequence diagram that shows how the inventory control supervisor in assignment 8 assigns a product to a bin in a warehouse.

B

Changing Screen Resolution and the IDE Layout

Appendix B explains how to change your screen resolution to the resolution used in this book. The appendix also explains how to rearrange windows and toolbars to change the layout of the Visual Basic .NET IDE, so that it is better suited to your preferred work habits.

Changing Screen Resolution

The following steps show how to change your screen's resolution from 800 by 600 pixels to 1024 by 768 pixels, which is the screen resolution used in this book.

To Change Screen Resolution

1. Click the Start button on the Windows taskbar, and then point to Control Panel on the Start menu.

The Start menu displays, and Control Panel is highlighted on the Start menu (Figure B-1).

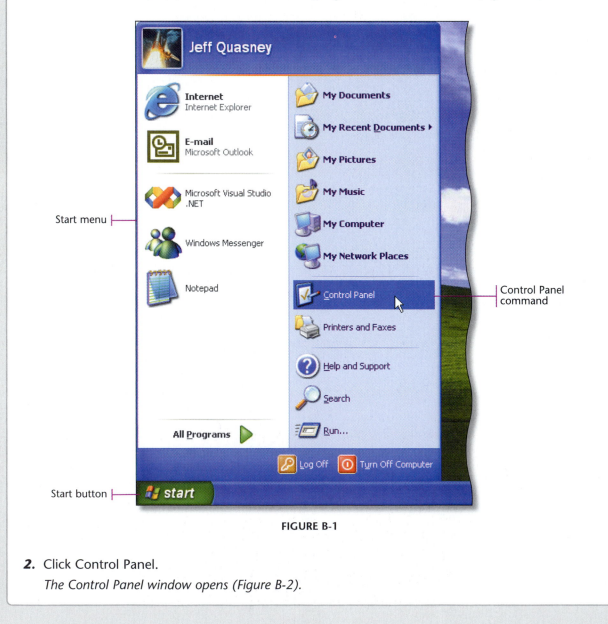

FIGURE B-1

2. Click Control Panel.

The Control Panel window opens (Figure B-2).

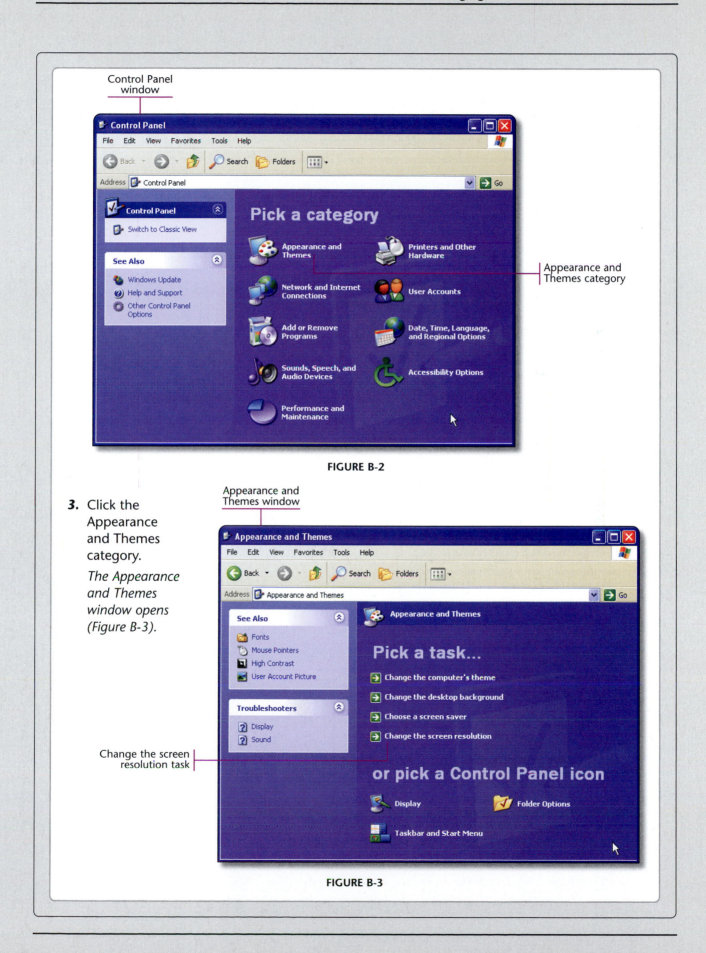

Control Panel window

FIGURE B-2

Appearance and Themes category

3. Click the Appearance and Themes category.

The Appearance and Themes window opens (Figure B-3).

Appearance and Themes window

Change the screen resolution task

FIGURE B-3

4. Click the Change the screen resolution task.

The Display Properties dialog box displays. The Settings tab is selected (Figure B-4). The current screen resolution displays in the screen resolution area.

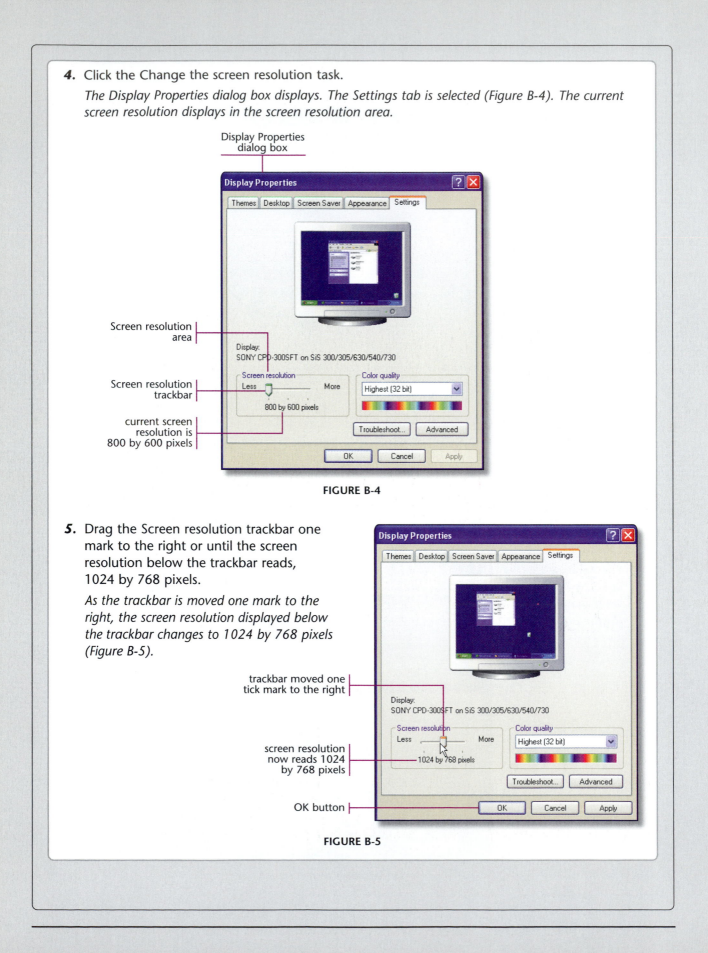

FIGURE B-4

5. Drag the Screen resolution trackbar one mark to the right or until the screen resolution below the trackbar reads, 1024 by 768 pixels.

As the trackbar is moved one mark to the right, the screen resolution displayed below the trackbar changes to 1024 by 768 pixels (Figure B-5).

FIGURE B-5

6. Click the OK button.

The Display Properties dialog box closes. The Windows desktop displays at a screen resolution of 1024 by 768 pixels, as shown in Figure B-6. Compare Figure B-6 with Figure B-3 to see the difference in the display between the 800 by 600 screen resolution and the 1024 by 768 screen resolution. With a higher resolution, more items can fit on the screen but the items, such as windows, text, and icons, display at a smaller size.

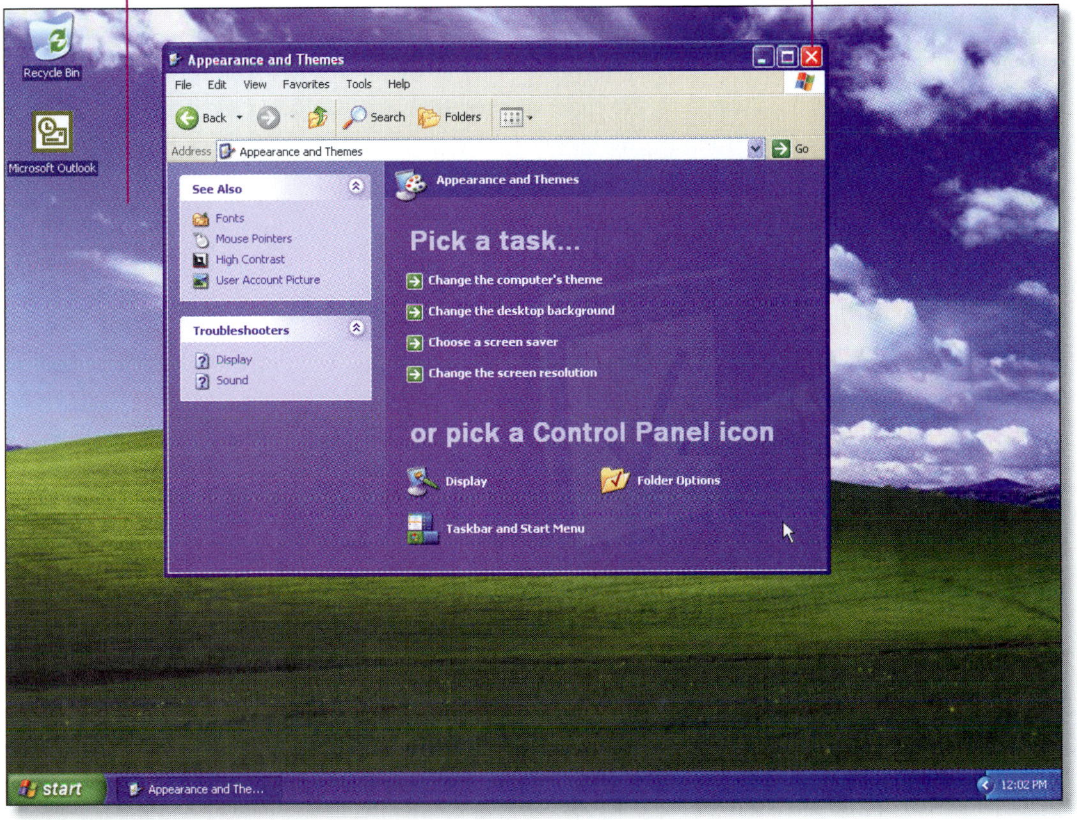

screen resolution
changed to 1024 by 768

Close button

FIGURE B-6

7. Click the Close button on the Appearance and Themes window title bar.

The new screen resolution is set.

You can experiment with various screen resolutions. Depending on your monitor and the video adapter installed in your computer, the screen resolutions available on your computer will vary.

When designing a user interface in the IDE, remember to take into consideration the screen resolutions available to the majority of the users of the application. A good rule of thumb is to test your application in all of the screen resolutions in which the application likely is to be used.

Changing the IDE Layout

The Visual Basic .NET IDE is fully customizable and allows you to arrange the contents of the IDE in a manner suitable to your work habits. This section contains some examples of various layouts used to get the most out of the IDE. You should experiment with various layouts to find the one that works best for you. If you need to change the layout back to the Visual Studio .NET default, you can open the Options dialog box from the Tools menu and then click the Reset Window Layout button.

Sample IDE Layouts

Figure B-7 shows a common layout for programmers developing Windows applications using Visual Basic .NET. The Task List, Command Window, and Output tabs display at the bottom of the IDE. The Full Screen toolbar is docked to the right of the Standard toolbar. Clicking the Full Screen button on the Full Screen toolbar quickly changes the view of the main work area to a larger view. The larger view makes it easier to focus on that which you are working. The Debug toolbar is docked to the right of the Layout toolbar.

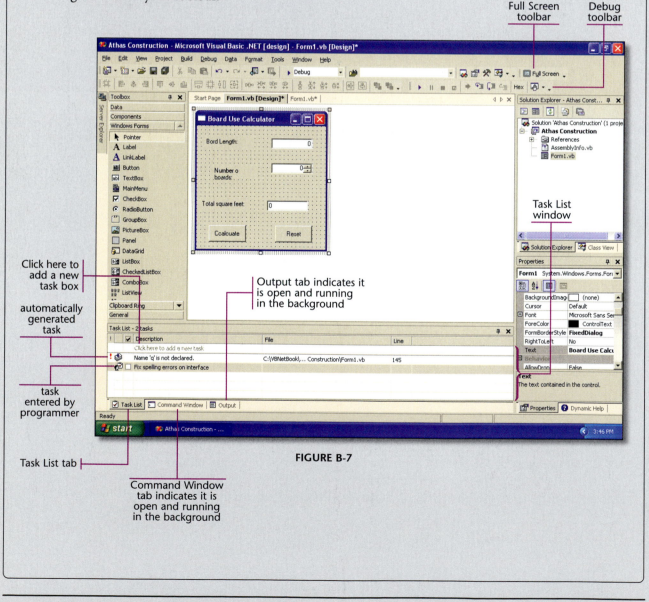

FIGURE B-7

As you are working, Visual Basic .NET automatically generates a new task in the **Task List** for any syntax errors in your code (Figure B-7). The tasks in the Task List serve as reminders of things that must be completed before you are done working on the code. You also can add tasks or reminders to the Task List by clicking the Click here to add a new task box directly above the Task List.

The **Command Window** allows you to test new code statements quickly without running the entire project (Figure B-7). The **Output window** displays the build results from the last time you ran the project. The contents of the Output window also serve as a reminder of bugs you must fix in the project. To view these windows, click the Command Window or Output tab at the bottom of the IDE.

Figure B-8 shows the result of undocking several of the windows from the IDE. This technique is useful if your computer only supports lower screen resolutions. By undocking the windows, you can move some windows out of the way, but still have quick access to the windows when necessary. To undock a window, drag the title bar of the window until you see a floating outline of the window, and then release the mouse button. To dock an undocked window, drag the window to the upper, lower, left, or right edge of the IDE. An outline of the window will snap to the edge as you move the mouse pointer towards the edge where you want to dock the window. When the window snaps to the desired position, release the mouse button to dock the window.

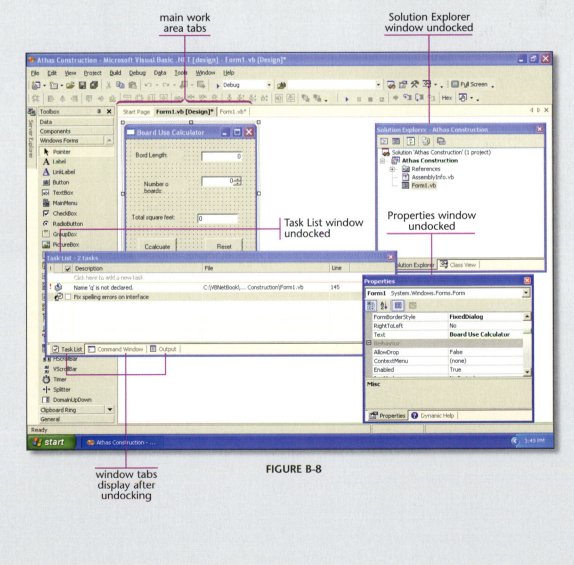

FIGURE B-8

Figure B-9 shows the main work area of the IDE in **Multiple Document Interface (MDI) mode**. In MDI mode, the IDE displays three separate windows in the main work area, instead of window tabs (Figure B-8 on the previous page). Using MDI mode is practical if you want to display a combination of form windows, code windows, and Help topics on the screen at one time. MDI mode also is useful for viewing multiple code windows, so that you can copy and paste code between the windows.

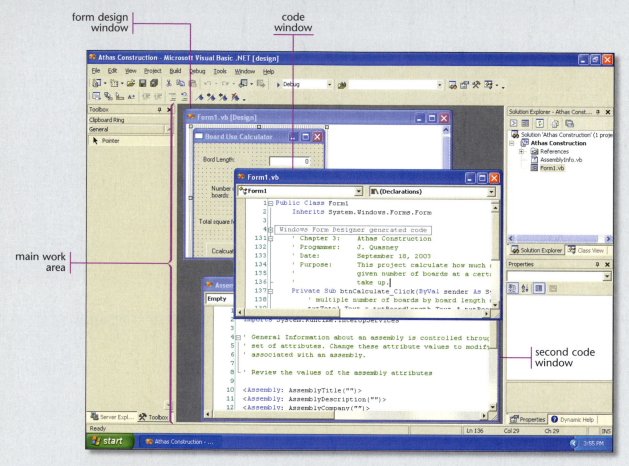

FIGURE B-9

Viewing the IDE at High Resolution

The higher the resolution you can tolerate while working in the IDE, the more information that you can make available on the screen at one time. Figure B-10 shows an example of the Visual Basic .NET IDE at 1280 by 1024 screen resolution. Much higher resolutions are possible with today's high-powered video cards and large monitors. In Figure B-10, the main work area illustrates a layout that displays a number of frequently used windows and toolbars in the IDE. The right side of the IDE is set up to display the Solution Explorer window, the Properties window, and the Dynamic Help window. Additional toolbars have been docked at the top of the IDE, including the Full Screen toolbar, the Debug toolbar, and the Query toolbar.

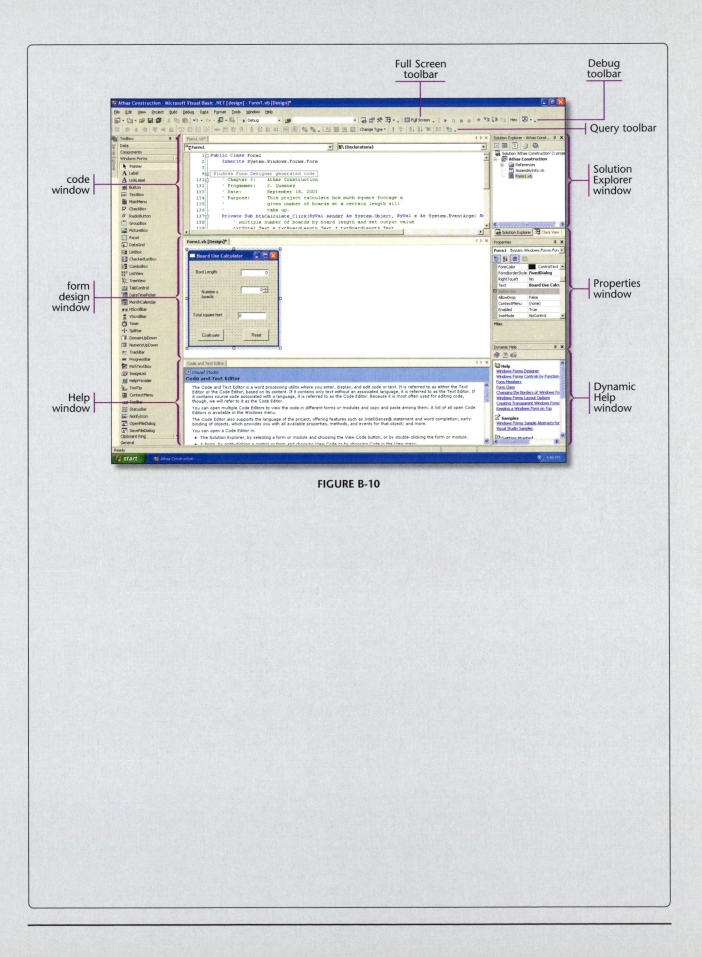

FIGURE B-10

A P P E N D I X

C

Visual Basic .NET Common Control Summary

Appendix C summarizes the commonly used properties, events, and methods for controls introduced in this book for developing applications in Visual Basic .NET.

Control Properties, Methods, and Events

The following tables summarize the properties, method, and events for the controls presented in this book. Default property values appear in bold font. The page number on which the control is first discussed in the book is shown next to the table title.

Common Properties of Controls

Table C-1 summarizes properties that are shared by a number of common Visual Basic .NET controls.

Table C-1   Common Properties of Controls (VB 3.39)

CATEGORY	PROPERTY	DESCRIPTION	PROPERTY VALUES
Appearance	BackColor	Sets the background color of the control	Select a color from a pop-up dialog box.
	Cursor	Defines which mouse pointer (cursor) displays when user moves the mouse over the control	Select a mouse pointer from a list of more than 20 mouse pointers.
	Font	Defines the text font to use if text displays in the control	Select a font style from a pop-up dialog box.
	ForeColor	Changes the foreground color, usually of the text that displays on the control	Select a color selected from a pop-up dialog box.
Behavior	Enabled	If True, control is usable at run time; if False, a user cannot change control value and control may display grayed out	**True** False
	TabStop	Determines whether the TAB key sets focus on the control during run time	**True** False
	TabIndex	Determines the order in which the TAB key navigates to the control	Any positive whole number
	Visible	If True, control displays at run time; if False, control does not display	**True** False
Data	Tag	Defines data to be stored with the control (data does not display to user)	Any text
Design	Locked	Ensures that a control cannot be moved during design time; prevents inadvertently moving the control once it is positioned	True **False**
	Name	Provides a descriptive, unique identifier for the control	Any text
	Size	Indicates height and width of the control in pixels	Two positive whole numbers, separated by a comma
	Location	Indicates distance from the top and left border of the form in pixels	Two positive whole numbers, separated by a comma

Common Control Methods and Events

Table C-2 summarizes the methods and events that are shared by a number of common Visual Basic .NET controls.

Table C-2   Common Methods and Events for Controls (N/A)

METHOD OR EVENT	DESCRIPTION
Enter event	Occurs when the control is entered
Focus method	Sets focus to the control
GotFocus event	Occurs when the control receives focus
Hide method	Conceals the control from the user
KeyPress event	Occurs when a key is pressed while the control has focus
LostFocus event	Occurs when the control loses focus; can be used to validate that the user has entered valid data
MouseMove event	Occurs when the mouse pointer is moved over the control
MouseWheel event	Occurs when the mouse wheel moves while the control has focus
Show method	Displays the control to the user

Form Properties

Table C-3 summarizes the more common properties of Form controls.

Table C-3   Form Properties (VB 3.22)

CATEGORY	PROPERTY	DESCRIPTION	PROPERTY VALUES
Appearance	BackColor	Sets background color of application window	Any color selected from dialog box
	ForeColor	Sets default color for controls that are dialog added to the form	Any color selected from box
	FormBorderStyle	Dictates appearance of form border; whether the form is sizable; and how the Minimize and Maximize buttons, Control menu box, and Help button behave	None FixedSingle Fixed3D FixedDialog **Sizable** FixedToolWindow SizableToolWindow
	Text	Sets title to display on title bar of application window	Any value
Behavior	Enabled	Sets form to be usable during run time	**True** False
Layout	WindowState	Dictates how a window should display initially during run time	**Normal** Minimized Maximized
Window Style	ControlBox	Determines if a Windows control box should display on the form	**True** False
	Icon	Defines the icon that displays on the top-left corner of the window title bar and on the taskbar at run time	Any icon selected from a file via a dialog box

Common Form Methods and Events

Table C-4 summarizes the more common methods and events of Form controls.

Table C-4   Common Form Methods and Events (VB 4.38)

METHOD OR EVENT	DESCRIPTION
Activate method	Activates the form and gives it focus
Activated event	Occurs when the form is activated in code or by the user
Click event	Occurs when the form is clicked
Close method	Closes the form
Closed event	Occurs when the form is closed in code or by the user
DragDrop event	Occurs when a drag-and-drop operation to the form is completed
Load event	Occurs before a form is displayed for the first time; if form subsequently is deactivated or hidden, and then reactivated or shown, event does not execute
Resize event	Event occurs when the Height or Width of the form is changed by the user or in code

TextBox Control Properties

Table C-5 summarizes the more common properties of the TextBox control.

Table C-5 TextBox Control Properties (VB 3.40)

CATEGORY	PROPERTY	DESCRIPTION	PROPERTY VALUES
Appearance	BorderStyle	Determines how the border of the TextBox control displays	None FixedSingle **Fixed3D**
	Text	Sets the text that displays inside the control	Any text with a character length up to the value specified in the MaxLength property
	TextAlign	Determines if text in the control displays left-aligned, right-aligned, or centered	**Left** Right Center
Behavior	AutoSize	Indicates whether the height of the control automatically changes when the font size in the control is changed	**True** False
	MaxLength	Sets the maximum number of characters a user can input into the text control	Any positive whole number from 0 through **32767**
	Multiline	Determines if text in the control displays on more than one line	True **False**
	ReadOnly	If True, a user cannot type or edit text in a control during run time; if False, user can type and edit text in control	True **False**

Table C-5 TextBox Control Properties (VB 3.40) (continued)

CATEGORY	PROPERTY	DESCRIPTION	PROPERTY VALUES
	WordWrap	If MultiLine is True, text in control wraps to next line when the text is longer than the width of the control	**True** False

Common TextBox Control Methods and Events

Table C-6 summarizes the more common methods and events of the TextBox control.

Table C-6 Common TextBox Control Methods and Events (VB 3.58)

METHOD OR EVENT	DESCRIPTION
AppendText method	Appends text to the current text of the control
Clear method	Clears all text from the control
Click event	Occurs when the control is clicked
Copy method	Copies the current selection in the control to the Clipboard
Cut method	Moves the current selection in the control to the Clipboard
DoubleClick event	Occurs when the control is double-clicked
Paste method	Replaces the current selection in the control with the contents of the Clipboard
SelectAll method	Selects all text in the text box
TextChanged	Occurs when the Text property value changes for any reason

Label Control Properties

Table C-7 summarizes the more common properties of the Label control.

Table C-7 Label Control Properties (VB 3.46)

CATEGORY	PROPERTY	DESCRIPTION	PROPERTY VALUES
Appearance	FlatStyle	Determines the 3D appearance of the control	Flat Popup **Standard** System
	Image	Sets an image to display on the visible portion of the Label control	Select a picture from the hard drive using a dialog box.
	ImageAlign	If the Image property is set, determines where the image displays	Select a location from a pop-up graphical display map. **(MiddleCenter)**
	Text	Defines the visible text that displays on the control	Any text with any character length

NumericUpDown Control Properties

Table C-8 summarizes the more common properties of the NumericUpDown control.

Table C-8   NumericUpDown Control Properties (VB 3.51)

CATEGORY	PROPERTY	DESCRIPTION	PROPERTY VALUES
Appearance	BorderStyle	Determines how the border of the control displays	None FixedSingle **Fixed3D**
	TextAlign	Defines if text in the control displays left-aligned, right-aligned, or centered	**Left** Right Center
	UpDownAlign	Determines if the up and down arrows on the control display on left or right side of the control	Left **Right**
	Value	Sets the value that displays in the control	Any value within the range set by the Minimum and Maximum property values
Behavior	InterceptArrowKeys	If True, user can use the UP ARROW and DOWN ARROW keys to change the value in the control; if False, the user cannot	**True** False
Data	DecimalPlaces	Defines numbers of decimal places that display in the value in the control	Any whole number from 0 to 99
	Increment	Defines amount to add or subtract from the displayed value each time user clicks the up or down arrow on control	Any positive number
	Maximum	Determines highest allowable value in the control; if user enters a higher value, the value is set automatically to the Maximum value	Any number
	Minimum	Determines lowest allowable value in the control; if a user enters a lower value, the value is set automatically to the Minimum value	Any number
	ThousandsSeparator	Determines if a Thousands separator character is used in the value, when appropriate; if True, value displays with a Thousands separator character set on user's system; if False, no Thousands separator character displays	True **False**

Common NumericUpDown Control Methods and Events

Table C-9 summarizes the more common methods and events of the NumericUpDown control.

Table C-9 Common NumericUpDown Control Methods and Events (VB 3.58)

METHOD OR EVENT	DESCRIPTION
DownButton method	Imitates the user clicking the down arrow on the control one time
UpButton method	Imitates the user clicking the up arrow on the control one time
ValueChanged event	Occurs when the Value property of the control has been changed in some way

Button Control Properties

Table C-10 summarizes the more common properties of the Button control.

Table C-10 Button Control Properties (VB 3.54)

CATEGORY	PROPERTY	DESCRIPTION	PROPERTY VALUES
Appearance	FlatStyle	Determines the 3D appearance of the control	Flat Popup **Standard** System
	Image	Sets an image to display on the visible portion of the Button control, along with the text	Select a picture from the hard drive using a dialog box.
	ImageAlign	Image property is set, determines where the image displays	Select a location from a pop-up graphical display map.
	TextAlign	Determines where text should display on the button	Select one of nine locations from a pop-up graphical display map.

Common Button Control Methods and Events

Table C-11 summarizes the more common methods and events of the Button control.

Table C-11 Common Button Control Methods and Events (VB 3.60)

METHOD OR EVENT	DESCRIPTION
Click event	Occurs when the user clicks the Button control
PerformClick method	Imitates a user clicking the Button control; causes the Click event to execute

GroupBox Control Properties

Table C-12 summarizes the more common properties of the GroupBox control.

Table C-12 **GroupBox Control Properties (VB 4.16)**

CATEGORY	PROPERTY	DESCRIPTION	PROPERTY VALUES
Appearance	FlatStyle	Determines the 3D appearance of the control	Flat Popup **Standard** System
	Text	Indicates the label to display on the upper-left edge of the control	Any value, or set blank if no label is desired
Design	GridSize: Width and Gridsize: Height	Determines the size of the positioning grid within the control	Width and Height properties can be any positive whole number **(8, 8)**

RadioButton Control Properties

Table C-13 summarizes the more common properties of the RadioButton control.

Table C-13 **RadioButton Control Properties (VB 4.19)**

CATEGORY	PROPERTY	DESCRIPTION	PROPERTY VALUES
Appearance	CheckAlign	Determines the location of the check box inside the control	Select a location from a pop-up graphical display map. **(MiddleLeft)**
	Checked	Determines whether the RadioButton is selected (checked) or not	True **False**
	FlatStyle	Determines the 3D appearance of the control	Flat Popup **Standard** System
	Image	Sets an image to display on the visible portion of the Label control along with the text	Select a picture from the hard drive using a dialog box.
	ImageAlign	If the Image property is set, determines where the image displays	Select a location from a pop-up graphical display map. **(MiddleCenter)**
	Text	Defines the visible text that displays on the control	Any text with any character length
Behavior	AutoCheck	Causes the RadioButton to change state (value of Checked property) automatically when clicked	**True** False

Common RadioButton Control Methods and Events

Table C-14 summarizes the more common methods and events of the RadioButton control.

Table C-14   Common RadioButton Control Methods and Events (VB 4.45)

METHOD OR EVENT	DESCRIPTION
CheckChanged event	Occurs when the value of the Checked property of the control changes

D

General Forms of Common Visual Basic .NET Statements

Appendix D summarizes the common Visual Basic .NET statements presented in this book along with their general forms.

General Forms of Visual Basic .NET Statements

Table D-1 summarizes the general forms of Visual Basic .NET statements introduced in this book and the page number on which the general forms appear.

Table D-1   General Forms of Common Visual Basic .NET Statements

STATEMENT	GENERAL FORM	PAGE NUMBER
Assignment	1. Object = newvalue 2. Object.Property = newvalue	VB 3.59
Comment	1. ' comment 2. REM comment	VB 3.60
Constant Declaration	1. Const name As type = value 2. Const name = value	VB 4.36
Dim (simple)	1. Dim variablename As datatype = initialvalue 2. Dim variablename As datatype 3. Dim variablename	VB 4.43
Option Strict	1. Option Strict On 2. Option Strict Off	VB 4.41

E

The .NET Framework Class Library Overview

Appendix E provides an overview of the .NET Framework class library, which consists of several namespaces. Each namespace contains classes that you can use in your programs. Use these classes to enhance your programs. They save you time by providing functionality that you do not need to code yourself, such as determining the square root of a number or the absolute value of a number. Additional namespaces can be added by creating them yourself or through third-party providers. The namespaces that Microsoft includes with the .NET Framework class library all begin with either Microsoft or System.

Namespaces and Classes

The following tables provide the namespaces and classes that may be useful to you as a beginning programmer. The .NET Framework class library contains several more namespaces than those listed and most of the namespaces contain many more classes than listed. Each class presented may contain many methods and attributes. Use the Visual Basic .NET Help system to find more information about each class.

The example below shows the use of the System.Math.Cos() method in the Math class of the System namespace. The Cos() method determines the cosine of a given angle.

```
Dim dblCosine as Double
dblCosine = System.Math.Cos(90.0)
```

Microsoft.VisualBasic Namespace

The **Microsoft.VisualBasic Namespace** (Table E-1) contains classes that are useful mostly for backwards compatibility with older versions of Visual Basic.

Table E-1   Microsoft.VisualBasic Namespace

CLASS	DESCRIPTION
Collection	The Collection class provides a convenient way to refer to a related group of items as a single object. Methods such as Add and Remove are used to modify the collection.
Conversion	The Conversion class contains methods used to perform various conversion operations. For example, Int() is used to convert a Double value to an Integer.
DateAndTime	The DateAndTime class contains methods and properties used in date and time operations. For example, the DateAdd() method adds an interval of time to a specified date.
ErrObject	The ErrObject class contains properties and procedures used to identify and handle run-time errors using the Err object. This should be used only for backward compatibility with older versions of Visual Basic.
FileSystem	The FileSystem module contains the procedures used to perform file, directory or folder, and system operations. This should only be used for backward compatibility with older versions of Visual Basic. For example, the FileCopy() function can be used to copy a file from one folder to another.
Financial	The Financial module contains procedures used to perform financial operations. For example, the Pv() function is used to determine a present value of an annuity based on periodic, fixed payments to be paid in the future and a fixed interest rate.
Globals	The Globals module contains script engine functions. For example, the ScriptEngine and ScriptEngineMajor properties give the version of the Visual Basic .NET run-time engine that you are using.
Information	The Information module contains the procedures used to return, test for, or verify information. For example, the IsDate() function returns a Boolean value indicating whether an expression can be converted to a date.

Table E-1   Microsoft.VisualBasic Namespace (continued)

CLASS	DESCRIPTION
Interaction	The Interaction module contains procedures used to interact with objects, applications, and systems. This should be used only for backward compatibility with older versions of Visual Basic. For example, the Beep() function causes the speaker to emit a brief tone.
Strings	The Strings module contains procedures used to perform string operations. For example, the StrComp() function can be used to compare the contents of two strings.
VbMath	The VbMath module contains procedures used to perform mathematical operations. For example, the Rnd() function can be used to return a random number of type Single.

Microsoft.Win32 Namespace

The **Microsoft.Win32 namespace** (Table E-2) provides two types of classes: (1) those that handle events raised by the operating system and (2) those that manipulate the system registry.

Table E-2   Microsoft.Win32 Namespace

CLASS	DESCRIPTION
Registry	Supplies the base RegistryKeys that access values and subkeys in the registry.
RegistryKey	Represents a key level node in the Windows registry. Use this class to manipulate registry keys you may need in your application.
SystemEvents	Provides a set of global system events to callers. System events include shutdown notifications and changes to user preferences.

System Namespace

The **System Namespace** (Table E-3) contains fundamental classes and base classes. It provides services supporting data type conversion, mathematics, local and remote program invocation, and application environment management.

Table E-3   System Namespace

CLASS	DESCRIPTION
Console	Represents the standard input, output, and error streams for console applications. For example, the Console.Write() method writes an expression to a console window.
Convert	Converts a base data type to another base data type. For example, the Convert.ToDouble() method converts a specified value to a double-precision floating point number.

(continued)

Table E-3   *System Namespace (continued)*

CLASS	DESCRIPTION
Exception	Represents errors that occur during application execution. Two categories of exceptions exist under the base class Exception: (1) The predefined common language runtime exception classes derived from SystemException; (2) The user-defined application exception classes derived from ApplicationException. For example, the ToString() method creates and returns a string representation of the current exception.
Math	Provides constants and static methods for trigonometric, logarithmic, and other common mathematical functions. For example, the Cos() method returns the cosine of the specified angle.
Object	Supports all classes in the .NET Framework class library hierarchy and provides low-level services to derived classes. This is the ultimate superclass of all classes in the .NET Framework; it is the root of the type hierarchy.
Random	Represents a pseudo-random number generator, a device that produces a sequence of numbers that meets certain statistical requirements for randomness. For example, the Next() method returns a random number.
String	Represents an immutable series of characters. For example, the Format() method replaces each format specification in a specified String with the textual equivalent of a corresponding object's value.
TimeZone	Represents a time zone. For example, the CurrentTimeZone property gets the time zone of the current computer system.
Type	Represents type declarations: class types, interface types, array types, value types, and enumeration types. Use the Type class to create your own data types.
Version	Represents the version number for a common language runtime assembly. For example, the Major property gets the value of the major component of the version number for this instance.

System.Collections Namespace

The **System.Collections namespace** (Table E-4) contains interfaces and classes that define various collections of objects, such as lists, queues, bit arrays, hashtables, and dictionaries.

Table E-4   *System.Collections Namespace*

CLASS	DESCRIPTION
ArrayList	Implements an interface using an array whose size is increased dynamically as required. Use the Add() method to add new items to the array.
Comparer	Compares two objects for equivalence, where string comparisons are case-sensitive. For example, the Compare() method performs a case-sensitive comparison of two objects of the same type and returns a value indicating whether one is less than, equal to, or greater than the other.
HashTable	Represents a collection of key-and-value pairs that are organized based on the hash code of the key. Use the Add() method to add new items to the array.

Table E-4 **System.Collections Namespace** *(continued)*

CLASS	DESCRIPTION
Queue	Represents a first-in, first-out collection of objects. Use the EnQueue() and DeQueue() methods to add and remove objects from the queue.
SortedList	Represents a collection of key-and-value pairs that are sorted by the keys and are accessible by key and by index. Use the Add() method to add an item to the list. Use the GetByIndex() method to access an item by the sort key.
Stack	Represents a simple last-in-first-out collection of objects. Use the Push() and Pop() methods to add and remove items from the stack.

System.Data Namespace

The **System.Data namespace** (Table E-5) consists mostly of the classes that constitute the ADO.NET architecture. The ADO.NET architecture enables you to build components that efficiently manage data from multiple data sources.

Table E-5 **System.Data Namespace**

CLASS	DESCRIPTION
DataColumn	Represents a schema, or definition, of a column in a data table.
DataColumnCollection	Represents all of the DataColumns for a data table. Defines the schema of the table.
DataRow	Represents one row of data in a table.
DataRowCollection	Represents a collection of rows in a table.
DataRowView	Represents a customized view of a DataRow exposed as a fully featured Windows Forms control.
DataSet	Represents an in-memory cache of data.
DataTable	Represents one table of in-memory data.
DataTableCollection	Represents the collection of tables for the DataSet.
DataView	Represents a databindable, customized view of a DataTable for sorting, filtering, searching, editing, and navigation.
DataViewManager	Contains a default DataViewSettingCollection for each DataTable in a DataSet.
DataViewSetting	Represents the default settings for ApplyDefaultSort, DataViewManager, RowFilter, RowStateFilter, Sort, and Table for DataViews created from the DataViewManager.

System.Data.OleDb Namespace

The **System.Data.OleDb namespace** (Table E-6) is the OLE DB .NET Data Provider. A .NET data provider describes a collection of classes used to access a data source, such as a database, in the managed space. Using the OleDbDataAdapter, you can fill a memory-resident DataSet, which you can use to query and update the datasource.

Table E-6 System.Data.OleDb Namespace

CLASS	DESCRIPTION
OleDbCommand	Represents an SQL statement or stored procedure to execute against a data source.
OleDbCommandBuilder	Provides a means of automatically generating single-table commands used to reconcile changes made to a DataSet with the associated database.
OleDbConnection	Represents an open connection to a data source.
OleDbDataReader	Provides a way of reading a forward-only stream of data rows from a data source.
OleDbErrorCollection	Collects all errors generated by the OLE DB .NET Data Provider.
OleDbTransaction	Represents an SQL transaction to be made at a data source.

System.Drawing Namespace

The **System.Drawing namespace** (Table E-7) provides access to basic graphics functionality. More advanced functionality is provided in the System.Drawing.Drawing2D, System.Drawing.Imaging, and System.Drawing.Text namespaces. The Graphics class provides methods for drawing to the display device. Classes such as Rectangle and Point encapsulate primitives. The Pen class is used to draw lines and curves, while classes derived from the abstract class Brush are used to fill the interiors of shapes.

Table E-7 System.Drawing Namespace

CLASS	DESCRIPTION
Bitmap	Encapsulates a bitmap, which consists of the pixel data for a graphics image and its attributes. A Bitmap object is an object used to work with images defined by pixel data.
Brush	Classes derived from this abstract base class define objects used to fill the interiors of graphical shapes such as rectangles, ellipses, pies, polygons, and paths.
Font	Defines a particular format for text, including font face, size, and style attributes.
Graphics	Encapsulates a drawing surface.
Icon	Represents a Windows icon, which is a small bitmap image used to represent an object. Icons can be thought of as transparent bitmaps, although their size is determined by the system.

Table E-7 System.Drawing Namespace (continued)

CLASS	DESCRIPTION
Image	An abstract base class that provides functionality for Bitmap, Icon, and Metafile descended classes.
Pen	Defines an object used to draw lines and curves.

System.Drawing.Printing Namespace

The **System.Drawing.Printing namespace** (Table E-8) provides print-related services. Typically, you create a new instance of the PrintDocument class, set the properties that describe what to print, and call the Print method actually to print the document.

Table E-8 System.Drawing.Printing Namespace

CLASS	DESCRIPTION
Margins	Specifies the margins of a printed page.
PageSettings	Specifies settings that apply to a single, printed page.
PaperSize	Specifies the size of a piece of paper.
PrintDocument	Defines a reusable object that sends output to a printer.
PrinterResolution	Represents the resolution supported by a printer.
PrinterSettings	Specifies information about how a document is printed, including the printer that prints it.
StandardPrintController	Specifies a print controller that sends information to a printer.

System.Drawing.Text Namespace

The **System.Drawing.Text namespace** (Table E-9) provides advanced typography functionality. Basic graphics functionality is provided by the System.Drawing namespace. The classes in this namespace allow users to create and use collections of fonts.

Table E-9 System.Drawing.Text Namespace

CLASS	DESCRIPTION
FontCollection	Base class for installed and private font collections. Provides a method to get a list of the font families contained in the collection.
InstalledFontCollection	Represents the fonts installed on the system.

System.IO Namespace

The **System.IO namespace** (Table E-10) contains types that allow synchronous and asynchronous reading and writing on data streams and files.

Table E-10   System.IO Namespace

CLASS	DESCRIPTION
Directory	Exposes static methods for creating, moving, and enumerating through directories and subdirectories.
DirectoryInfo	Exposes instance methods for creating, moving, and enumerating through directories and subdirectories.
File	Provides static methods for the creation, copying, deletion, moving, and opening of files, and aids in the creation of FileStream objects. For example, the Copy() method copies an existing file to a new file.
FileInfo	Provides instance methods for the creation, copying, deletion, moving, and opening of files, and aids in the creation of FileStream objects. For example, the Name property gets the name of the file.
FileStream	Exposes a Stream around a file, supporting both synchronous and asynchronous read and write operations.
Path	Performs operations on String instances that contain file or directory path information. These operations are performed in a cross-platform manner. For example, the Combine() method combines two path strings.
Stream	Provides a generic view of a sequence of bytes.
StreamReader	Implements a TextReader that reads characters from a byte stream in a particular encoding.
StreamWriter	Implements a TextWriter for writing characters to a stream in a particular encoding.
StringReader	Implements a TextReader that reads from a string.
StringWriter	Writes information to a string. The information is stored in an underlying StringBuilder.
TextReader	Represents a reader that can read a sequential series of characters.
TextWriter	Represents a writer that can write a sequential series of characters.

System.Web Namespace

The **System.Web namespace** (Table E-11) supplies classes and interfaces that enable browser-server communication.

Table E-11   System.Web Namespace

CLASS	DESCRIPTION
HttpApplication	Defines the methods, properties, and events common to all application objects within a Web application. For example, the Session property gets the intrinsic session object that provides access to session data.
HttpApplicationState	Enables sharing of global information across multiple sessions and requests within a Web application. For example, the Item property gives you access to the state information regarding the user's session.
HttpBrowserCapabilities	Enables the server to gather information on the capabilities of the browser that is running on the client. For example, the JavaScript property gets a value indicating whether the client browser supports JavaScript.
HttpCookie	Provides a type-safe way to create and manipulate individual HTTP cookies. For example, the Name and Value properties give you the name and value of a cookie.
HttpCookieCollection	Provides a type-safe way to manipulate HTTP cookies. For example, the Add() method adds the specified cookie to the cookie collection.
HttpResponse	Encapsulates HTTP response information from a Web operation. For example, the Cookies property gets the response cookie collection.
HttpWriter	Provides a TextWriter object that is accessed through the intrinsic HttpResponse object. For example, the Write() method sends HTTP output to the client.

System.Web.Mail Namespace

The **System.Web.Mail namespace** (Table E-12) contains classes that enable you to construct and send messages. The mail message is delivered either through the SMTP mail service built into Microsoft Windows or through an arbitrary SMTP server.

Table E-12   System.Web.Mail Namespace

CLASS	DESCRIPTION
MailAttachment	Provides properties and methods for constructing an e-mail attachment. For example, the FileName property gets the name of the file attachment.
MailMessage	Provides properties and methods for constructing an e-mail message. For example, the Subject property gets or sets the subject line of the e-mail message.
SmtpMail	Provides properties and methods for sending messages. For example, the Send() method sends an email message.

System.Web.Services Namespace

The **System.Web.Services namespace** (Table E-13) consists of the classes that enable you to create XML Web services.

Table E-13 System.Web.Services Namespace

CLASS	DESCRIPTION
WebMethodAttribute	Adding this attribute to a method within an XML Web service created using ASP.NET makes the method callable from remote Web clients.
WebService	Defines the optional base class for XML Web services, which provides direct access to common ASP.NET objects, such as application and session state.
WebServiceAttribute	Used to add additional information to an XML Web service, such as a string describing its functionality.

System.Web.UI.WebControls Namespace

The **System.Web.UI.WebControls namespace** (Table E-14) is a collection of classes that allows you to create Web server controls on a Web page. Web server controls run on the server and include form controls such as buttons and text boxes. They also include special-purpose controls such as a calendar. Because Web server controls run on the server, you can control these elements programmatically. Web server controls are more abstract than HTML server controls.

Table E-14 System.Web.UI.WebControls Namespace

CATEGORY OR CLASS	DESCRIPTION
Controls	A category of classes that include all of the controls listed in the Web Forms tab of the Toolbox when creating a Web application. For example, the TextBox, Label, and Button controls are included.
WebControl	Serves as the base class that defines the methods, properties, and events common to all controls in the System.Web.UI.WebControls namespace.
Xml	Displays an XML document without formatting or using Extensible Stylesheet Language Transformations (XSLT).

System.Windows.Forms Namespace

The **System.Windows.Forms namespace** (Table E-15) contains classes for creating Windows-based applications that take full advantage of the rich user interface features available in the Microsoft Windows operating system.

Table E-15 System.Windows.Forms Namespace

CATEGORY OR CLASS	DESCRIPTION
Application	Provides shared methods and properties to manage an application, such as methods to start and stop an application, to process Windows messages, and properties to get information about an application.
Common Dialog Boxes	A category of classes that includes such classes as the SaveFileDialog, OpenFileDialog, FontDialog, and PrintDialog classes.
Components	A category of classes that includes the Tooltip class, Menu related classes, and Help classes.
Control	A high-level class from which the Controls and Form classes are derived.
Controls	A category of classes that includes all of the Windows Forms controls you see in the Toolbox window. For example, the TextBox, Label, and Button controls are included.
Form	Represents a window or dialog box that makes up an application's user interface.
Screen	Represents a display device or multiple display devices on a single system.
UserControl	Provides an empty control that can be used to create other controls.

System.Xml Namespace

The **System.Xml namespace** (Table E-16) provides standards-based support for processing XML.

Table E-16 System.Xml Namespace

CLASS	DESCRIPTION
XmlAttribute	Represents an attribute. Valid and default values for the attribute are defined in a DTD or schema.
XmlDocument	Represents an XML document.
XmlDocumentType	Represents the document type declaration.
XmlElement	Represents an element.
XmlNameTable	Table of atomized string objects.
XmlNode	Represents a single node in the XML document.
XmlNodeList	Represents an ordered collection of nodes.
XmlNodeReader	Represents a reader that provides fast, non-cached forward-only access to XML data in an XmlNode.
XmlReader	Represents a reader that provides fast, non-cached, forward-only access to XML data.
XmlText	Represents the text content of an element or attribute.
XmlTextReader	Represents a reader that provides fast, non-cached, forward-only access to XML data.

(continued)

Table E-16 System.Xml Namespace *(continued)*

CLASS	DESCRIPTION
XmlTextWriter	Represents a writer that provides a fast, non-cached, forward-only way of generating streams or files containing XML data that conforms to the W3C Extensible Markup Language (XML) 1.0 and the Namespaces in XML recommendations.
XmlWhitespace	Represents white space in element content.
XmlWriter	Represents a writer that provides a fast, non-cached, forward-only means of generating streams or files containing XML data that conforms to the W3C Extensible Markup Language (XML) 1.0 and the Namespaces in XML recommendations.

F

ASCII
Character Codes

Appendix F lists all 256 ASCII decimal codes and their corresponding characters. The characters shown in Table F-1 on the next page for codes 128 to 255 represent the default character set for a console application. These codes may differ based on the selected typeface in which they are displayed. Foreign character sets also may be represented by these decimal codes.

ASCII Character Set

Table F-1 illustrates the ASCII character set. Decimal codes 0 to 31 are considered control characters and are not printable; thus the corresponding characters for these codes are blank. Code 32 is the space character.

Table F-1   ASCII Character Set

DECIMAL CODE	CHARACTER	DECIMAL CODE	CHARACTER	DECIMAL CODE	CHARACTER	DECIMAL CODE	CHARACTER	DECIMAL CODE	CHARACTER
0		51	3	102	f	153	ö	204	╠
1		52	4	103	g	154	Ü	205	=
2		53	5	104	h	155	¢	206	╬
3		54	6	105	i	156	£	207	╧
4		55	7	106	j	157	¥	208	╨
5		56	8	107	k	158	₧	209	╤
6		57	9	108	l	159	ƒ	210	╥
7		58	:	109	m	160	á	211	╙
8		59	;	110	n	161	í	212	╘
9		60	<	111	o	162	ó	213	╒
10		61	=	112	p	163	ú	214	╓
11		62	>	113	q	164	ñ	215	╫
12		63	?	114	r	165	Ñ	216	╪
13		64	@	115	s	166	ª	217	┘
14		65	A	116	t	167	º	218	┌
15		66	B	117	u	168	¿	219	█
16		67	C	118	v	169	⌐	220	▄
17		68	D	119	w	170	¬	221	▌
18		69	E	120	x	171	½	222	▐
19		70	F	121	y	172	¼	223	▀
20		71	G	122	z	173	¡	224	∝
21		72	H	123	{	174	«	225	ß
22		73	I	124	¦	175	»	226	Γ
23		74	J	125	}	176	▒	227	Π
24		75	K	126	~	177	▒	228	Σ
25		76	L	127	⌂	178	▓	229	σ
26		77	M	128	Ç	179	│	230	µ
27		78	N	129	ü	180	┤	231	Υ
28		79	O	130	é	181	╡	232	Φ
29		80	P	131	â	182	╢	233	θ
30	▲	81	Q	132	ä	183	╖	234	Ω
31	▼	82	R	133	à	184	╕	235	δ
32		83	S	134	å	185	╣	236	∞
33	!	84	T	135	ç	186	║	237	φ
34	"	85	U	136	ê	187	╗	238	∈
35	#	86	V	137	ë	188	╝	239	∩
36	$	87	W	138	è	189	╜	240	≡
37	%	88	X	139	ï	190	╛	241	±
38	&	89	Y	140	î	191	┐	242	≥
39	'	90	Z	141	ì	192	└	243	≤
40	(	91	[	142	Ä	193	┴	244	⌠
41	)	92	\	143	Å	194	┬	245	⌡
42	*	93	]	144	É	195	├	246	÷
43	+	94	^	145	æ	196	─	247	≈
44	,	95	_	146	Æ	197	┼	248	°
45	-	96	`	147	ô	198	╞	249	·
46	.	97	a	148	ö	199	╟	250	·
47	/	98	b	149	ò	200	╚	251	√
48	0	99	c	150	û	201	╔	252	ⁿ
49	1	100	d	151	ù	202	╩	253	²
50	2	101	e	152	ÿ	203	╦	254	■
								255	

Index